volume

4

ASADORA!

NAOKI URASAWA

Chapter 24 ◉ The Day It Appears

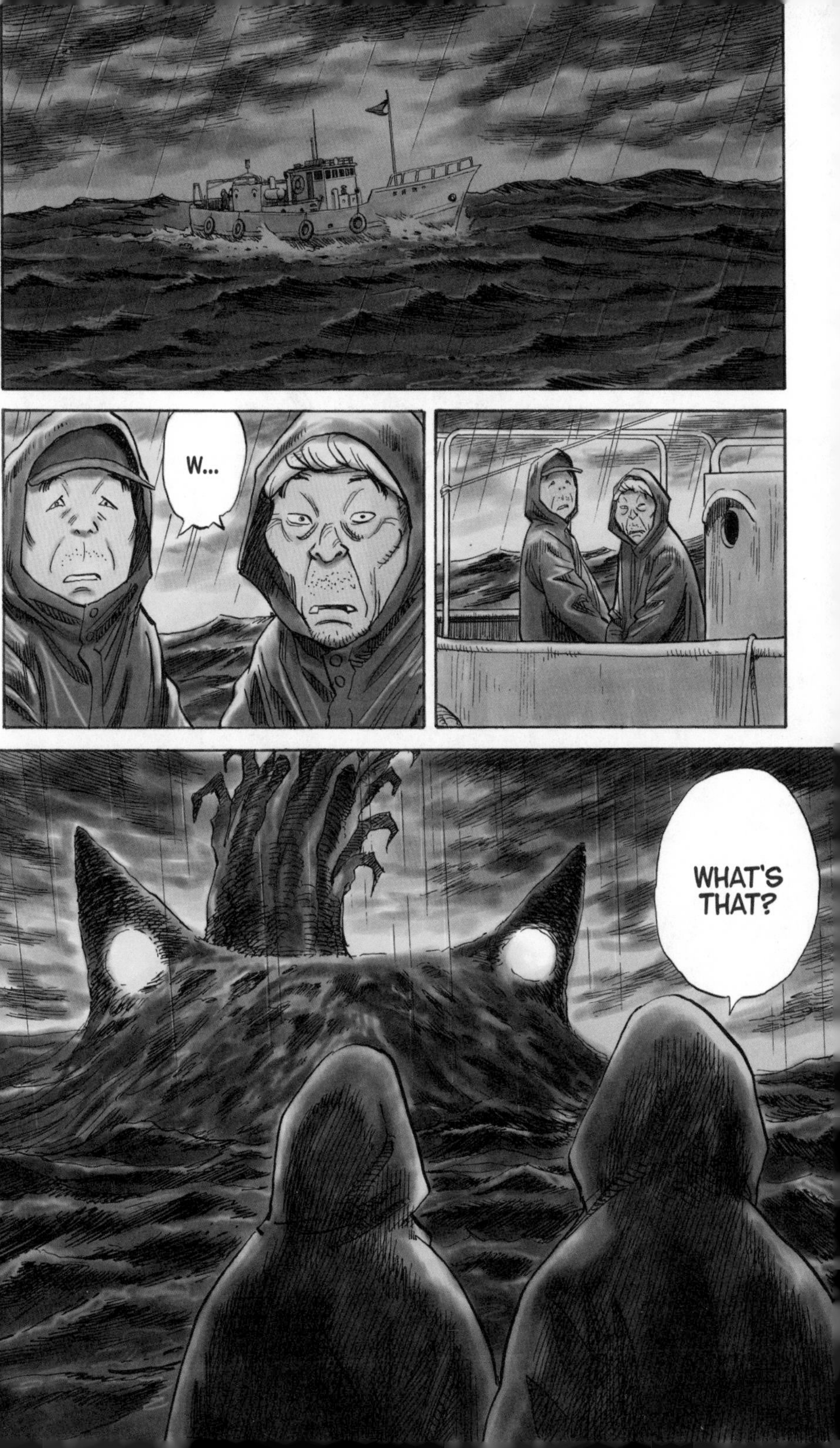
W...
WHAT'S THAT?

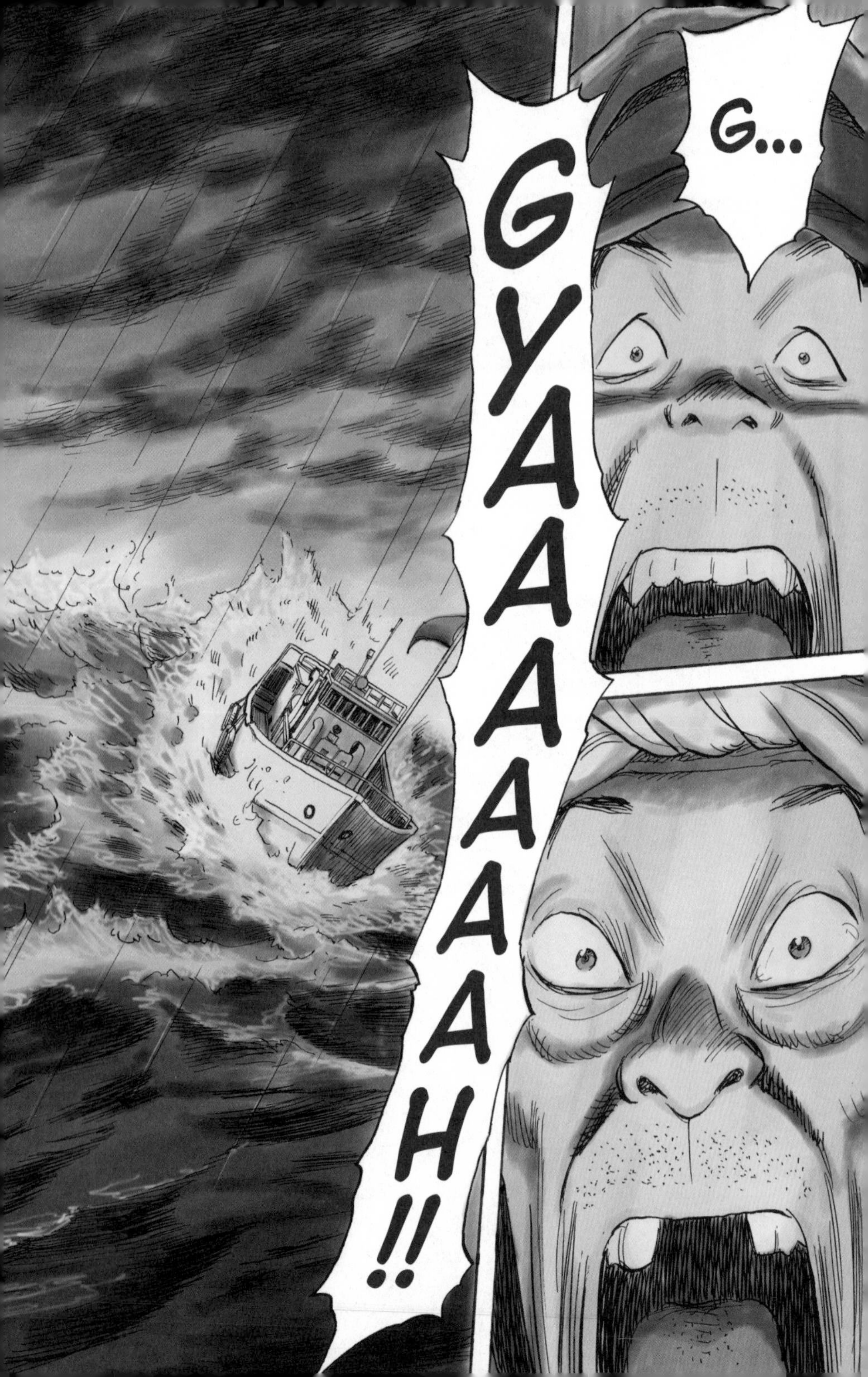
G...
GYAAAAAAH!!

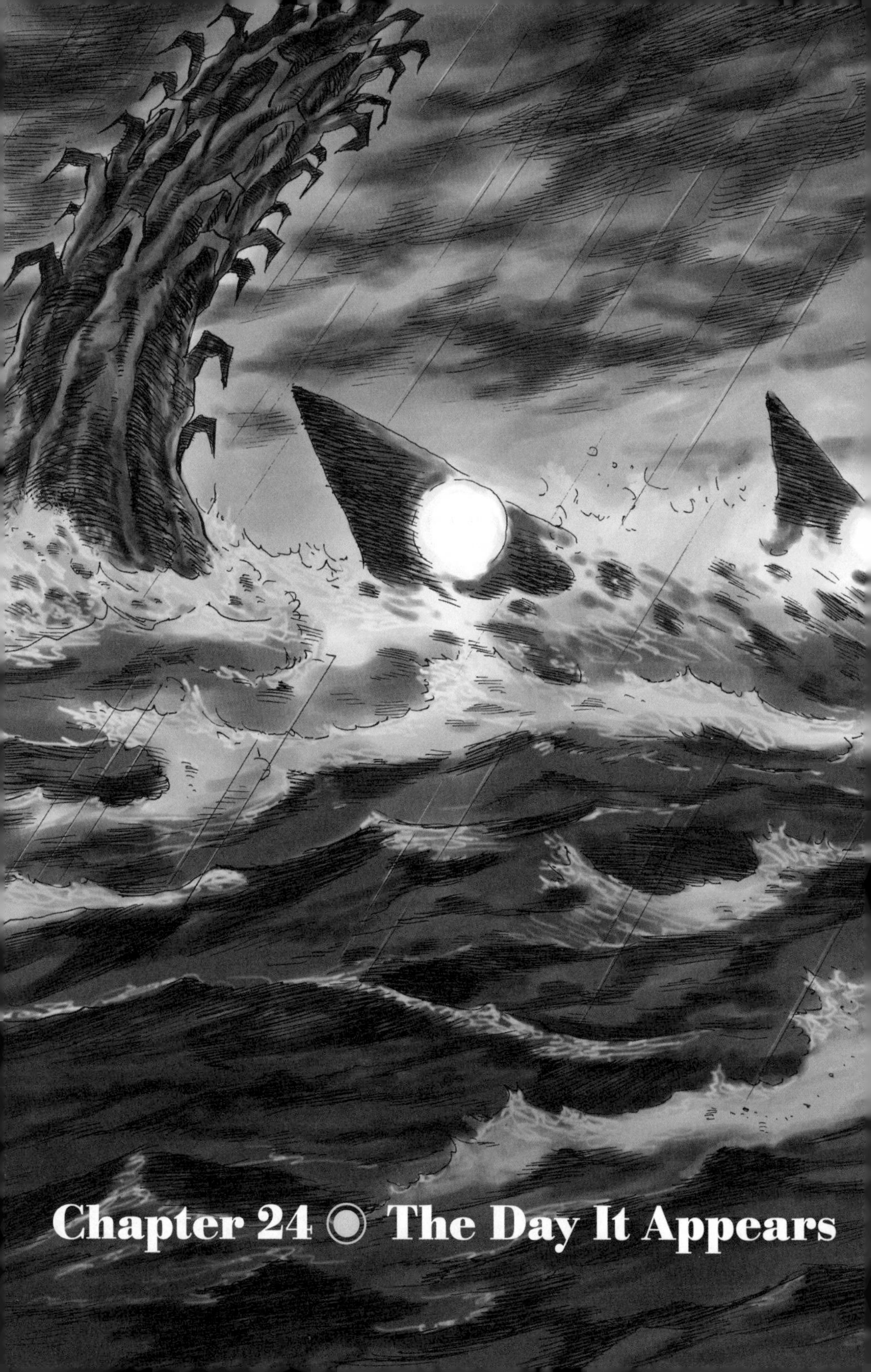
Chapter 24 ◎ The Day It Appears

Characters

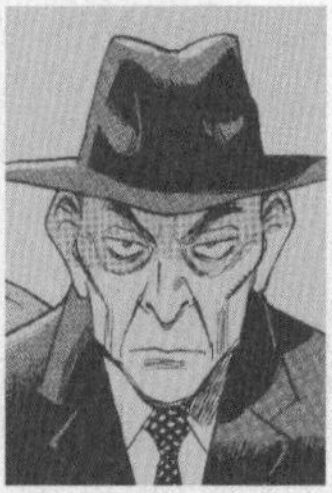

Minoru Jissoji

A mysterious man in the government who was once Kasuga's superior officer. He has asked Asa and Kasuga to help next time "that thing" appears.

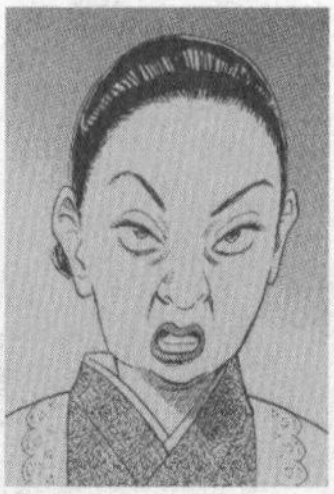

Kinuyo

Once the proprietress of a small diner in Nagoya. She took in Asa and her surviving siblings and now runs a restaurant in Tokyo.

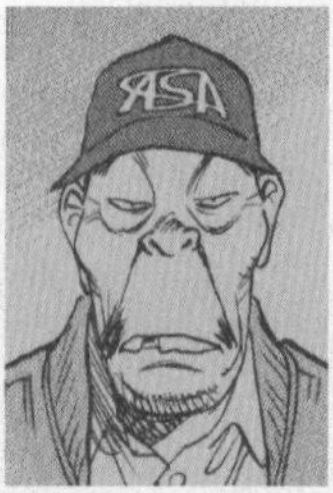

Mister Kasuga (Haruo Kasuga)

A skilled pilot during World War II. Five years ago, he kidnapped Asa, but now they run an aviation company together.

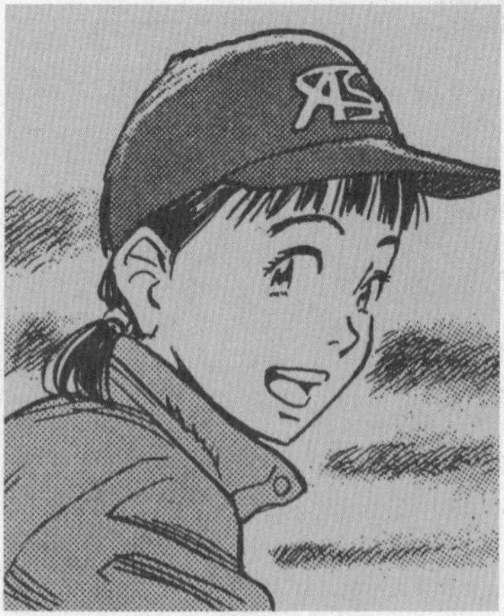

Asa Asada

Airplane pilot, 17 years old. She was born into a large family in Nagoya but lost her parents and many siblings in the Isewan Typhoon. That was when she saw "that thing" from the sky.

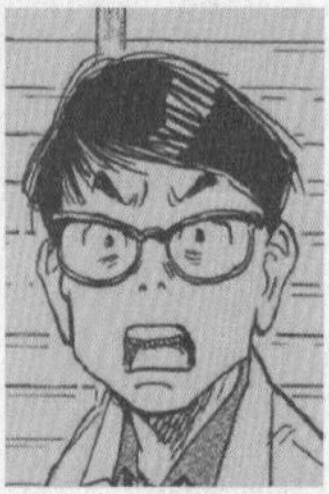

Keiichi Nakaido

Professor Yodogawa's pupil. Since his mentor passed away, he has preserved documents regarding "that thing."

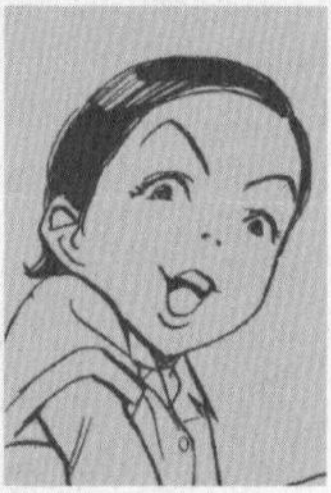

Miyako

Asa's classmate. She hopes that she, Asa, and Yone will become a pop trio, but...

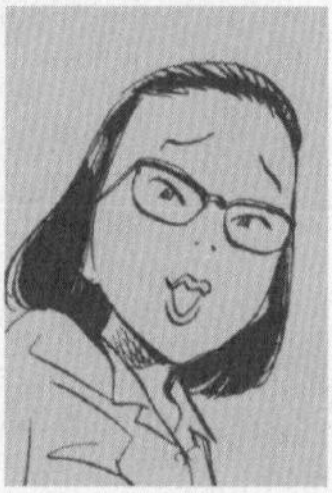

Yone

Asa's classmate. An entertainment agency scouted her (and only her) in Ginza.

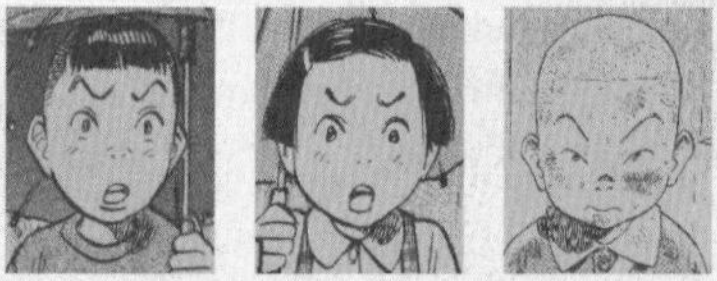

Shinroku, Hazuki, Koshichi

Asa's younger siblings. These three survived the typhoon.

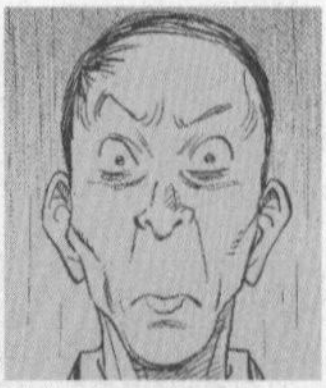

Newspaper Reporter

A reporter for the *Daily Every*. Why is he snooping around Asa and Kasuga?

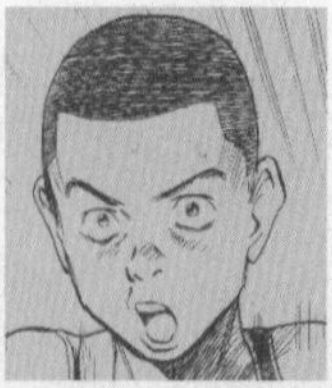

Sho (Shota Hayata)

Asa's childhood friend. He was planning to run in the Olympic marathon, but...

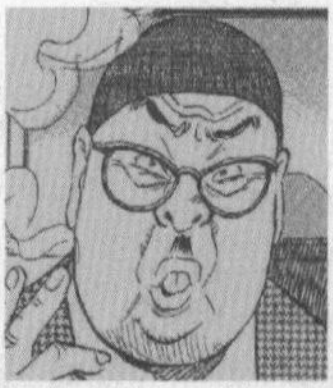

Noro

Nakaido's relative. He plans to open a sex museum in a red-light district.

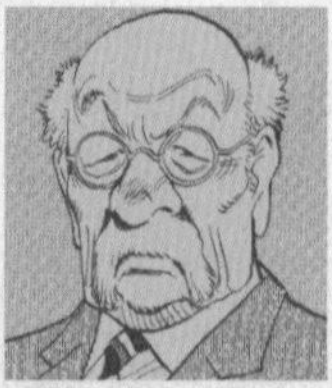

Professor Yodogawa

A renegade biologist who researched "that thing." Deceased.

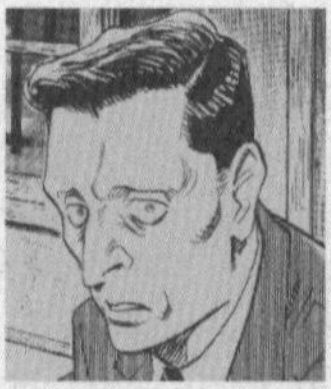

A-kura

A mysterious man serving under Jissoji.

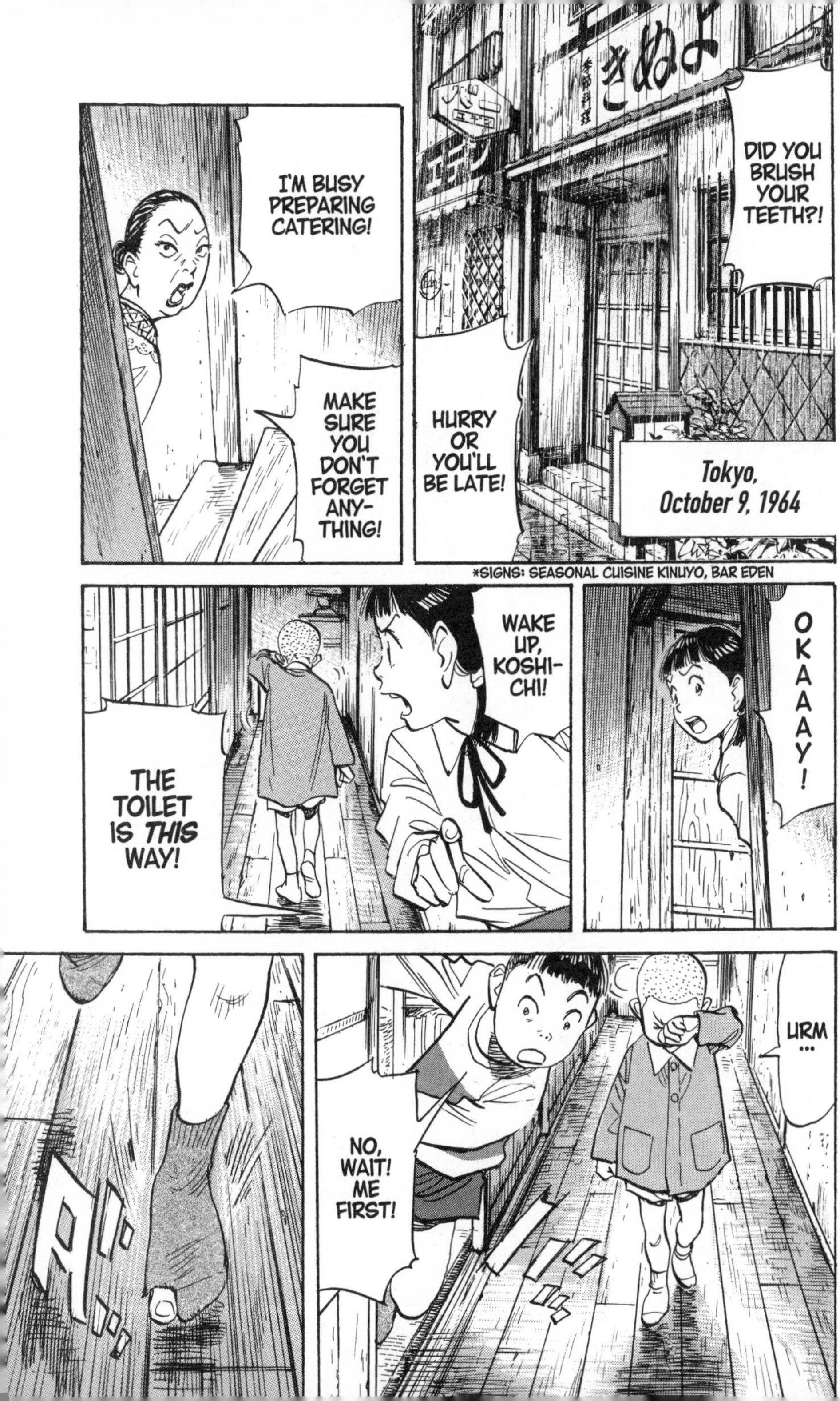
きぬよ
DID YOU BRUSH YOUR TEETH?!
HURRY OR YOU'LL BE LATE!
Tokyo, October 9, 1964
I'M BUSY PREPARING CATERING!
MAKE SURE YOU DON'T FORGET ANY-THING!
OKAAAAY!
WAKE UP, KOSHI-CHI!
THE TOILET IS *THIS* WAY!
URM ...
NO, WAIT! ME FIRST!

*SIGNS: SEASONAL CUISINE KINUYO, BAR EDEN

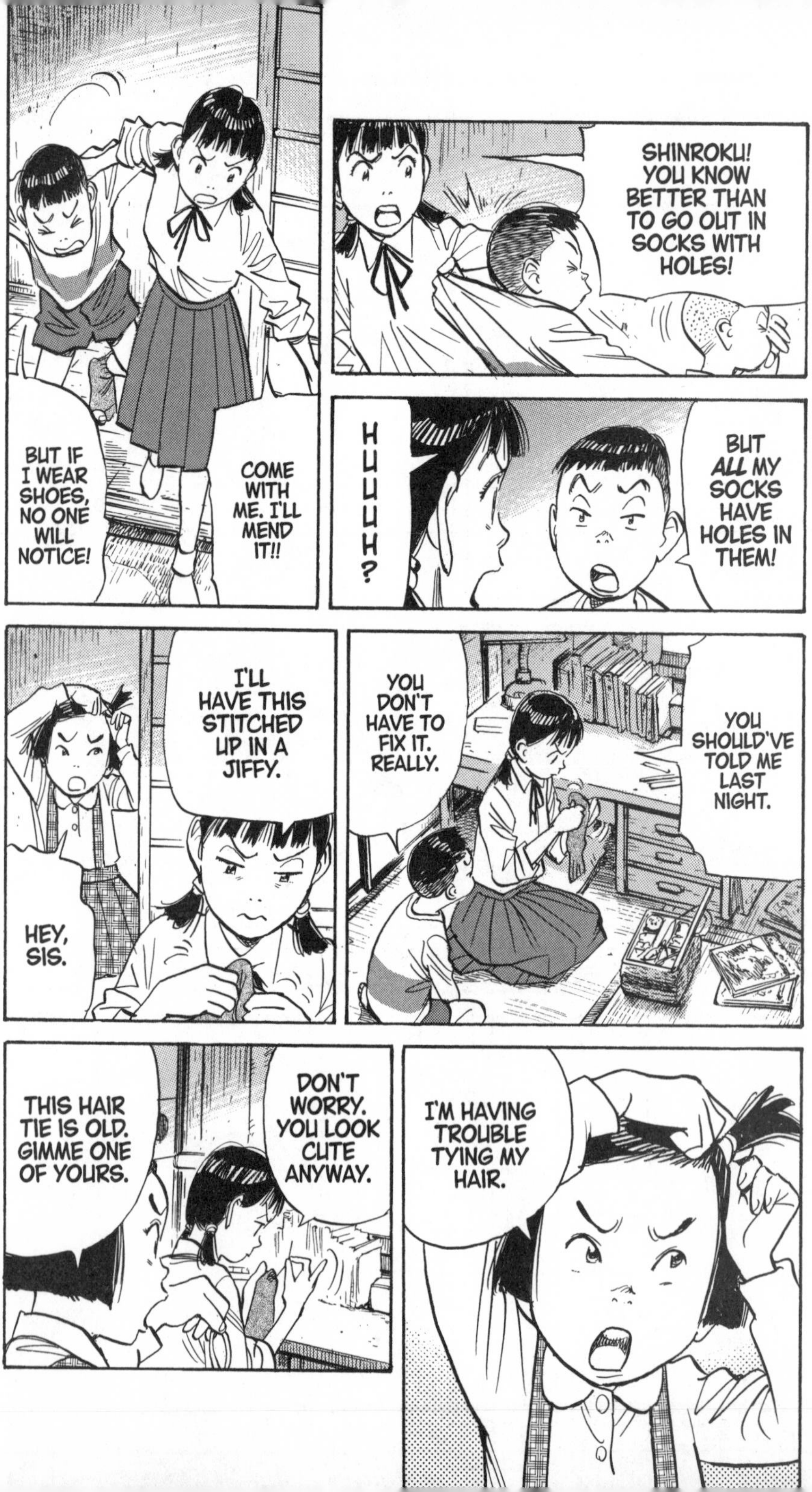
SHINROKU! YOU KNOW BETTER THAN TO GO OUT IN SOCKS WITH HOLES!
BUT ALL MY SOCKS HAVE HOLES IN THEM!
HUUUUH?
COME WITH ME. I'LL MEND IT!!
BUT IF I WEAR SHOES, NO ONE WILL NOTICE!
YOU SHOULD'VE TOLD ME LAST NIGHT.
YOU DON'T HAVE TO FIX IT. REALLY.
I'LL HAVE THIS STITCHED UP IN A JIFFY.
HEY, SIS.
I'M HAVING TROUBLE TYING MY HAIR.
DON'T WORRY. YOU LOOK CUTE ANYWAY.
THIS HAIR TIE IS OLD. GIMME ONE OF YOURS.

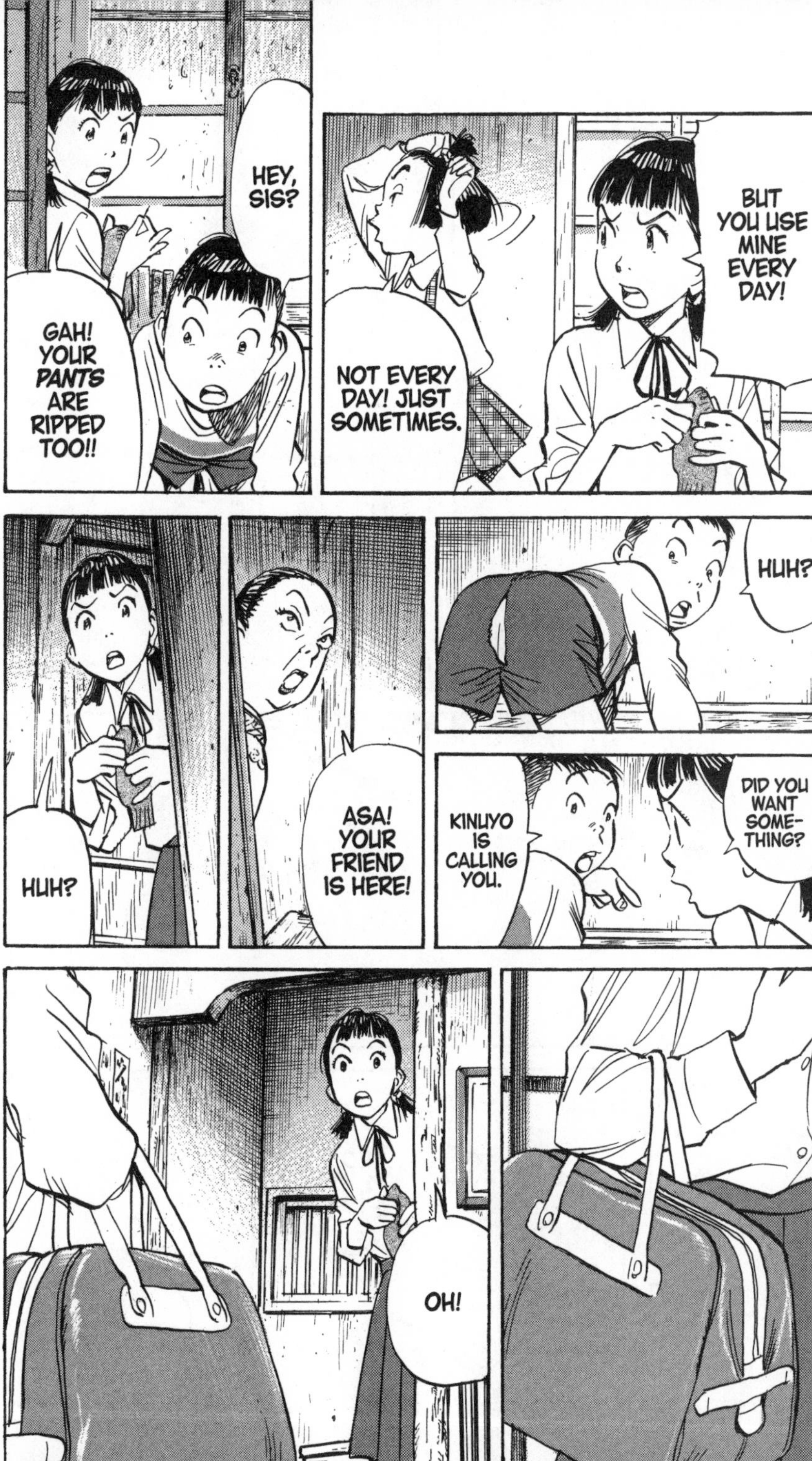
BUT YOU USE MINE EVERY DAY!
NOT EVERY DAY! JUST SOMETIMES.
HEY, SIS?
GAH! YOUR PANTS ARE RIPPED TOO!!
HUH?
DID YOU WANT SOMETHING?
KINUYO IS CALLING YOU.
ASA! YOUR FRIEND IS HERE!
HUH?
OH!

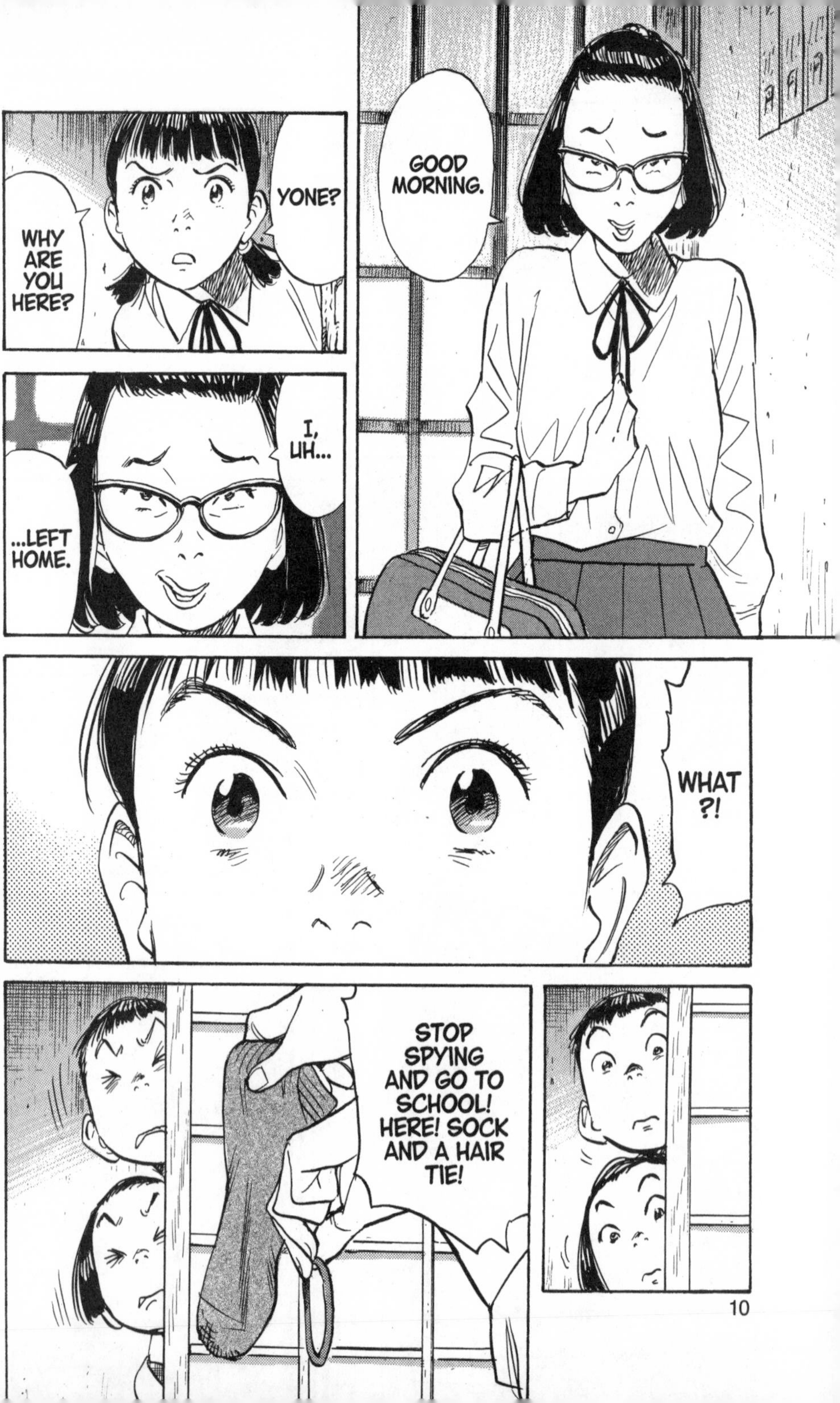
GOOD MORNING.
YONE?
WHY ARE YOU HERE?
I, UH...
...LEFT HOME.
WHAT?!
STOP SPYING AND GO TO SCHOOL! HERE! SOCK AND A HAIR TIE!

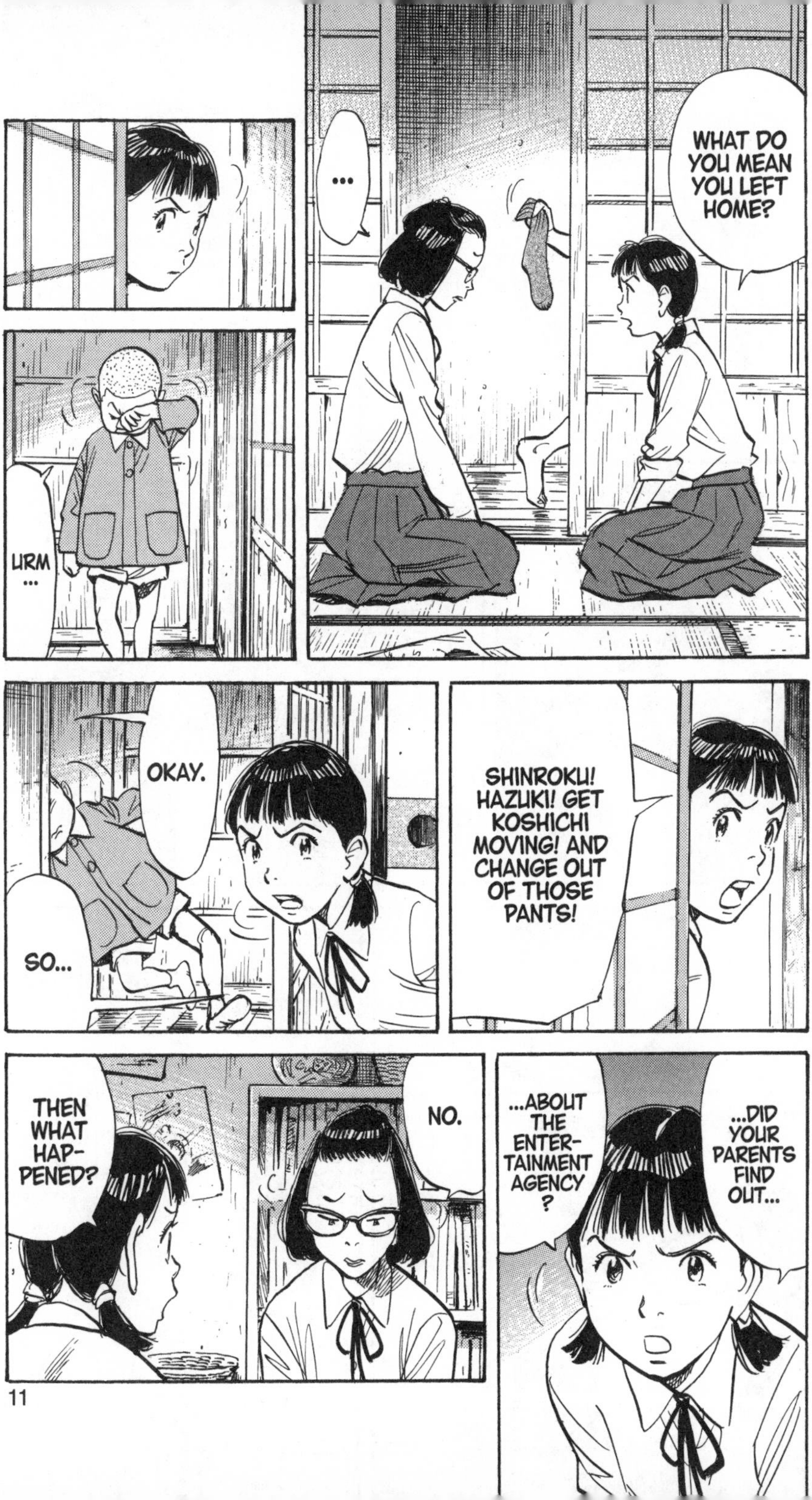
WHAT DO YOU MEAN YOU LEFT HOME?
...
URM ...
SHINROKU! HAZUKI! GET KOSHICHI MOVING! AND CHANGE OUT OF THOSE PANTS!
OKAY.
SO...
...DID YOUR PARENTS FIND OUT...
...ABOUT THE ENTER-TAINMENT AGENCY?
NO.
THEN WHAT HAP-PENED?

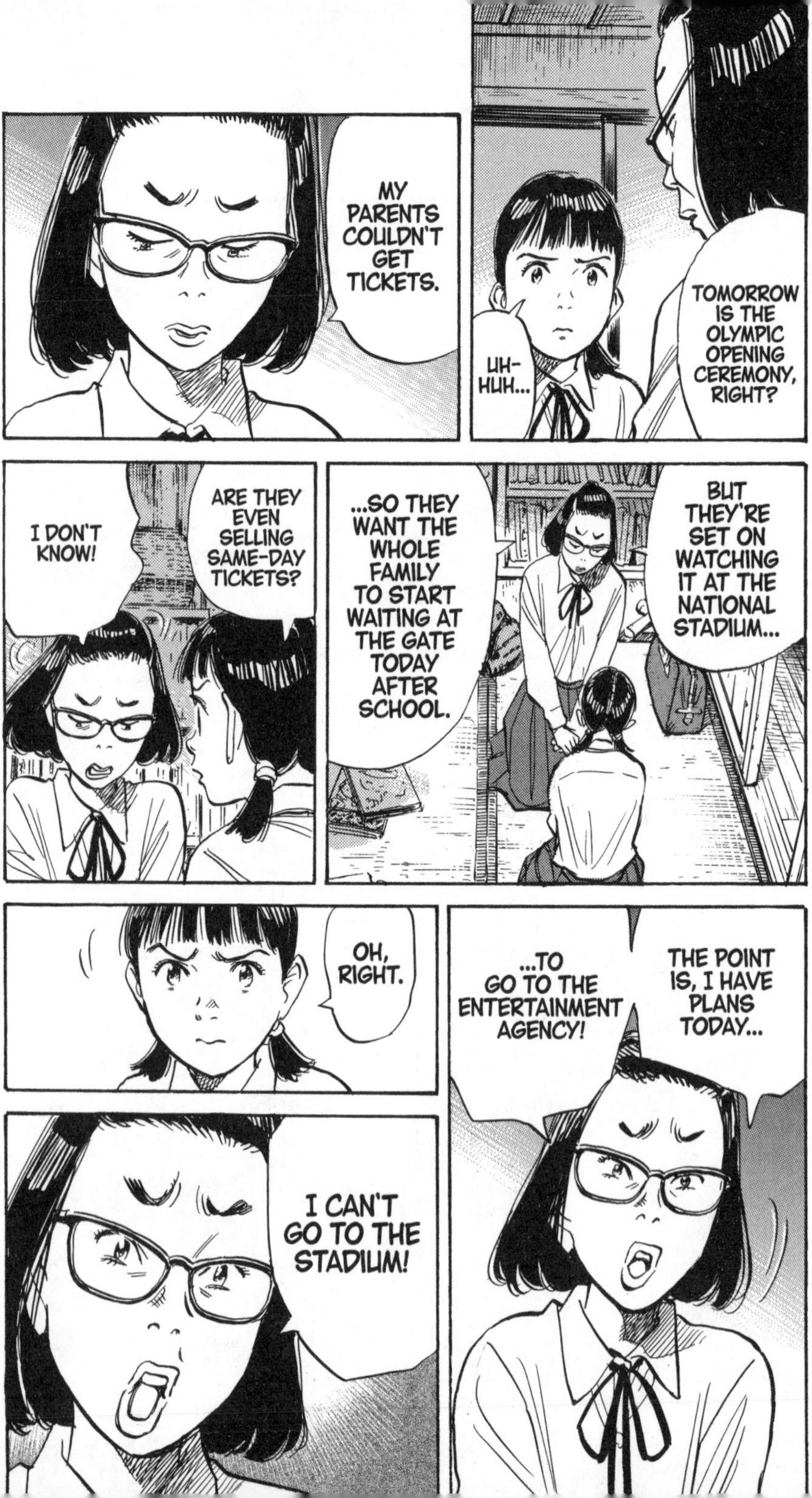
TOMORROW IS THE OLYMPIC OPENING CEREMONY, RIGHT?
UH-HUH...
MY PARENTS COULDN'T GET TICKETS.
BUT THEY'RE SET ON WATCHING IT AT THE NATIONAL STADIUM...
...SO THEY WANT THE WHOLE FAMILY TO START WAITING AT THE GATE TODAY AFTER SCHOOL.
ARE THEY EVEN SELLING SAME-DAY TICKETS?
I DON'T KNOW!
THE POINT IS, I HAVE PLANS TODAY...
...TO GO TO THE ENTERTAINMENT AGENCY!
OH, RIGHT.
I CAN'T GO TO THE STADIUM!

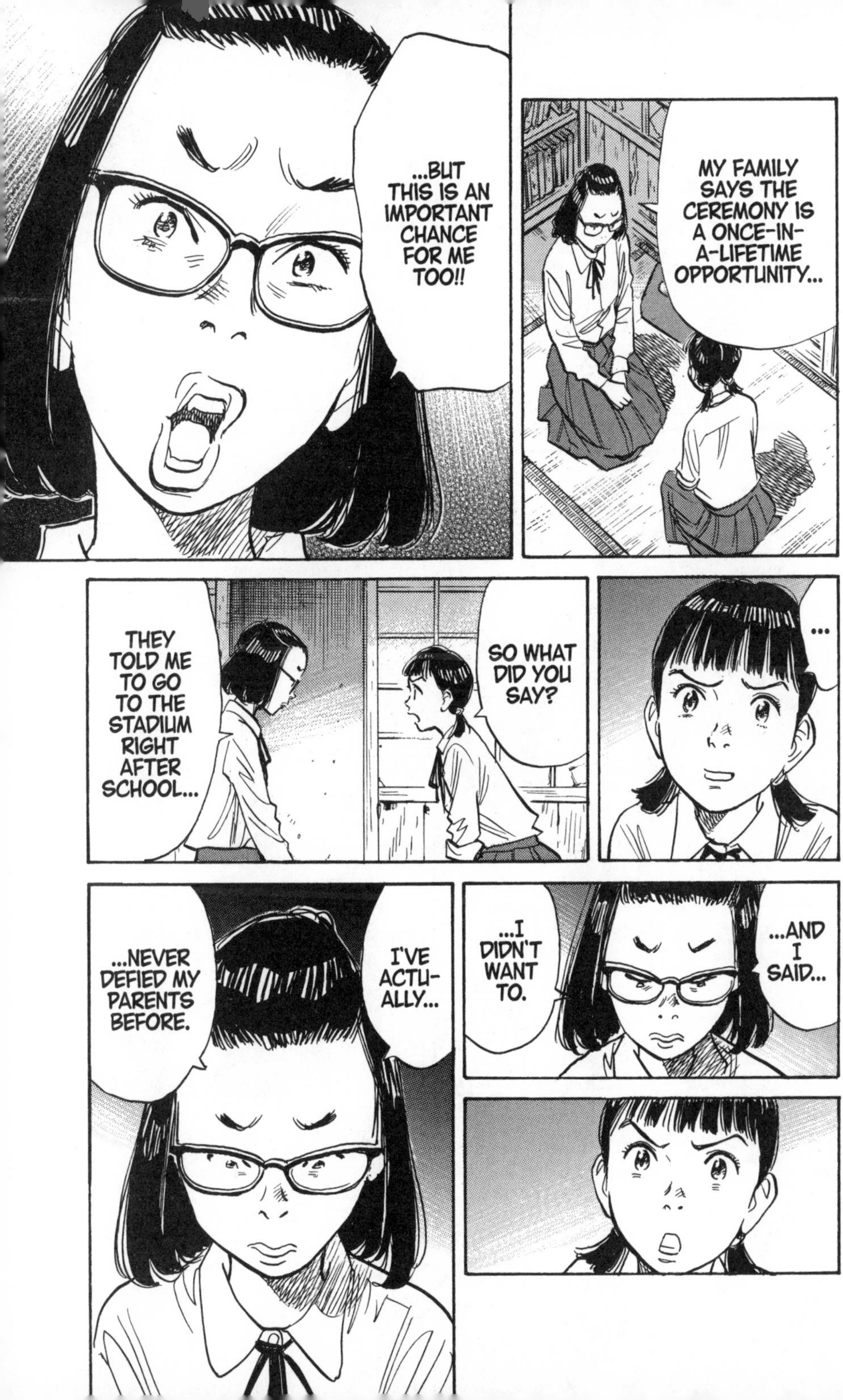
MY FAMILY SAYS THE CEREMONY IS A ONCE-IN-A-LIFETIME OPPORTUNITY...
...BUT THIS IS AN IMPORTANT CHANCE FOR ME TOO!!
...
SO WHAT DID YOU SAY?
THEY TOLD ME TO GO TO THE STADIUM RIGHT AFTER SCHOOL...
...AND I SAID...
...I DIDN'T WANT TO.
I'VE ACTUALLY...
...NEVER DEFIED MY PARENTS BEFORE.

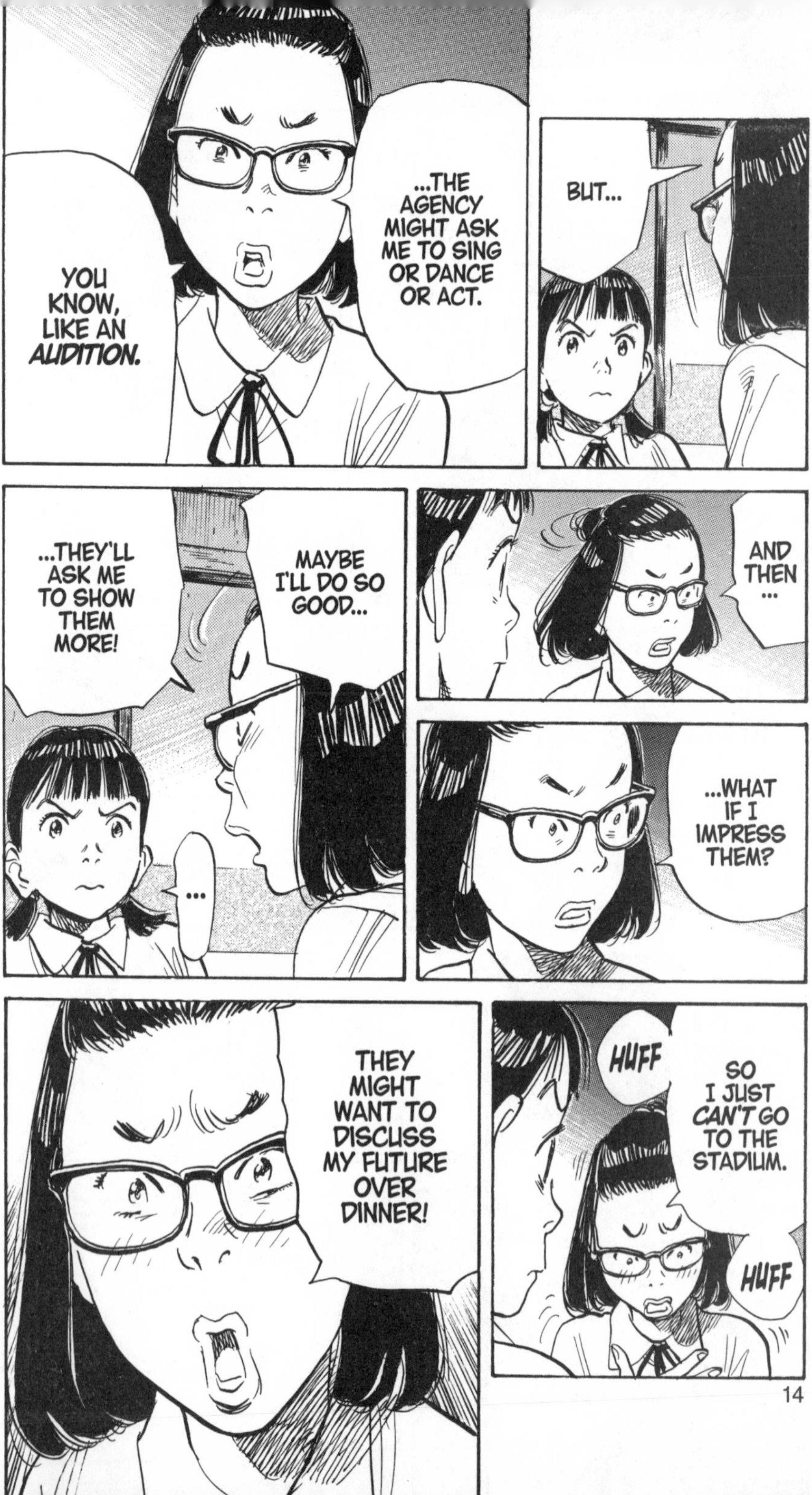
BUT...
...THE AGENCY MIGHT ASK ME TO SING OR DANCE OR ACT.
YOU KNOW, LIKE AN *AUDITION.*
AND THEN...
...WHAT IF I IMPRESS THEM?
MAYBE I'LL DO SO GOOD...
...THEY'LL ASK ME TO SHOW THEM MORE!
...
HUFF
SO I JUST *CAN'T* GO TO THE STADIUM.
HUFF
THEY MIGHT WANT TO DISCUSS MY FUTURE OVER DINNER!

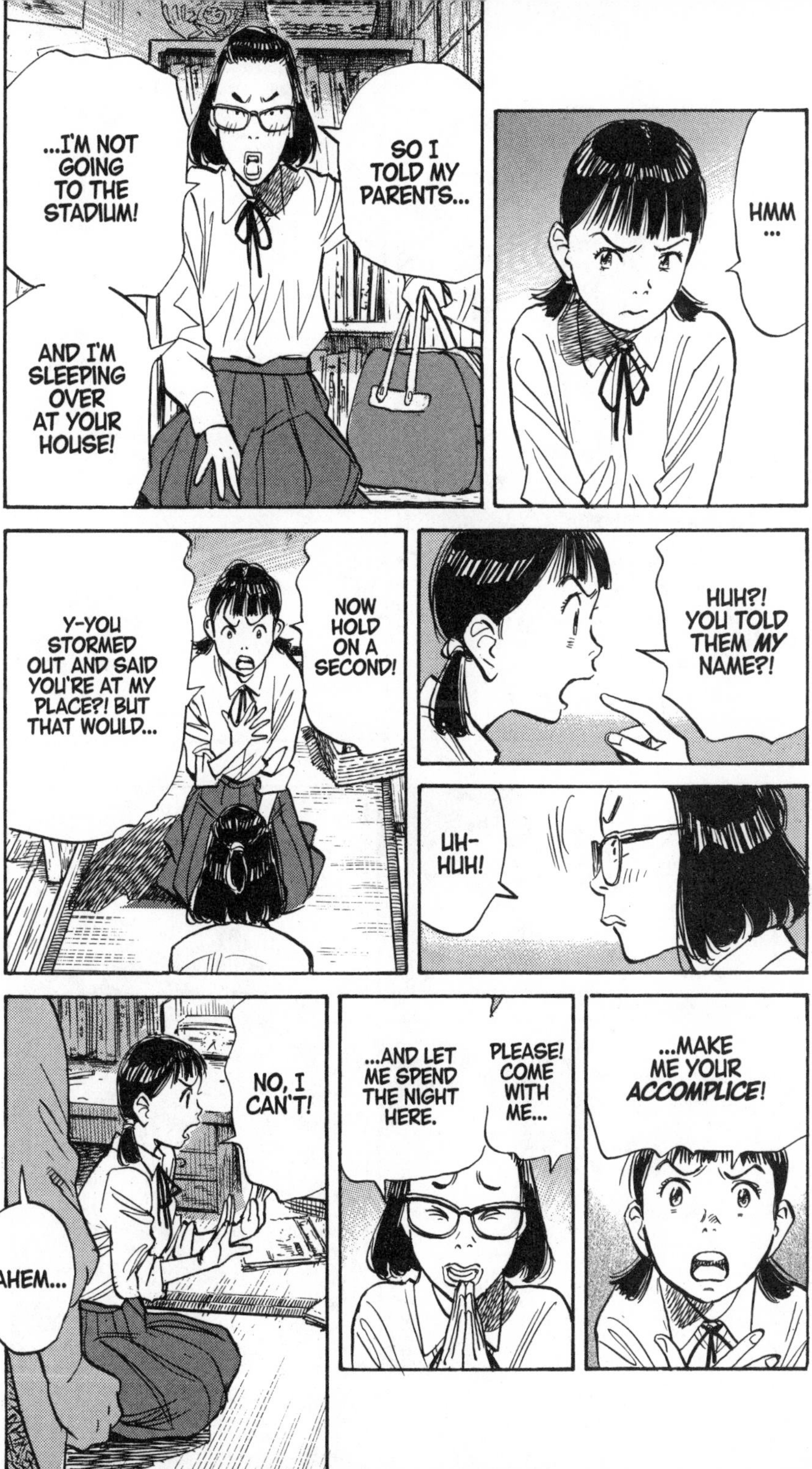
HMM ...
SO I TOLD MY PARENTS...
...I'M NOT GOING TO THE STADIUM!
AND I'M SLEEPING OVER AT YOUR HOUSE!
HUH?! YOU TOLD THEM *MY* NAME?!
UH-HUH!
NOW HOLD ON A SECOND!
Y-YOU STORMED OUT AND SAID YOU'RE AT MY PLACE?! BUT THAT WOULD...
...MAKE ME YOUR *ACCOMPLICE*!
PLEASE! COME WITH ME...
...AND LET ME SPEND THE NIGHT HERE.
NO, I CAN'T!
AHEM...

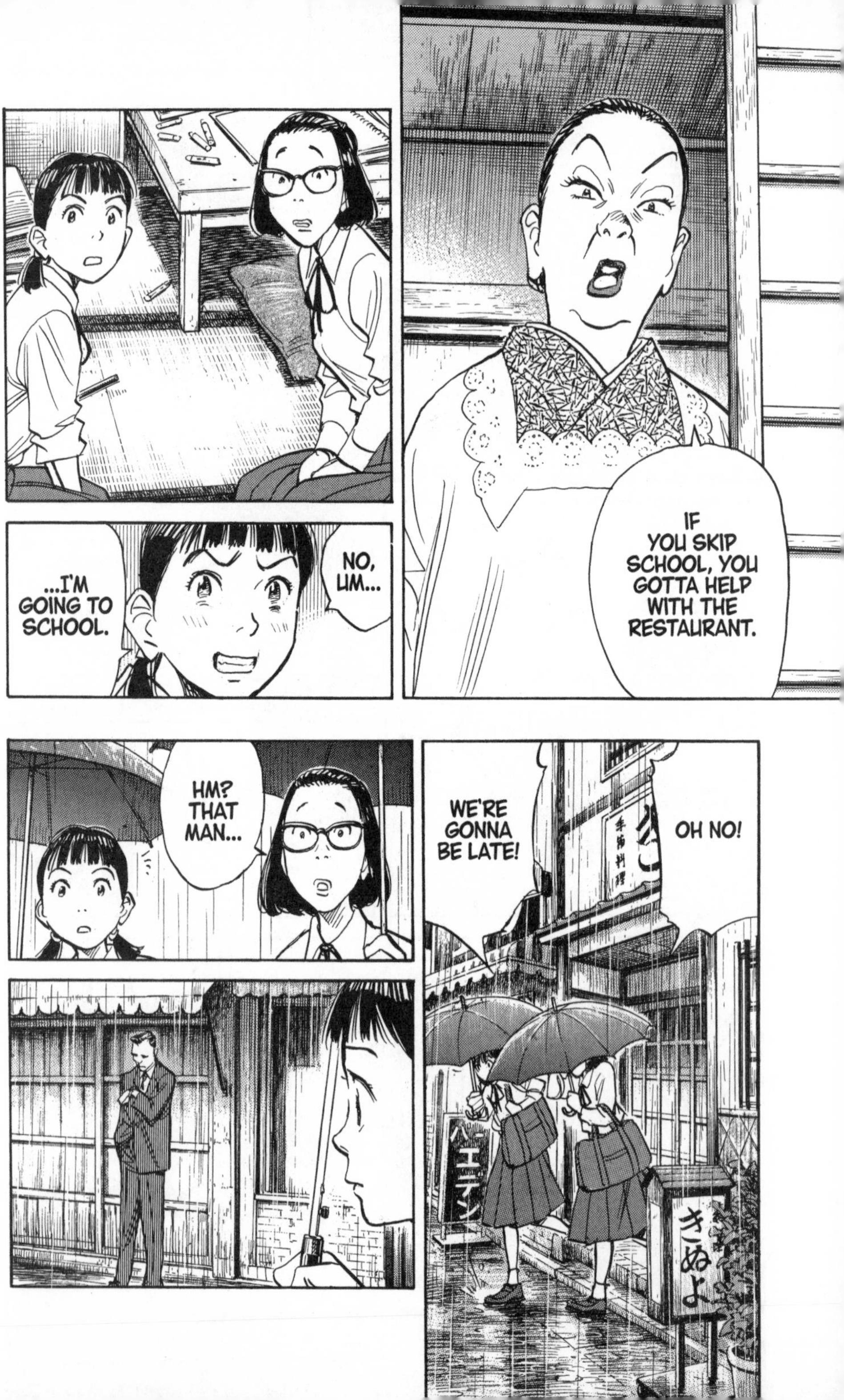
IF YOU SKIP SCHOOL, YOU GOTTA HELP WITH THE RESTAURANT.
NO, UM...
...I'M GOING TO SCHOOL.
季節料理
OH NO!
WE'RE GONNA BE LATE!
きぬよ
HM? THAT MAN...

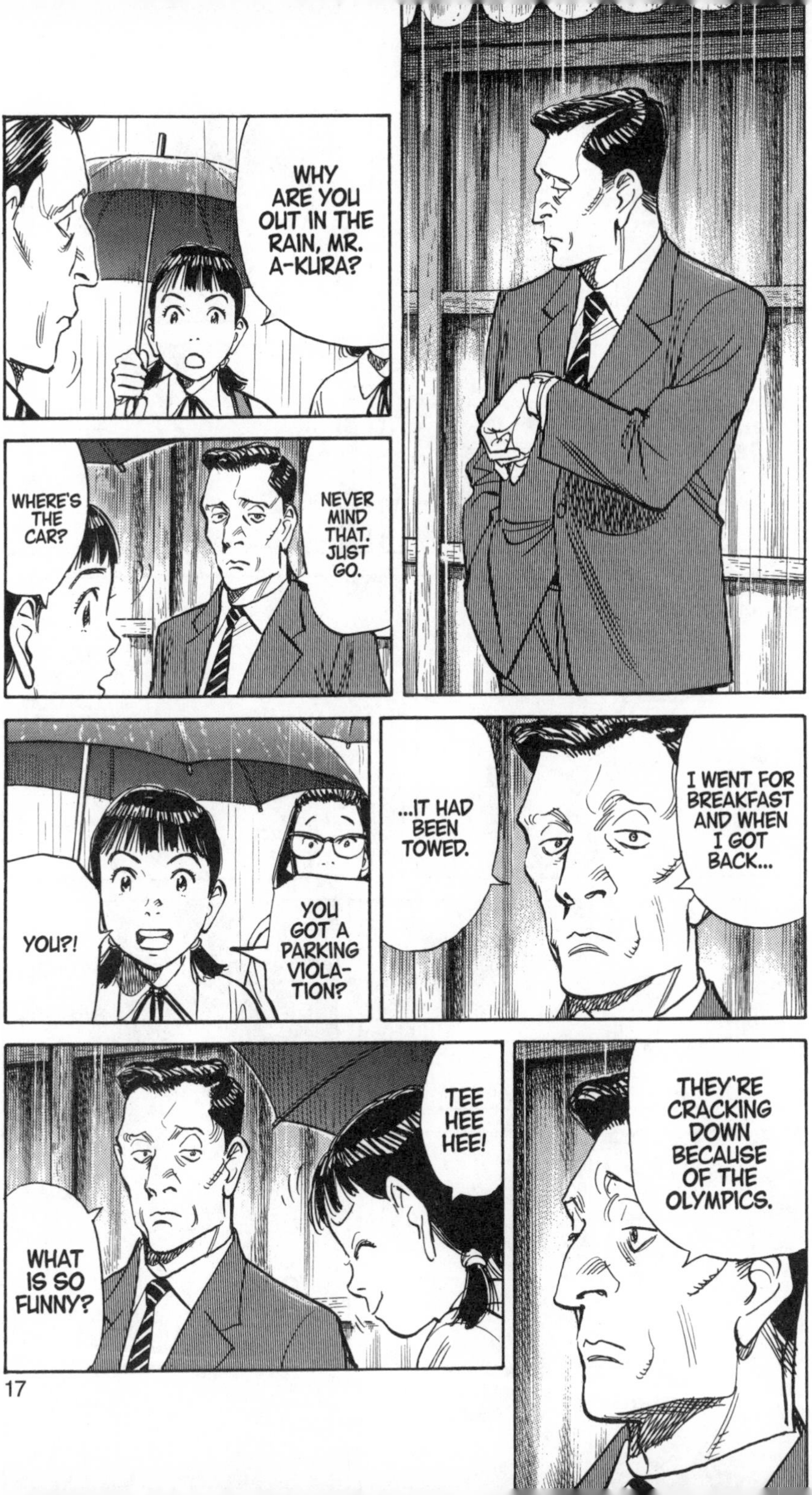
WHY ARE YOU OUT IN THE RAIN, MR. A-KURA?
WHERE'S THE CAR?
NEVER MIND THAT. JUST GO.
I WENT FOR BREAKFAST AND WHEN I GOT BACK...
...IT HAD BEEN TOWED.
YOU GOT A PARKING VIOLATION?
YOU?!
THEY'RE CRACKING DOWN BECAUSE OF THE OLYMPICS.
TEE HEE HEE!
WHAT IS SO FUNNY?

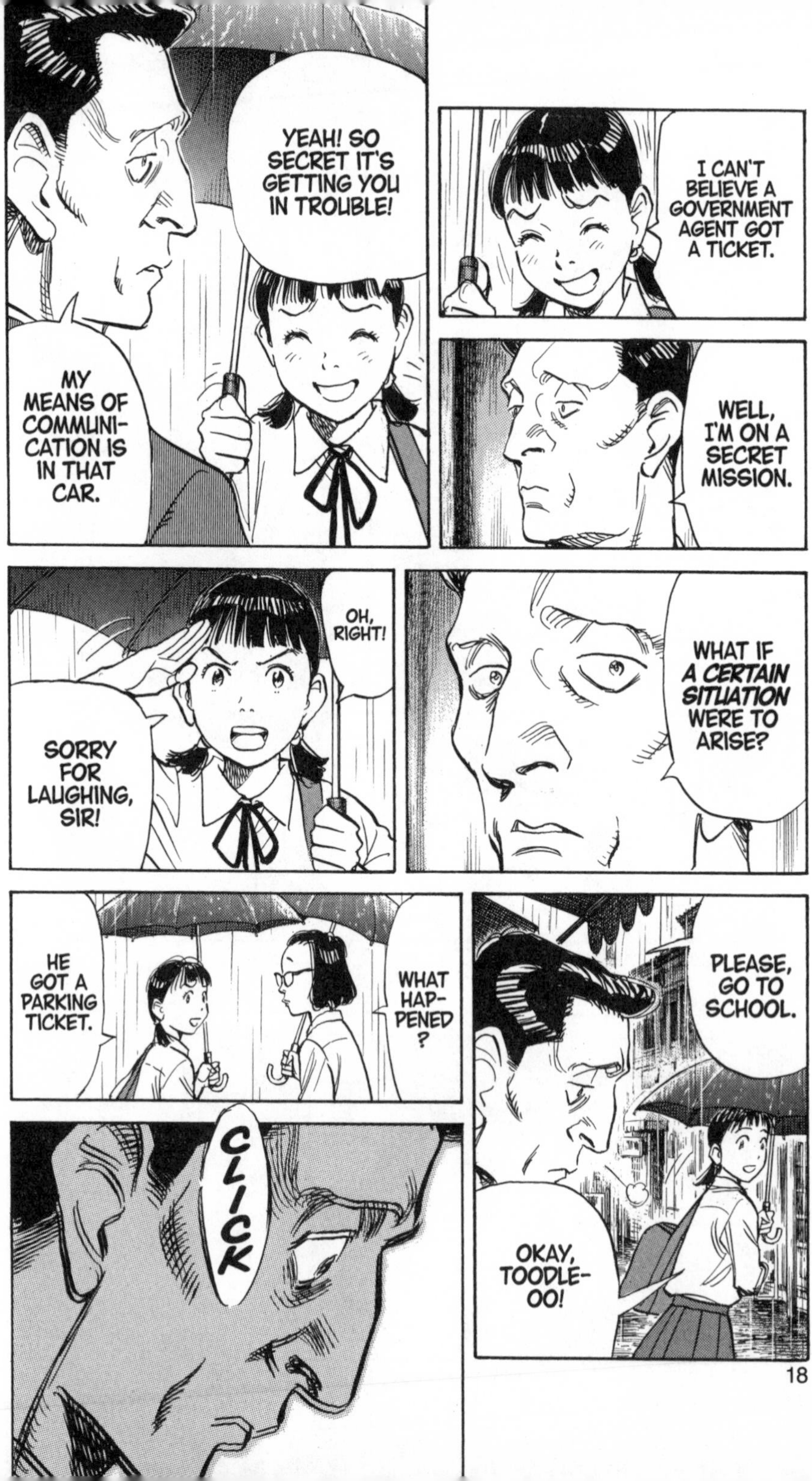
I CAN'T BELIEVE A GOVERNMENT AGENT GOT A TICKET.
WELL, I'M ON A SECRET MISSION.
YEAH! SO SECRET IT'S GETTING YOU IN TROUBLE!
MY MEANS OF COMMUNI-CATION IS IN THAT CAR.
WHAT IF A *CERTAIN SITUATION* WERE TO ARISE?
OH, RIGHT!
SORRY FOR LAUGHING, SIR!
PLEASE, GO TO SCHOOL.
OKAY, TOODLE-OO!
WHAT HAP-PENED?
HE GOT A PARKING TICKET.
CLICK

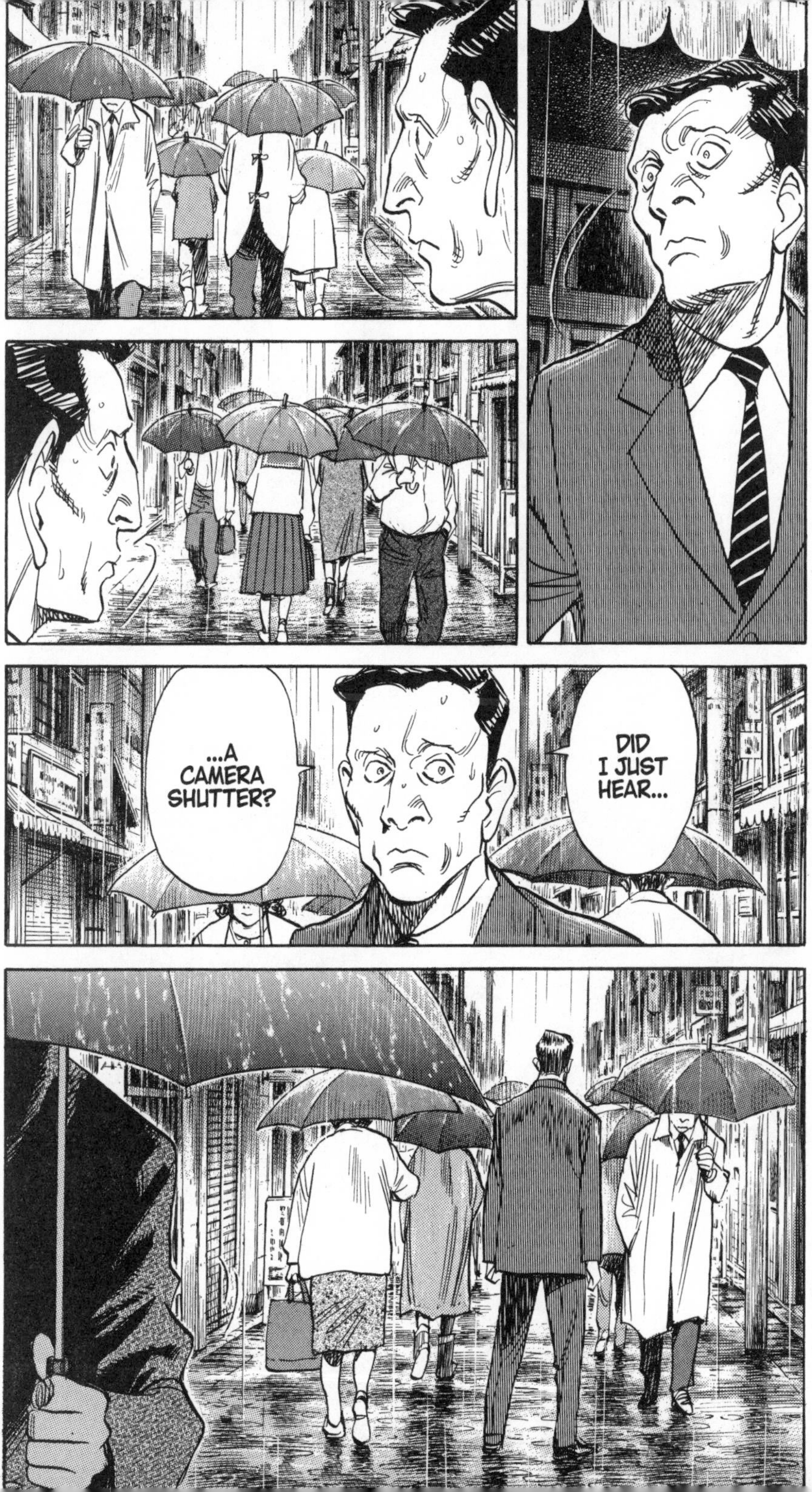
DID I JUST HEAR...
...A CAMERA SHUTTER?

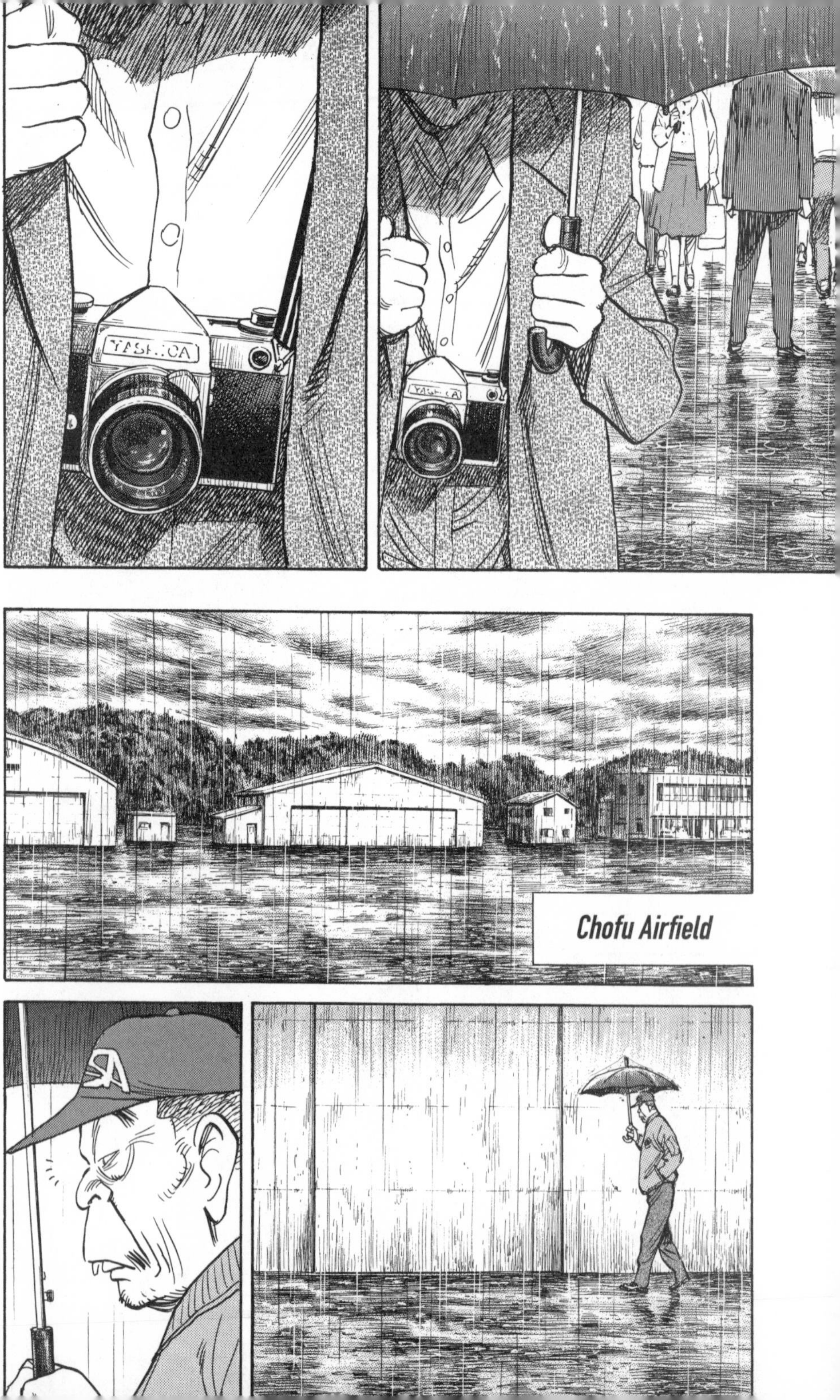
Chofu Airfield

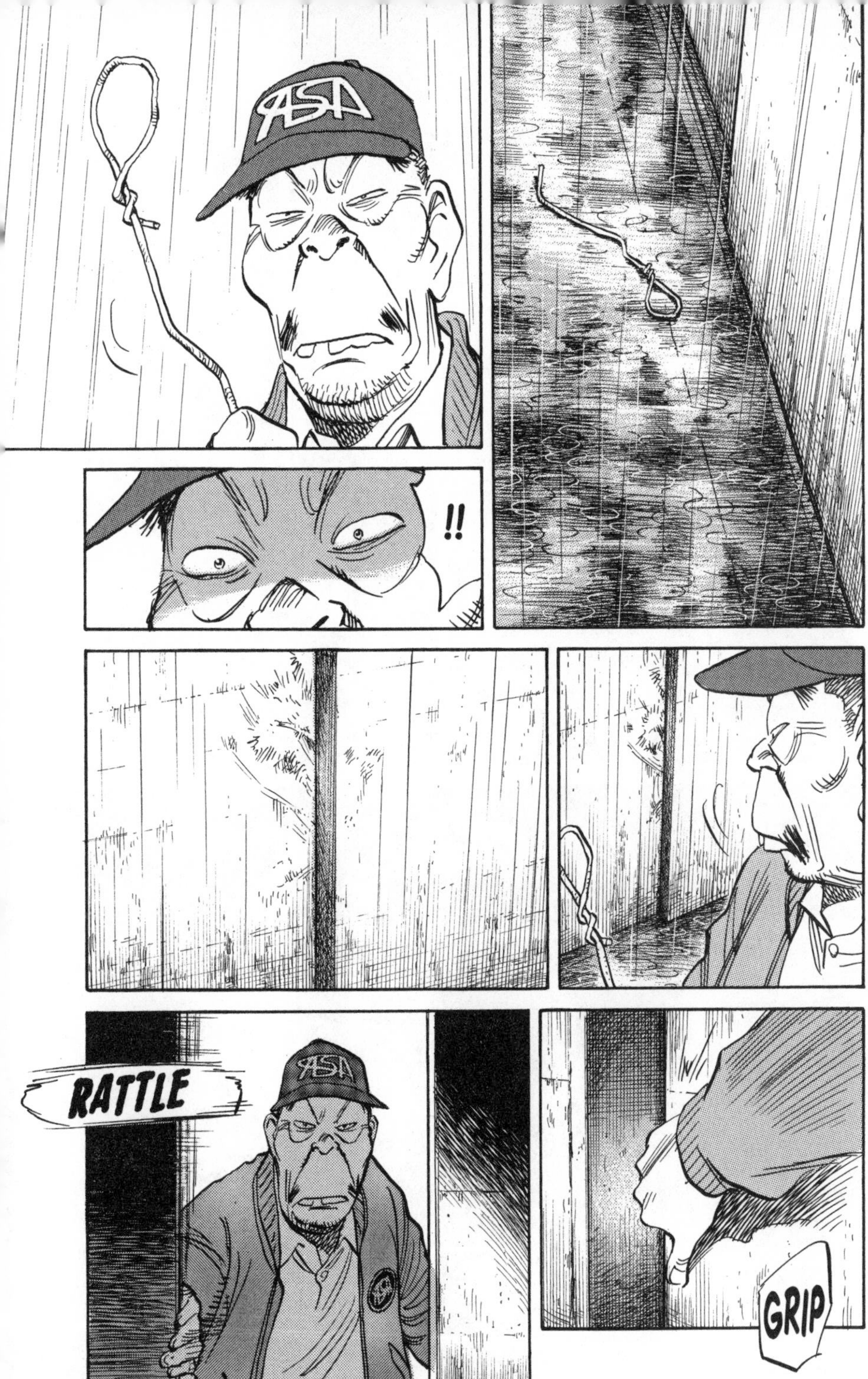
!!
GRIP
RATTLE

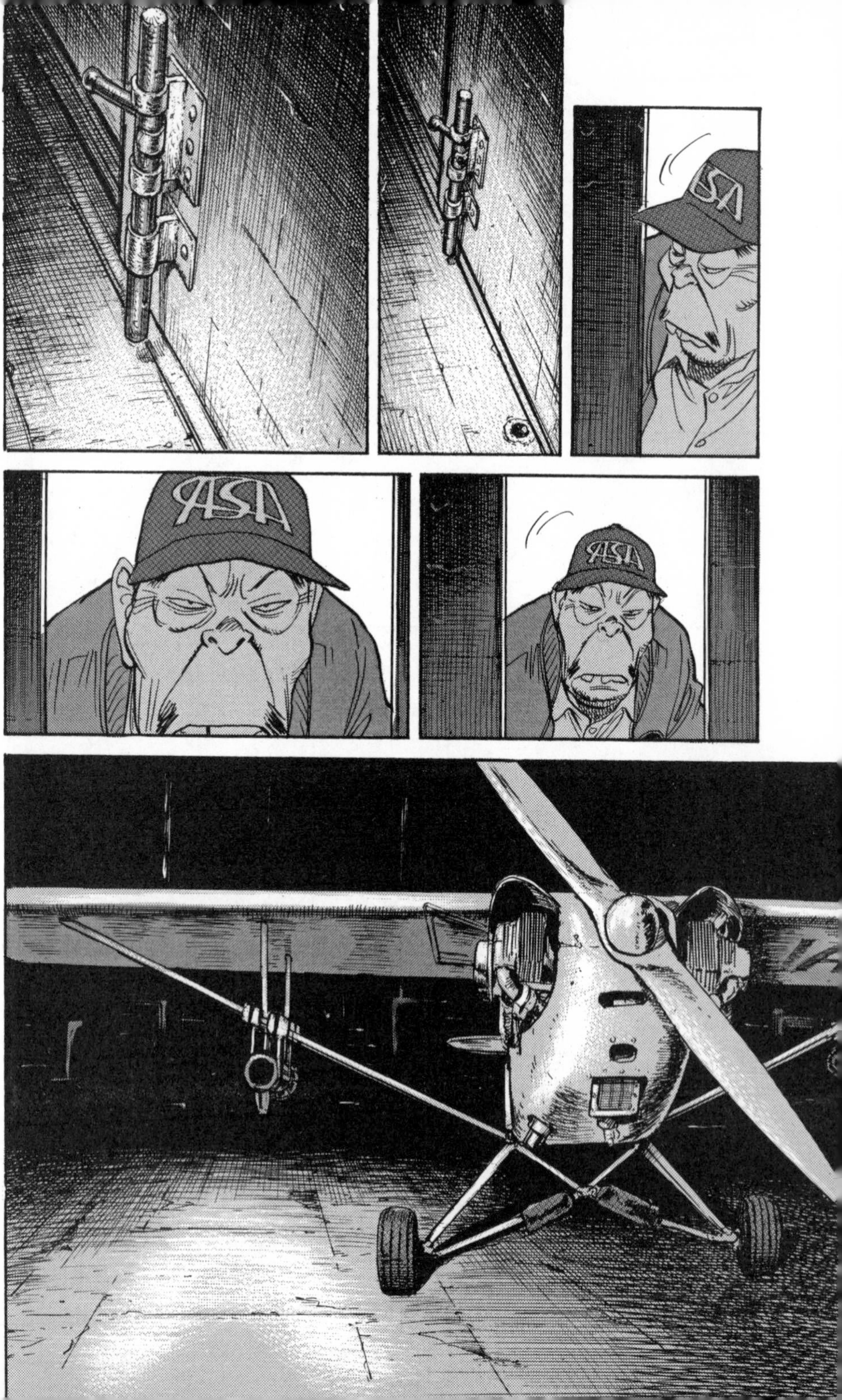

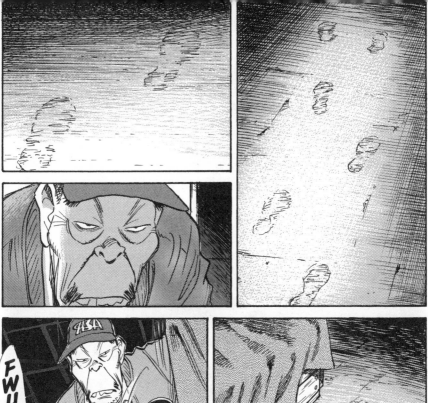

FWUP

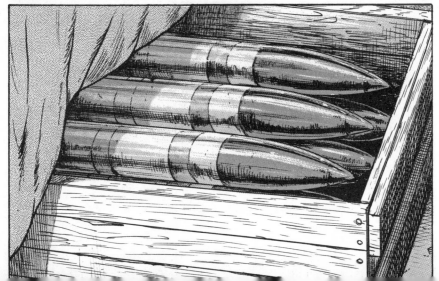

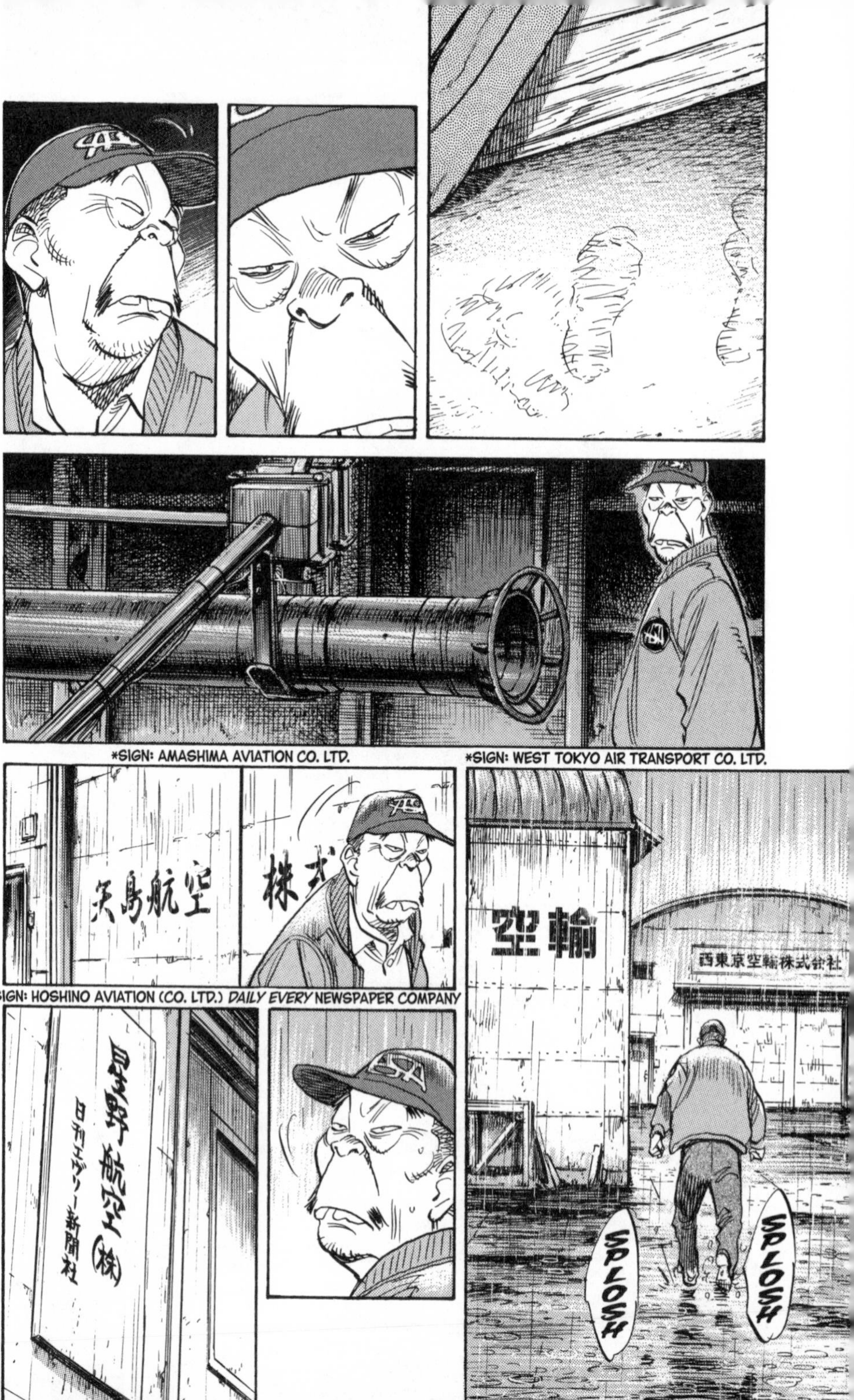
*SIGN: WEST TOKYO AIR TRANSPORT CO. LTD.
空輸
西東京空輸株式会社
SPLOSH
SPLOSH
*SIGN: AMASHIMA AVIATION CO. LTD.
株式
天島航空
*SIGN: HOSHINO AVIATION (CO. LTD.) *DAILY EVERY* NEWSPAPER COMPANY
星野航空(株)
日刊エヴリー新聞社

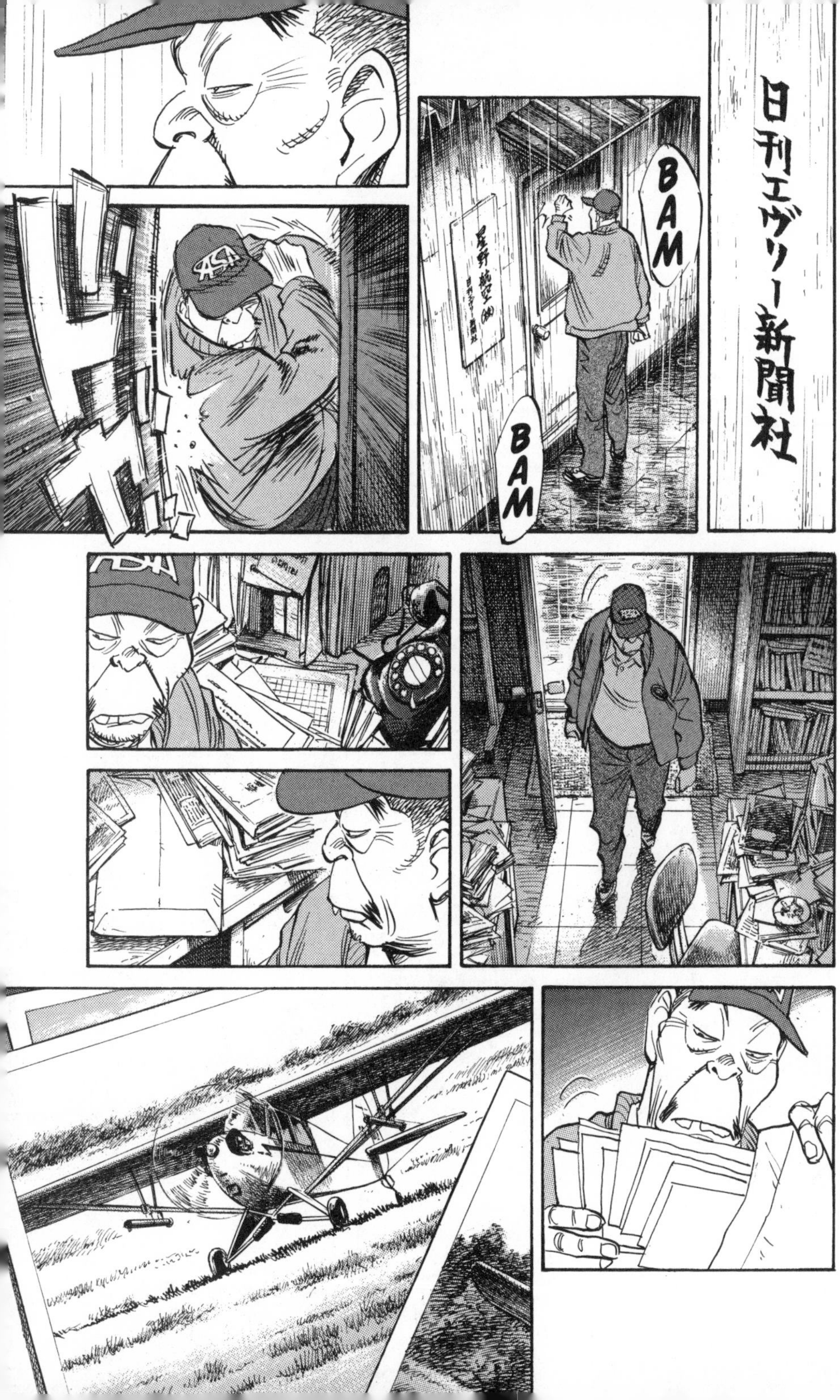
日刊エヴリー新聞社
BAM
BAM
星野航空(株)
日刊エヴリー新聞社

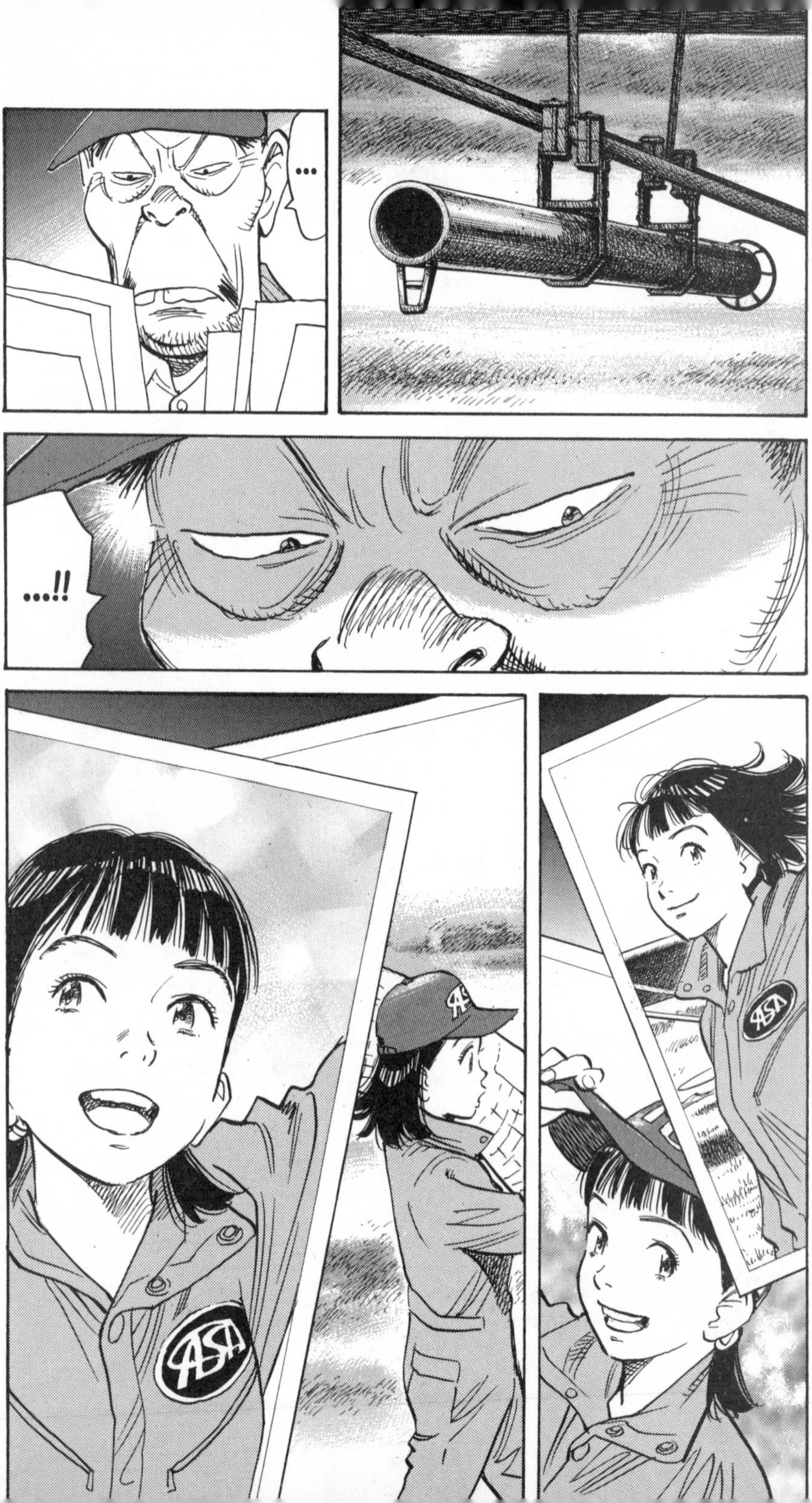
...
...!!

ASADORA!

ASADORA!

Chapter 25 ● Communication Breakdown

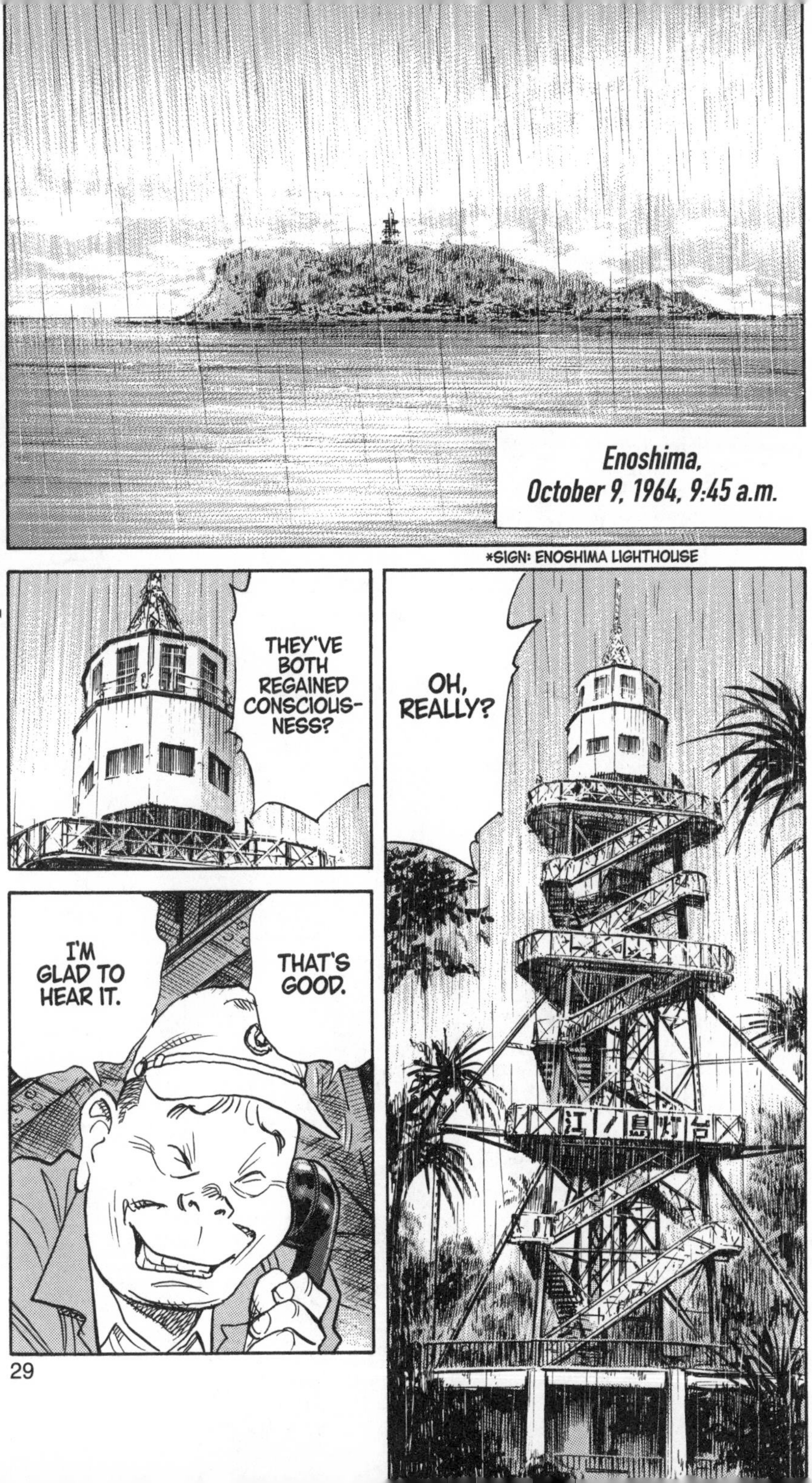
Enoshima,
October 9, 1964, 9:45 a.m.
*SIGN: ENOSHIMA LIGHTHOUSE
OH, REALLY?
江ノ島灯台
THEY'VE BOTH REGAINED CONSCIOUS-NESS?
THAT'S GOOD.
I'M GLAD TO HEAR IT.

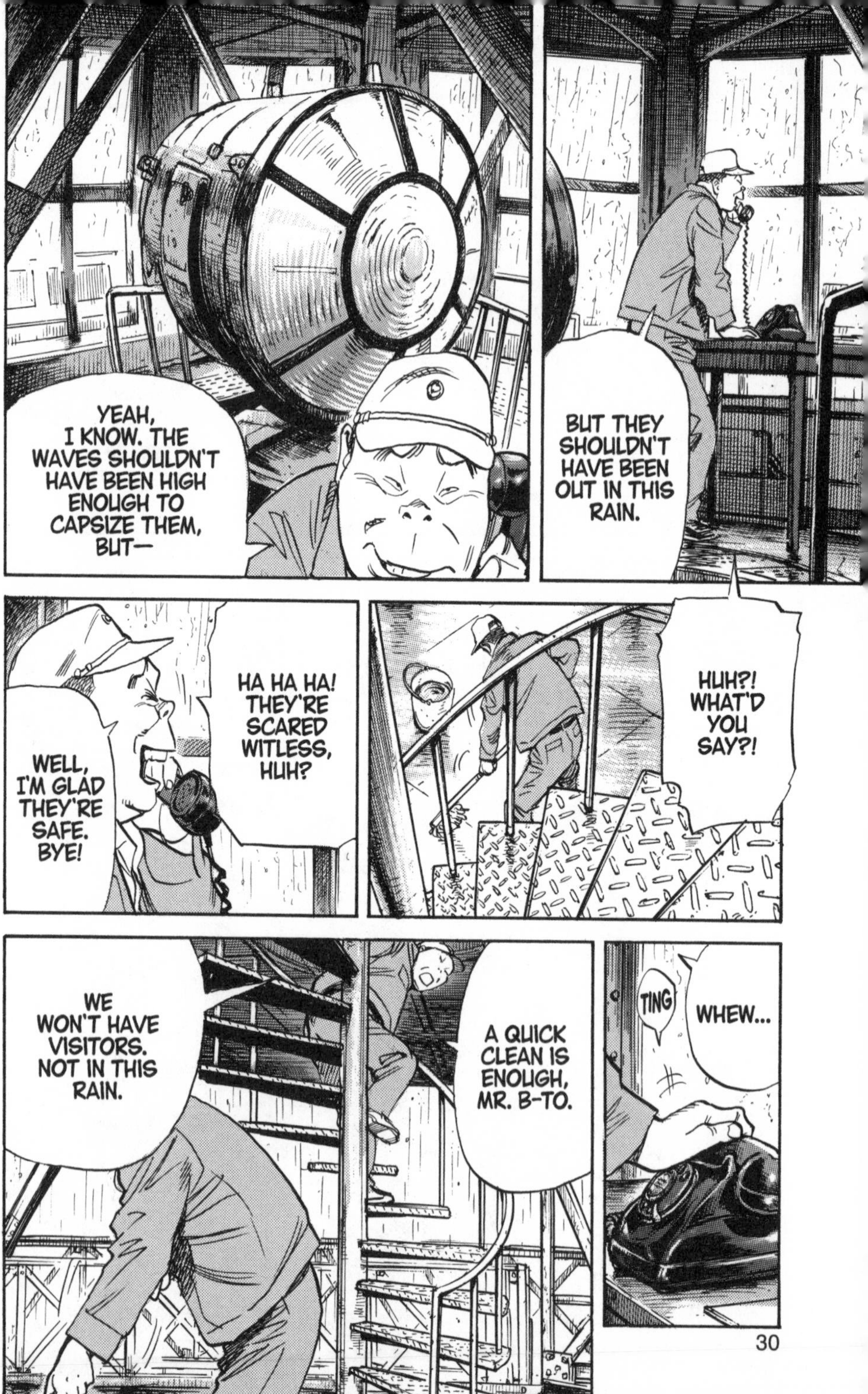
BUT THEY SHOULDN'T HAVE BEEN OUT IN THIS RAIN.
YEAH, I KNOW. THE WAVES SHOULDN'T HAVE BEEN HIGH ENOUGH TO CAPSIZE THEM, BUT—
HUH?! WHAT'D YOU SAY?!
HA HA HA! THEY'RE SCARED WITLESS, HUH?
WELL, I'M GLAD THEY'RE SAFE. BYE!
TING
WHEW...
A QUICK CLEAN IS ENOUGH, MR. B-TO.
WE WON'T HAVE VISITORS. NOT IN THIS RAIN.

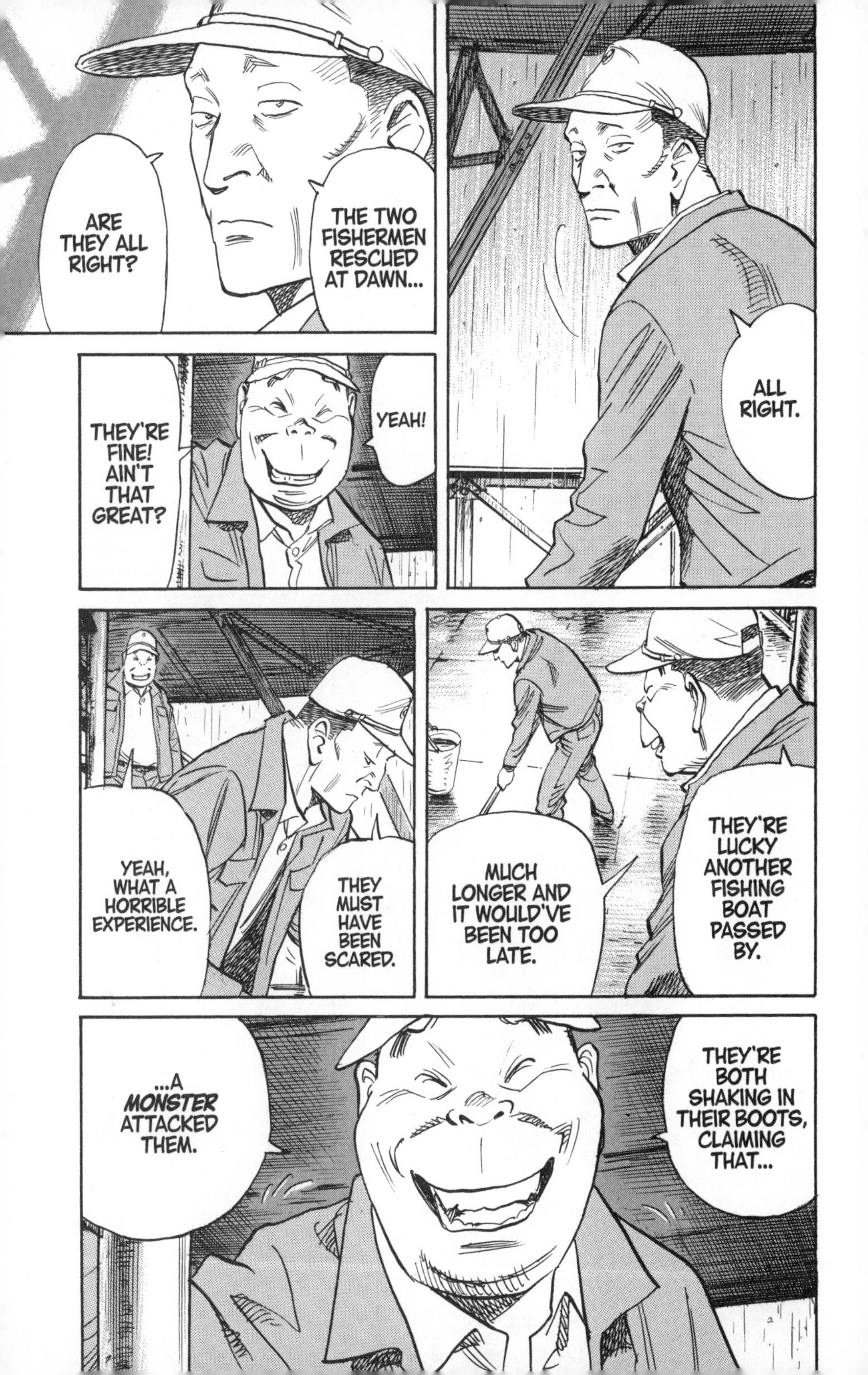
ALL RIGHT.
THE TWO FISHERMEN RESCUED AT DAWN...
ARE THEY ALL RIGHT?
YEAH!
THEY'RE FINE! AIN'T THAT GREAT?
THEY'RE LUCKY ANOTHER FISHING BOAT PASSED BY.
MUCH LONGER AND IT WOULD'VE BEEN TOO LATE.
THEY MUST HAVE BEEN SCARED.
YEAH, WHAT A HORRIBLE EXPERIENCE.
THEY'RE BOTH SHAKING IN THEIR BOOTS, CLAIMING THAT...
...A *MONSTER* ATTACKED THEM.

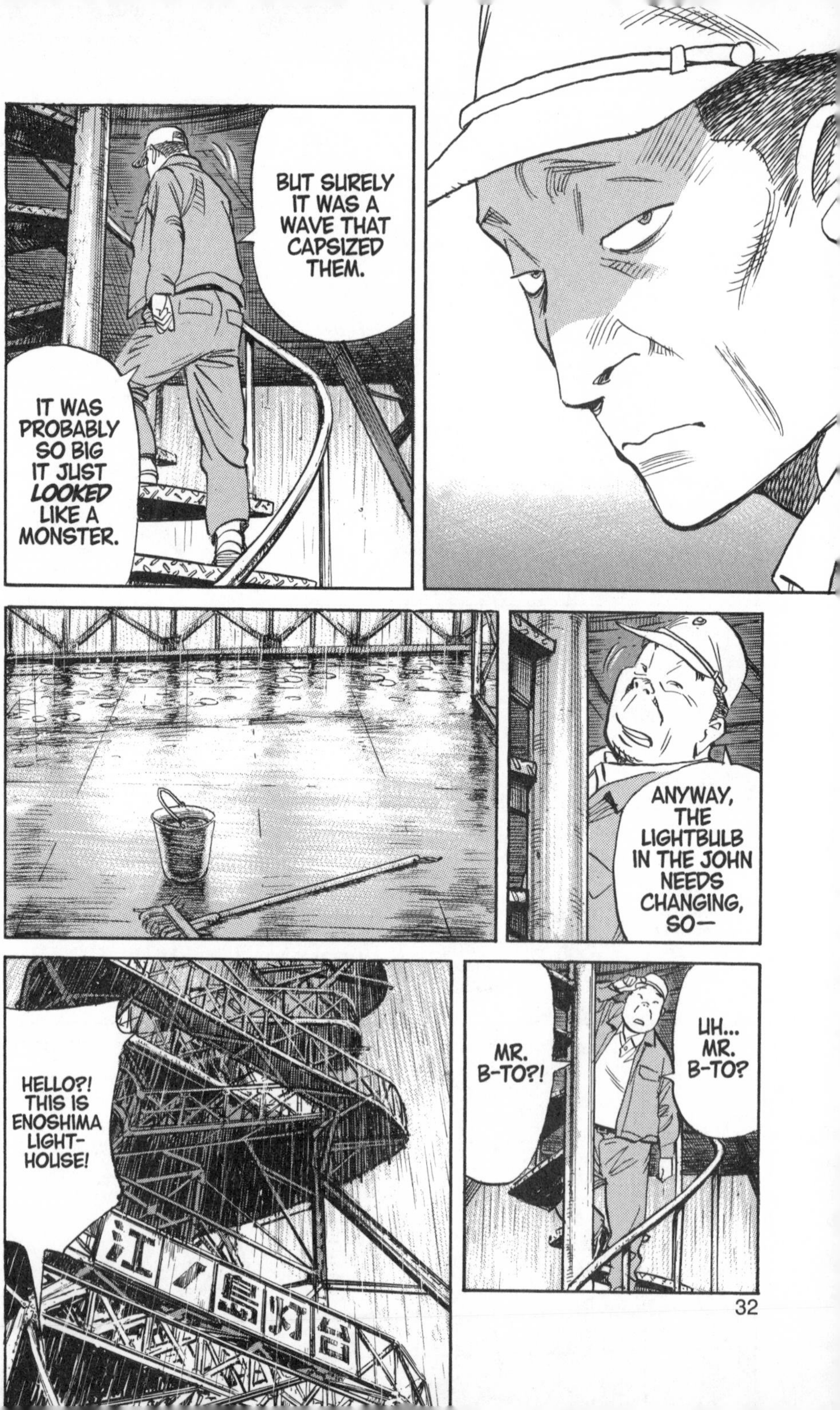
BUT SURELY IT WAS A WAVE THAT CAPSIZED THEM.
IT WAS PROBABLY SO BIG IT JUST *LOOKED* LIKE A MONSTER.
ANYWAY, THE LIGHTBULB IN THE JOHN NEEDS CHANGING, SO—
UH... MR. B-TO?
MR. B-TO?!
HELLO?! THIS IS ENOSHIMA LIGHT-HOUSE!
江ノ島灯台

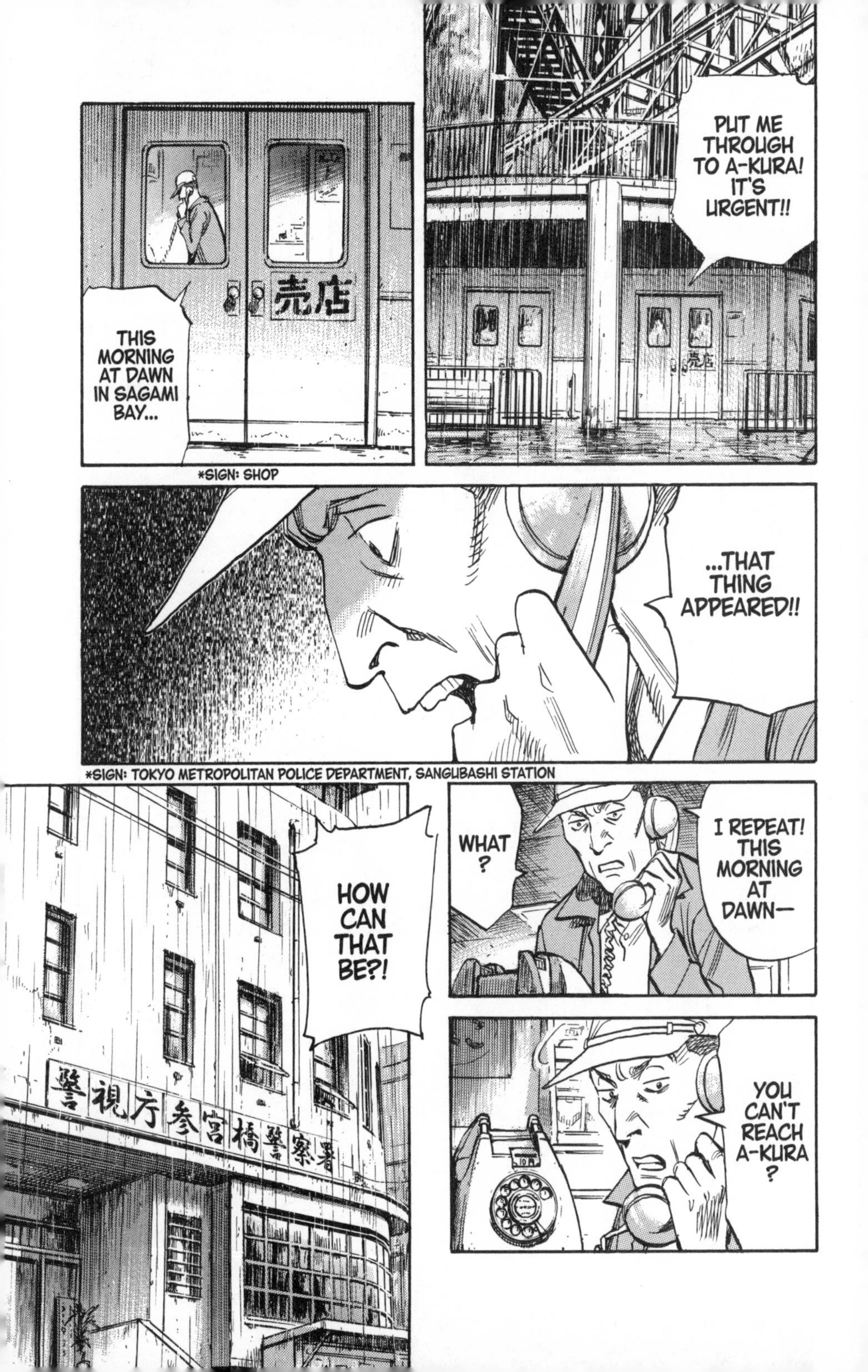
PUT ME THROUGH TO A-KURA! IT'S URGENT!!
THIS MORNING AT DAWN IN SAGAMI BAY...
売店
*SIGN: SHOP
...THAT THING APPEARED!!
*SIGN: TOKYO METROPOLITAN POLICE DEPARTMENT, SANGUBASHI STATION
I REPEAT! THIS MORNING AT DAWN—
WHAT?
YOU CAN'T REACH A-KURA?
警視庁参宮橋警察署
HOW CAN THAT BE?!

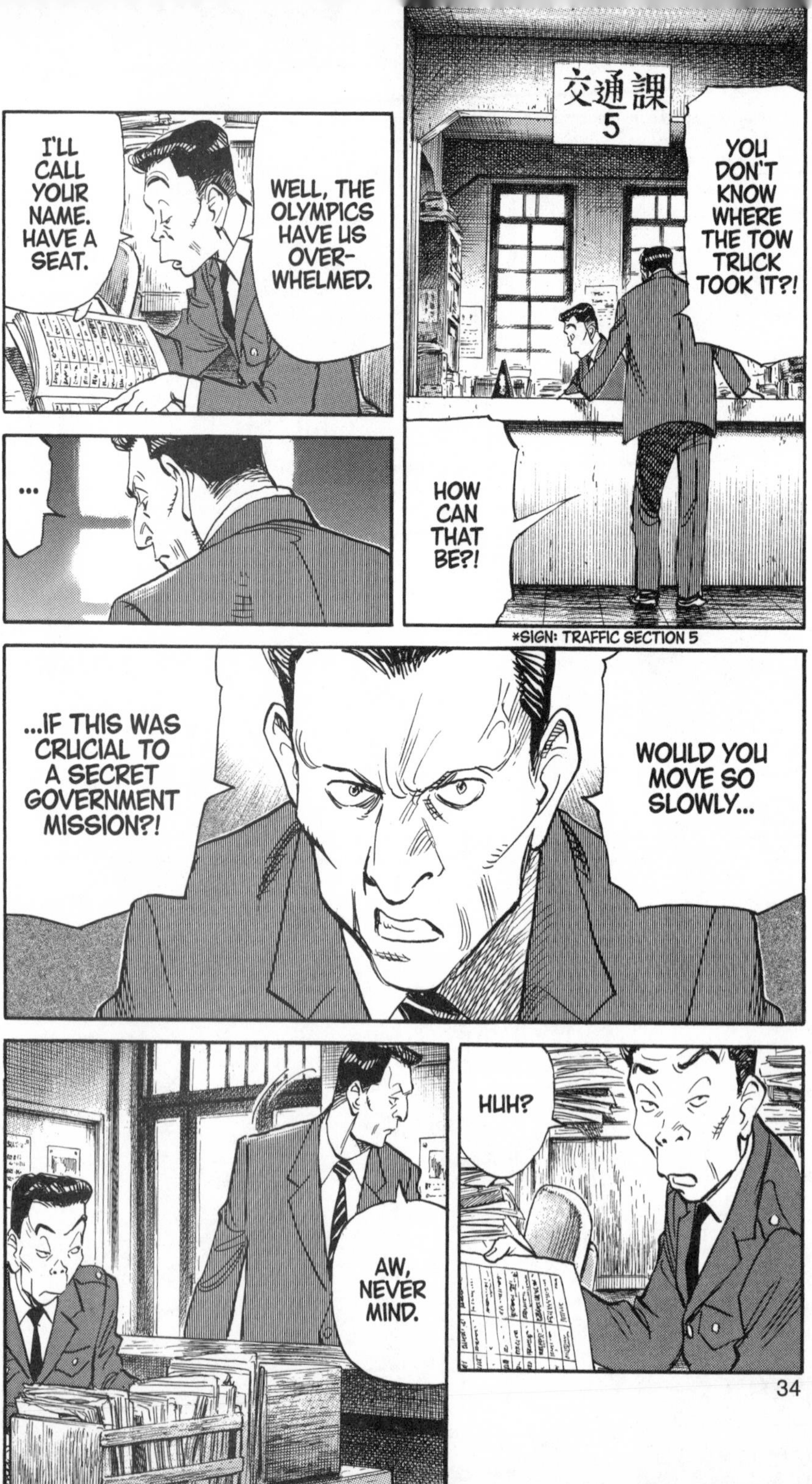
交通課
5
YOU DON'T KNOW WHERE THE TOW TRUCK TOOK IT?!
HOW CAN THAT BE?!
WELL, THE OLYMPICS HAVE US OVER-WHELMED.
I'LL CALL YOUR NAME. HAVE A SEAT.
...
*SIGN: TRAFFIC SECTION 5
WOULD YOU MOVE SO SLOWLY...
...IF THIS WAS CRUCIAL TO A SECRET GOVERNMENT MISSION?!
HUH?
AW, NEVER MIND.

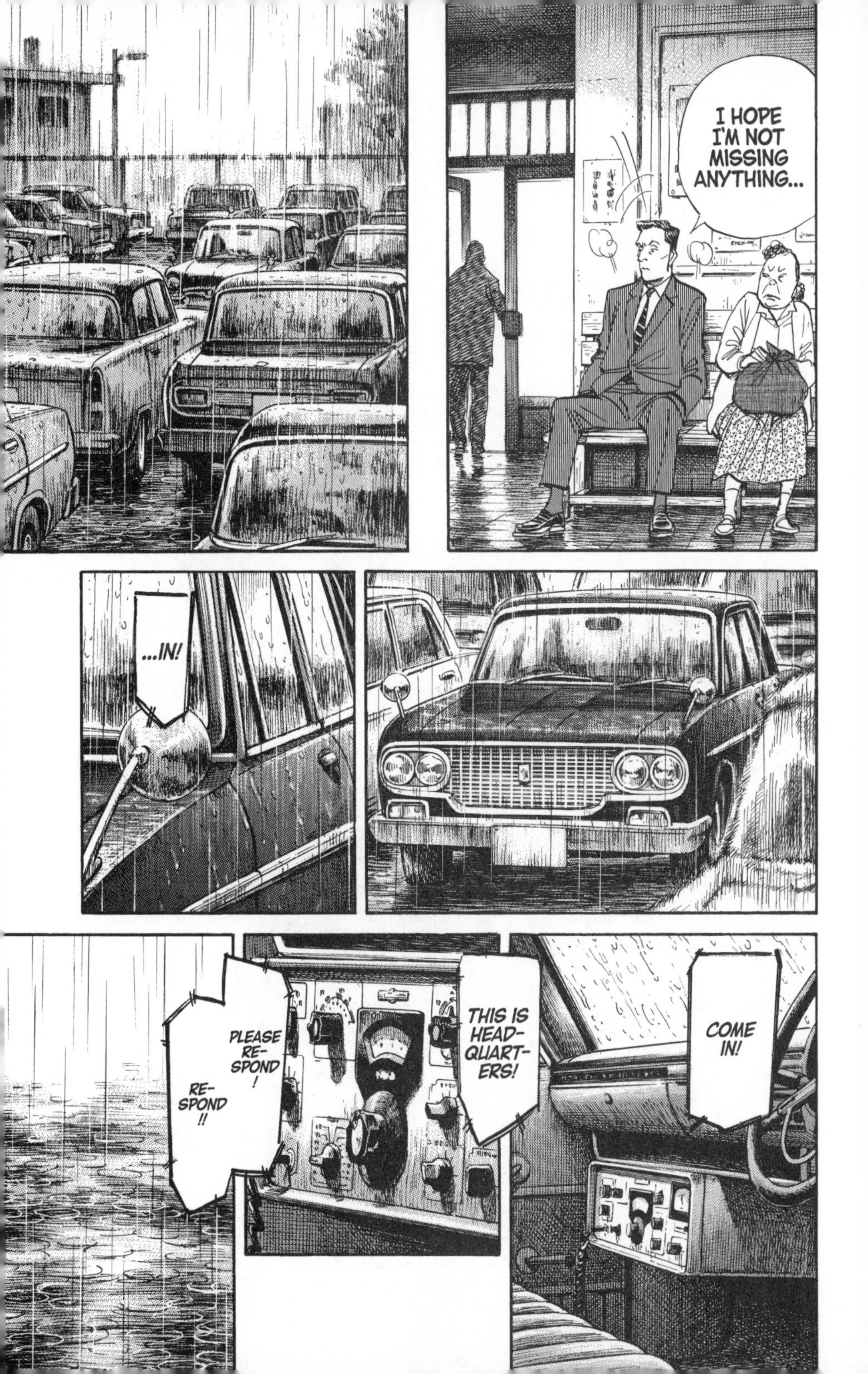
I HOPE I'M NOT MISSING ANYTHING...
...IN!
COME IN!
THIS IS HEADQUARTERS!
PLEASE RESPOND!
RESPOND!!

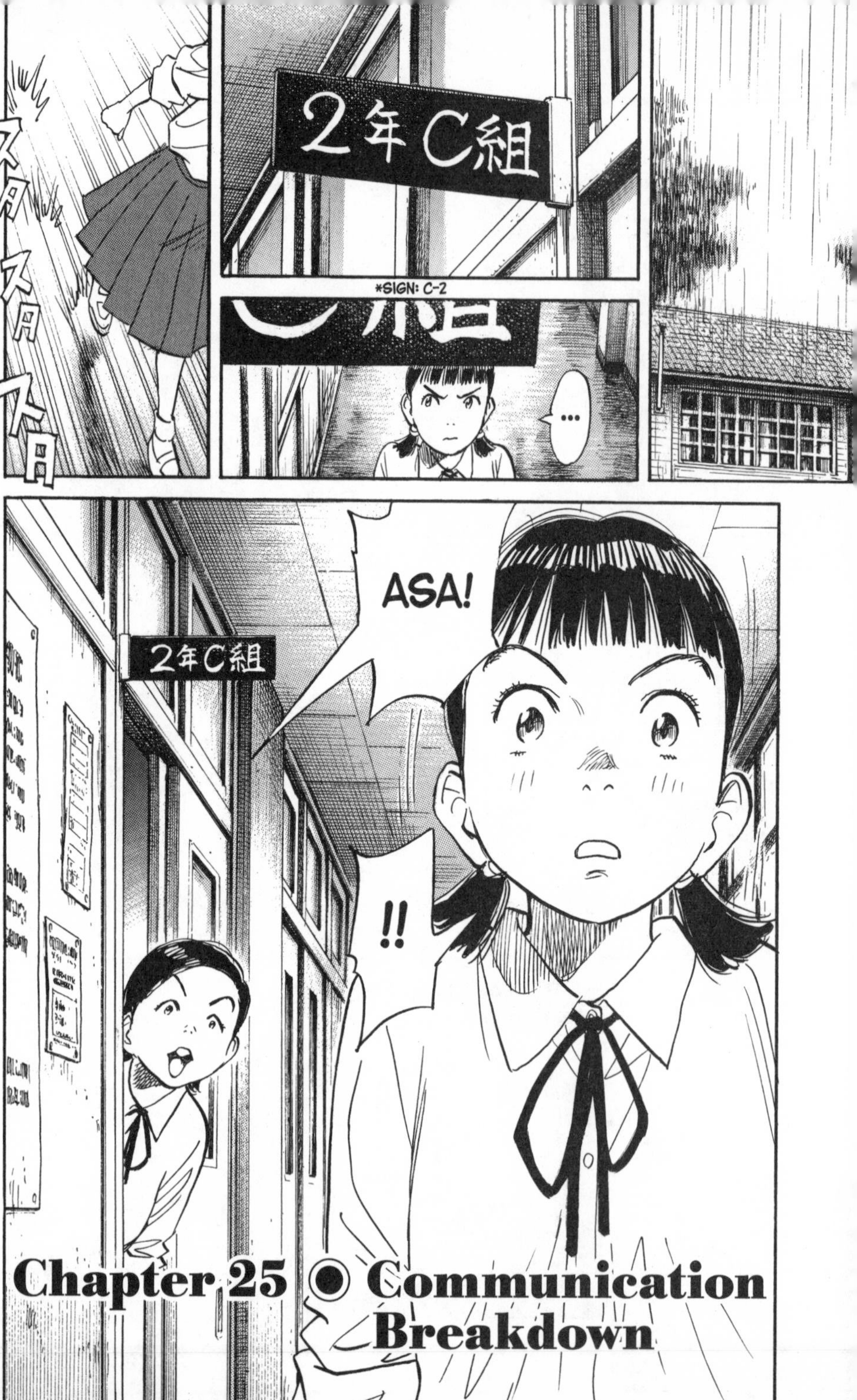
2年C組
*SIGN: C-2
...
スタスタスタ
ASA!
2年C組
!!
Chapter 25 ● Communication Breakdown

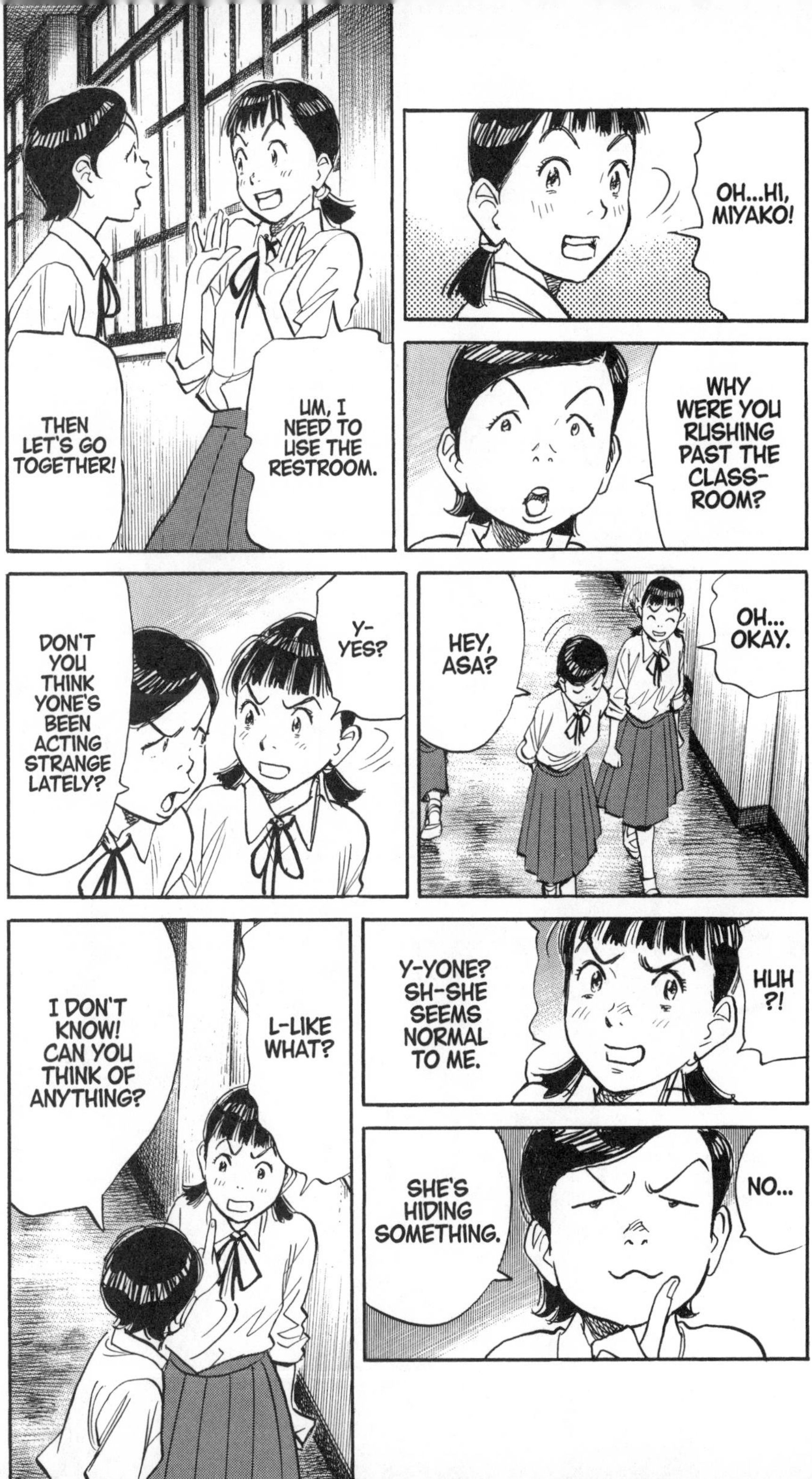
OH...HI, MIYAKO!
WHY WERE YOU RUSHING PAST THE CLASS-ROOM?
UM, I NEED TO USE THE RESTROOM.
THEN LET'S GO TOGETHER!
OH... OKAY.
HEY, ASA?
Y-YES?
DON'T YOU THINK YONE'S BEEN ACTING STRANGE LATELY?
HUH ?!
Y-YONE? SH-SHE SEEMS NORMAL TO ME.
NO...
SHE'S HIDING SOMETHING.
L-LIKE WHAT?
I DON'T KNOW! CAN YOU THINK OF ANYTHING?

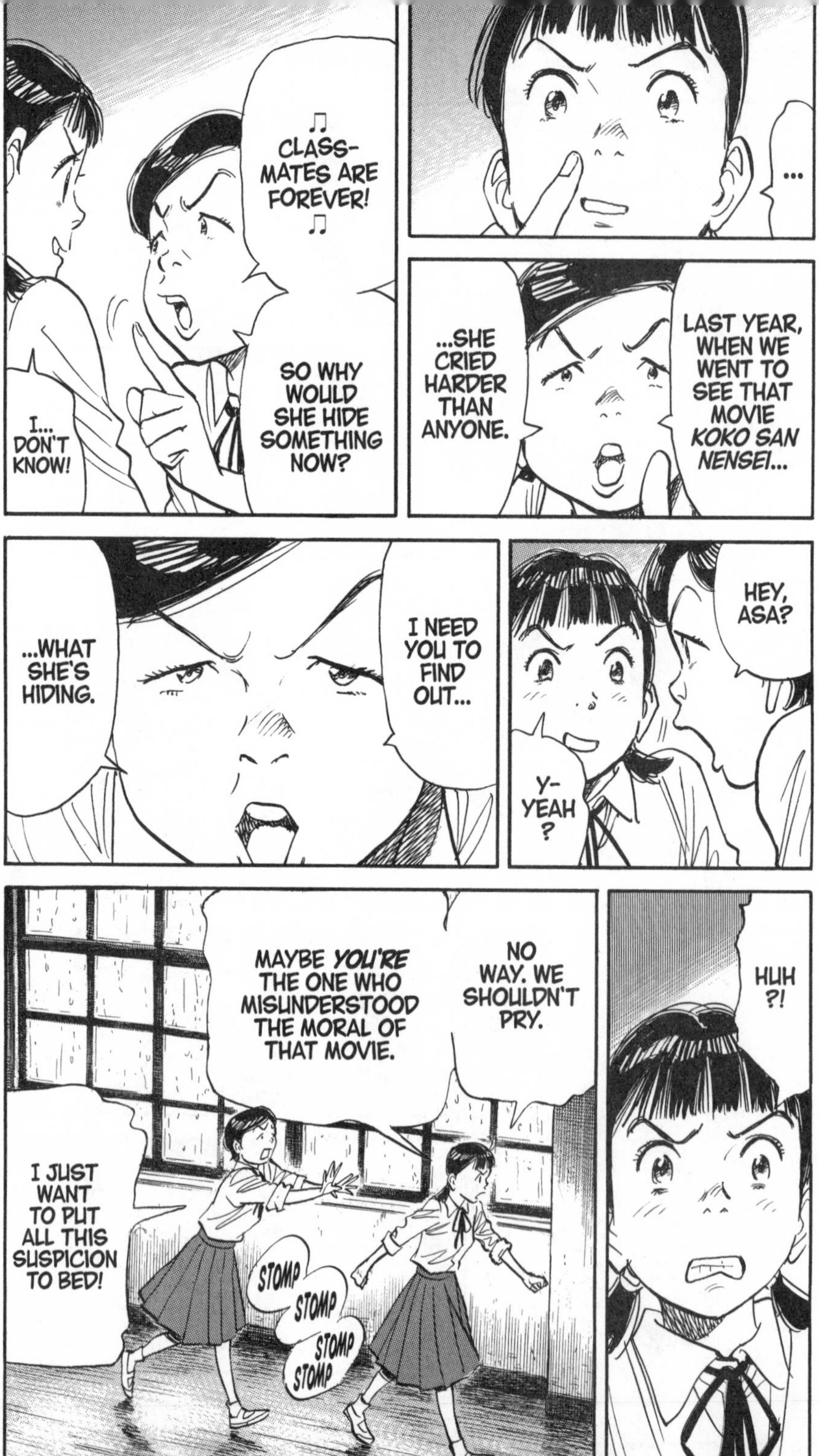
...
LAST YEAR, WHEN WE WENT TO SEE THAT MOVIE *KOKO SAN NENSEI*...
...SHE CRIED HARDER THAN ANYONE.
♫ CLASS-MATES ARE FOREVER! ♫
SO WHY WOULD SHE HIDE SOMETHING NOW?
I... DON'T KNOW!
HEY, ASA?
Y-YEAH?
I NEED YOU TO FIND OUT...
...WHAT SHE'S HIDING.
HUH?!
NO WAY. WE SHOULDN'T PRY.
MAYBE *YOU'RE* THE ONE WHO MISUNDERSTOOD THE MORAL OF THAT MOVIE.
I JUST WANT TO PUT ALL THIS SUSPICION TO BED!
STOMP
STOMP
STOMP
STOMP

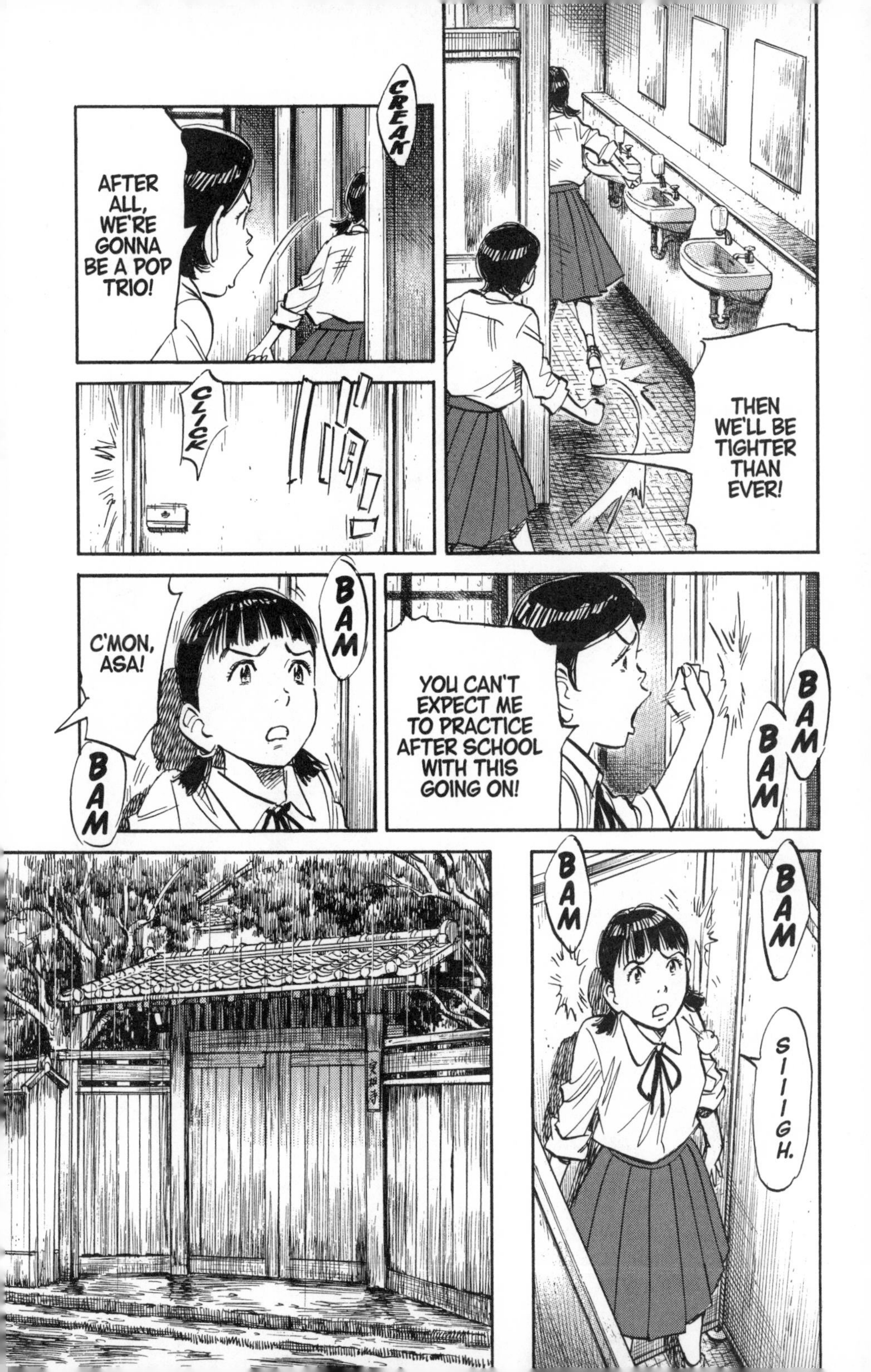
THEN WE'LL BE TIGHTER THAN EVER!
CREAK
AFTER ALL, WE'RE GONNA BE A POP TRIO!
CLICK
BAM BAM
YOU CAN'T EXPECT ME TO PRACTICE AFTER SCHOOL WITH THIS GOING ON!
BAM BAM
BAM
C'MON, ASA!
BAM
BAM
BAM
SIIIGH.

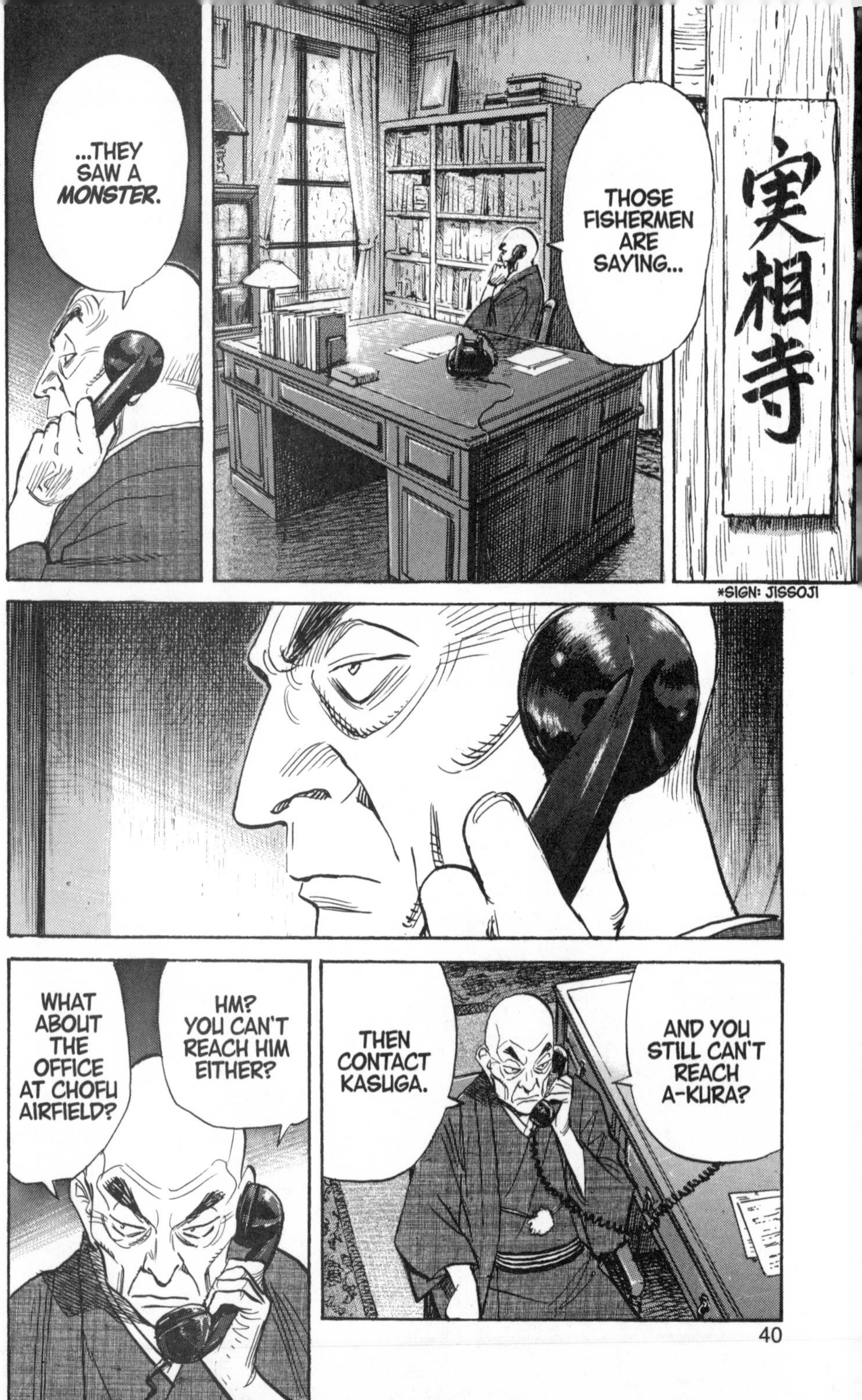
実相寺
THOSE FISHERMEN ARE SAYING...
...THEY SAW A *MONSTER*.
*SIGN: JISSOJI
AND YOU STILL CAN'T REACH A-KURA?
THEN CONTACT KASUGA.
HM? YOU CAN'T REACH HIM EITHER?
WHAT ABOUT THE OFFICE AT CHOFU AIRFIELD?

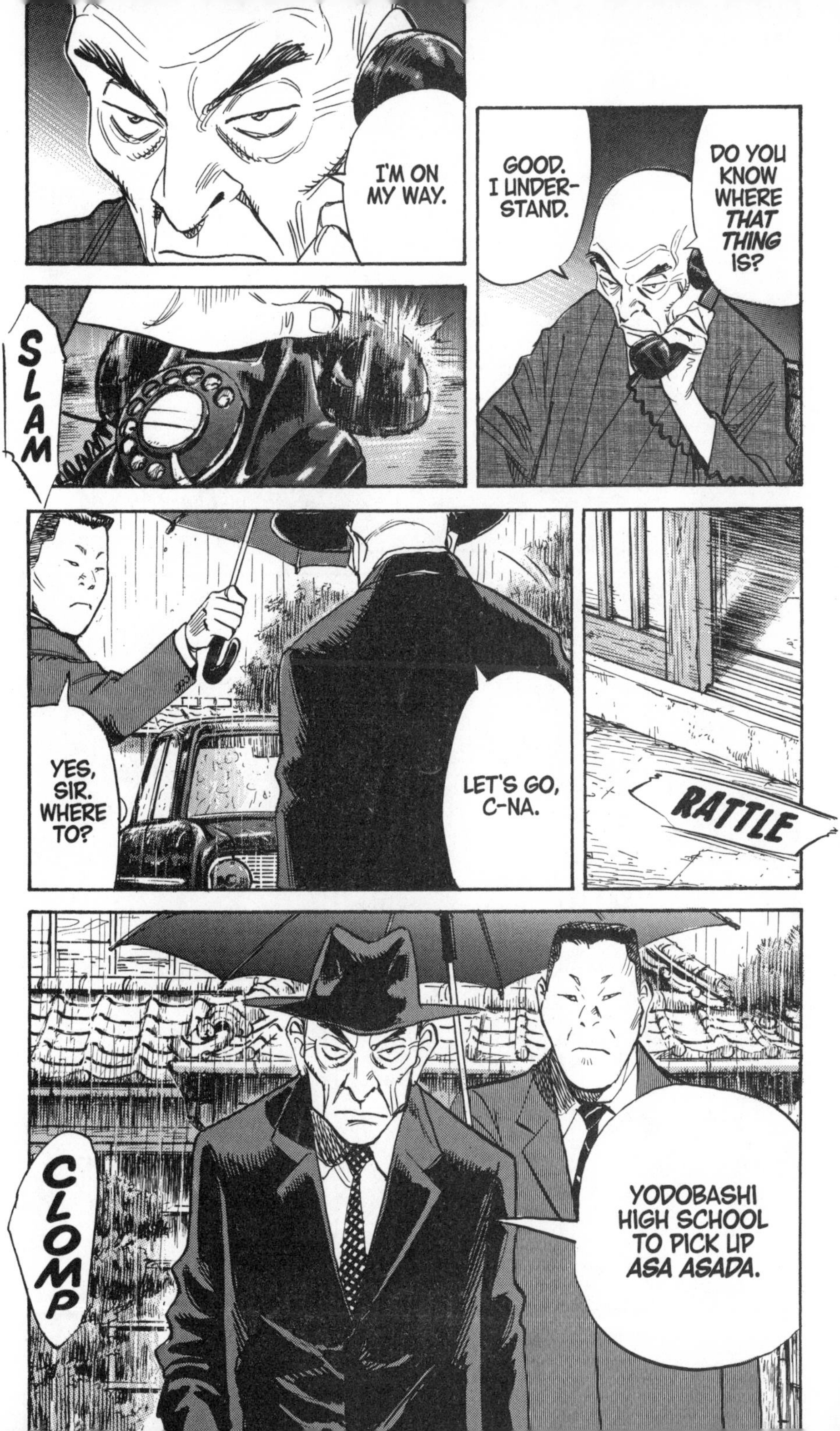
DO YOU KNOW WHERE *THAT THING* IS?
GOOD. I UNDER-STAND.
I'M ON MY WAY.
SLAM
RATTLE
LET'S GO, C-NA.
YES, SIR. WHERE TO?
YODOBASHI HIGH SCHOOL TO PICK UP ASA ASADA.
CLOMP

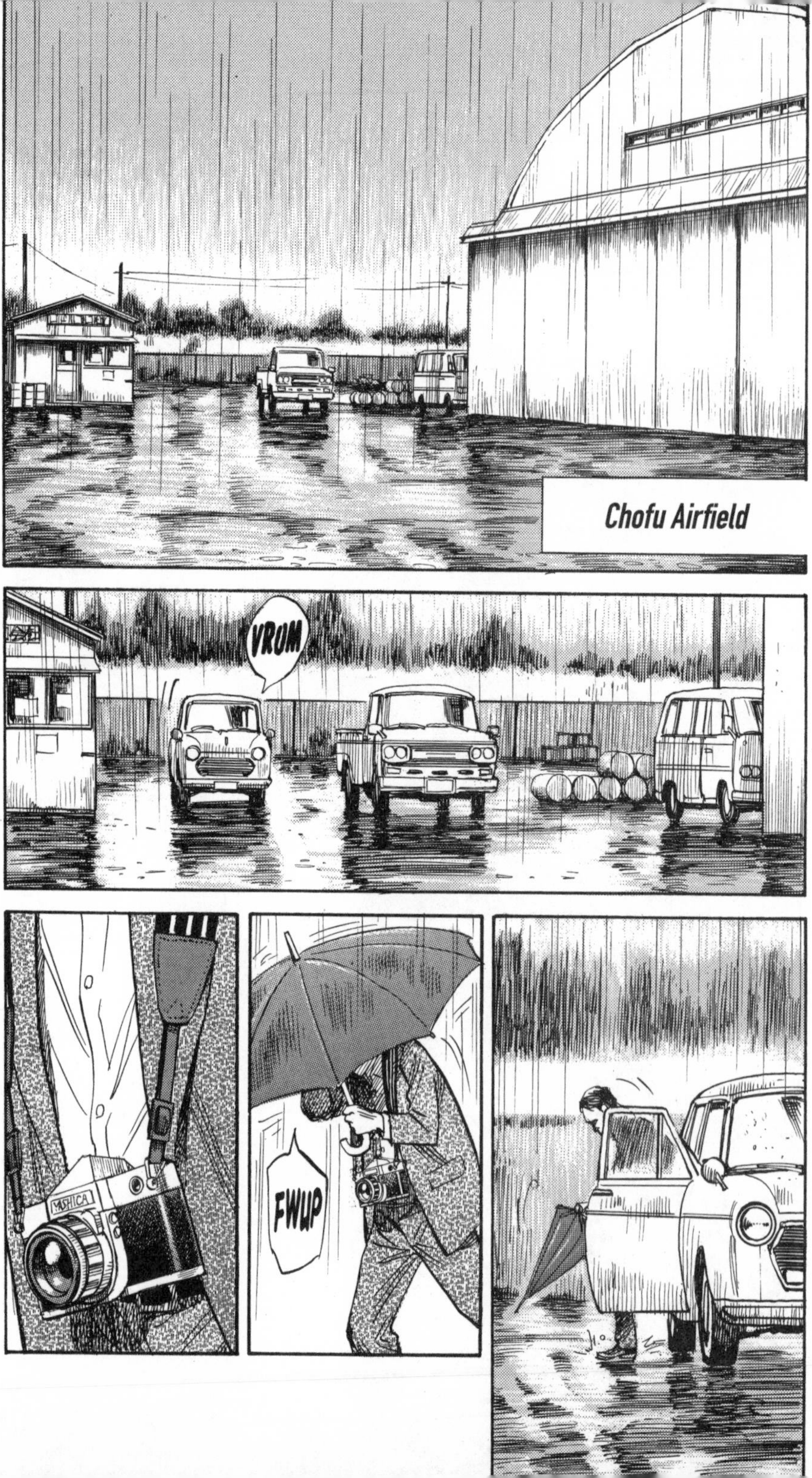
Chofu Airfield
VRUM
FWUP
YASHICA

*SIGN: HOSHINO AVIATION (CO. LTD.)
DAILY EVERY NEWSPAPER COMPANY

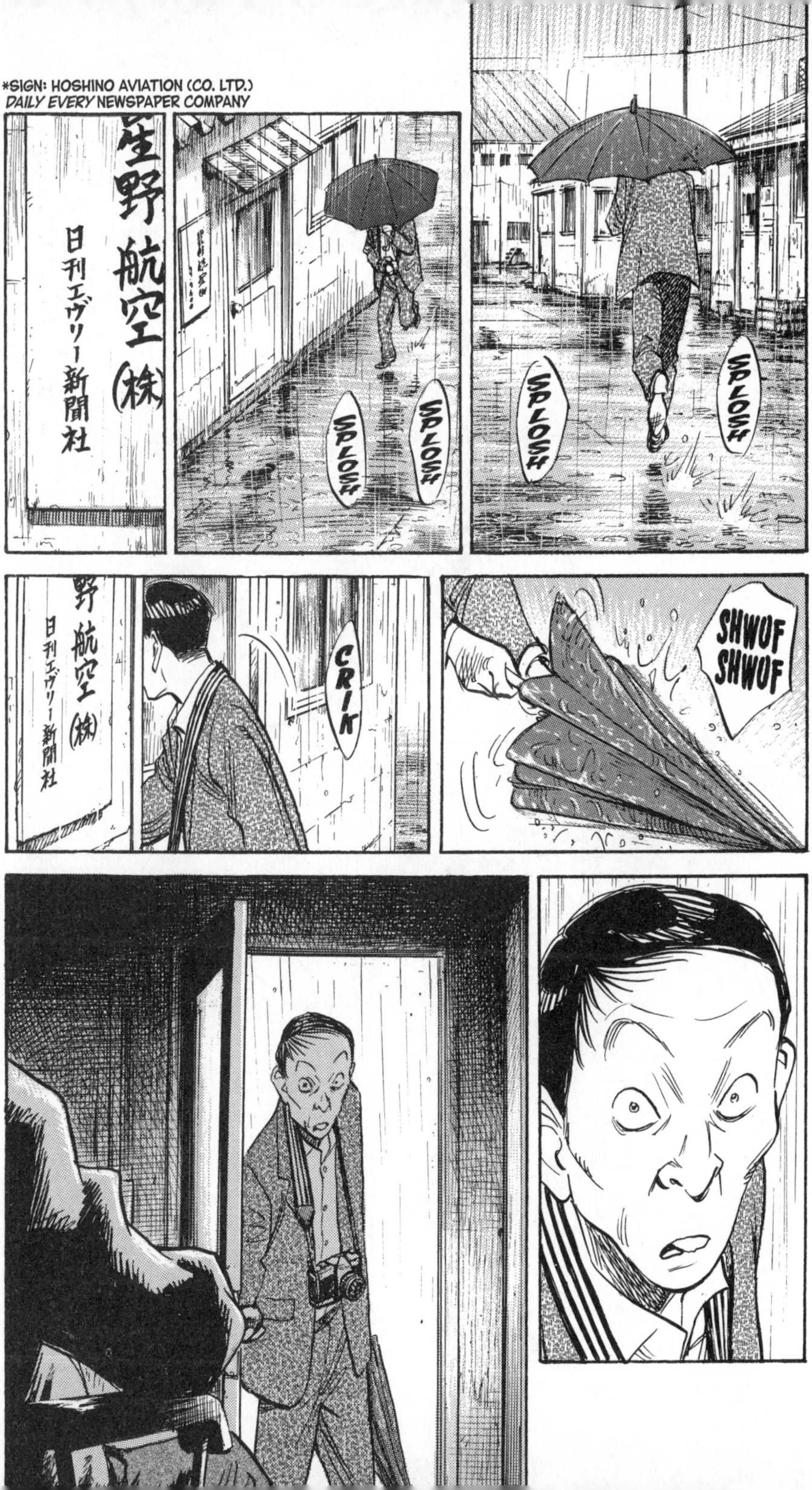
SPLOSH
SPLOSH
SPLOSH
SPLOSH
星野航空(株)
日刊エヴリー新聞社
SHWUF SHWUF
CRIK
野航空(株)
日刊エヴリー新聞社

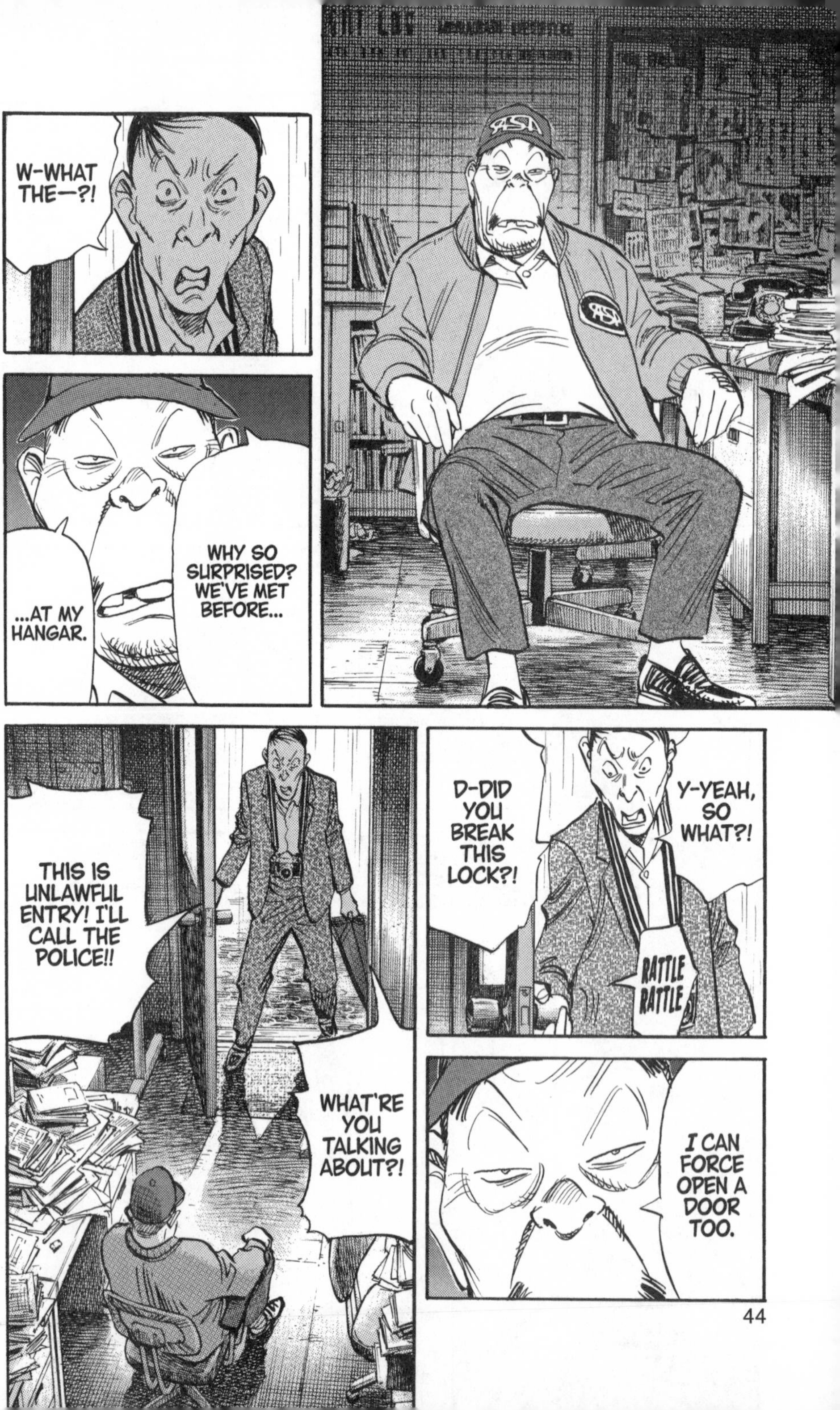
W-WHAT THE—?!
WHY SO SURPRISED? WE'VE MET BEFORE...
...AT MY HANGAR.
D-DID YOU BREAK THIS LOCK?!
Y-YEAH, SO WHAT?!
RATTLE RATTLE
I CAN FORCE OPEN A DOOR TOO.
THIS IS UNLAWFUL ENTRY! I'LL CALL THE POLICE!!
WHAT'RE YOU TALKING ABOUT?!

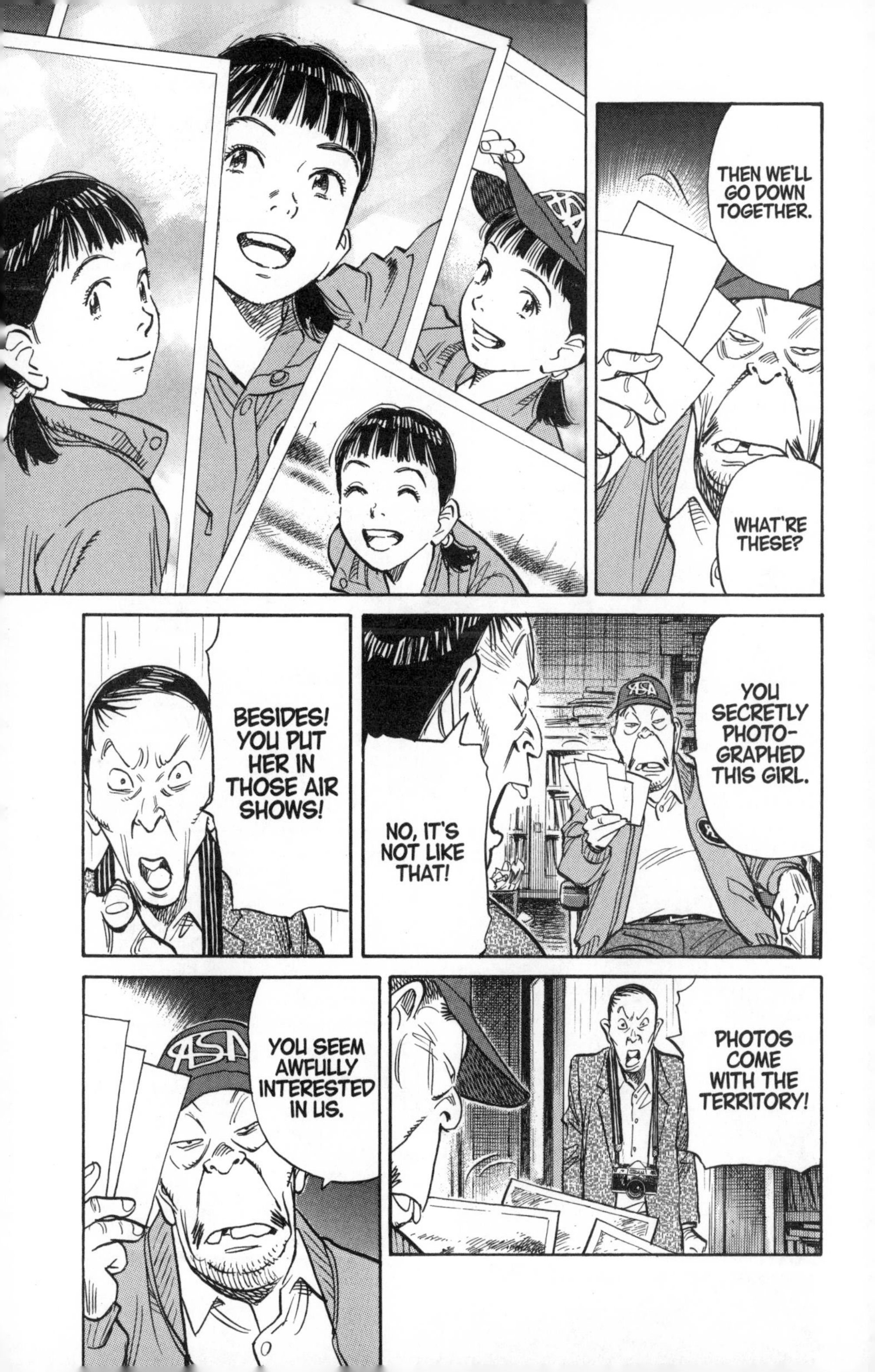
THEN WE'LL GO DOWN TOGETHER.
WHAT'RE THESE?
YOU SECRETLY PHOTO-GRAPHED THIS GIRL.
NO, IT'S NOT LIKE THAT!
BESIDES! YOU PUT HER IN THOSE AIR SHOWS!
PHOTOS COME WITH THE TERRITORY!
YOU SEEM AWFULLY INTERESTED IN US.

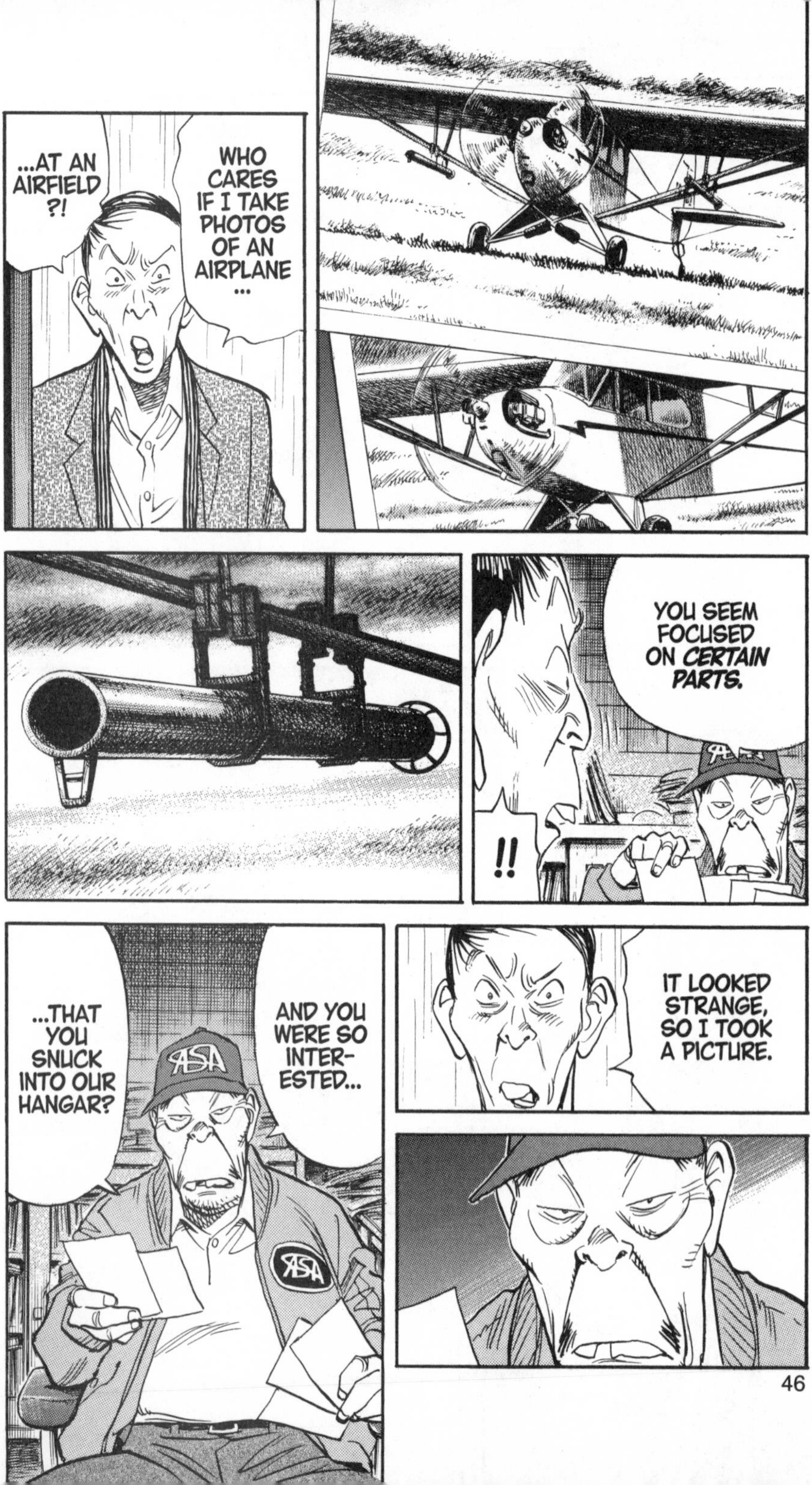
WHO CARES IF I TAKE PHOTOS OF AN AIRPLANE...
...AT AN AIRFIELD?!
YOU SEEM FOCUSED ON *CERTAIN* PARTS.
!!
IT LOOKED STRANGE, SO I TOOK A PICTURE.
AND YOU WERE SO INTER-ESTED...
...THAT YOU SNUCK INTO OUR HANGAR?

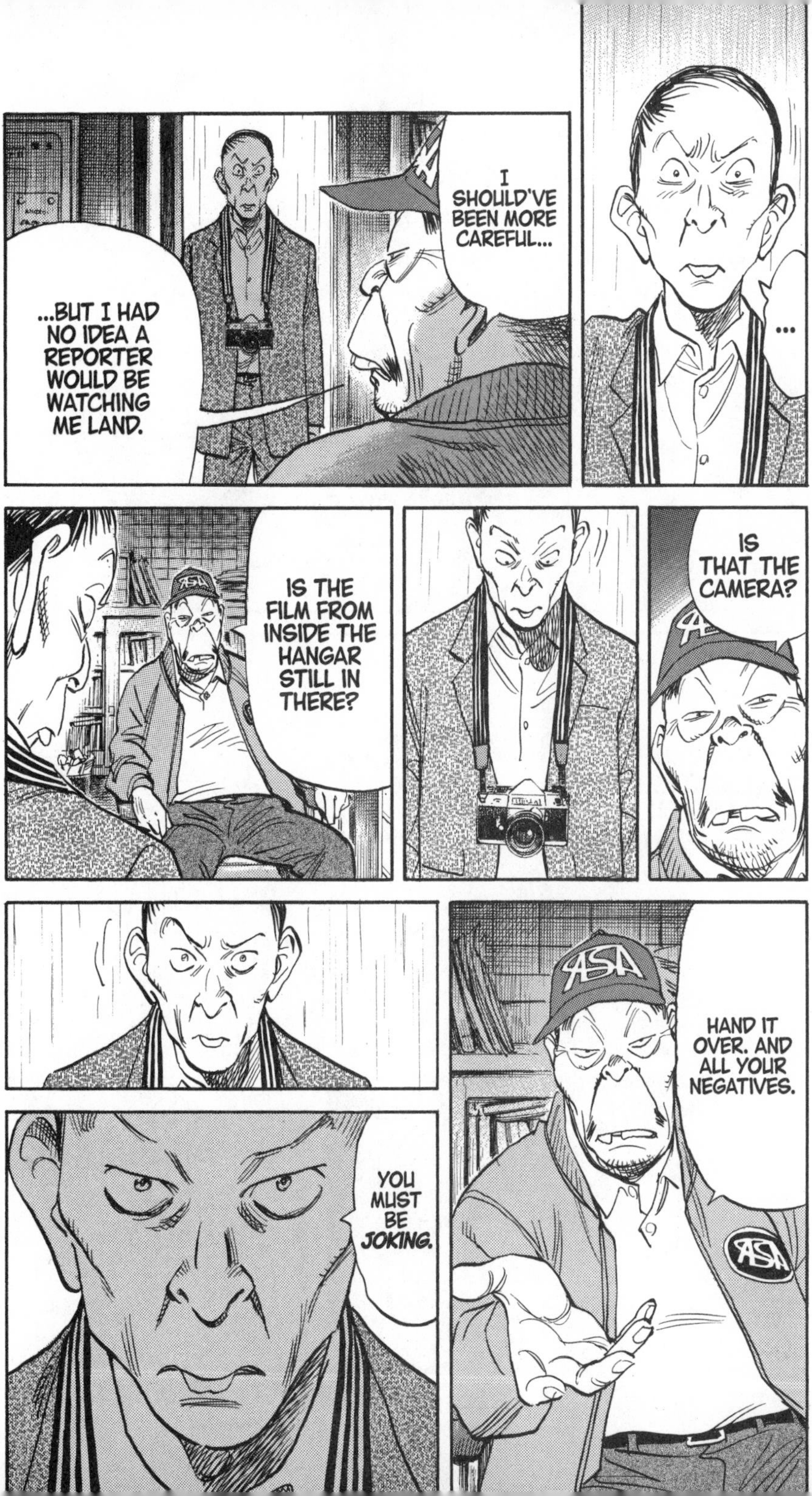
...
I SHOULD'VE BEEN MORE CAREFUL...
...BUT I HAD NO IDEA A REPORTER WOULD BE WATCHING ME LAND.
IS THAT THE CAMERA?
IS THE FILM FROM INSIDE THE HANGAR STILL IN THERE?
HAND IT OVER. AND ALL YOUR NEGATIVES.
YOU MUST BE *JOKING.*

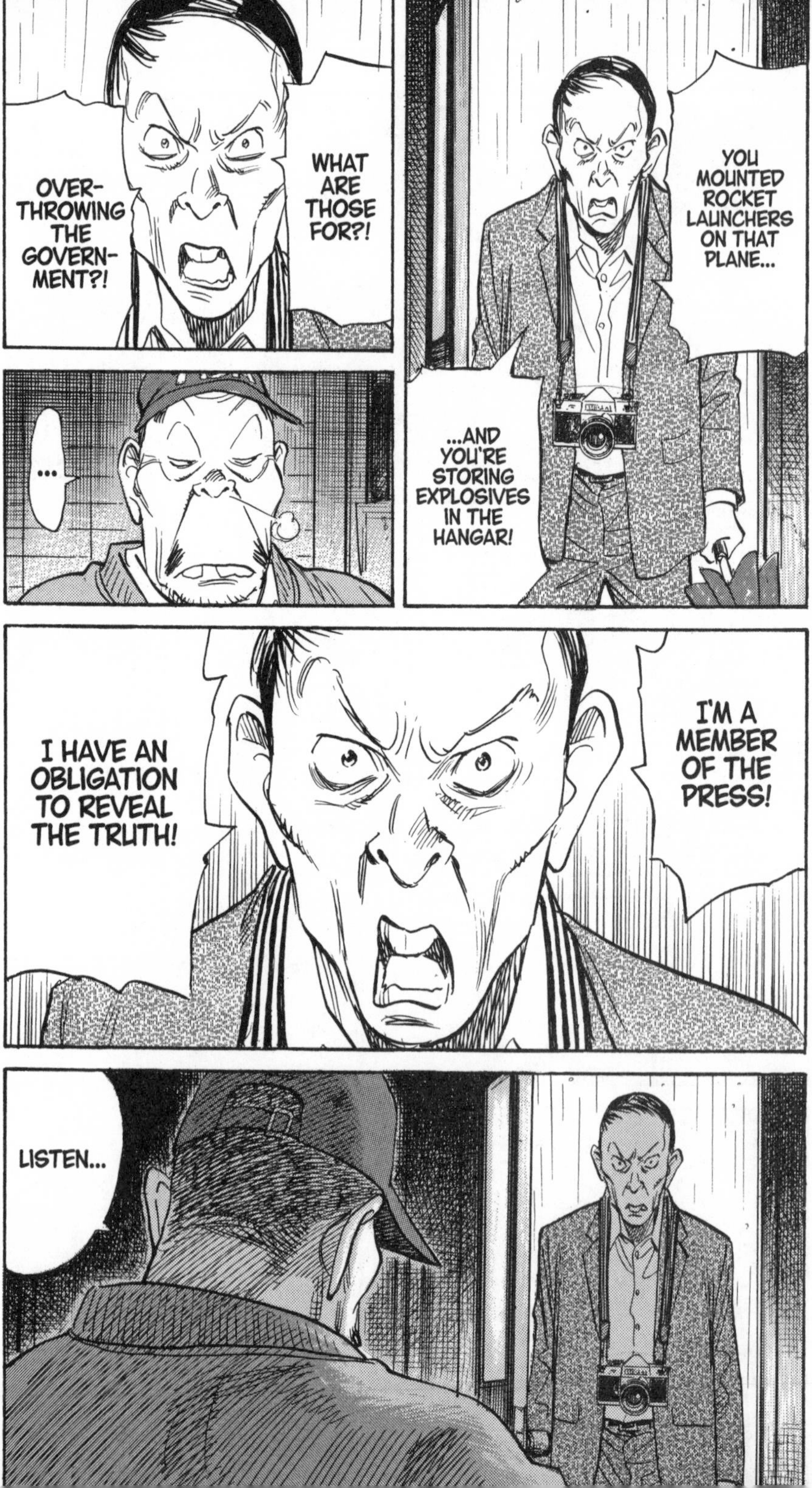
YOU MOUNTED ROCKET LAUNCHERS ON THAT PLANE...
WHAT ARE THOSE FOR?!
OVER-THROWING THE GOVERN-MENT?!
...AND YOU'RE STORING EXPLOSIVES IN THE HANGAR!
...
I'M A MEMBER OF THE PRESS!
I HAVE AN OBLIGATION TO REVEAL THE TRUTH!
LISTEN...

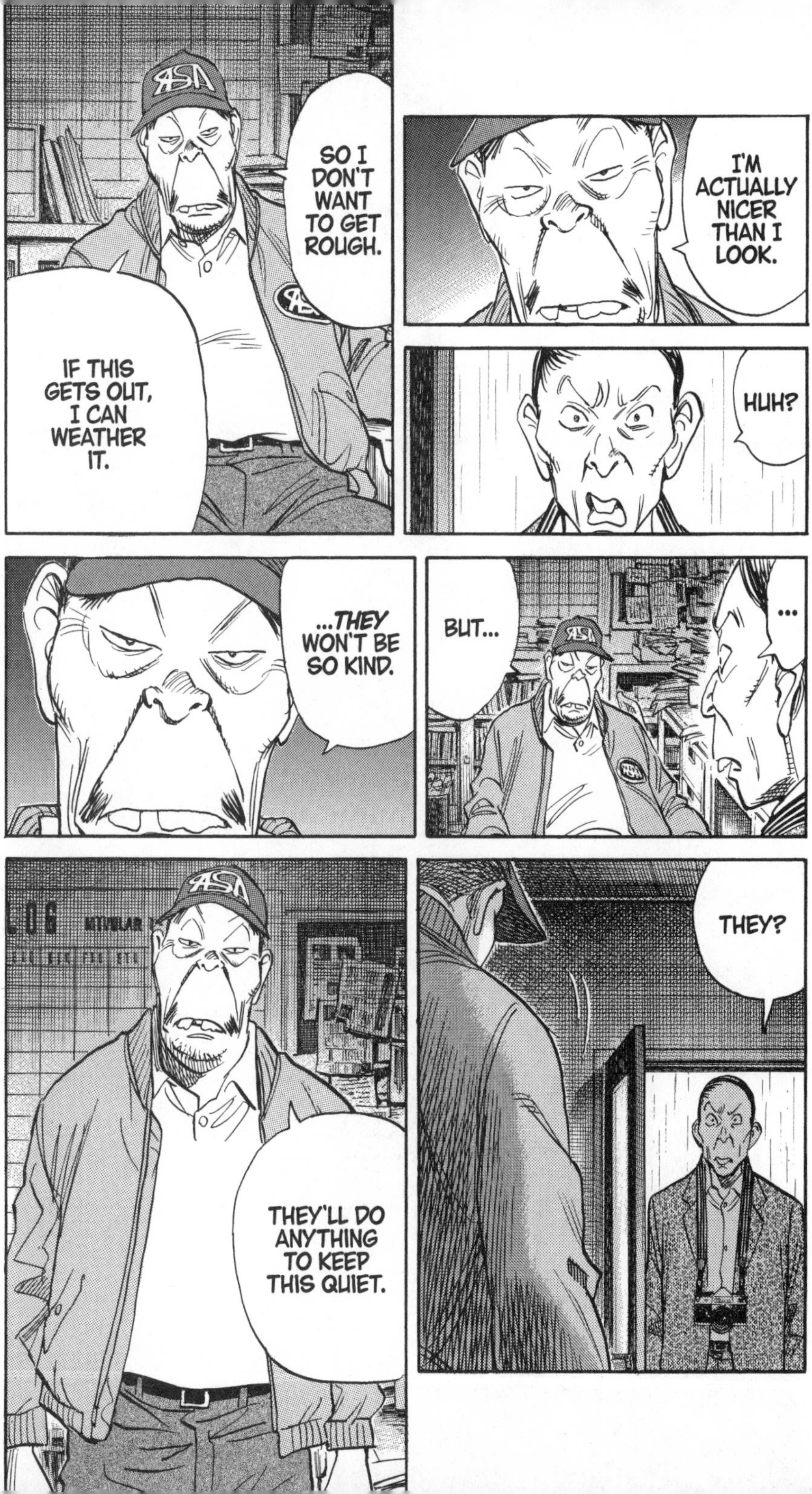
I'M ACTUALLY NICER THAN I LOOK.
HUH?
SO I DON'T WANT TO GET ROUGH.
IF THIS GETS OUT, I CAN WEATHER IT.
...
BUT...
...*THEY* WON'T BE SO KIND.
THEY?
THEY'LL DO ANYTHING TO KEEP THIS QUIET.

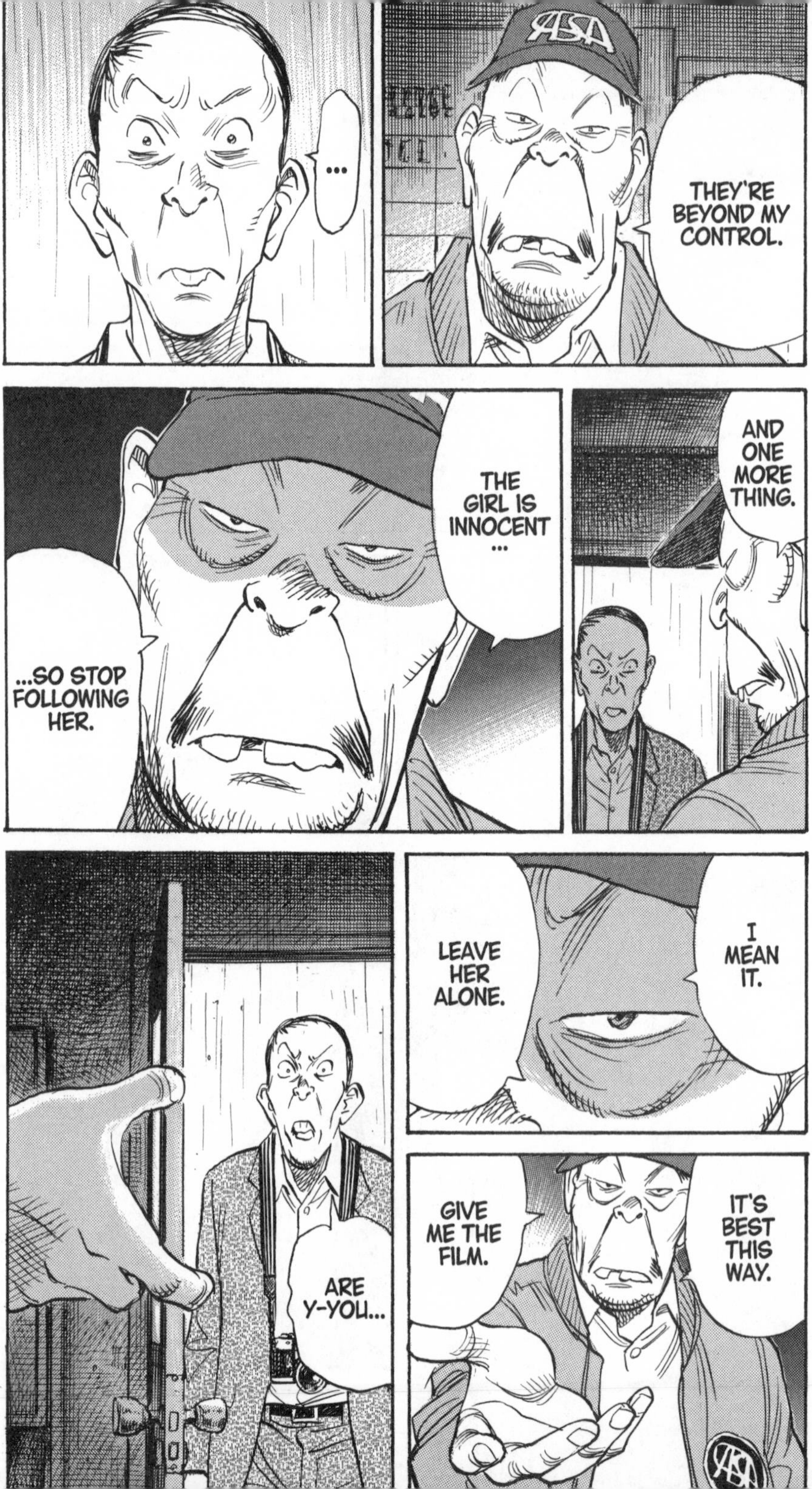
THEY'RE BEYOND MY CONTROL.
...
AND ONE MORE THING.
THE GIRL IS INNOCENT ...
...SO STOP FOLLOWING HER.
I MEAN IT.
LEAVE HER ALONE.
IT'S BEST THIS WAY.
GIVE ME THE FILM.
ARE Y-YOU...

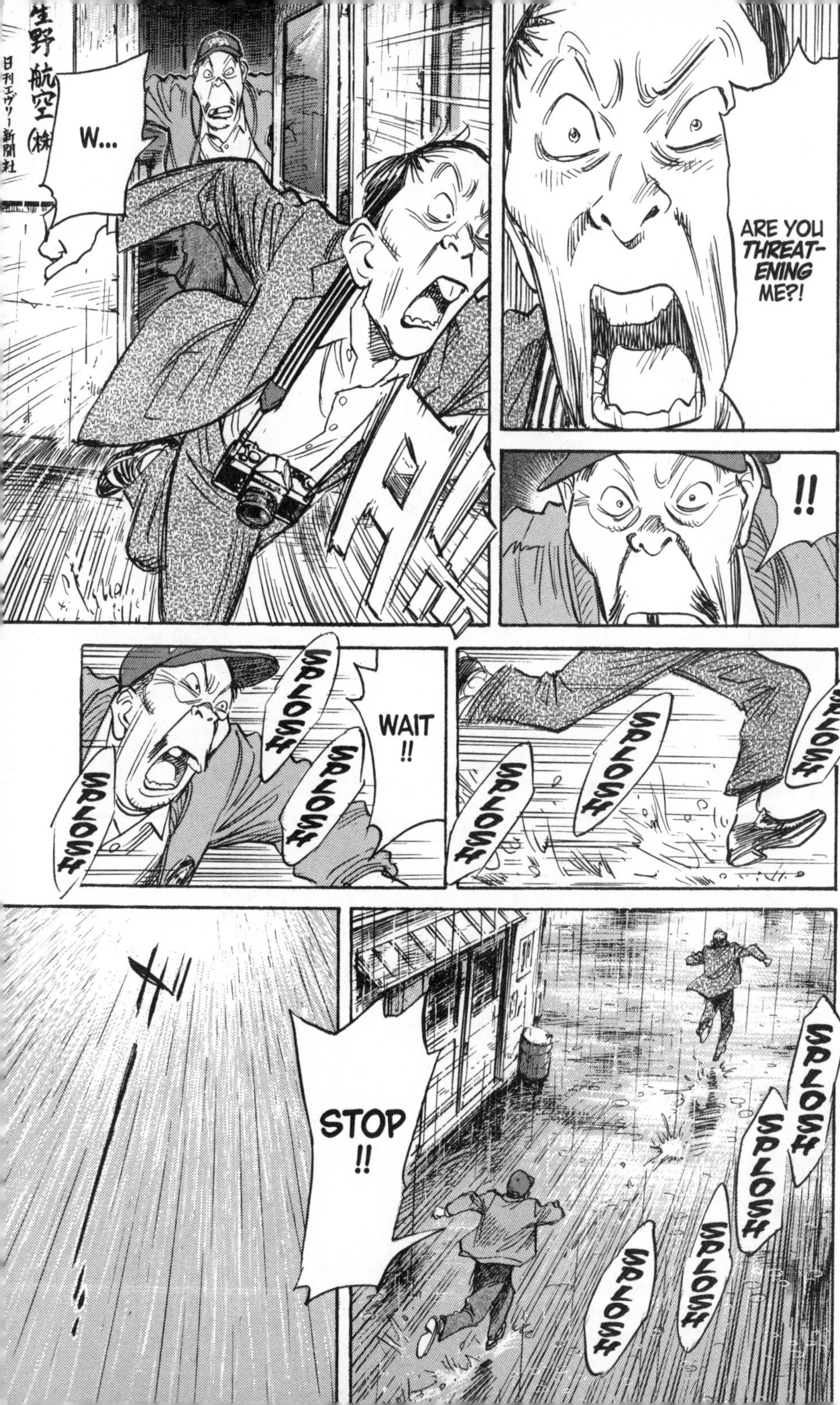
ARE YOU THREAT-ENING ME?!
!!
生野航空(株)
日刊エヴリー新聞社
W...
SPLOSH
SPLOSH
SPLOSH
WAIT !!
SPLOSH
SPLOSH
SPLOSH
STOP !!
SPLOSH
SPLOSH
SPLOSH
SPLOSH
SPLOSH

I FINALLY...

...GOT MY CAR BACK.

PLEASE COME IN!

TUNK

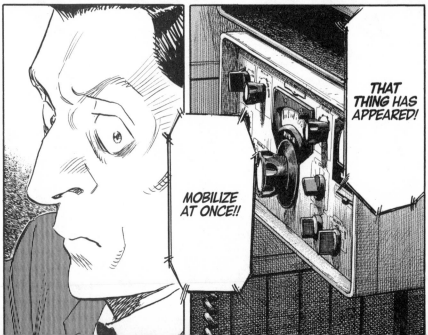

THAT THING HAS APPEARED!

MOBILIZE AT ONCE!!

ASADORA!

ASADORA!

Chapter 26 ● Garbage

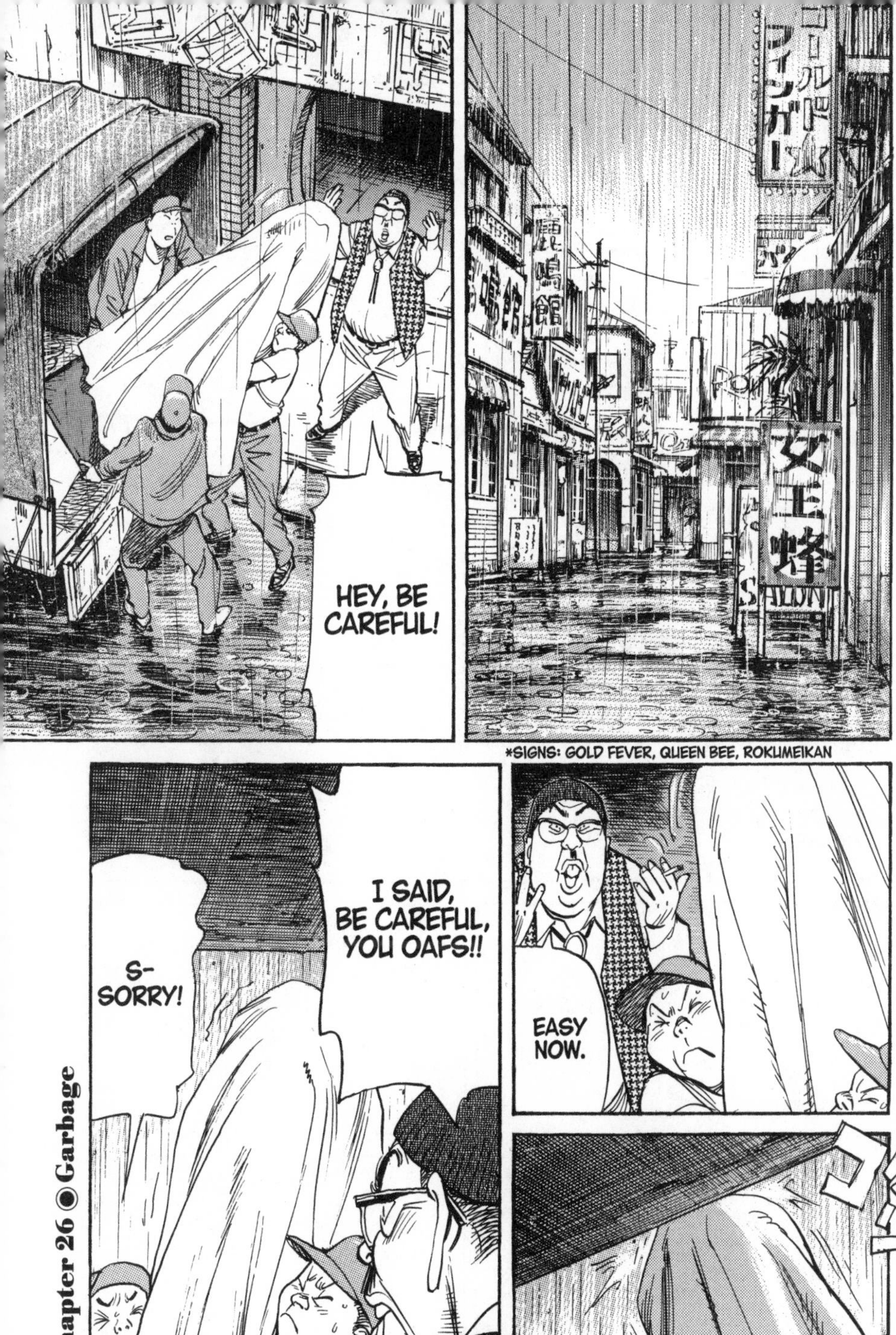
*SIGNS: GOLD FEVER, QUEEN BEE, ROKUMEIKAN
HEY, BE CAREFUL!
EASY NOW.
I SAID, BE CAREFUL, YOU OAFS!!
S-SORRY!

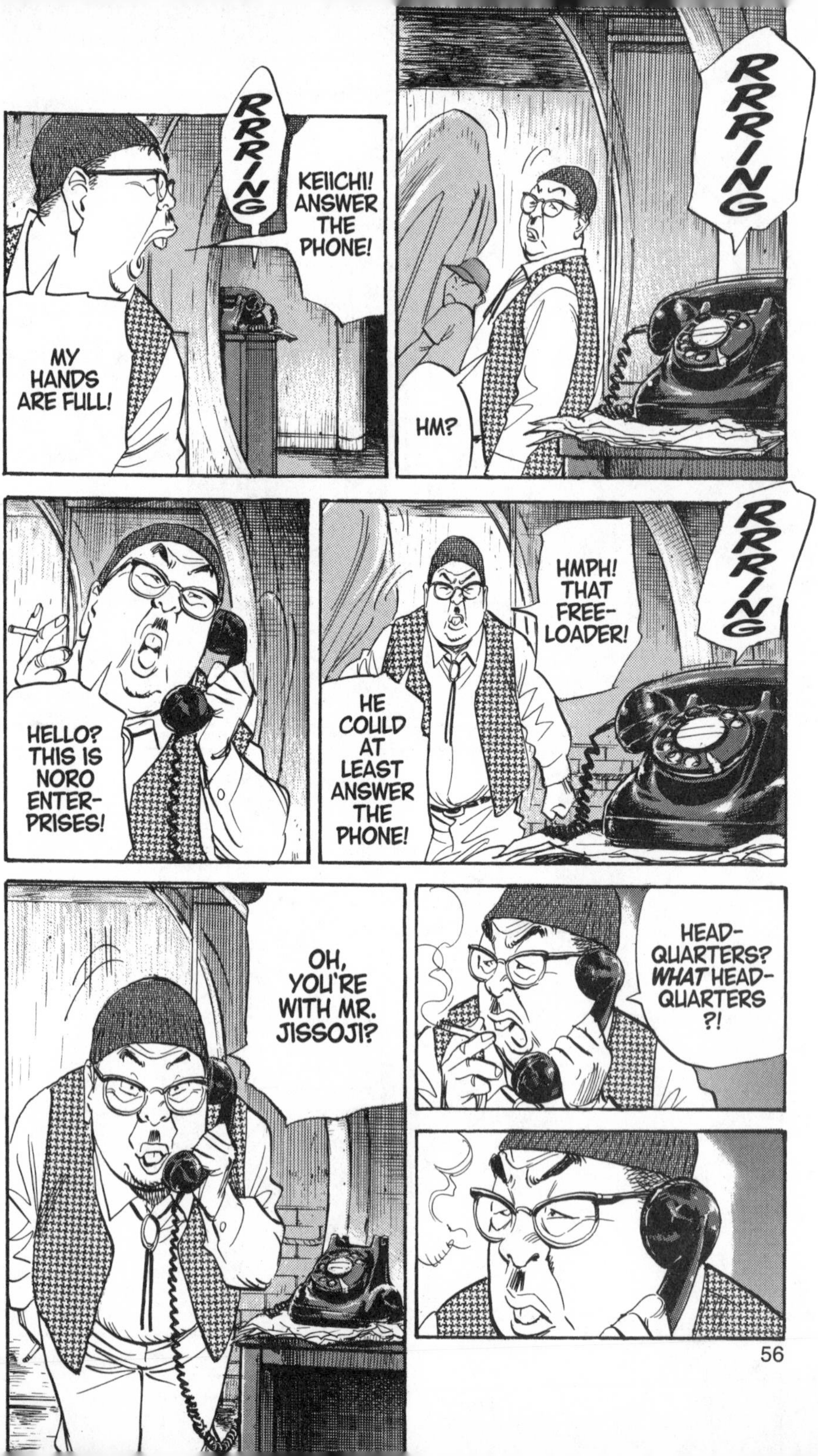
RRRING
HM?
RRRING
KEIICHI! ANSWER THE PHONE!
MY HANDS ARE FULL!
RRRING
HMPH! THAT FREE-LOADER!
HE COULD AT LEAST ANSWER THE PHONE!
HELLO? THIS IS NORO ENTER-PRISES!
HEAD-QUARTERS? *WHAT* HEAD-QUARTERS?!
OH, YOU'RE WITH MR. JISSOJI?

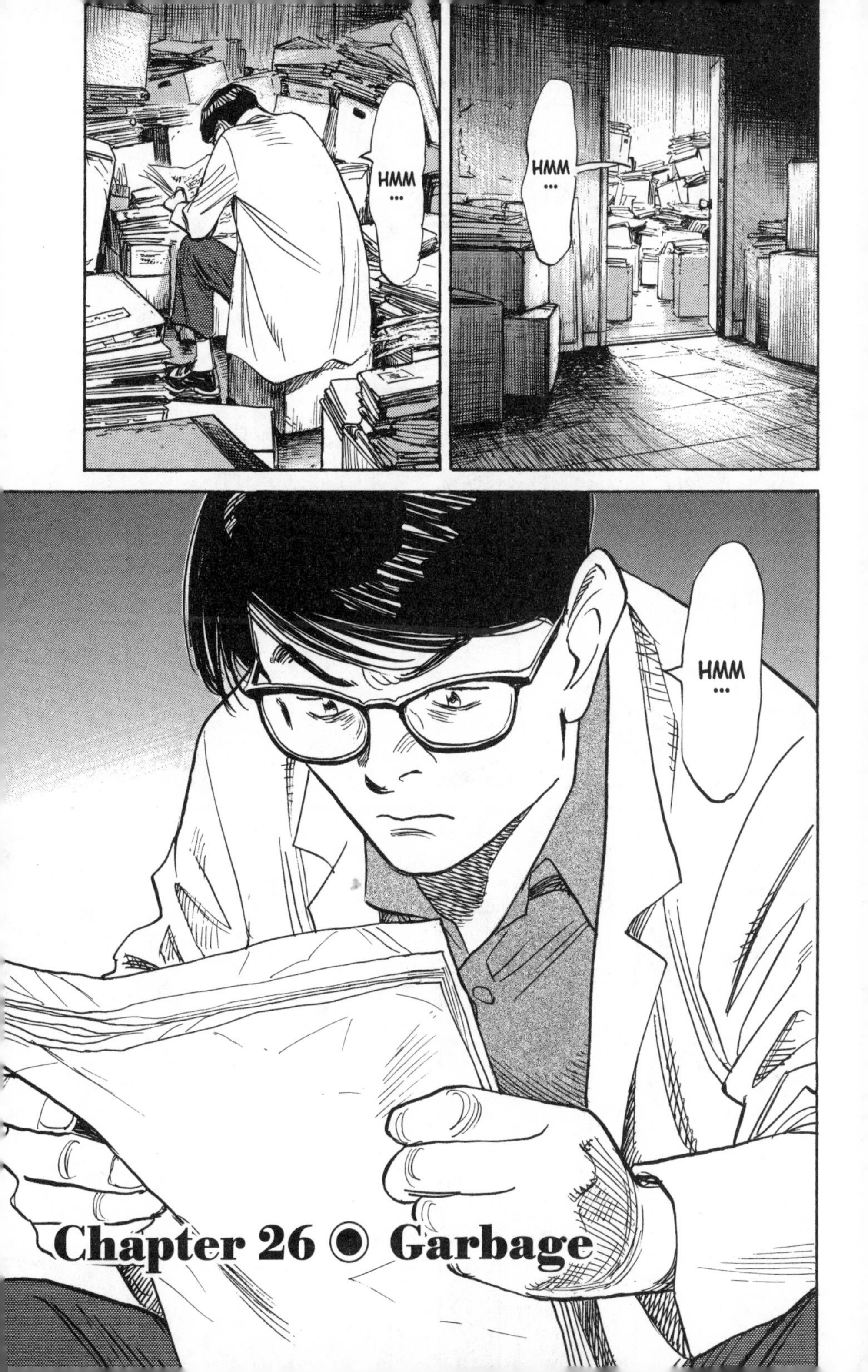
HMM...
HMM...
HMM...
Chapter 26 ● Garbage

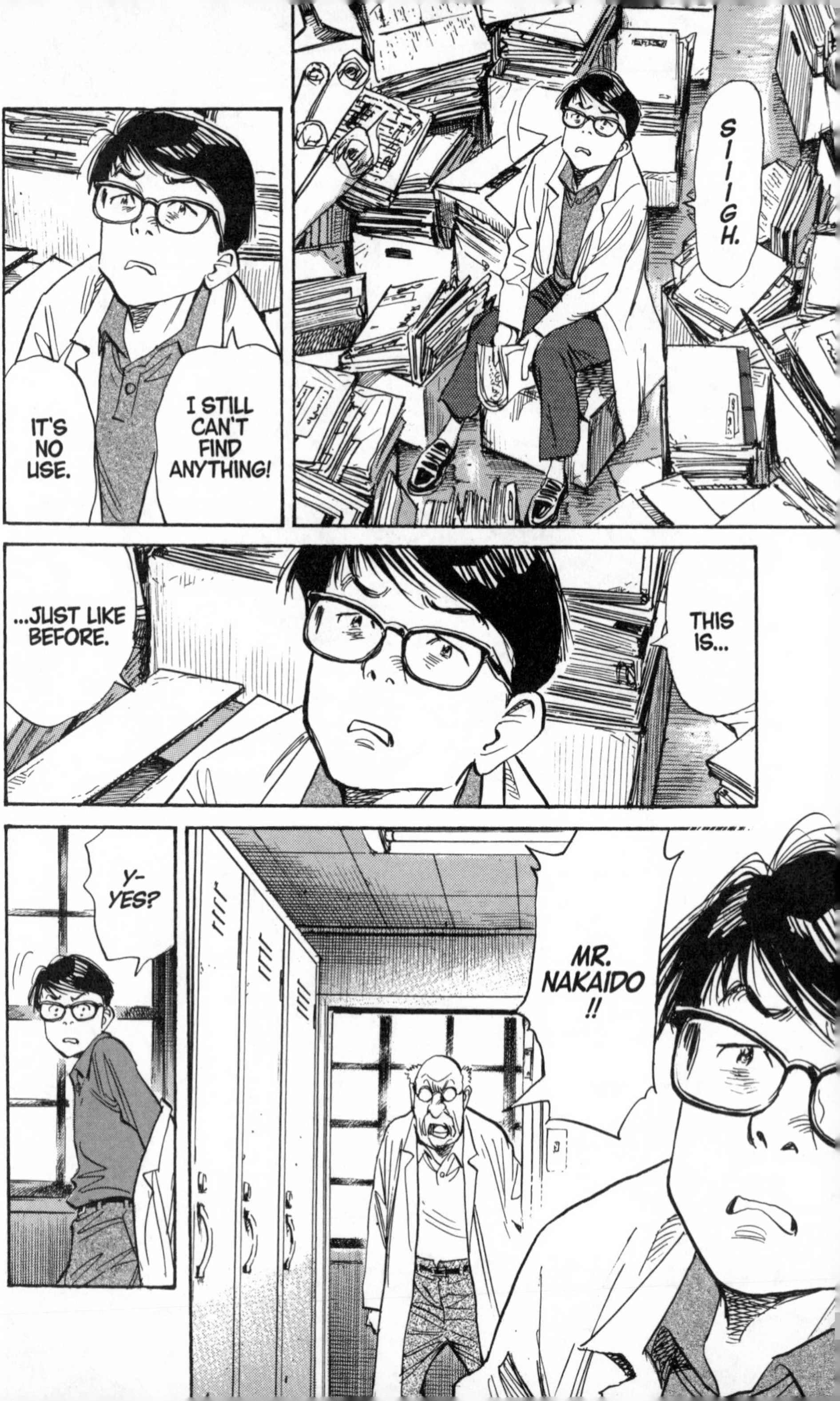
SIIIGH.
I STILL CAN'T FIND ANYTHING!
IT'S NO USE.
THIS IS...
...JUST LIKE BEFORE.
MR. NAKAIDO !!
Y- YES?

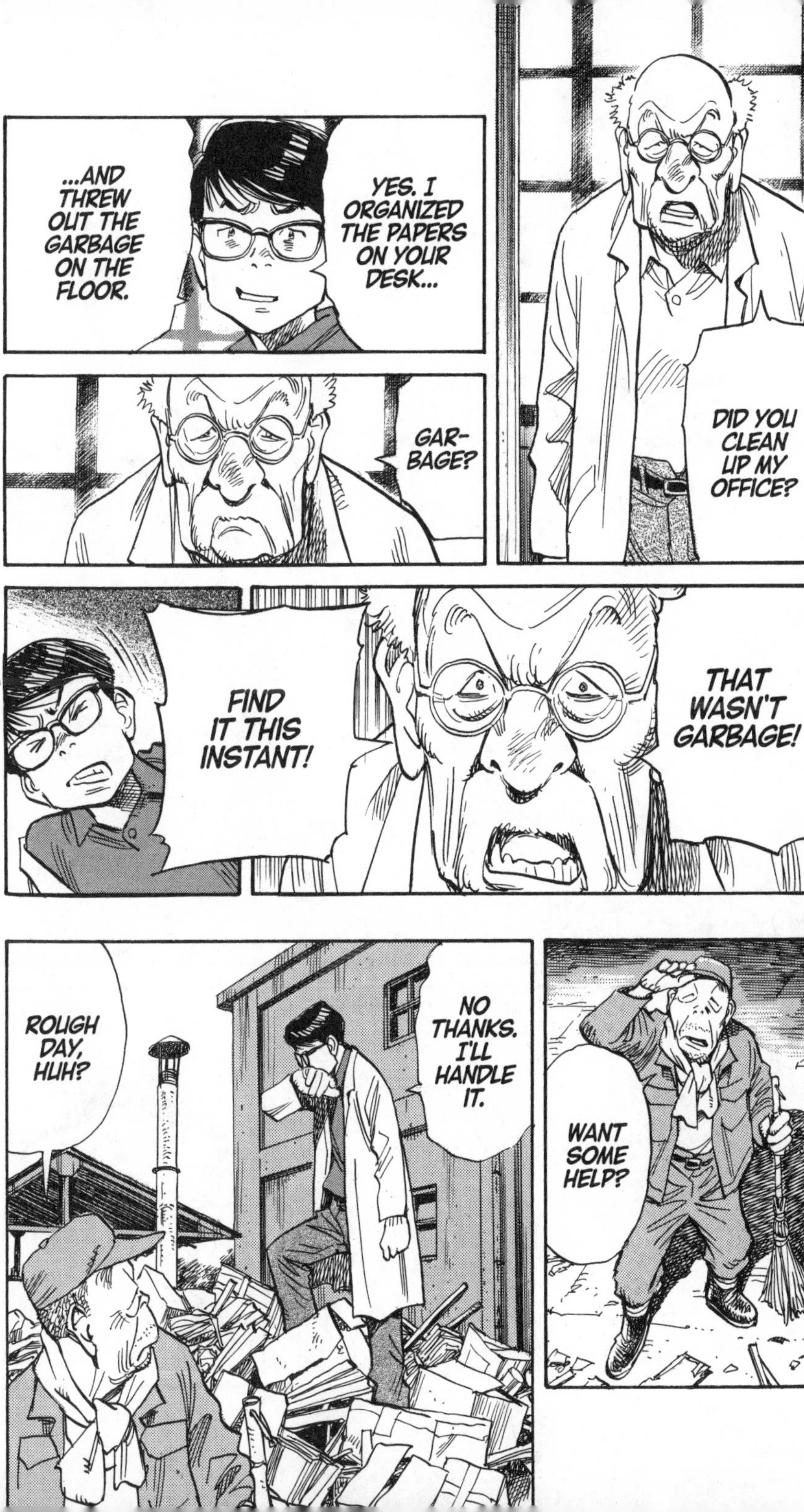
DID YOU CLEAN UP MY OFFICE?
YES. I ORGANIZED THE PAPERS ON YOUR DESK...
...AND THREW OUT THE GARBAGE ON THE FLOOR.
GAR-BAGE?
THAT WASN'T GARBAGE!
FIND IT THIS INSTANT!
WANT SOME HELP?
NO THANKS. I'LL HANDLE IT.
ROUGH DAY, HUH?

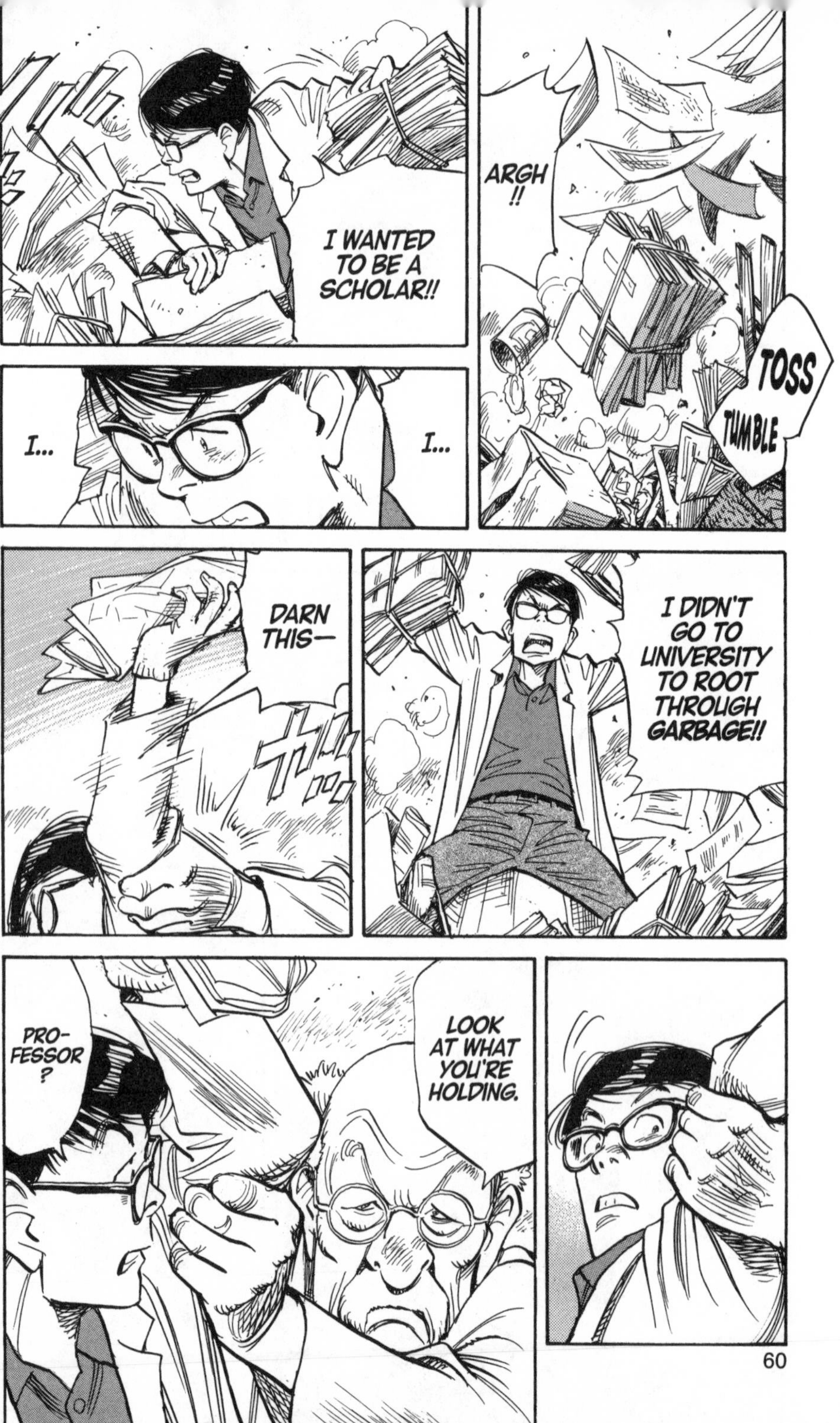
ARGH!!
TOSS
TUMBLE
I WANTED TO BE A SCHOLAR!!
I...
I...
I DIDN'T GO TO UNIVERSITY TO ROOT THROUGH GARBAGE!!
DARN THIS—
LOOK AT WHAT YOU'RE HOLDING.
PRO-FESSOR?

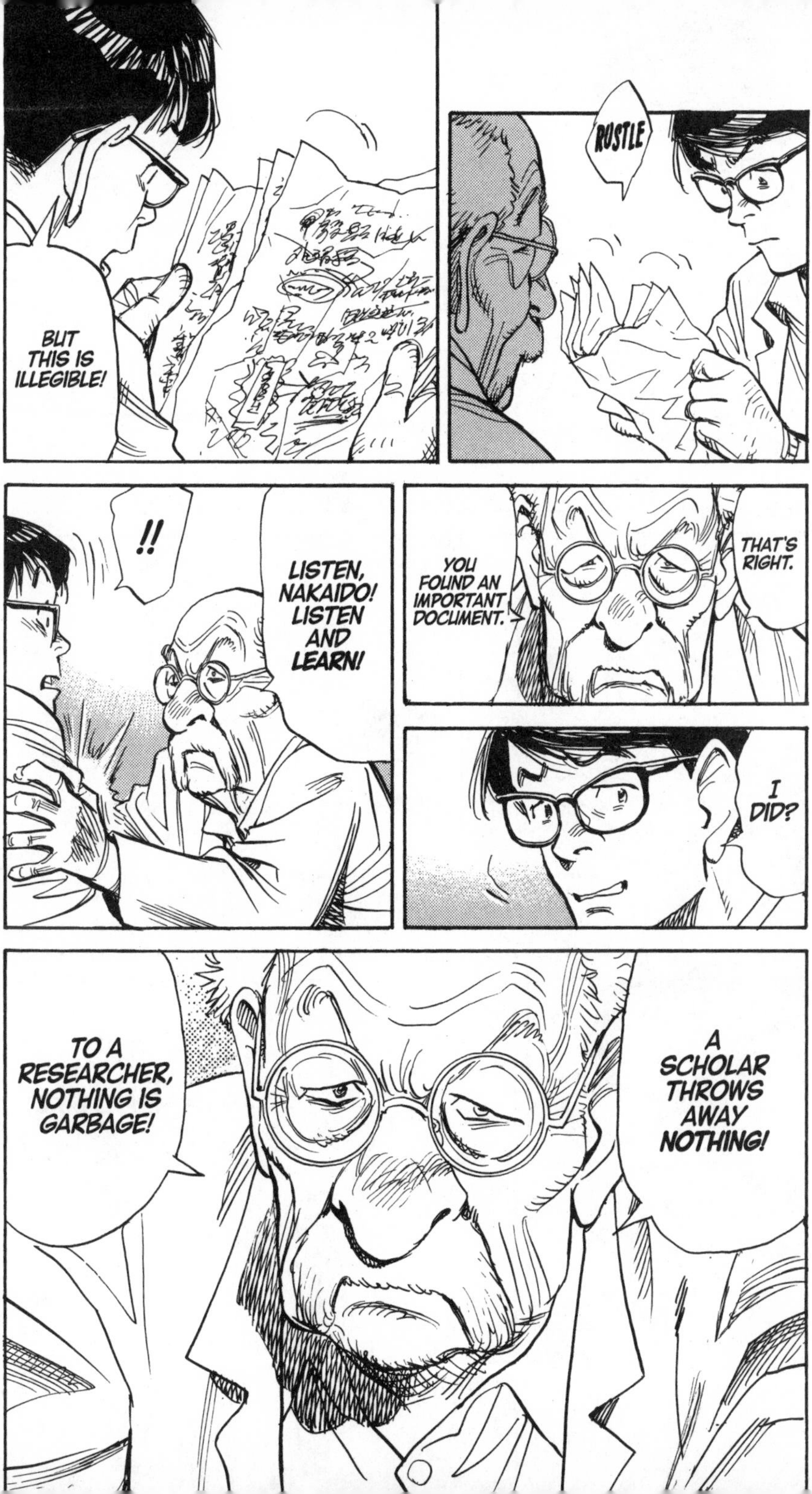
RUSTLE
BUT THIS IS ILLEGIBLE!
THAT'S RIGHT.
YOU FOUND AN IMPORTANT DOCUMENT.
I DID?
LISTEN, NAKAIDO! LISTEN AND LEARN!
!!
A SCHOLAR THROWS AWAY NOTHING!
TO A RESEARCHER, NOTHING IS GARBAGE!

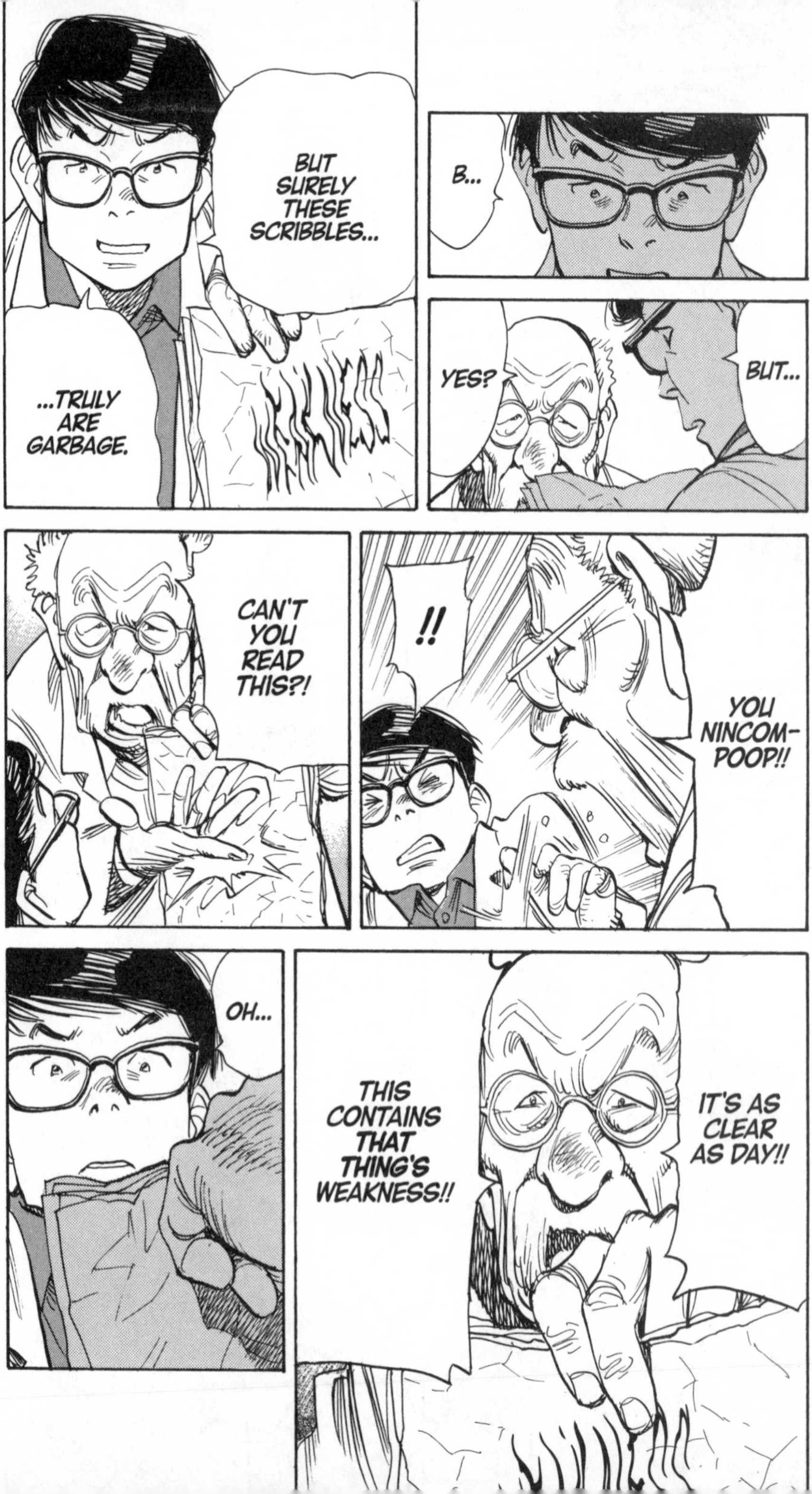
B...
BUT...
YES?
BUT SURELY THESE SCRIBBLES...
...TRULY ARE GARBAGE.
YOU NINCOM-POOP!!
!!
CAN'T YOU READ THIS?!
IT'S AS CLEAR AS DAY!!
THIS CONTAINS THAT THING'S WEAKNESS!!
OH...

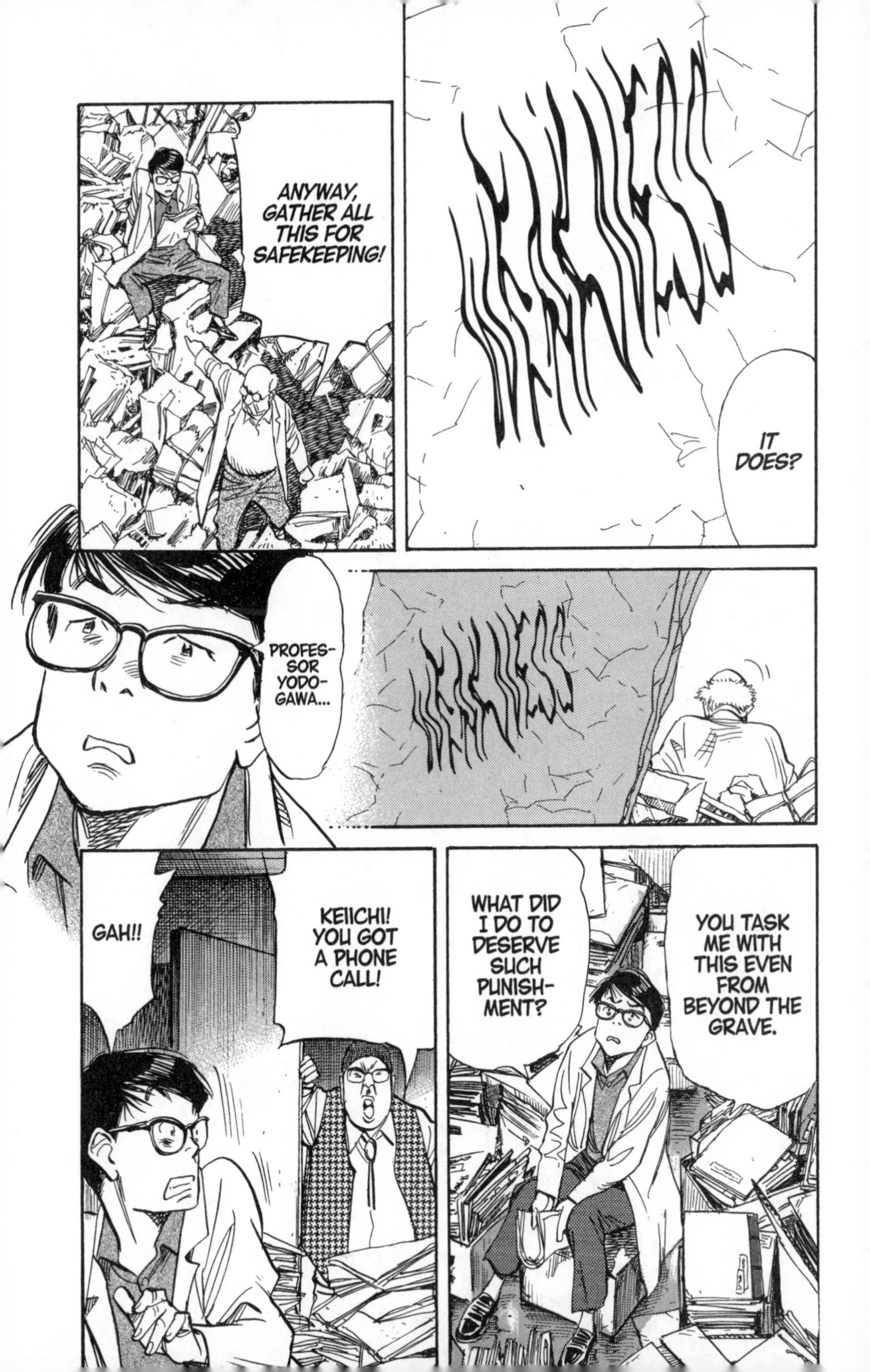
IT DOES?
ANYWAY, GATHER ALL THIS FOR SAFEKEEPING!
PROFES-SOR YODO-GAWA...
YOU TASK ME WITH THIS EVEN FROM BEYOND THE GRAVE.
WHAT DID I DO TO DESERVE SUCH PUNISH-MENT?
KEIICHI! YOU GOT A PHONE CALL!
GAH!!

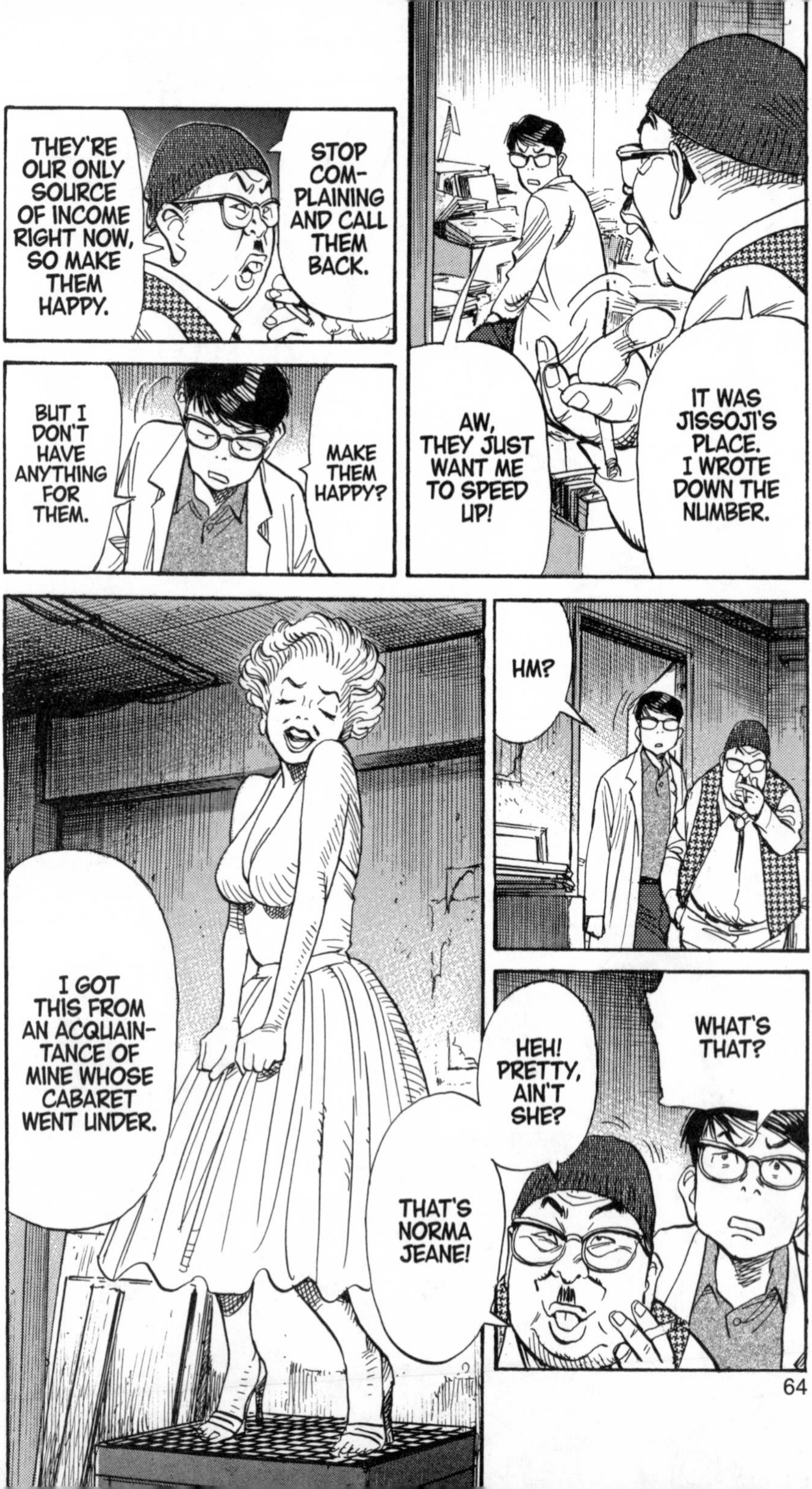
IT WAS JISSOJI'S PLACE. I WROTE DOWN THE NUMBER.
AW, THEY JUST WANT ME TO SPEED UP!
STOP COM-PLAINING AND CALL THEM BACK.
THEY'RE OUR ONLY SOURCE OF INCOME RIGHT NOW, SO MAKE THEM HAPPY.
MAKE THEM HAPPY?
BUT I DON'T HAVE ANYTHING FOR THEM.
HM?
WHAT'S THAT?
HEH! PRETTY, AIN'T SHE?
THAT'S NORMA JEANE!
I GOT THIS FROM AN ACQUAIN-TANCE OF MINE WHOSE CABARET WENT UNDER.

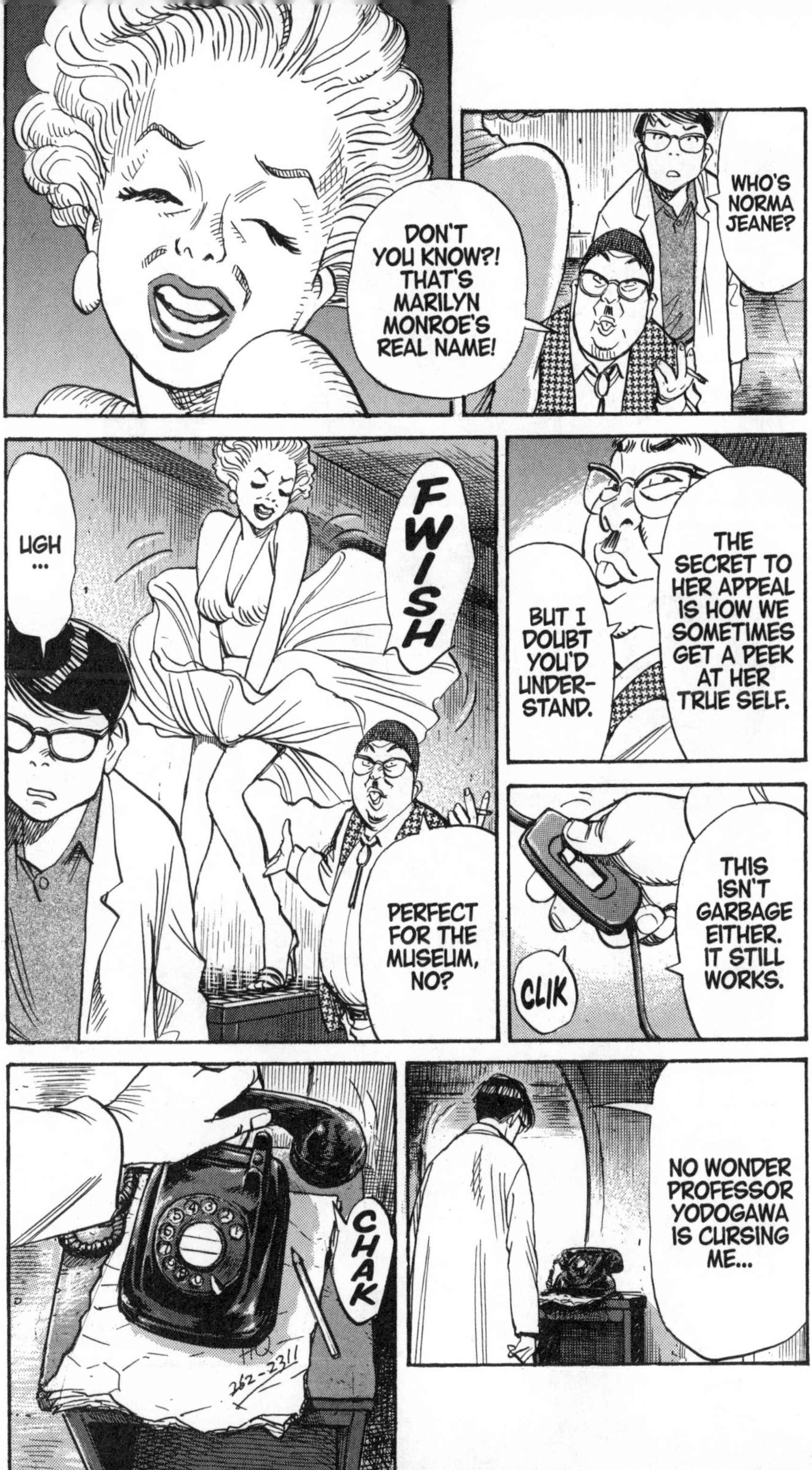
WHO'S NORMA JEANE?
DON'T YOU KNOW?! THAT'S MARILYN MONROE'S REAL NAME!
THE SECRET TO HER APPEAL IS HOW WE SOMETIMES GET A PEEK AT HER TRUE SELF.
BUT I DOUBT YOU'D UNDER-STAND.
THIS ISN'T GARBAGE EITHER. IT STILL WORKS.
CLIK
FWISH
PERFECT FOR THE MUSEUM, NO?
UGH ...
NO WONDER PROFESSOR YODOGAWA IS CURSING ME...
CHAK
262-2311

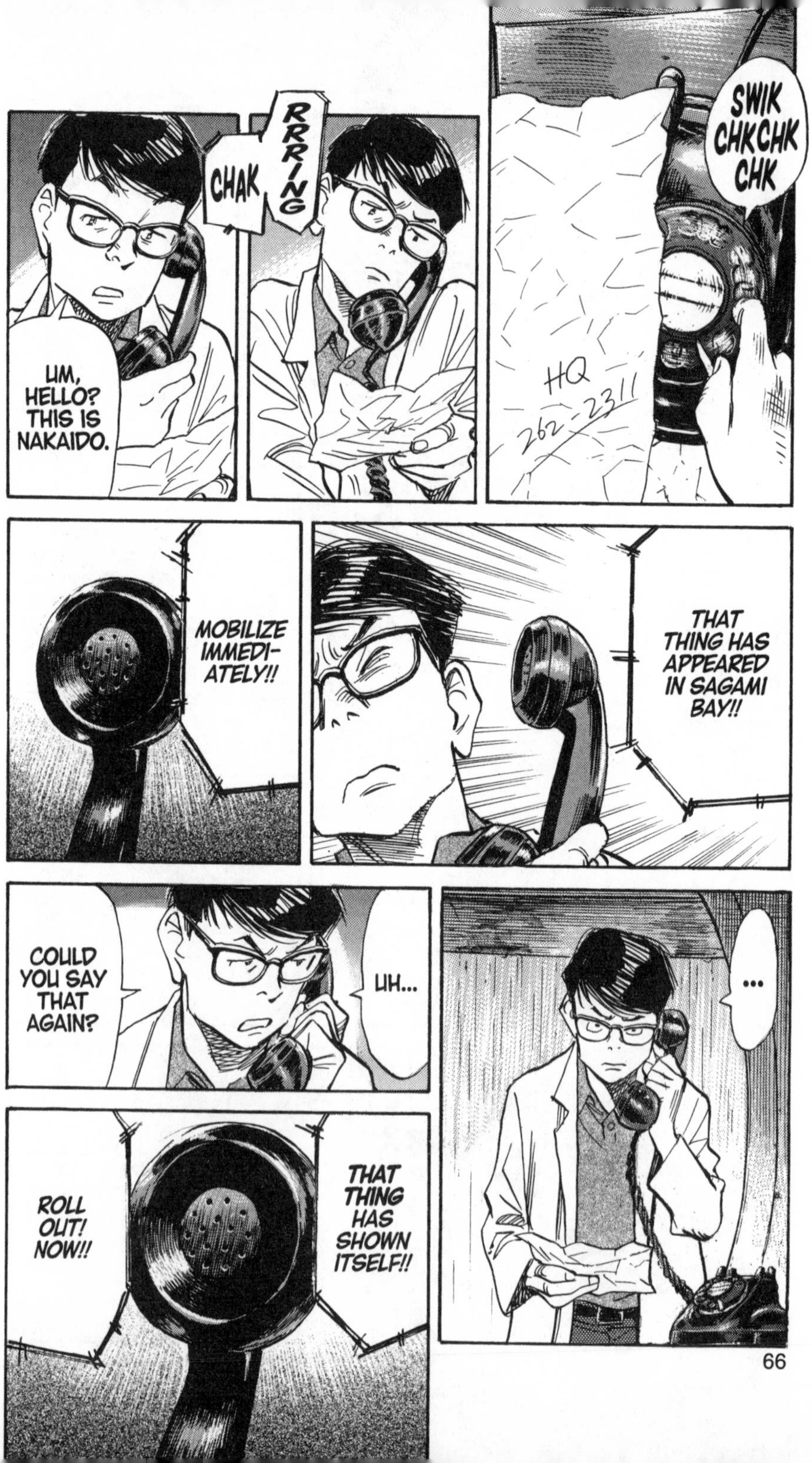
SWIK CHKCHK CHK
HQ 262-2311
RRRING
CHAK
UM, HELLO? THIS IS NAKAIDO.
THAT THING HAS APPEARED IN SAGAMI BAY!!
MOBILIZE IMMEDI-ATELY!!
...
UH...
COULD YOU SAY THAT AGAIN?
THAT THING HAS SHOWN ITSELF!!
ROLL OUT! NOW!!

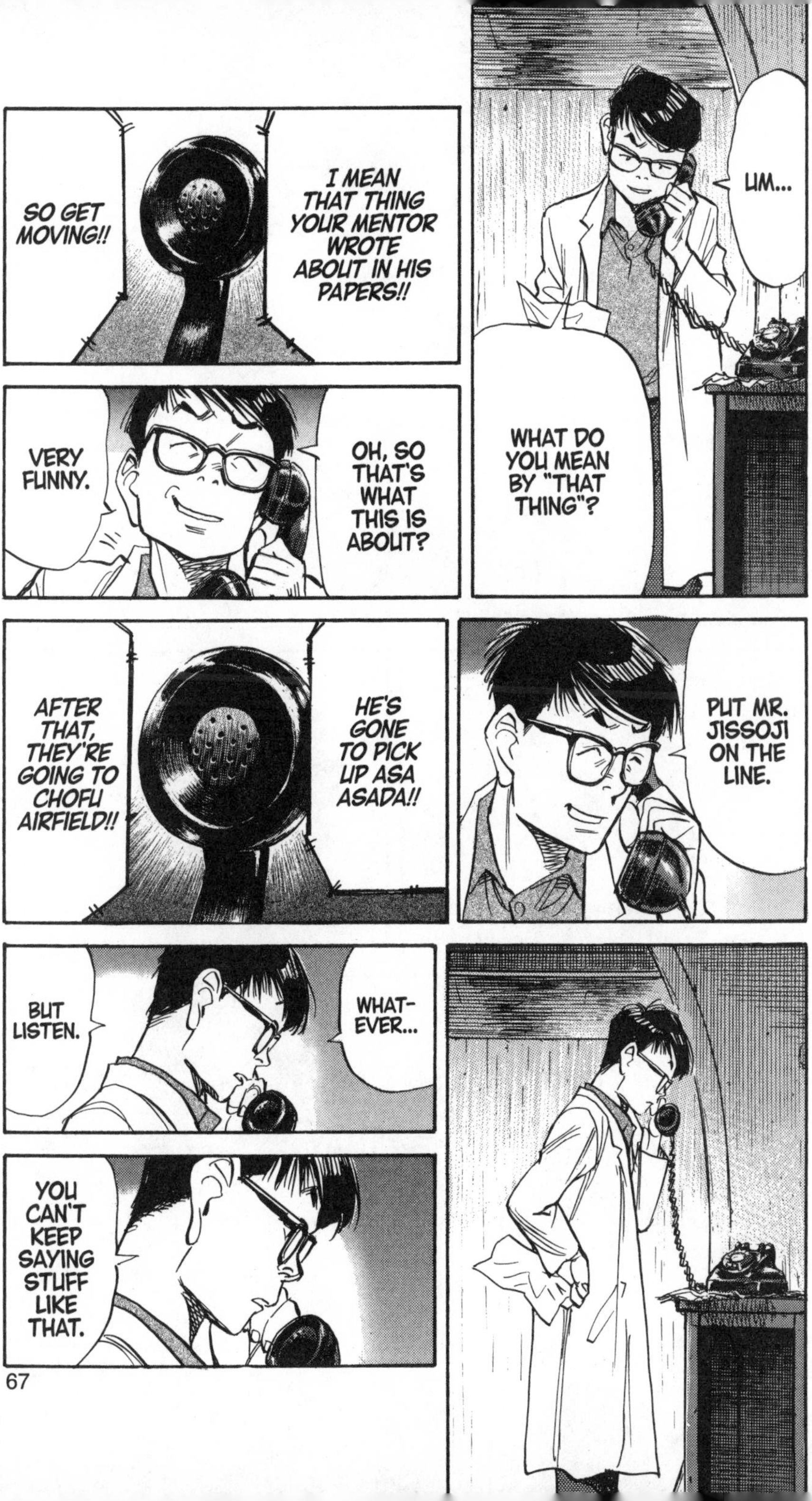
UM...
WHAT DO YOU MEAN BY "THAT THING"?
I MEAN THAT THING YOUR MENTOR WROTE ABOUT IN HIS PAPERS!!
SO GET MOVING!!
OH, SO THAT'S WHAT THIS IS ABOUT?
VERY FUNNY.
PUT MR. JISSOJI ON THE LINE.
HE'S GONE TO PICK UP ASA ASADA!!
AFTER THAT, THEY'RE GOING TO CHOFU AIRFIELD!!
WHAT-EVER...
BUT LISTEN.
YOU CAN'T KEEP SAYING STUFF LIKE THAT.

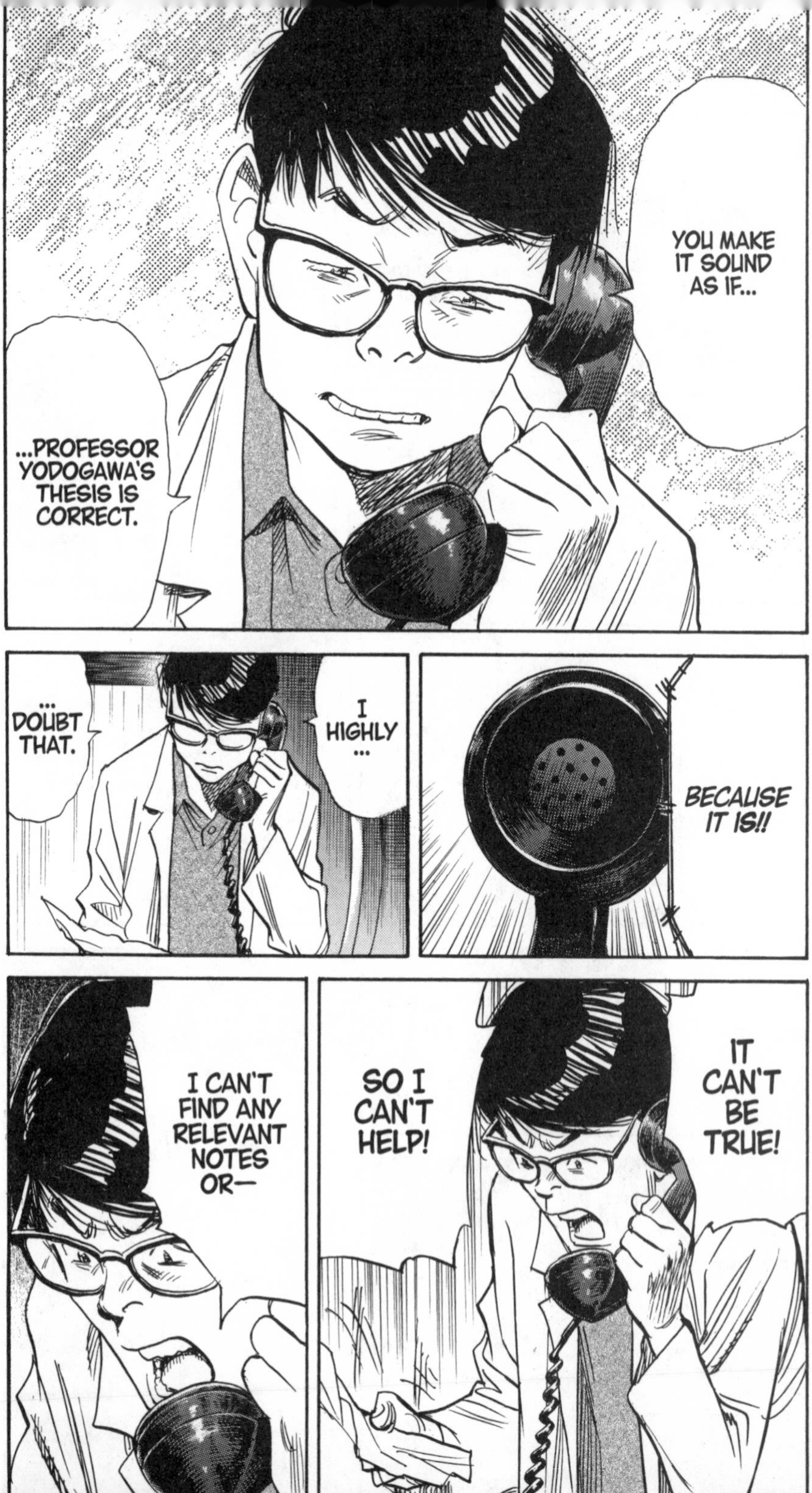
YOU MAKE IT SOUND AS IF...
...PROFESSOR YODOGAWA'S THESIS IS CORRECT.
BECAUSE IT IS!!
I HIGHLY ...
... DOUBT THAT.
IT CAN'T BE TRUE!
SO I CAN'T HELP!
I CAN'T FIND ANY RELEVANT NOTES OR—

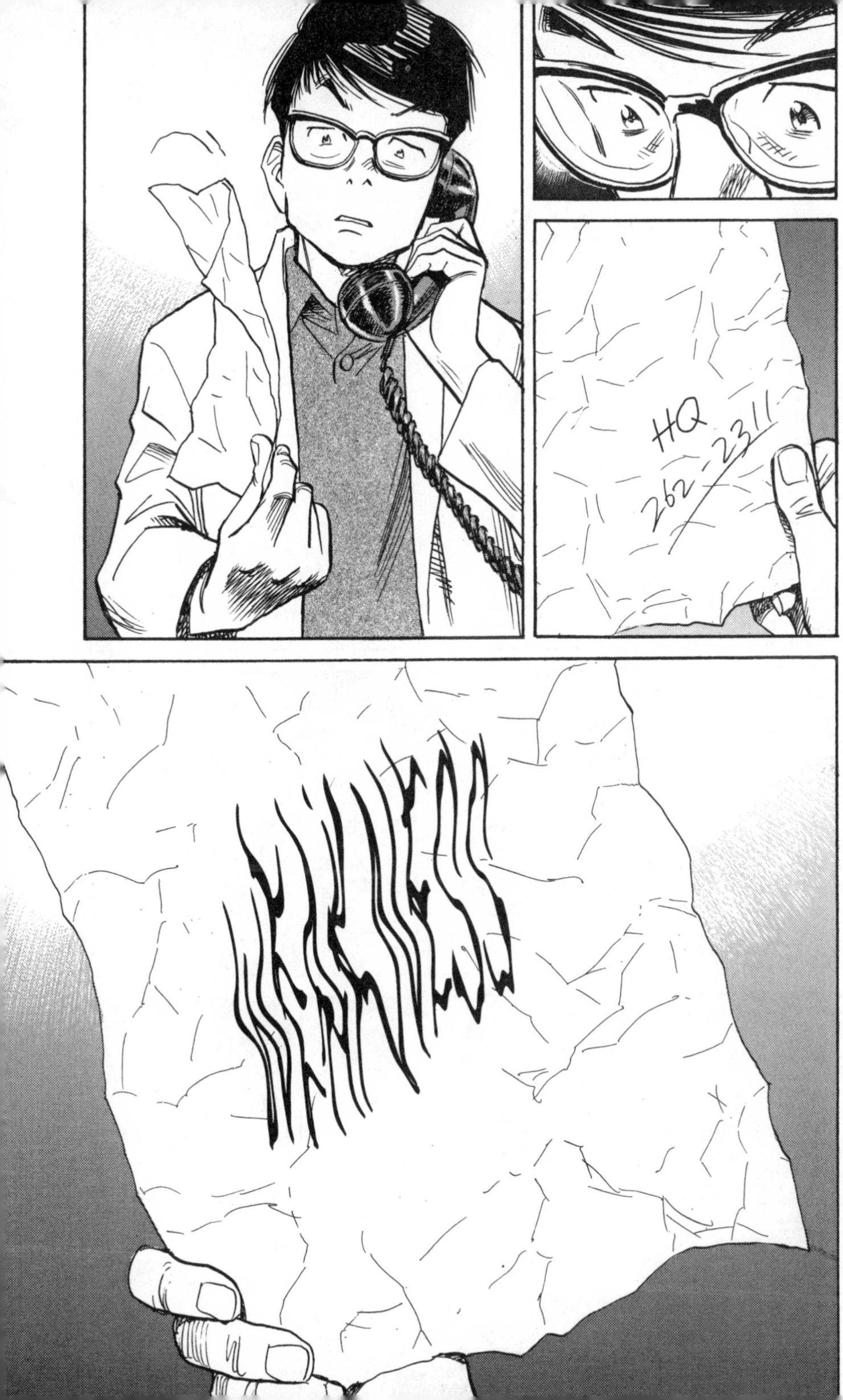
HQ
262-2311

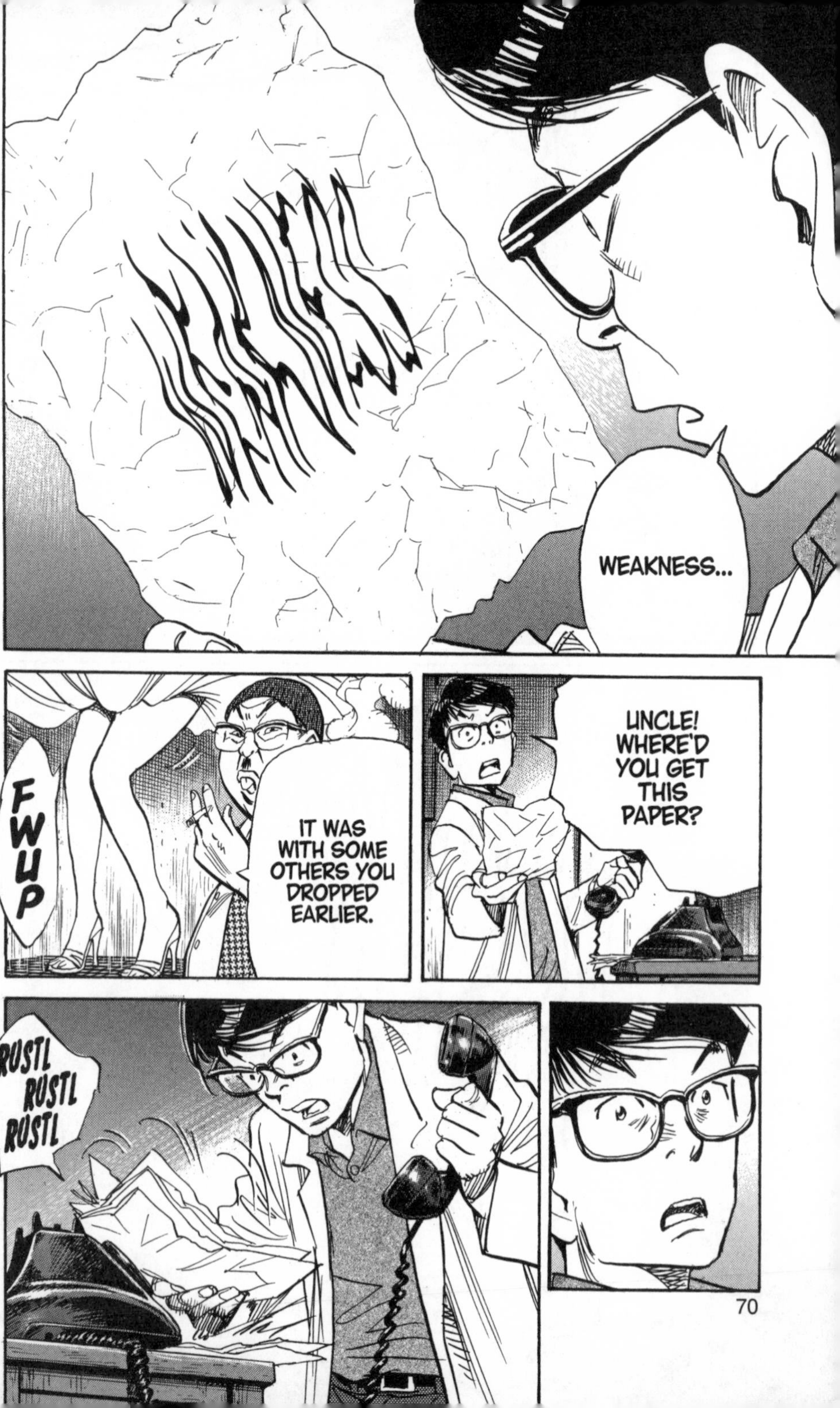
WEAKNESS...
UNCLE! WHERE'D YOU GET THIS PAPER?
IT WAS WITH SOME OTHERS YOU DROPPED EARLIER.
FWUP
RUSTL RUSTL RUSTL

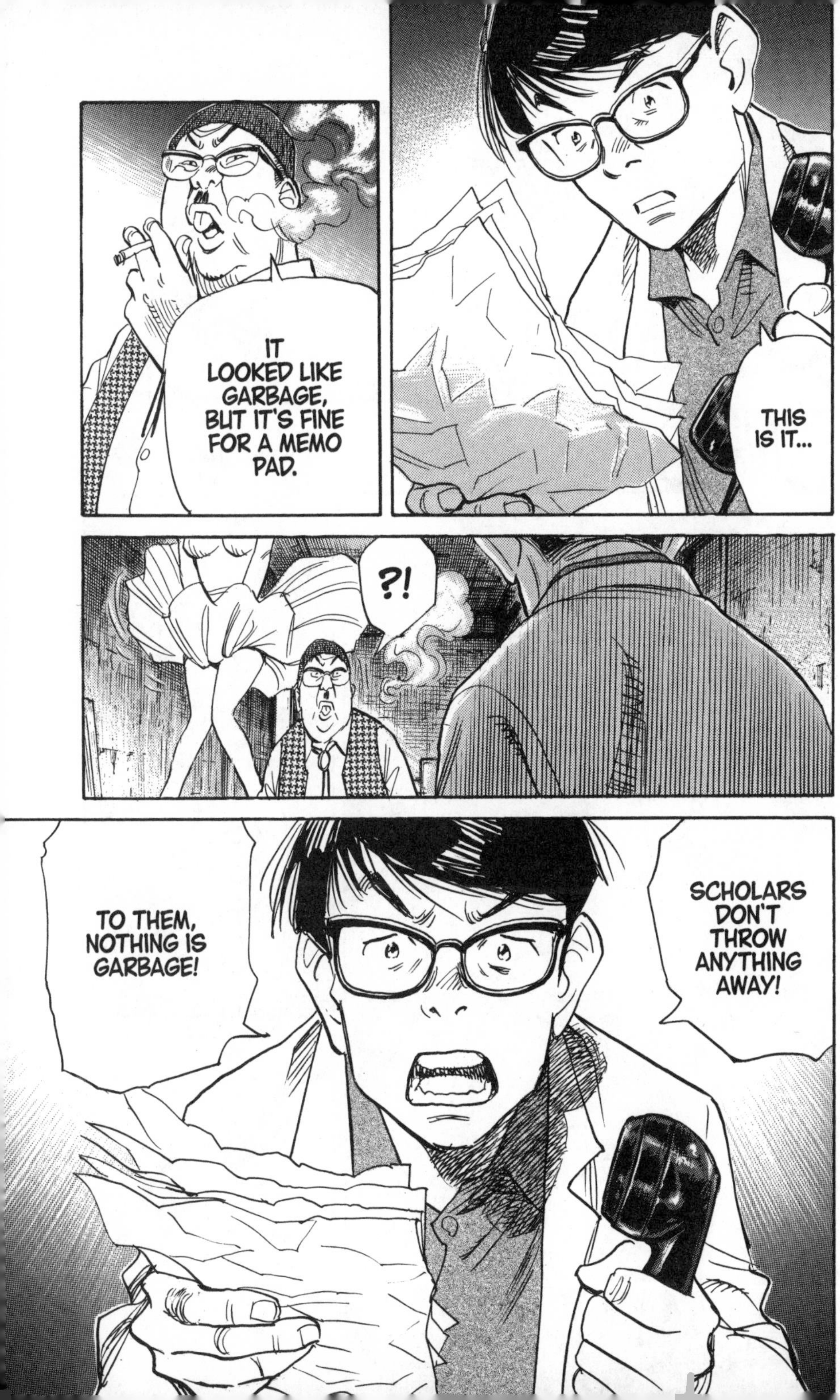
THIS IS IT...
IT LOOKED LIKE GARBAGE, BUT IT'S FINE FOR A MEMO PAD.
?!
SCHOLARS DON'T THROW ANYTHING AWAY!
TO THEM, NOTHING IS GARBAGE!

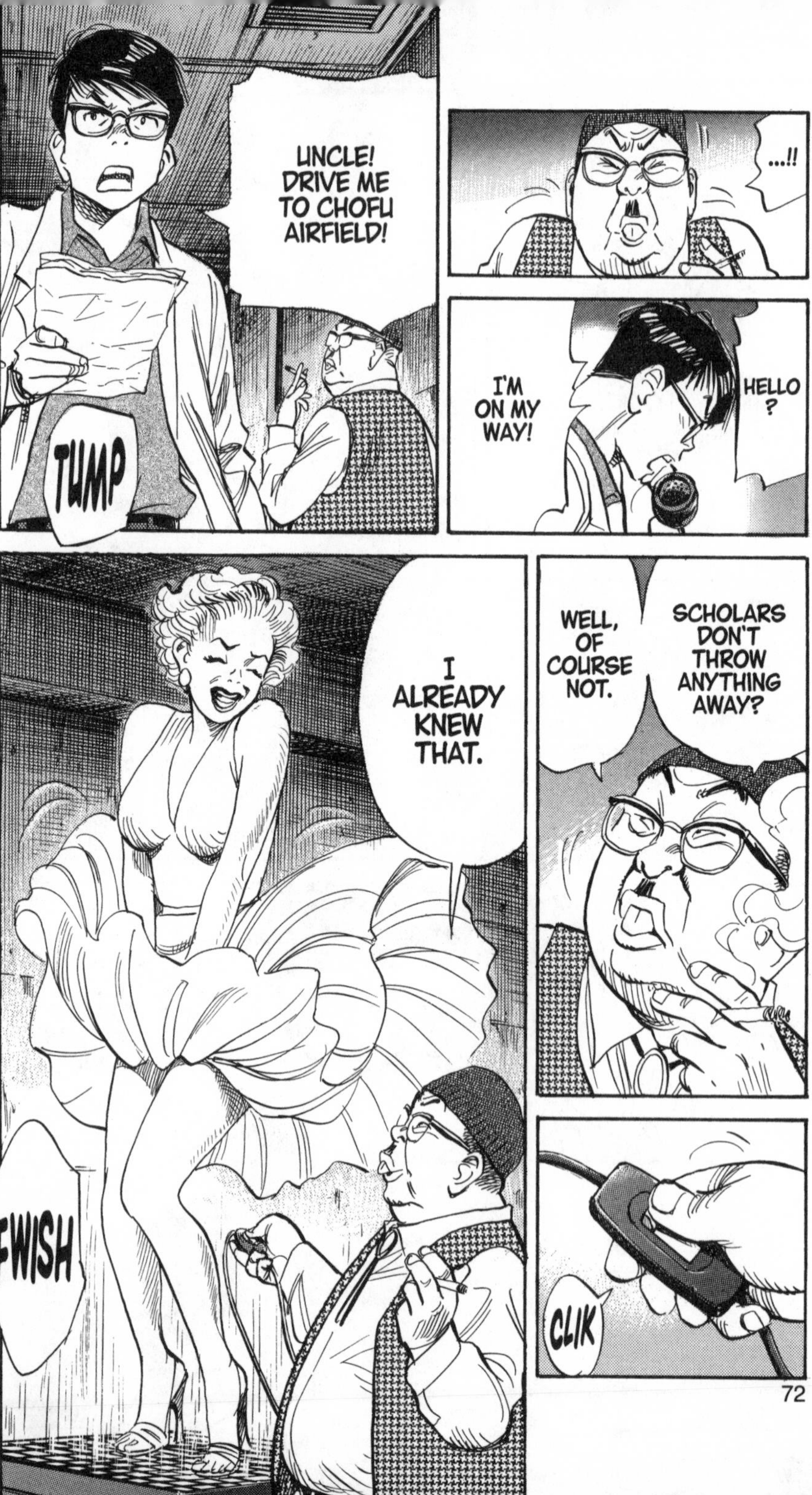
...!!
HELLO ?
I'M ON MY WAY!
UNCLE! DRIVE ME TO CHOFU AIRFIELD!
TUMP
SCHOLARS DON'T THROW ANYTHING AWAY?
WELL, OF COURSE NOT.
CLIK
I ALREADY KNEW THAT.
FWISH

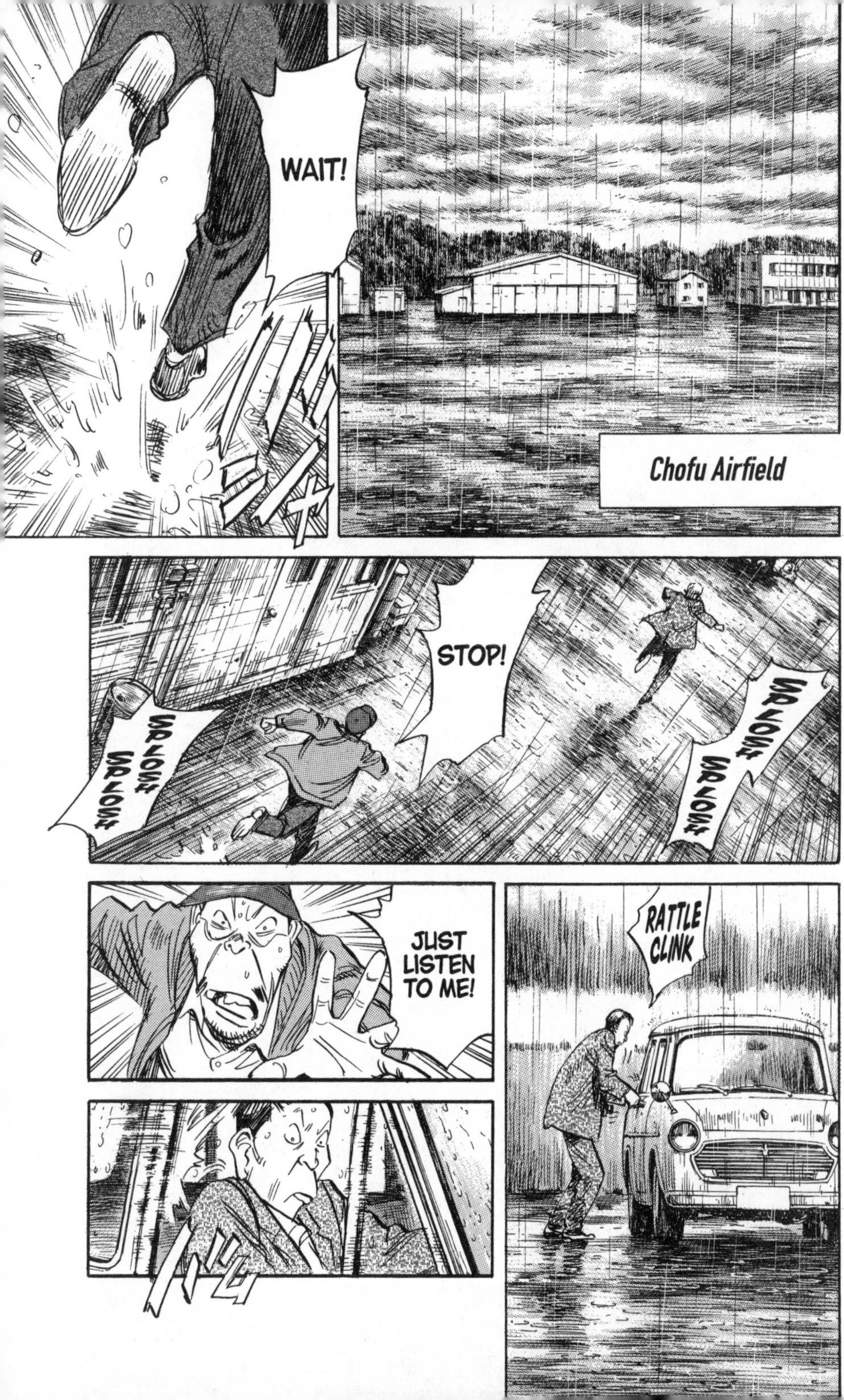
Chofu Airfield
WAIT!
STOP!
SPLOOSH SPLOOSH
SPLOOSH SPLOOSH
RATTLE CLINK
JUST LISTEN TO ME!

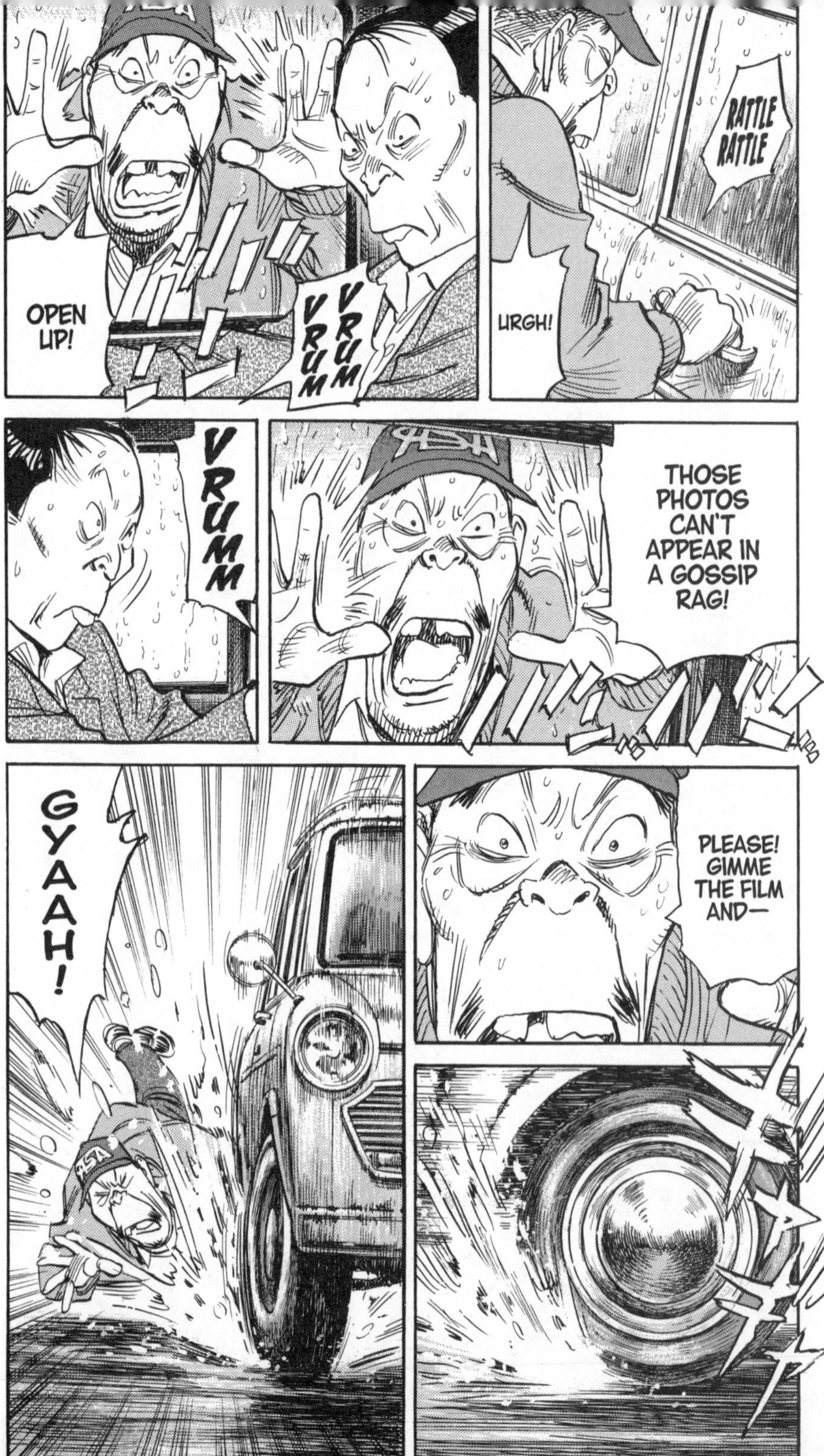
RATTLE RATTLE
URGH!
OPEN UP!
VRUM VRUM
THOSE PHOTOS CAN'T APPEAR IN A GOSSIP RAG!
VRUMM
PLEASE! GIMME THE FILM AND—
GYAAAH!

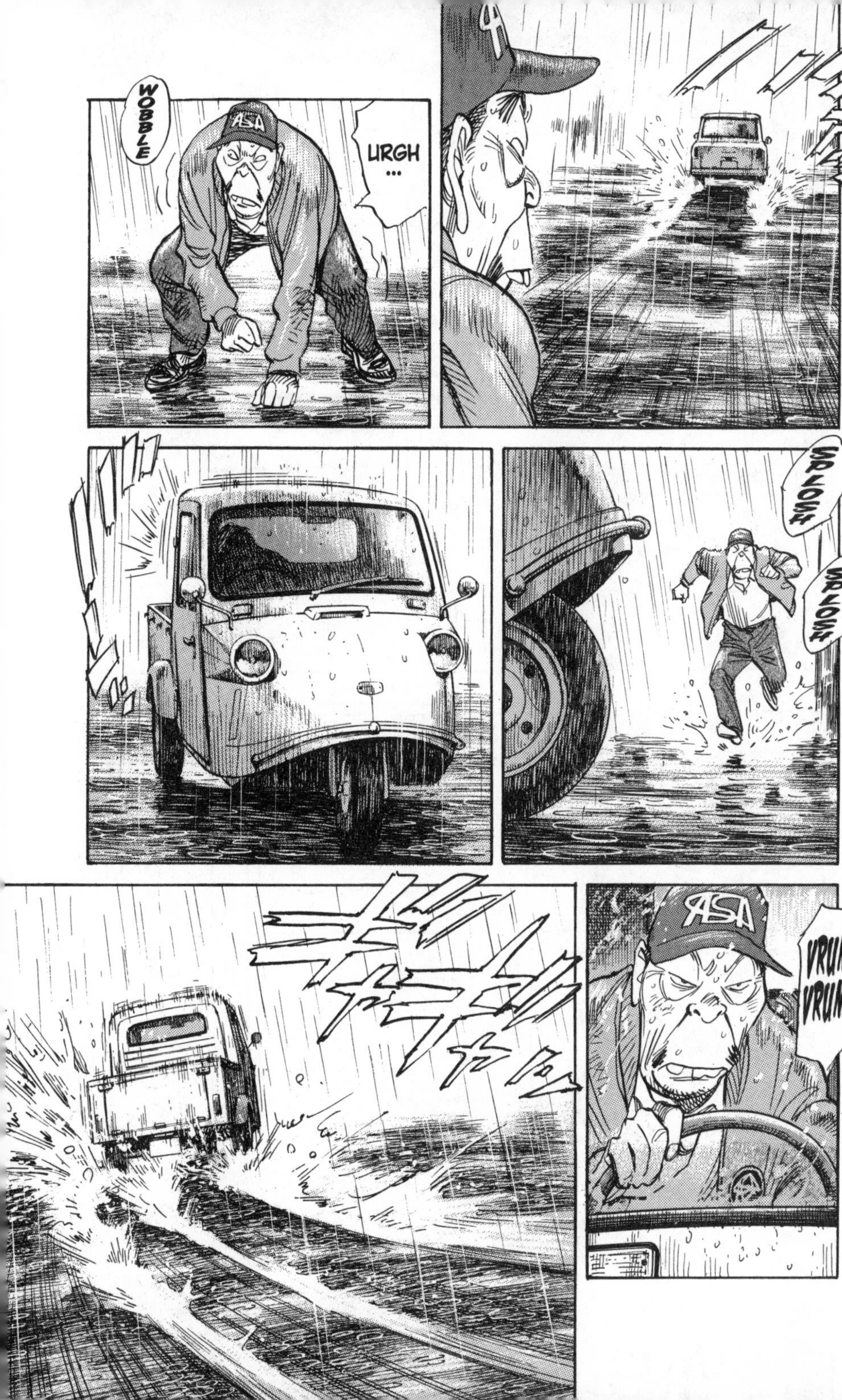
WOBBLE
URGH ...
VROOSH
VROOSH
VRUM VRUM

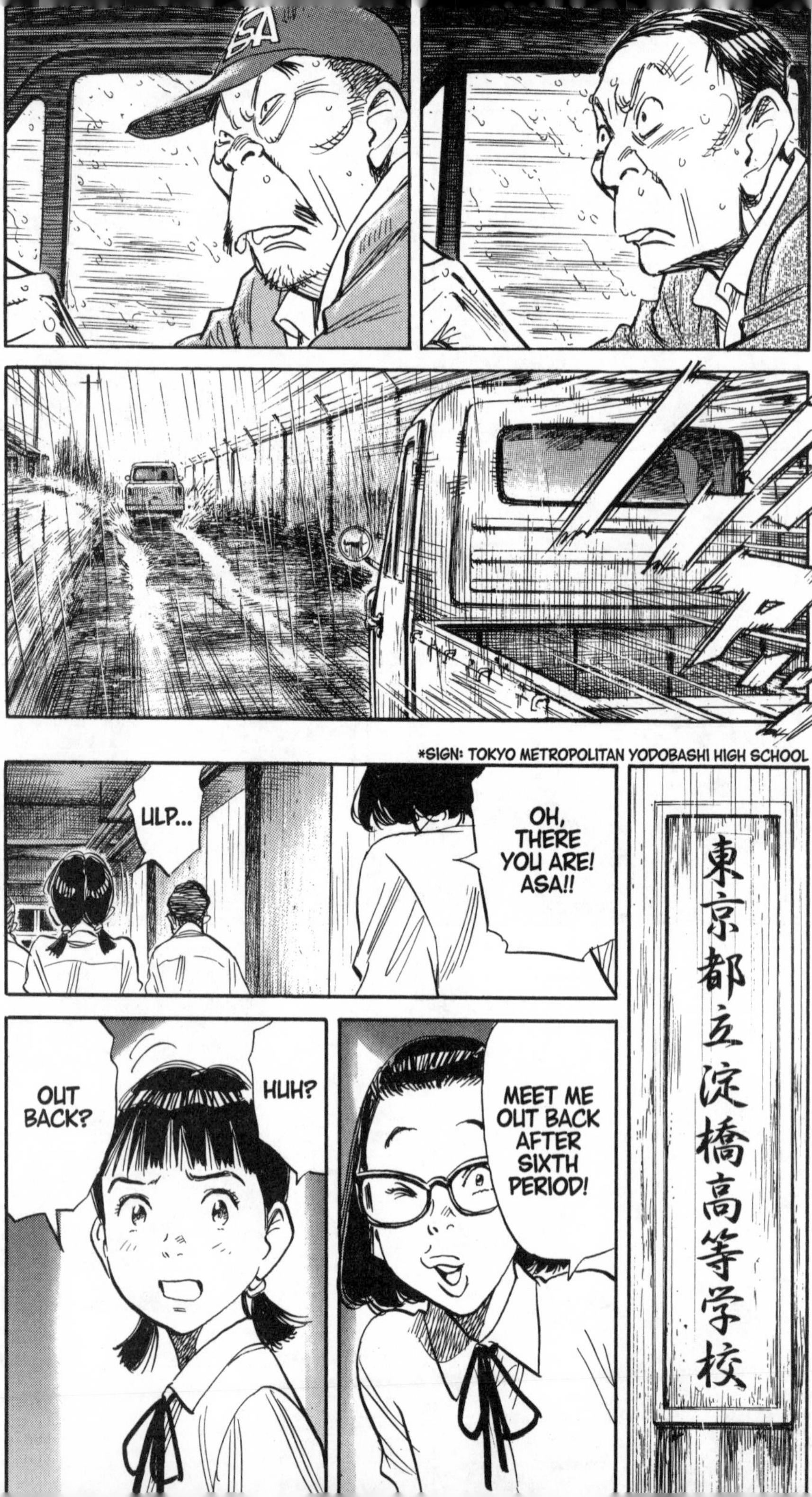
*SIGN: TOKYO METROPOLITAN YODOBASHI HIGH SCHOOL
東京都立淀橋高等学校
OH, THERE YOU ARE! ASA!!
ULP...
MEET ME OUT BACK AFTER SIXTH PERIOD!
HUH?
OUT BACK?

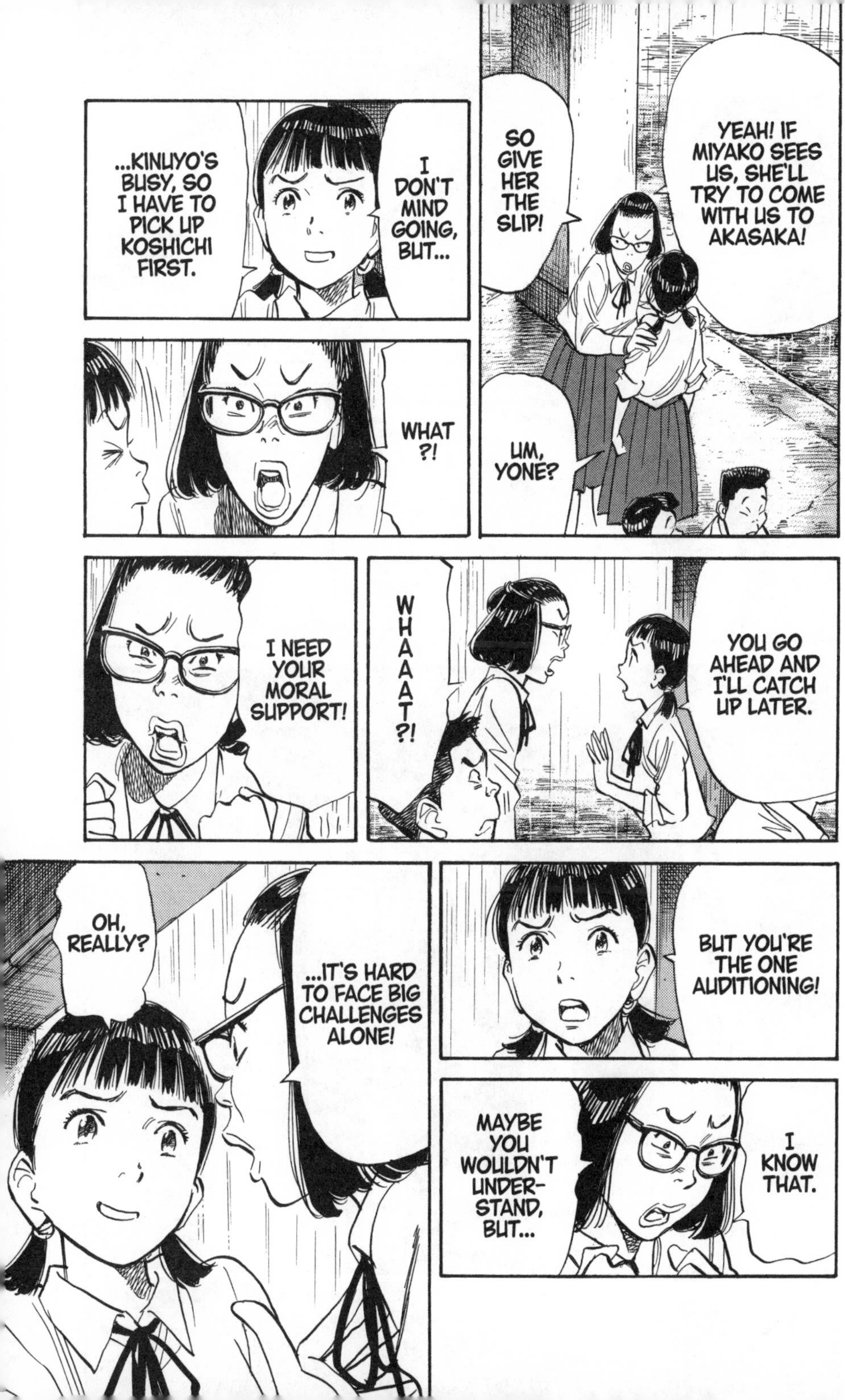
YEAH! IF MIYAKO SEES US, SHE'LL TRY TO COME WITH US TO AKASAKA!
SO GIVE HER THE SLIP!
UM, YONE?
I DON'T MIND GOING, BUT...
...KINUYO'S BUSY, SO I HAVE TO PICK UP KOSHICHI FIRST.
WHAT?!
YOU GO AHEAD AND I'LL CATCH UP LATER.
WHAAAT?!
I NEED YOUR MORAL SUPPORT!
BUT YOU'RE THE ONE AUDITIONING!
I KNOW THAT.
MAYBE YOU WOULDN'T UNDER-STAND, BUT...
...IT'S HARD TO FACE BIG CHALLENGES ALONE!
OH, REALLY?

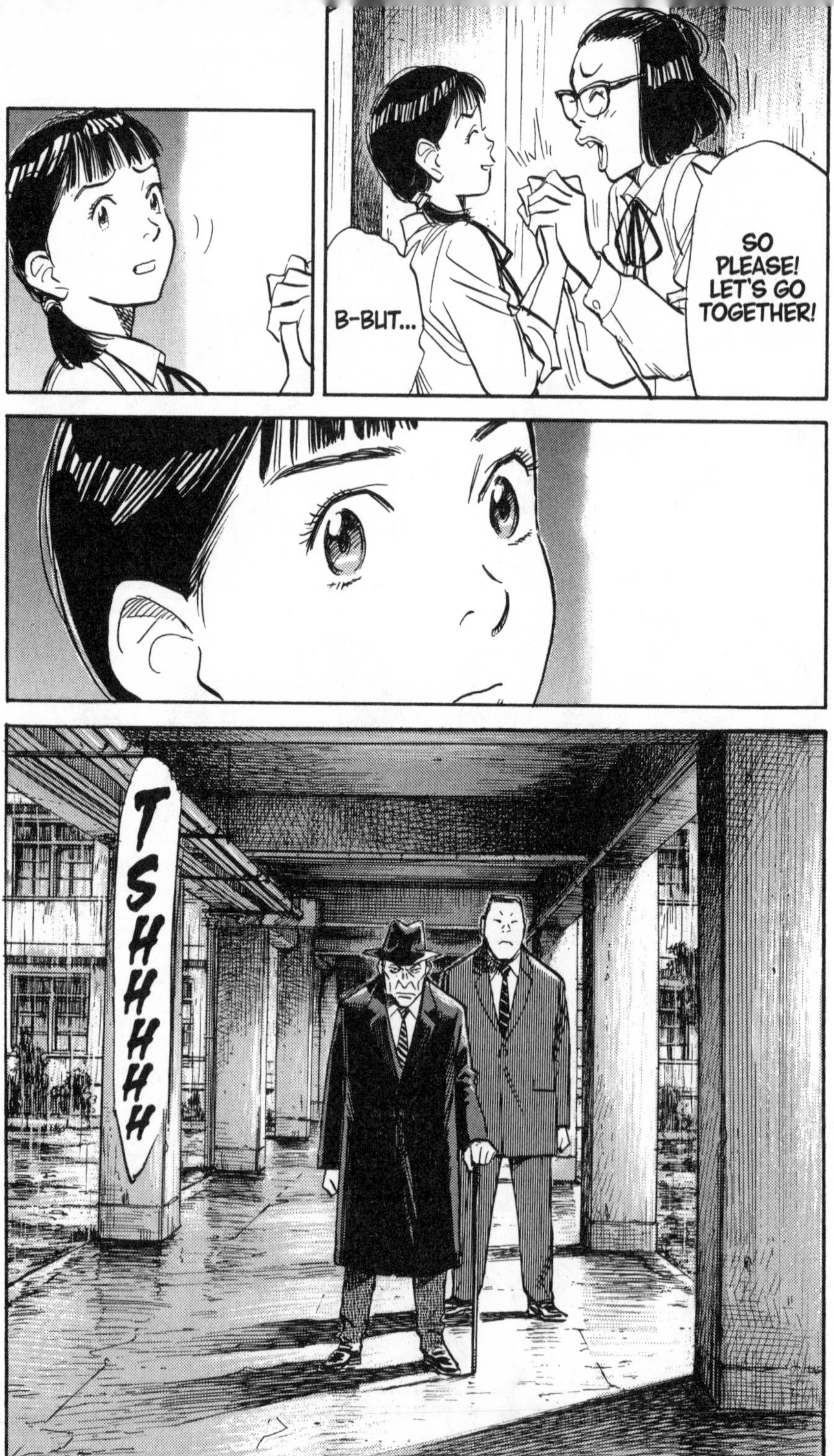
SO PLEASE! LET'S GO TOGETHER!
B-BUT...
TSHHHHHH

Chapter 27 ● A Big Sister's Job

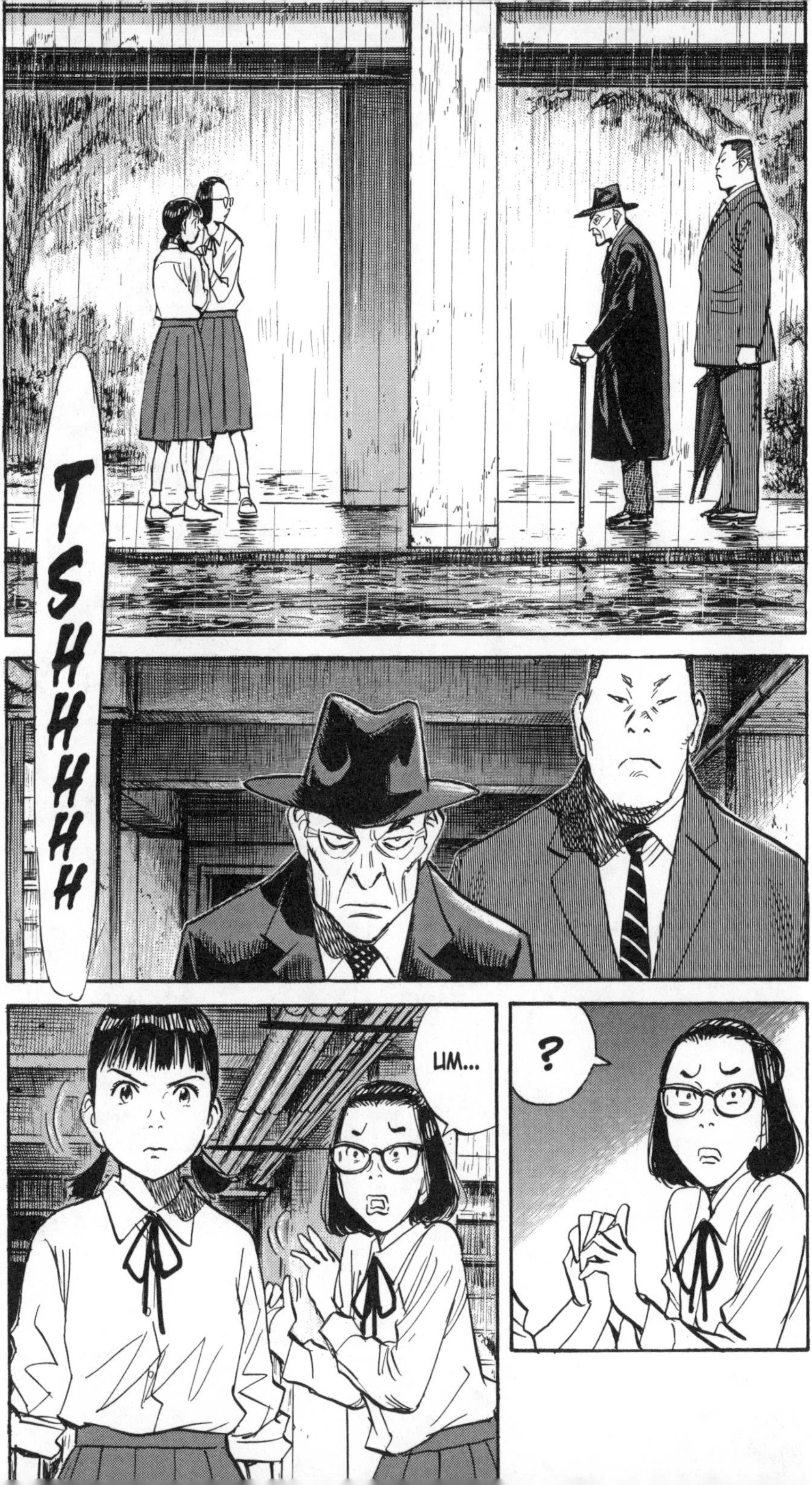

TSHHHHHH
?
UM...

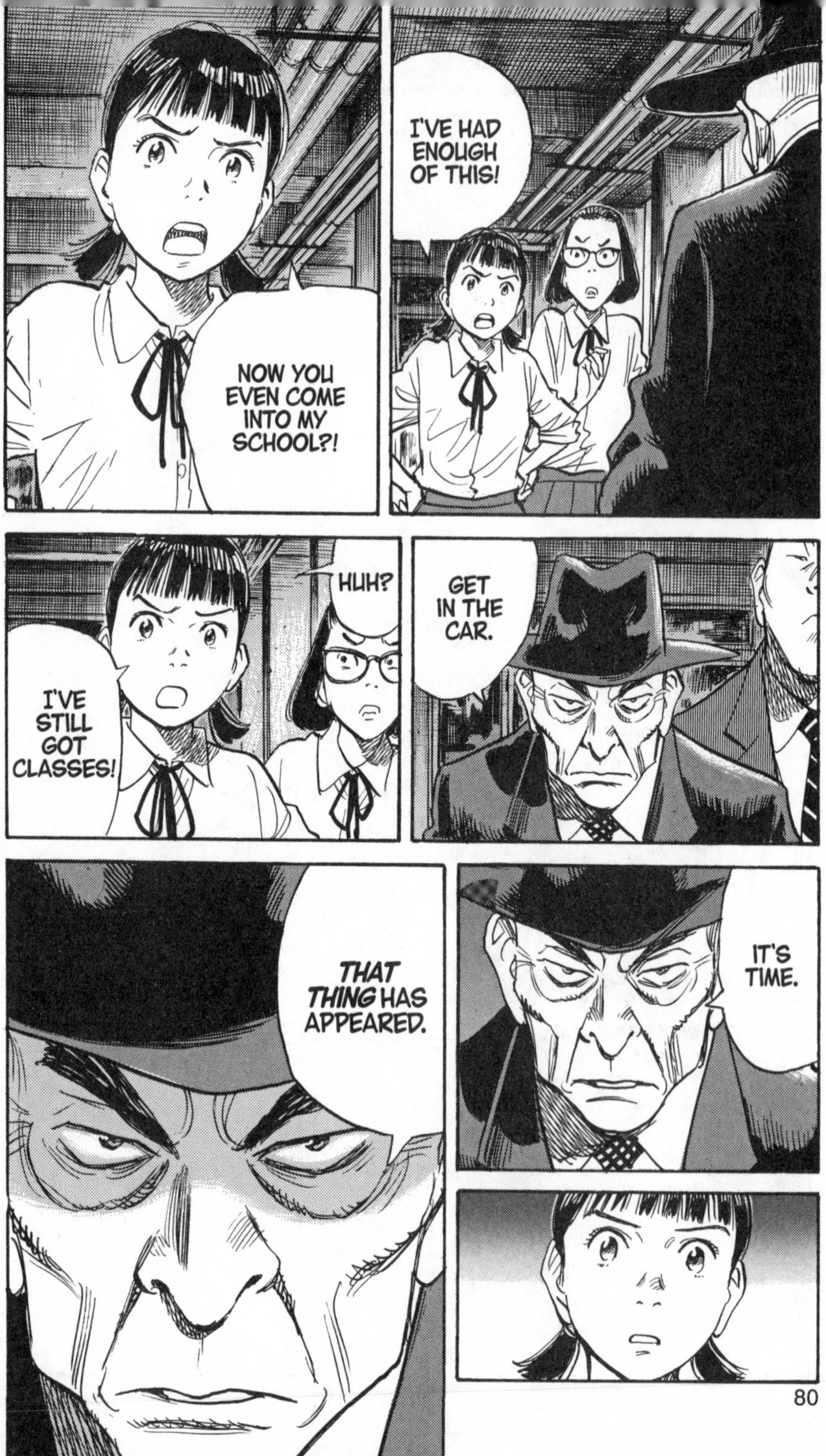
I'VE HAD ENOUGH OF THIS!
NOW YOU EVEN COME INTO MY SCHOOL?!
GET IN THE CAR.
HUH?
I'VE STILL GOT CLASSES!
IT'S TIME.
THAT THING HAS APPEARED.

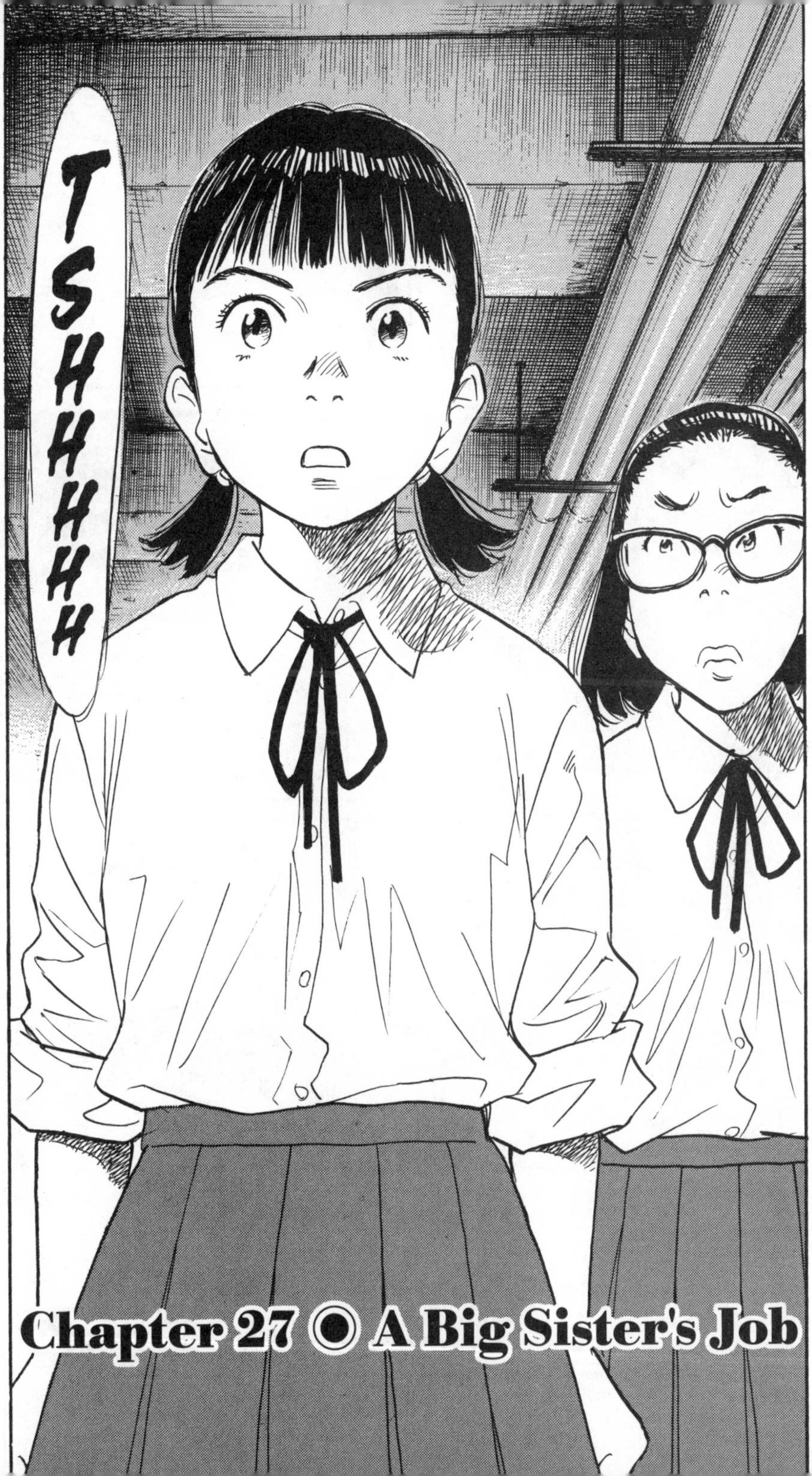
TSHHHHHHH
Chapter 27 ◉ A Big Sister's Job

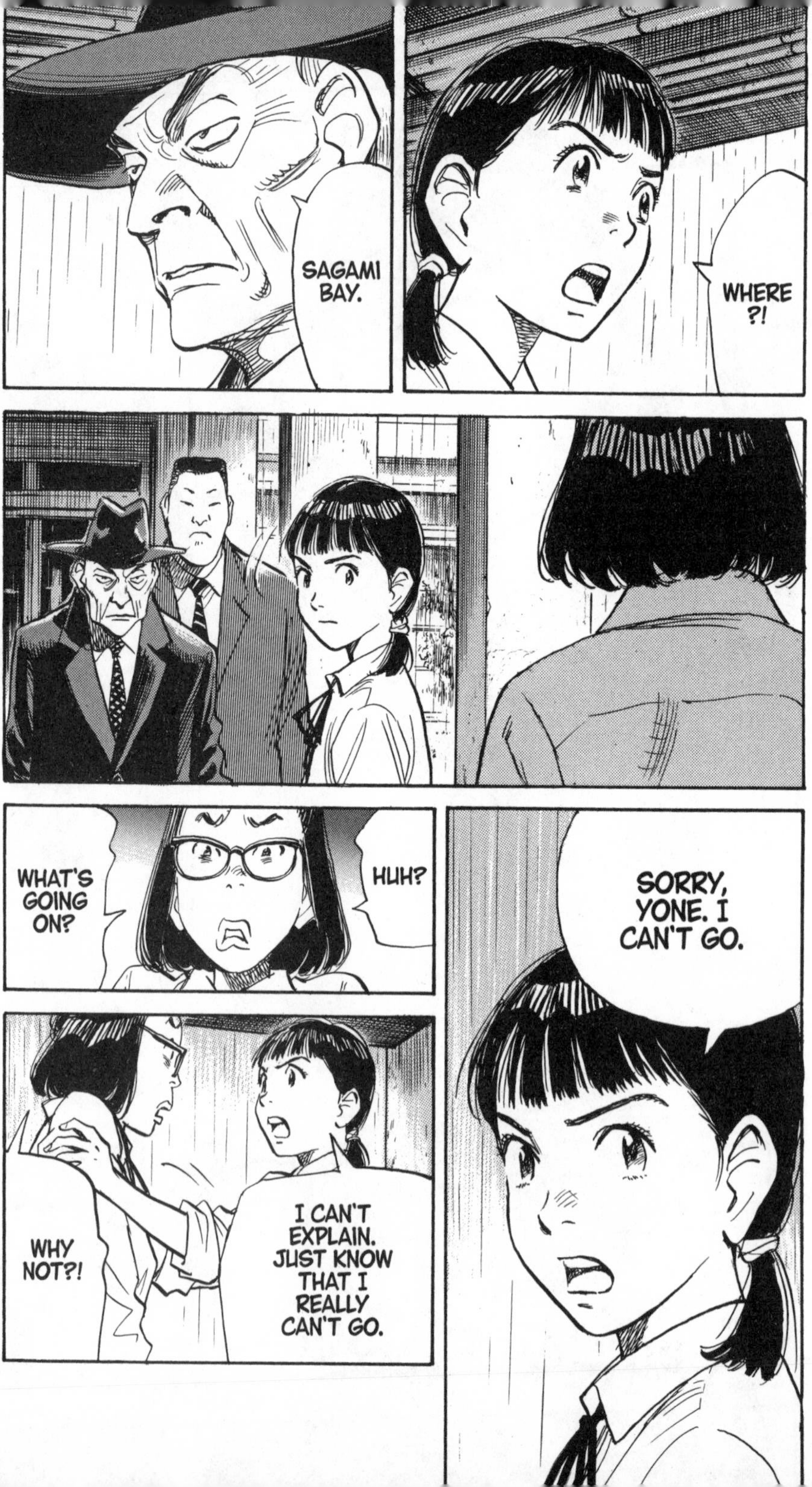
WHERE ?!
SAGAMI BAY.
SORRY, YONE. I CAN'T GO.
HUH?
WHAT'S GOING ON?
I CAN'T EXPLAIN. JUST KNOW THAT I REALLY CAN'T GO.
WHY NOT?!

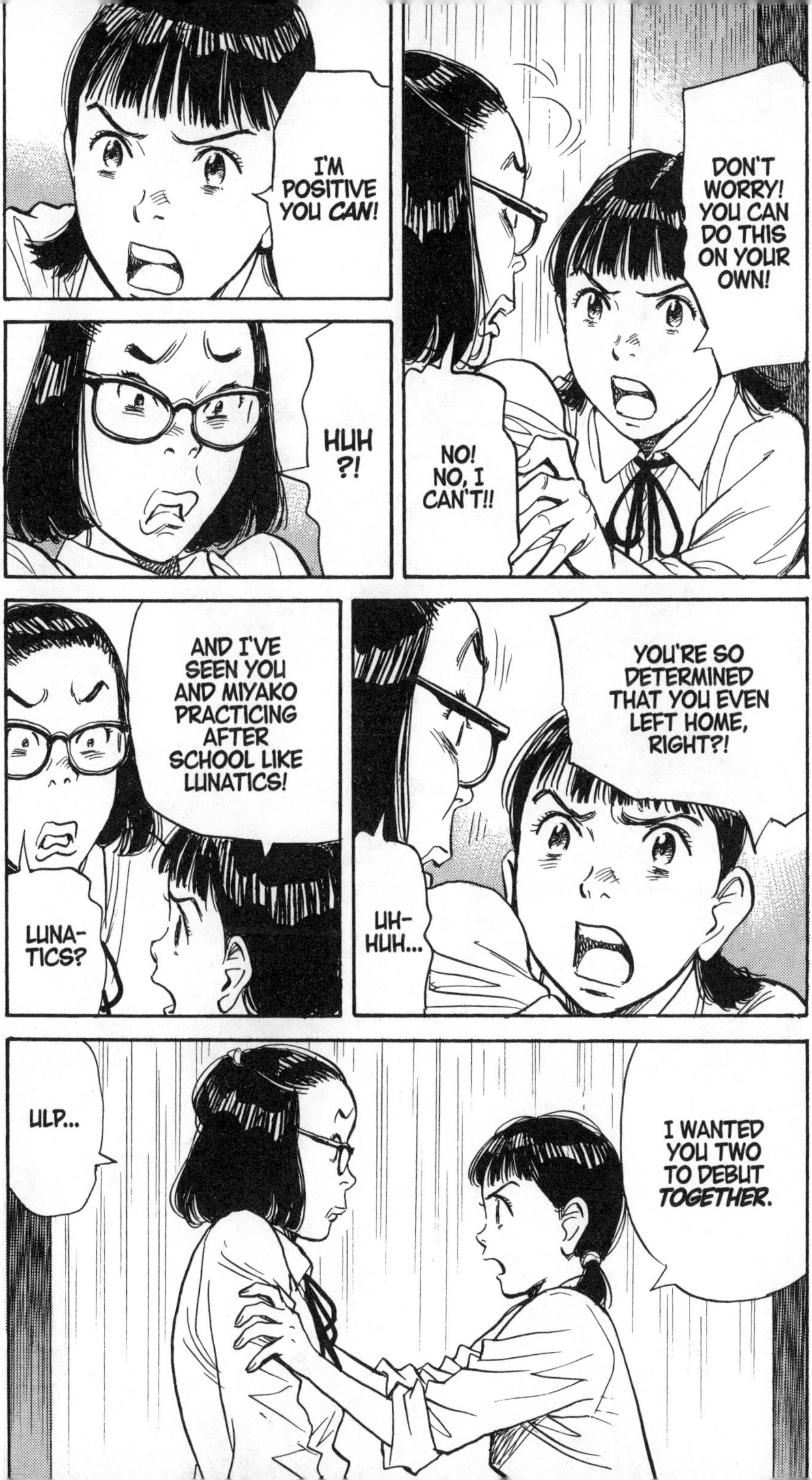
DON'T WORRY! YOU CAN DO THIS ON YOUR OWN!
NO! NO, I CAN'T!!
I'M POSITIVE YOU *CAN*!
HUH ?!
YOU'RE SO DETERMINED THAT YOU EVEN LEFT HOME, RIGHT?!
UH-HUH...
AND I'VE SEEN YOU AND MIYAKO PRACTICING AFTER SCHOOL LIKE LUNATICS!
LUNA-TICS?
I WANTED YOU TWO TO DEBUT *TOGETHER*.
ULP...

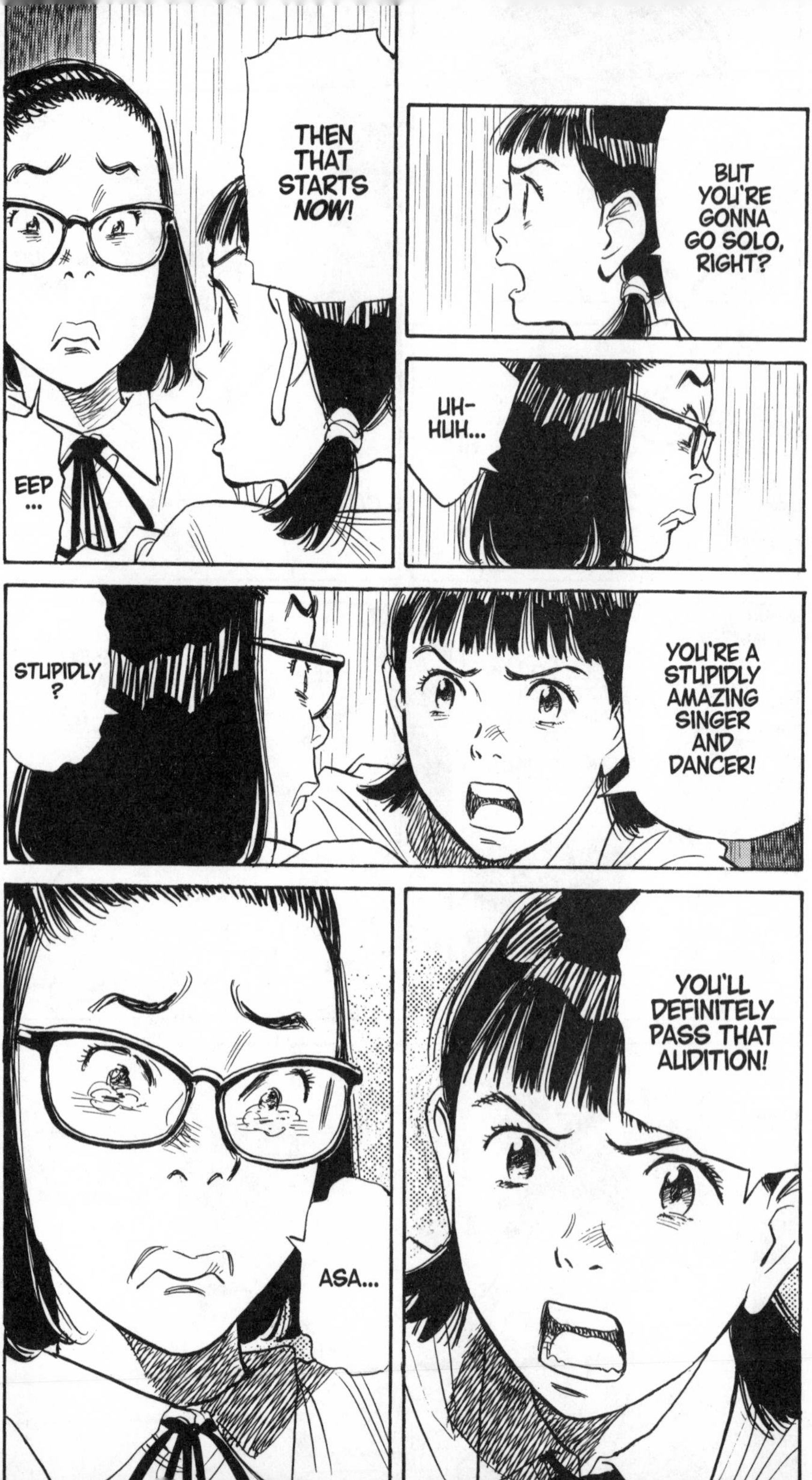
BUT YOU'RE GONNA GO SOLO, RIGHT?
UH-HUH...
THEN THAT STARTS *NOW*!
EEP...
YOU'RE A STUPIDLY AMAZING SINGER AND DANCER!
STUPIDLY?
YOU'LL DEFINITELY PASS THAT AUDITION!
ASA...

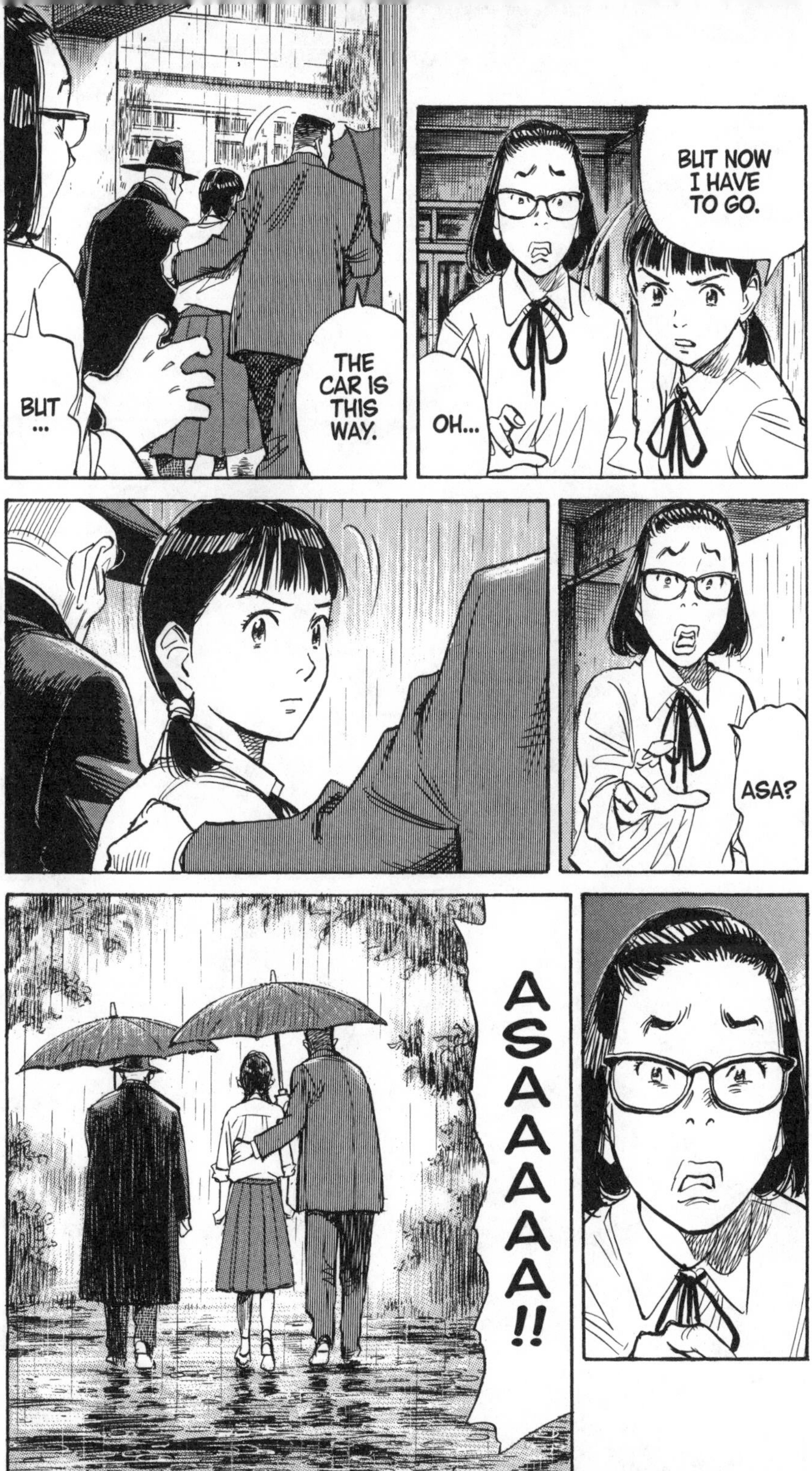
BUT NOW I HAVE TO GO.
OH...
THE CAR IS THIS WAY.
BUT ...
ASA?
ASAAAAA!!

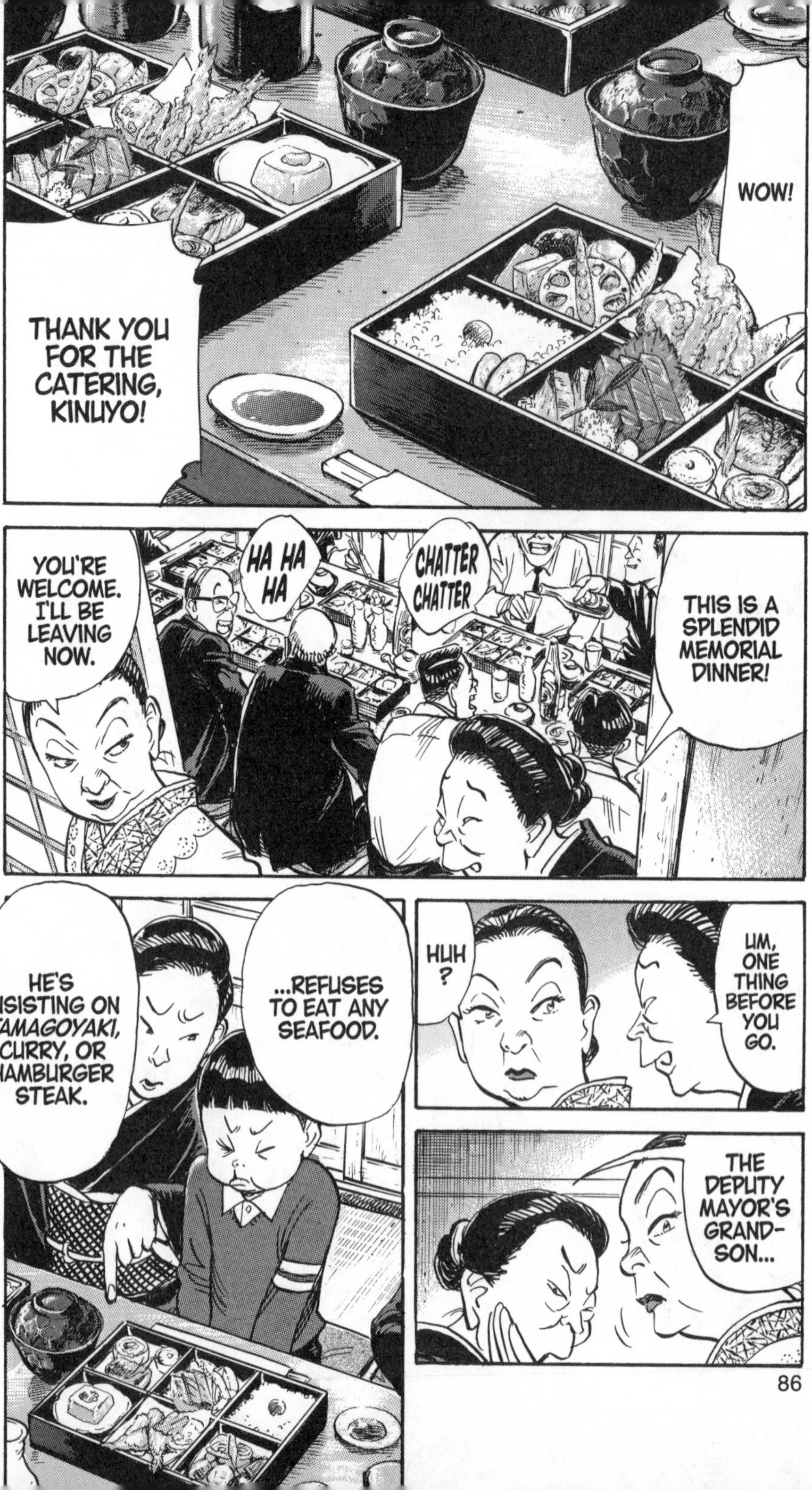
WOW!
THANK YOU FOR THE CATERING, KINUYO!
THIS IS A SPLENDID MEMORIAL DINNER!
CHATTER CHATTER
HA HA HA
YOU'RE WELCOME. I'LL BE LEAVING NOW.
UM, ONE THING BEFORE YOU GO.
HUH?
THE DEPUTY MAYOR'S GRAND-SON...
...REFUSES TO EAT ANY SEAFOOD.
HE'S INSISTING ON *TAMAGOYAKI*, CURRY, OR HAMBURGER STEAK.

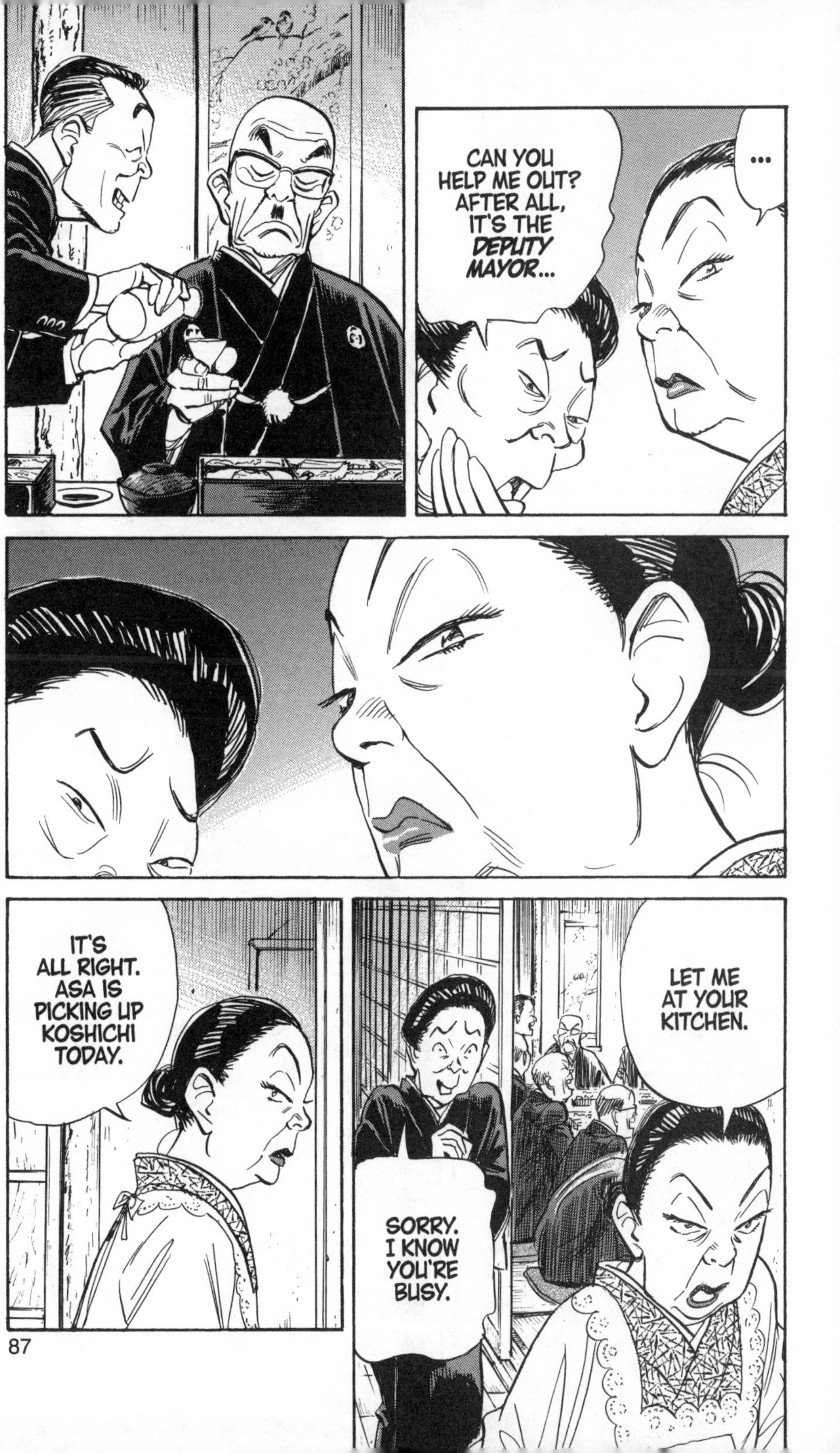
CAN YOU HELP ME OUT? AFTER ALL, IT'S THE DEPUTY MAYOR...
...
LET ME AT YOUR KITCHEN.
SORRY. I KNOW YOU'RE BUSY.
IT'S ALL RIGHT. ASA IS PICKING UP KOSHICHI TODAY.

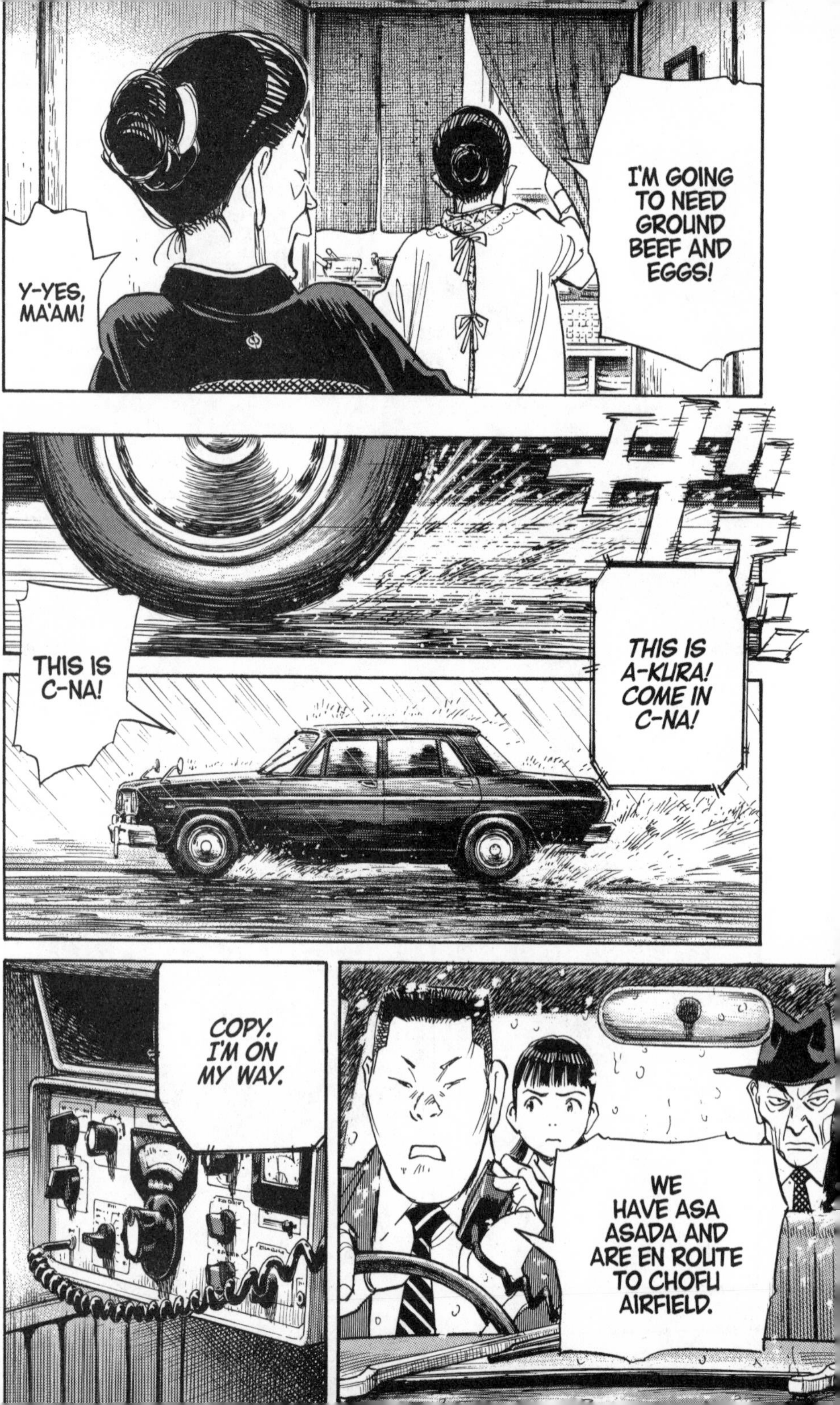
I'M GOING TO NEED GROUND BEEF AND EGGS!
Y-YES, MA'AM!
THIS IS A-KURA! COME IN C-NA!
THIS IS C-NA!
WE HAVE ASA ASADA AND ARE EN ROUTE TO CHOFU AIRFIELD.
COPY. I'M ON MY WAY.

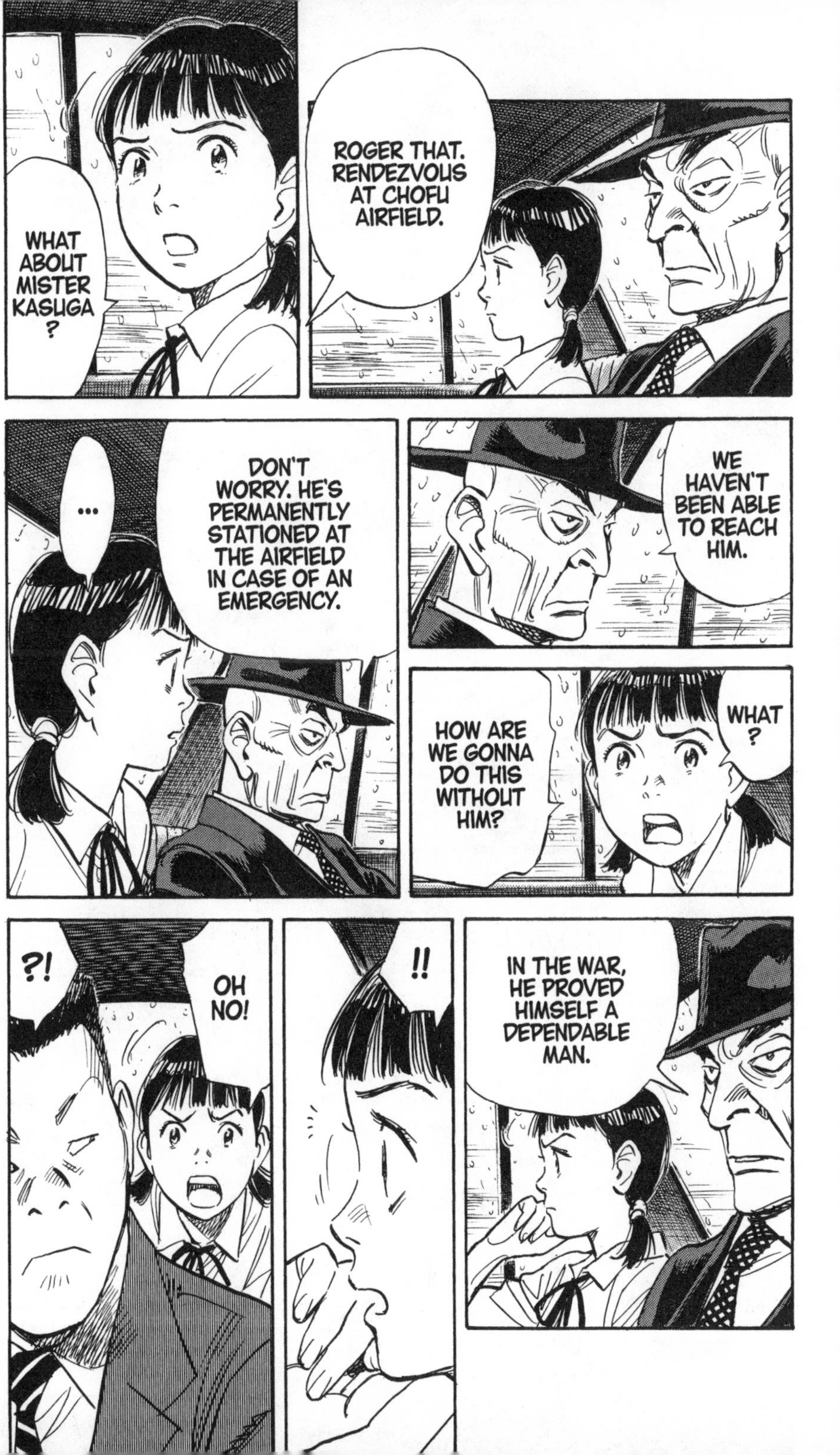
ROGER THAT. RENDEZVOUS AT CHOFU AIRFIELD.
WHAT ABOUT MISTER KASUGA ?
WE HAVEN'T BEEN ABLE TO REACH HIM.
WHAT ?
HOW ARE WE GONNA DO THIS WITHOUT HIM?
DON'T WORRY. HE'S PERMANENTLY STATIONED AT THE AIRFIELD IN CASE OF AN EMERGENCY.
...
IN THE WAR, HE PROVED HIMSELF A DEPENDABLE MAN.
!!
OH NO!
?!

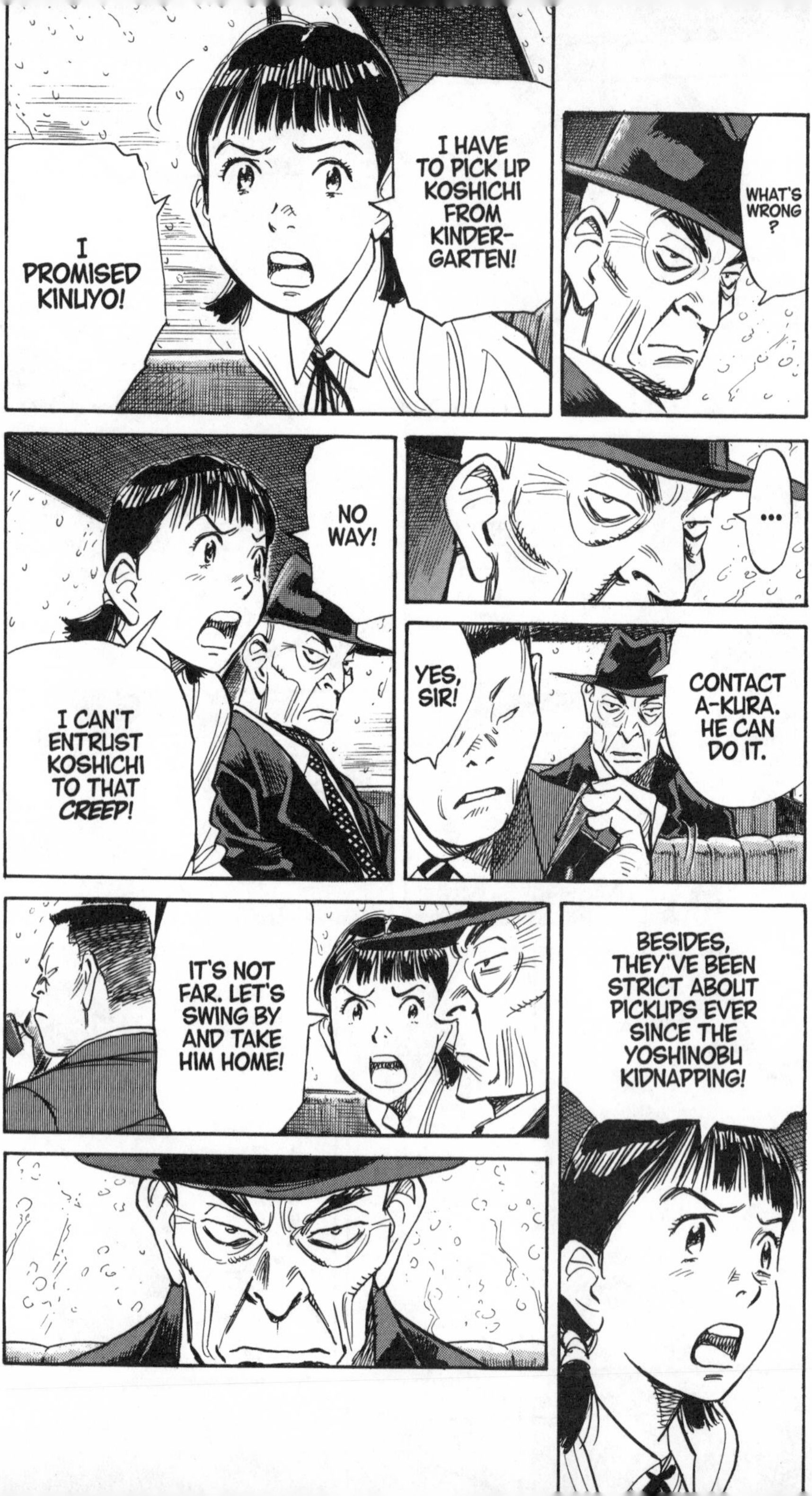
WHAT'S WRONG?
I HAVE TO PICK UP KOSHICHI FROM KINDER-GARTEN!
I PROMISED KINUYO!
...
CONTACT A-KURA. HE CAN DO IT.
YES, SIR!
NO WAY!
I CAN'T ENTRUST KOSHICHI TO THAT *CREEP*!
BESIDES, THEY'VE BEEN STRICT ABOUT PICKUPS EVER SINCE THE YOSHINOBU KIDNAPPING!
IT'S NOT FAR. LET'S SWING BY AND TAKE HIM HOME!

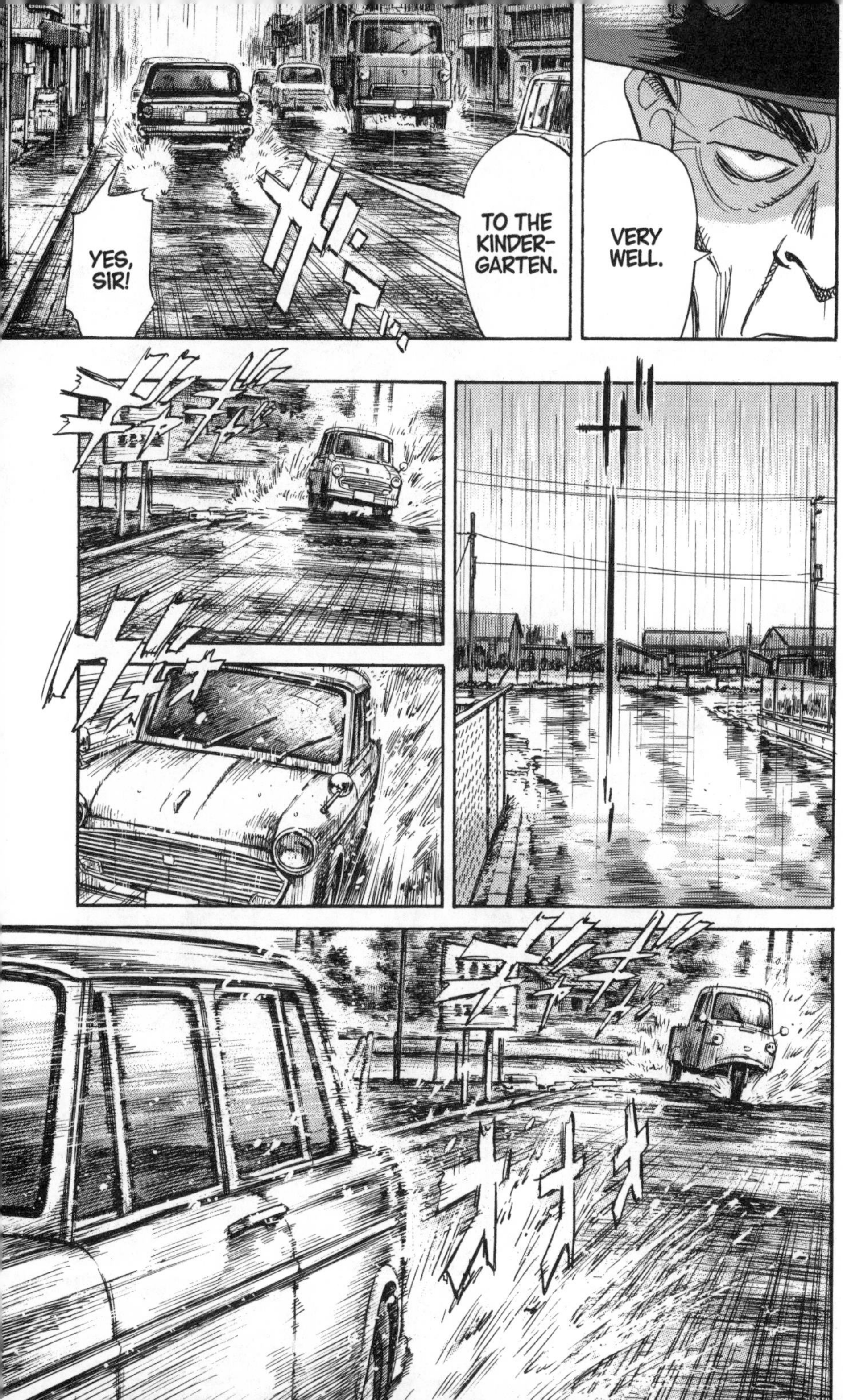
VERY WELL.
TO THE KINDER-GARTEN.
YES, SIR!

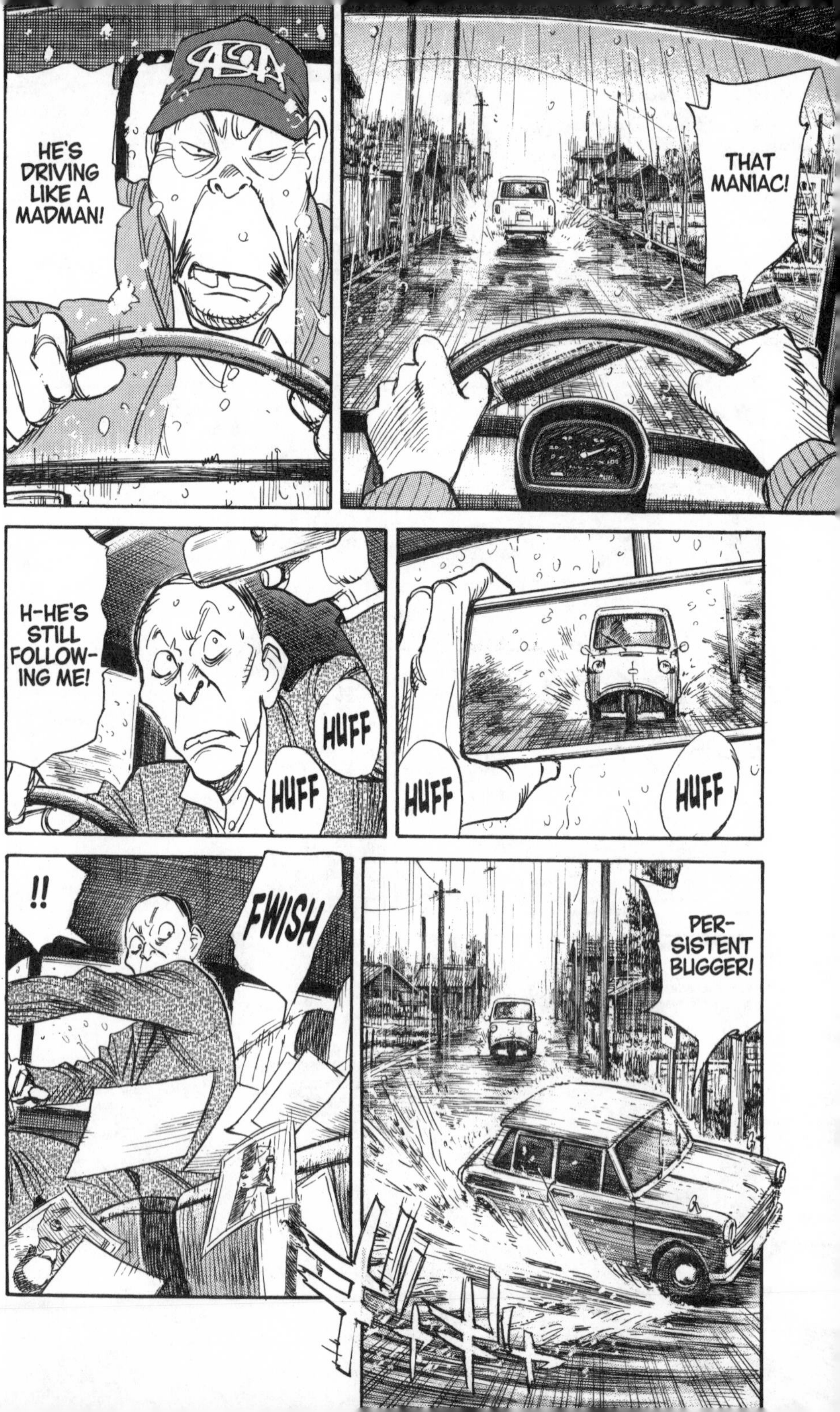
THAT MANIAC!
HE'S DRIVING LIKE A MADMAN!
HUFF
HUFF
H-HE'S STILL FOLLOW-ING ME!
HUFF
HUFF
PER-SISTENT BUGGER!
!!
FWISH

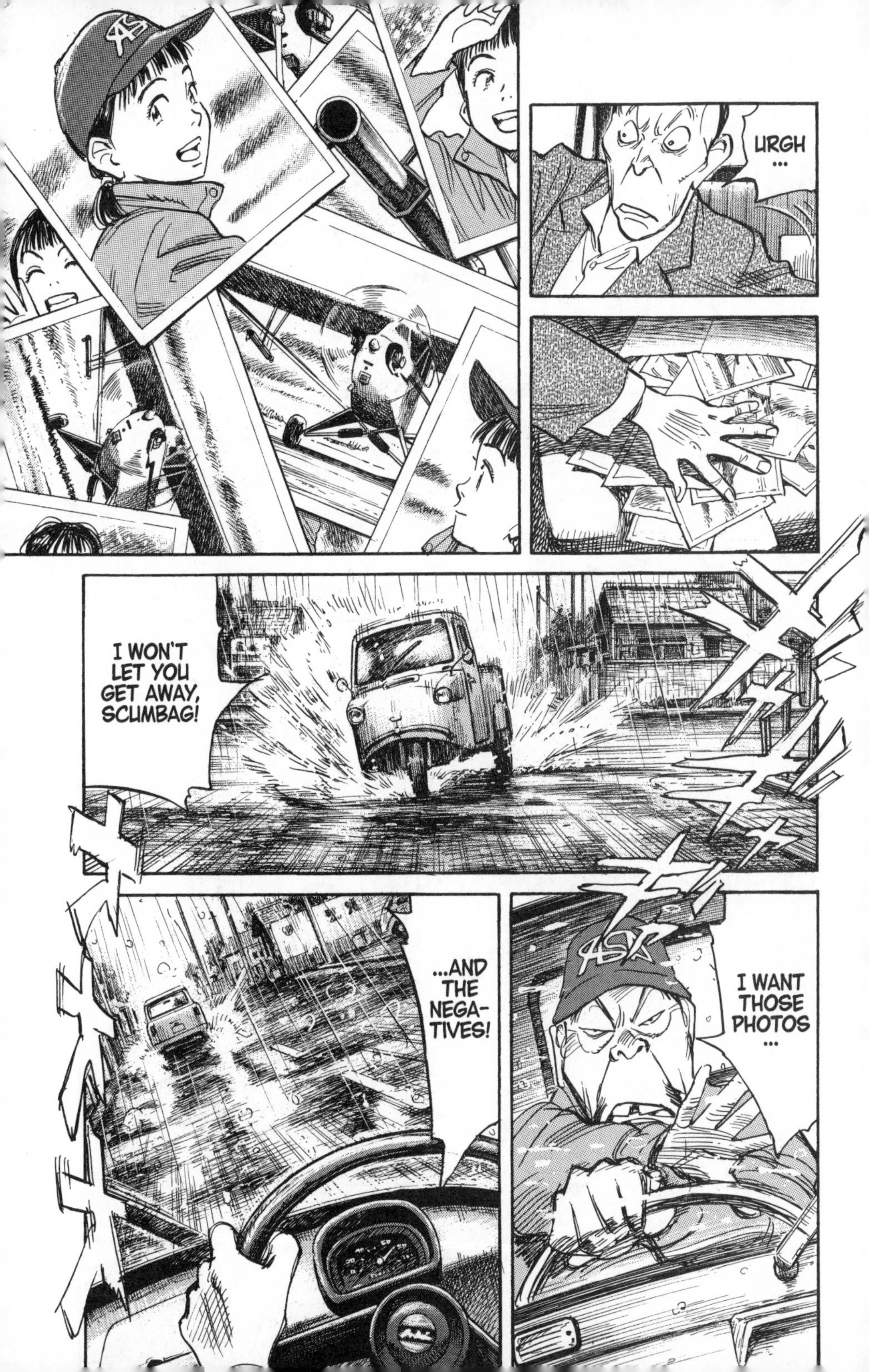
URGH ...
I WON'T LET YOU GET AWAY, SCUMBAG!
I WANT THOSE PHOTOS ...
...AND THE NEGA-TIVES!

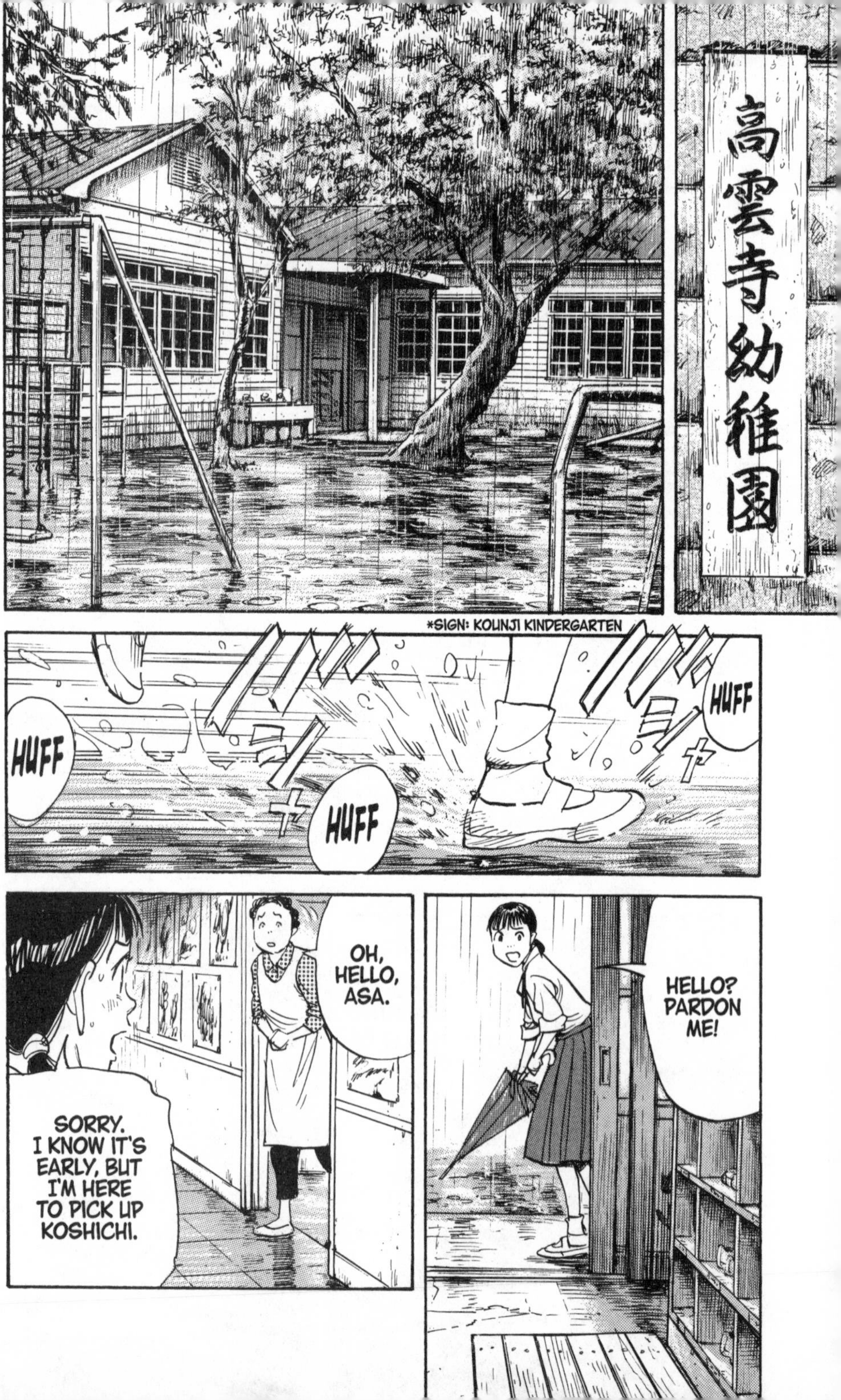
高雲寺幼稚園
*SIGN: KOUNJI KINDERGARTEN
HUFF
HUFF
HUFF
HELLO? PARDON ME!
OH, HELLO, ASA.
SORRY. I KNOW IT'S EARLY, BUT I'M HERE TO PICK UP KOSHICHI.

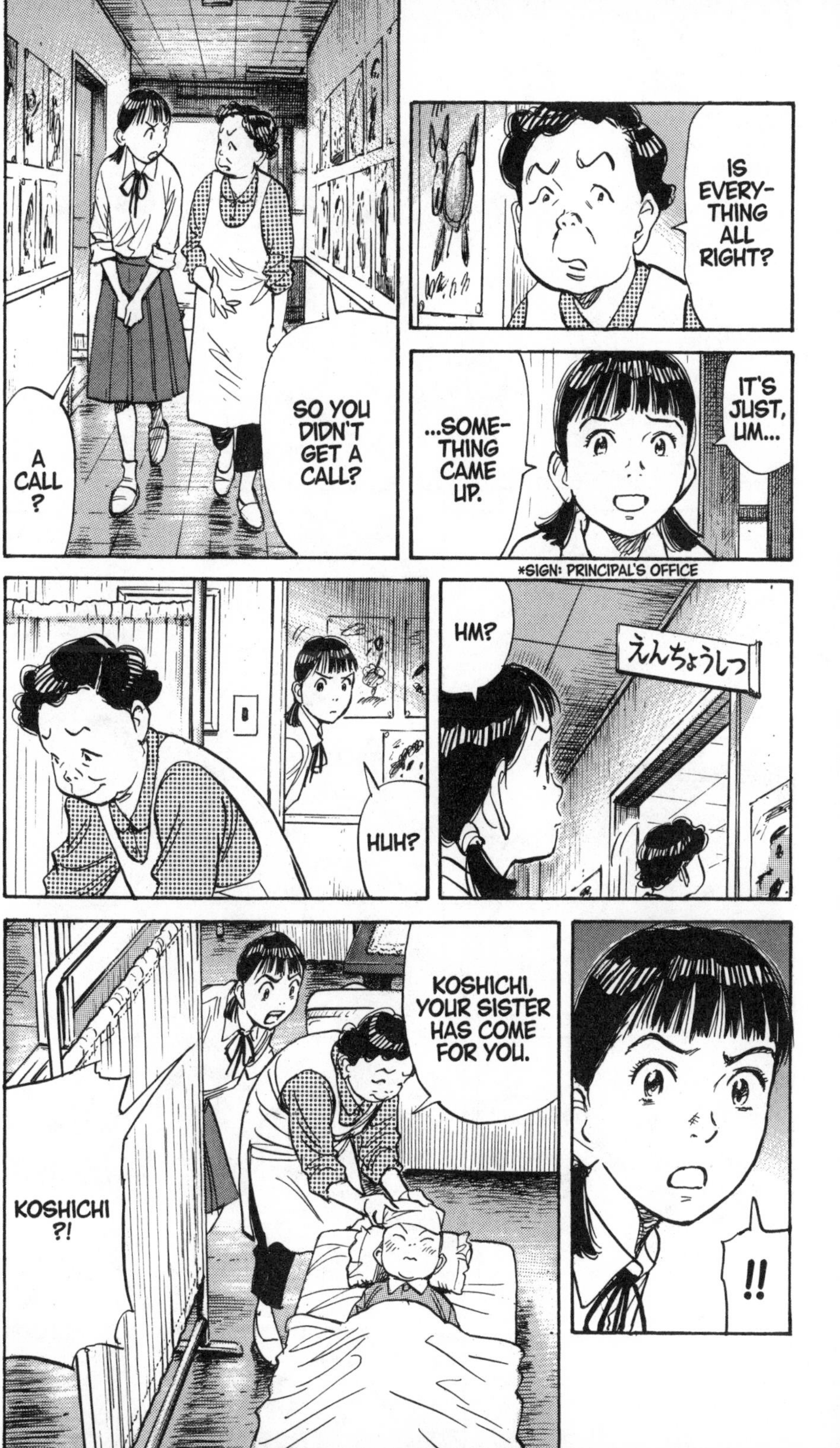
IS EVERYTHING ALL RIGHT?
IT'S JUST, UM...
...SOMETHING CAME UP.
SO YOU DIDN'T GET A CALL?
A CALL?
*SIGN: PRINCIPAL'S OFFICE
えんちょうしつ
HM?
HUH?
!!
KOSHICHI, YOUR SISTER HAS COME FOR YOU.
KOSHICHI?!

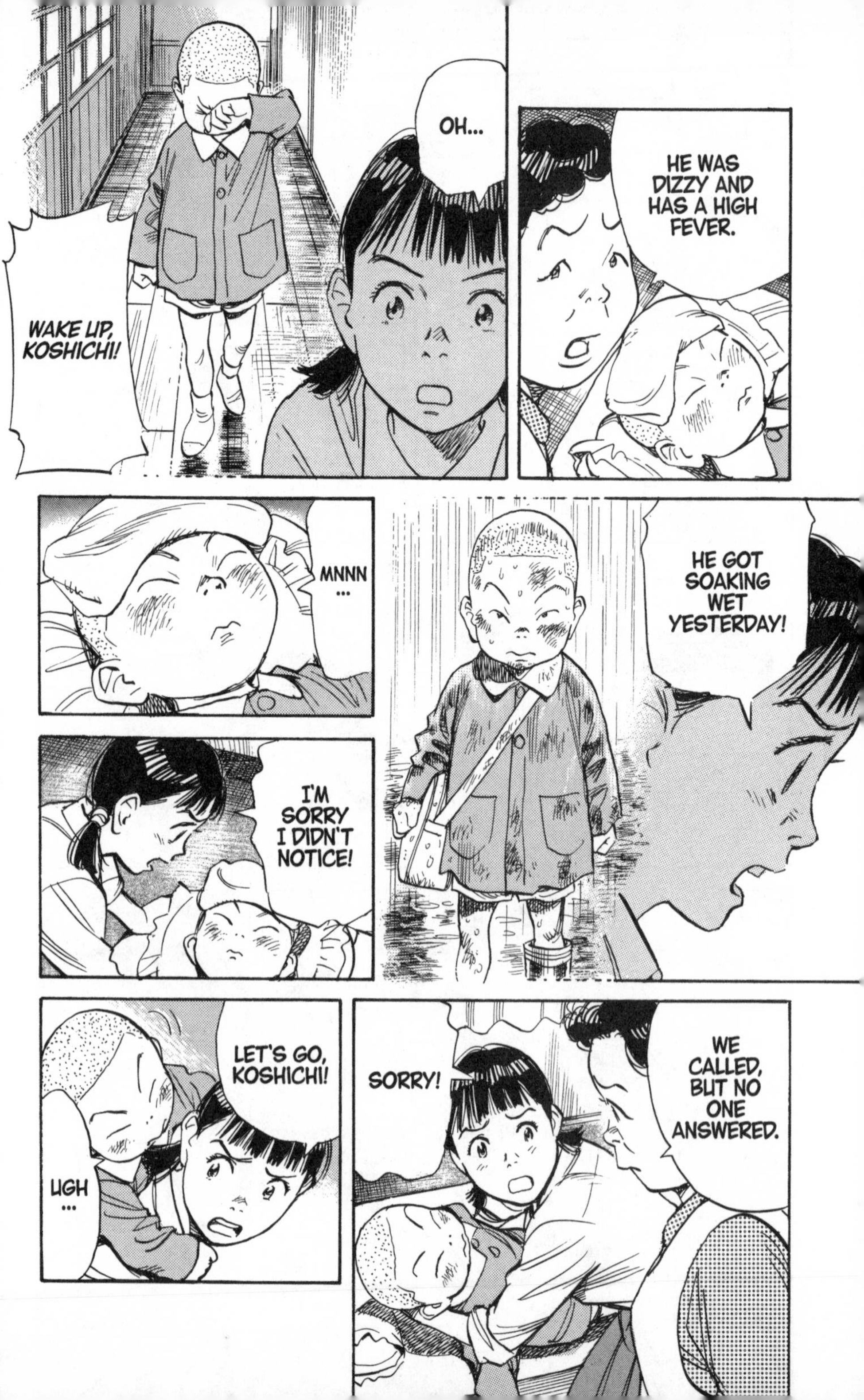
HE WAS DIZZY AND HAS A HIGH FEVER.
OH...
WAKE UP, KOSHICHI!
HE GOT SOAKING WET YESTERDAY!
MNNN ...
I'M SORRY I DIDN'T NOTICE!
WE CALLED, BUT NO ONE ANSWERED.
SORRY!
LET'S GO, KOSHICHI!
UGH ...

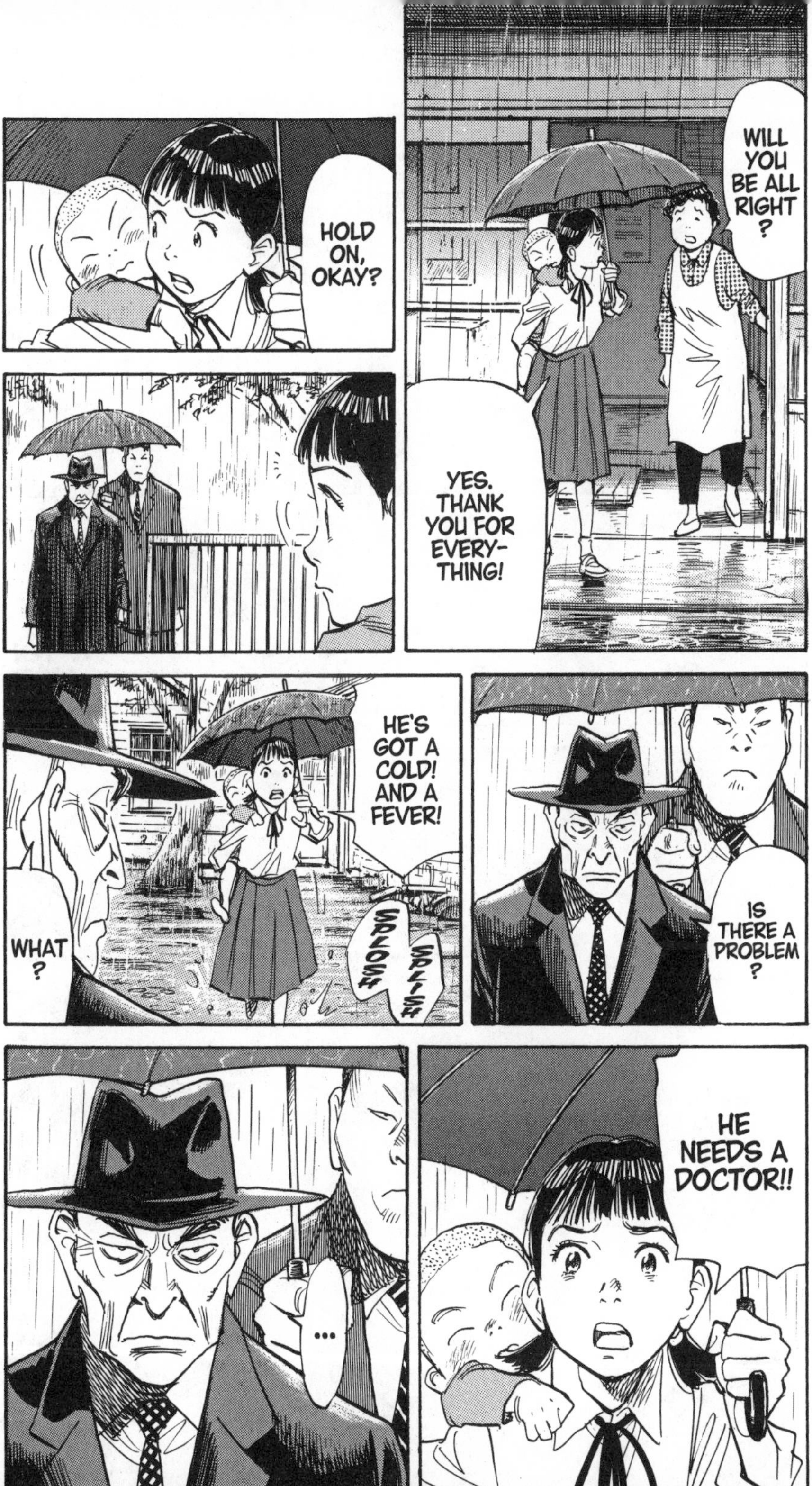
WILL YOU BE ALL RIGHT?
YES. THANK YOU FOR EVERY-THING!
HOLD ON, OKAY?
IS THERE A PROBLEM?
HE'S GOT A COLD! AND A FEVER!
SPLISH
SPLOSH
WHAT?
HE NEEDS A DOCTOR!!
...

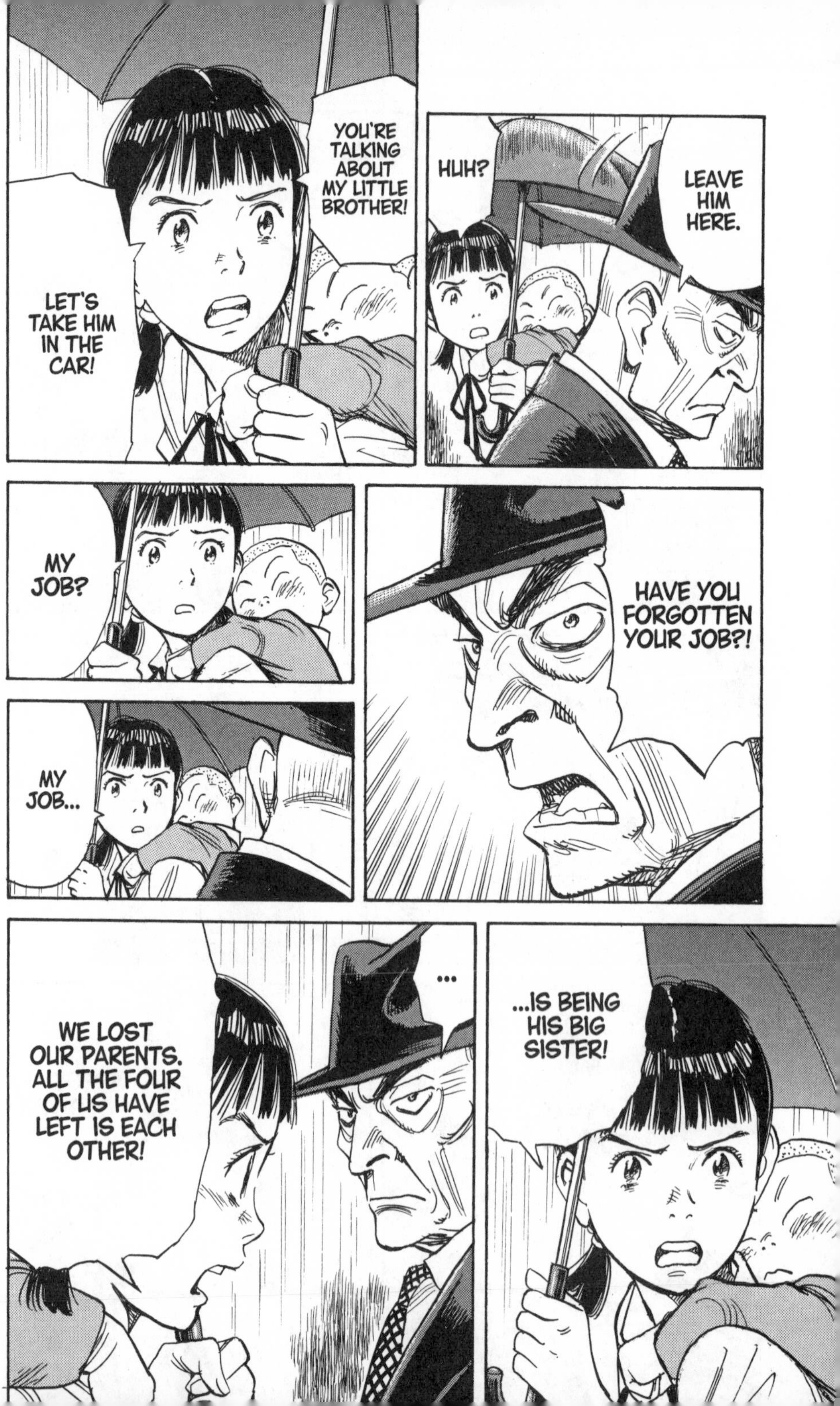
LEAVE HIM HERE.
HUH?
YOU'RE TALKING ABOUT MY LITTLE BROTHER!
LET'S TAKE HIM IN THE CAR!
HAVE YOU FORGOTTEN YOUR JOB?!
MY JOB?
MY JOB...
...IS BEING HIS BIG SISTER!
...
WE LOST OUR PARENTS. ALL THE FOUR OF US HAVE LEFT IS EACH OTHER!

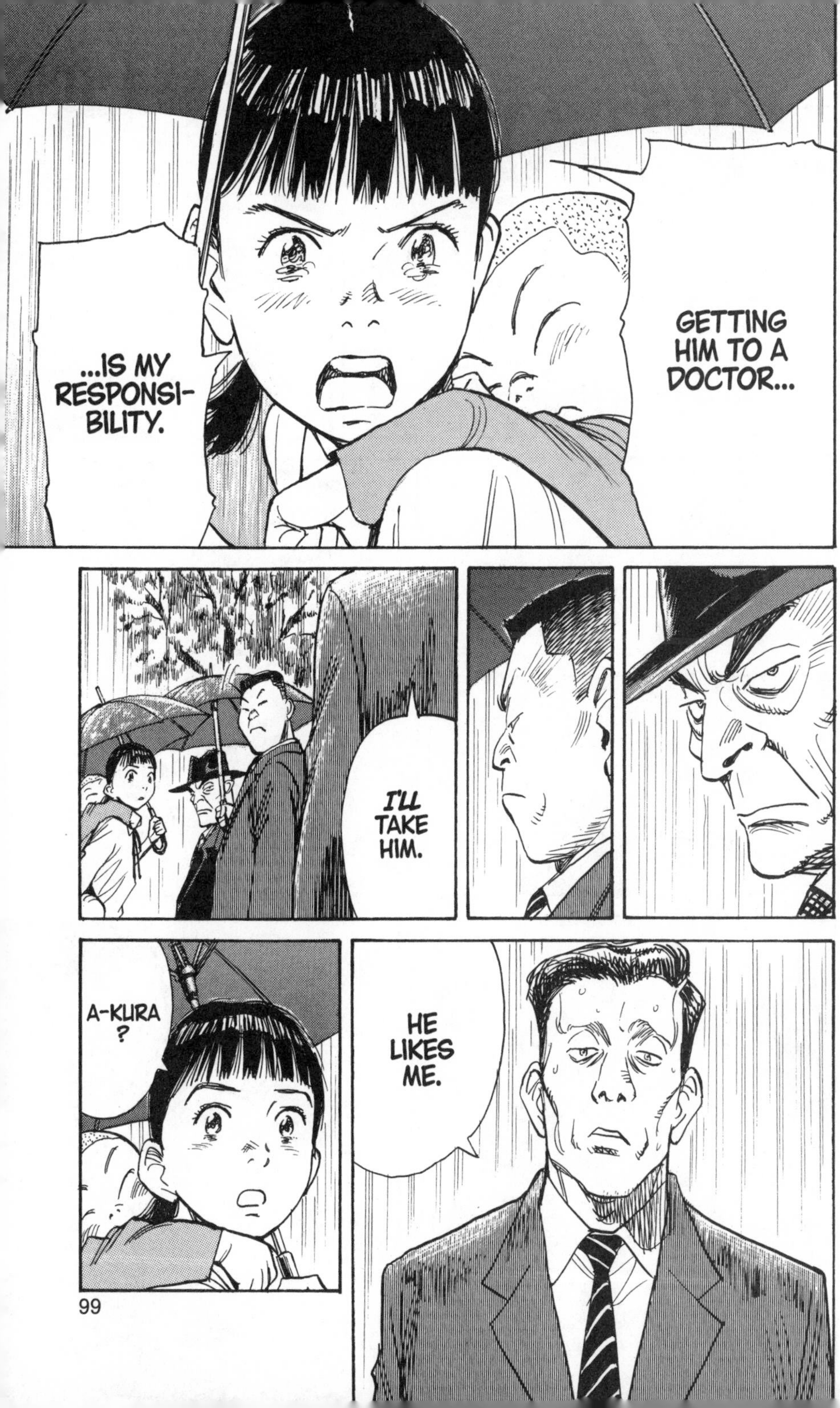
GETTING HIM TO A DOCTOR...
...IS MY RESPONSI-BILITY.
I'LL TAKE HIM.
HE LIKES ME.
A-KURA?

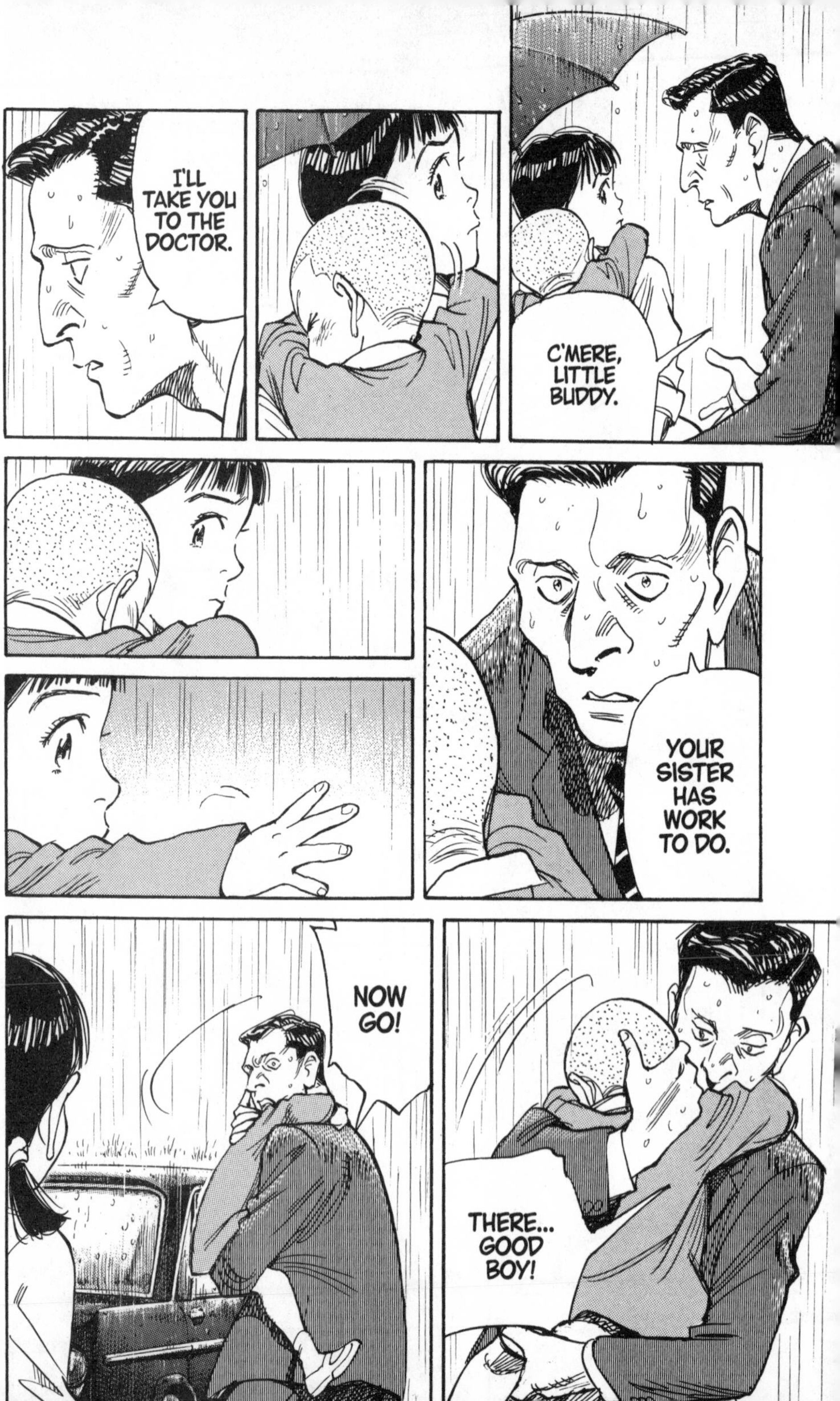
C'MERE, LITTLE BUDDY.
I'LL TAKE YOU TO THE DOCTOR.
YOUR SISTER HAS WORK TO DO.
THERE... GOOD BOY!
NOW GO!

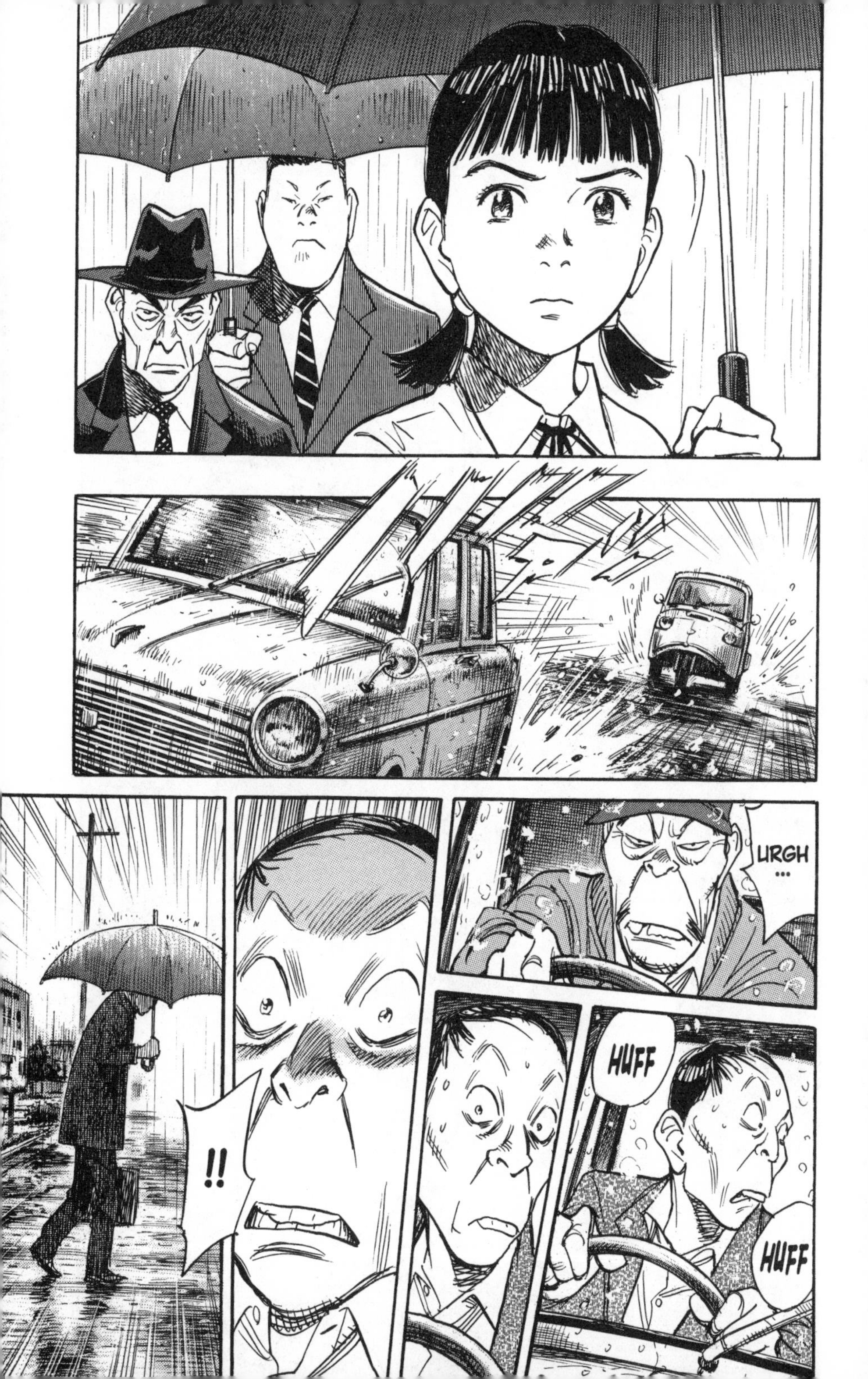
URGH ...
HUFF
HUFF
!!

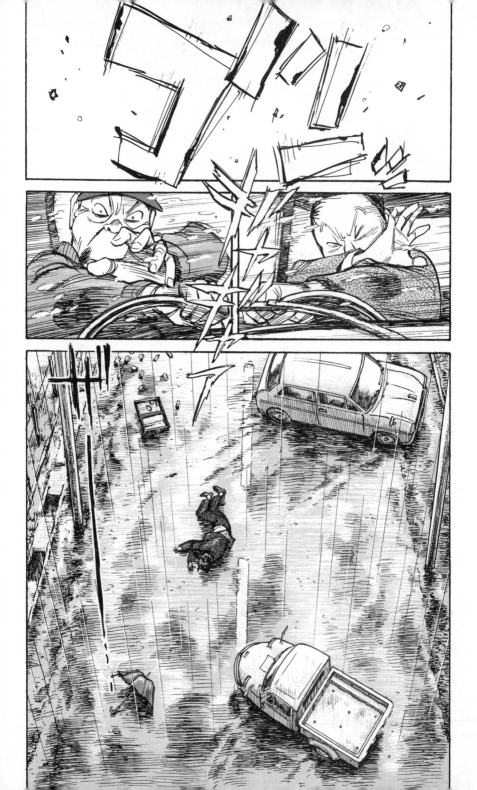

Chapter 28 ● The Accident

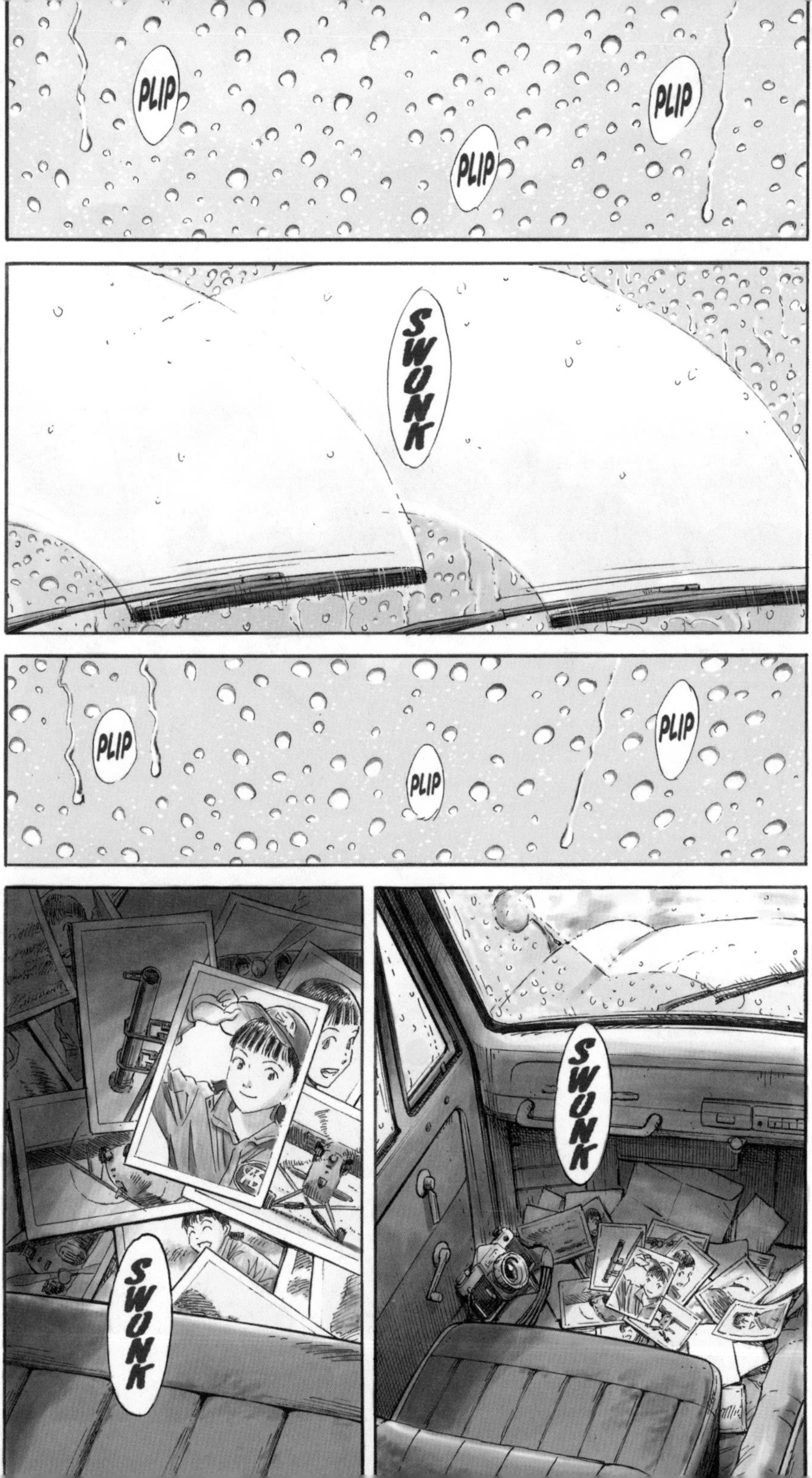

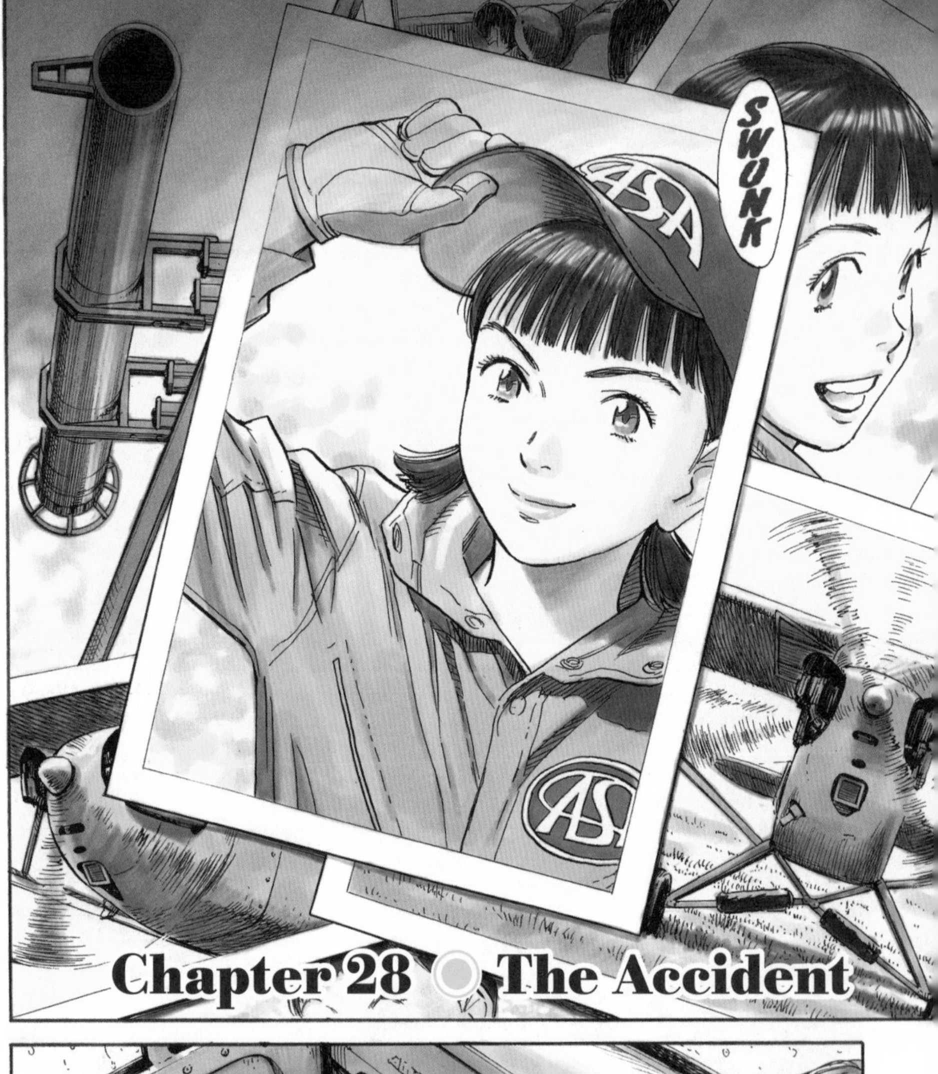
SWONK

Chapter 28 ● The Accident

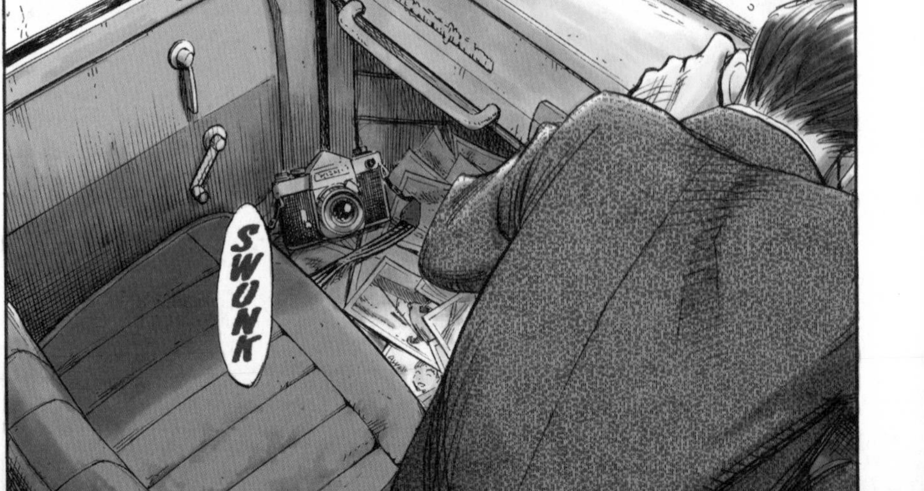
SWONK

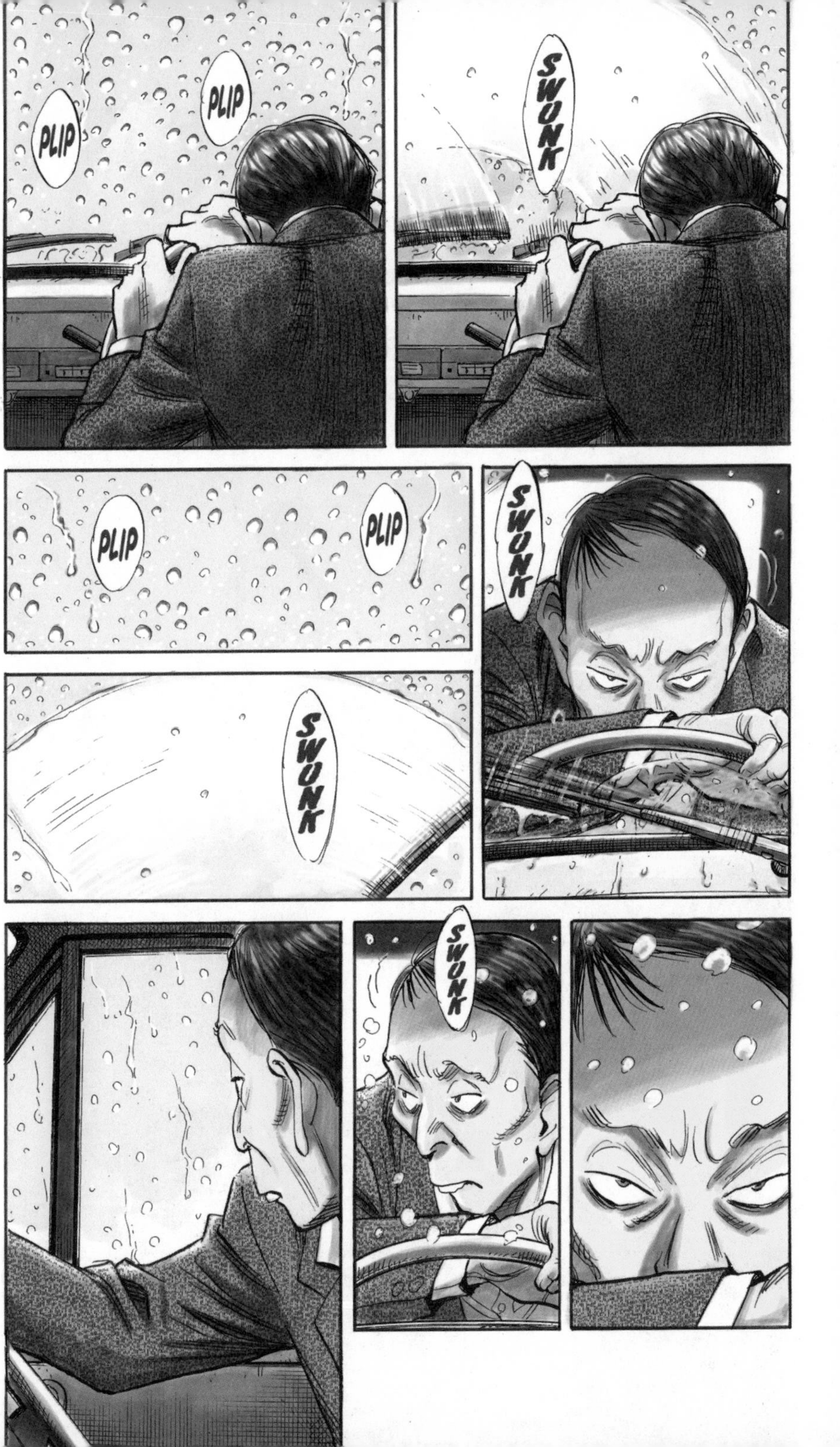
SWUNK
PLIP
PLIP
SWUNK
PLIP
PLIP
SWUNK
SWUNK

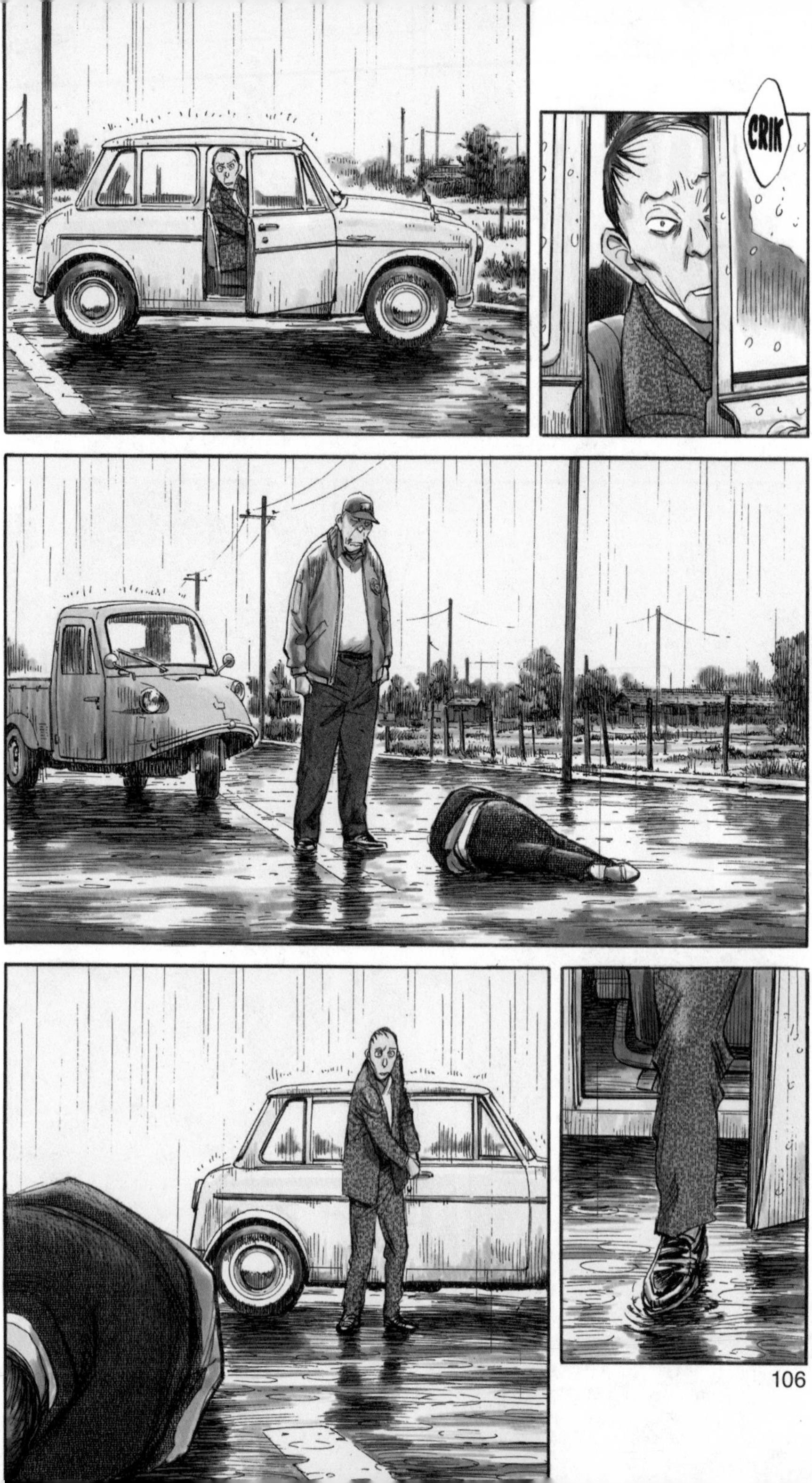
CRIK

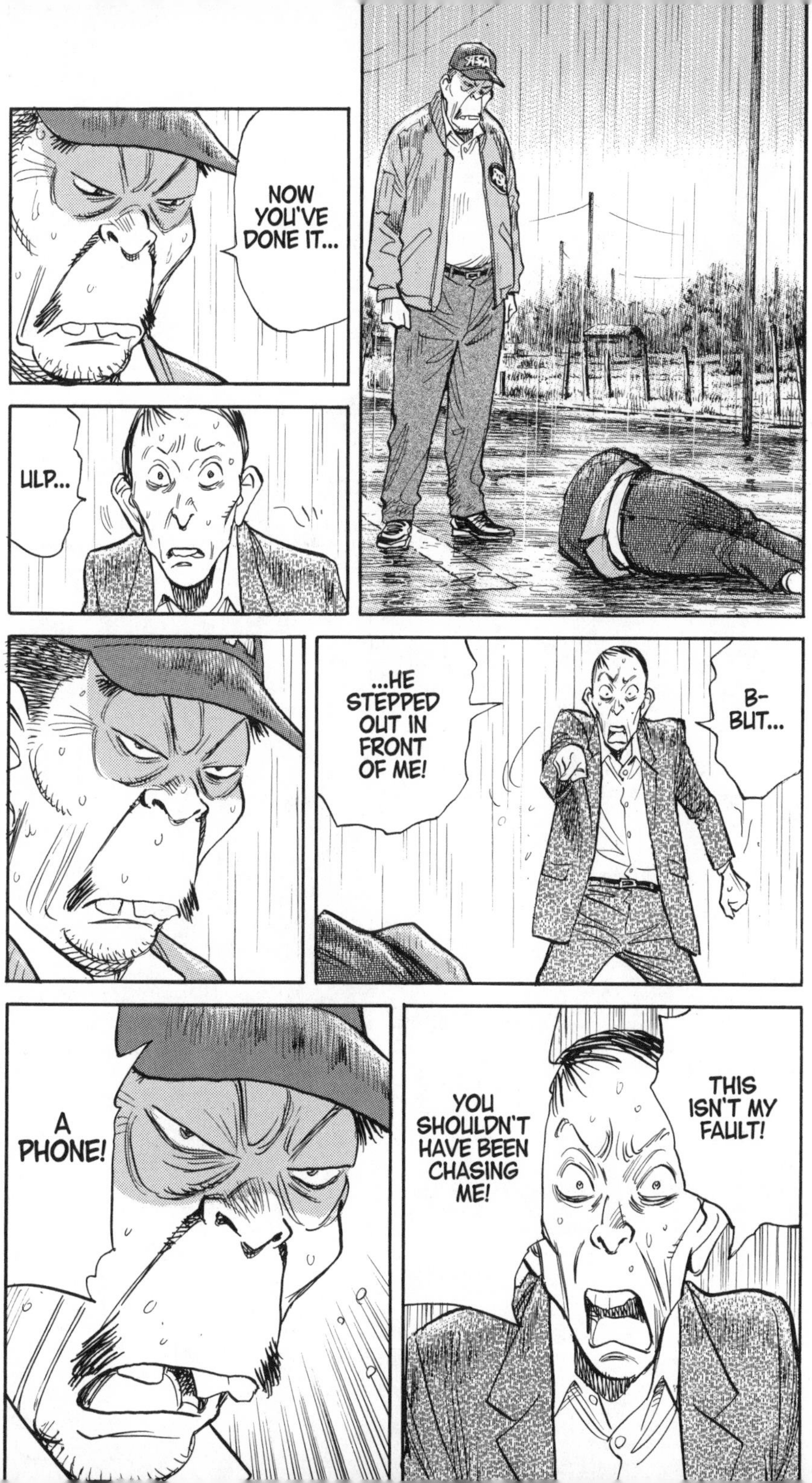
NOW YOU'VE DONE IT...
ULP...
B-BUT...
...HE STEPPED OUT IN FRONT OF ME!
THIS ISN'T MY FAULT!
YOU SHOULDN'T HAVE BEEN CHASING ME!
A PHONE!

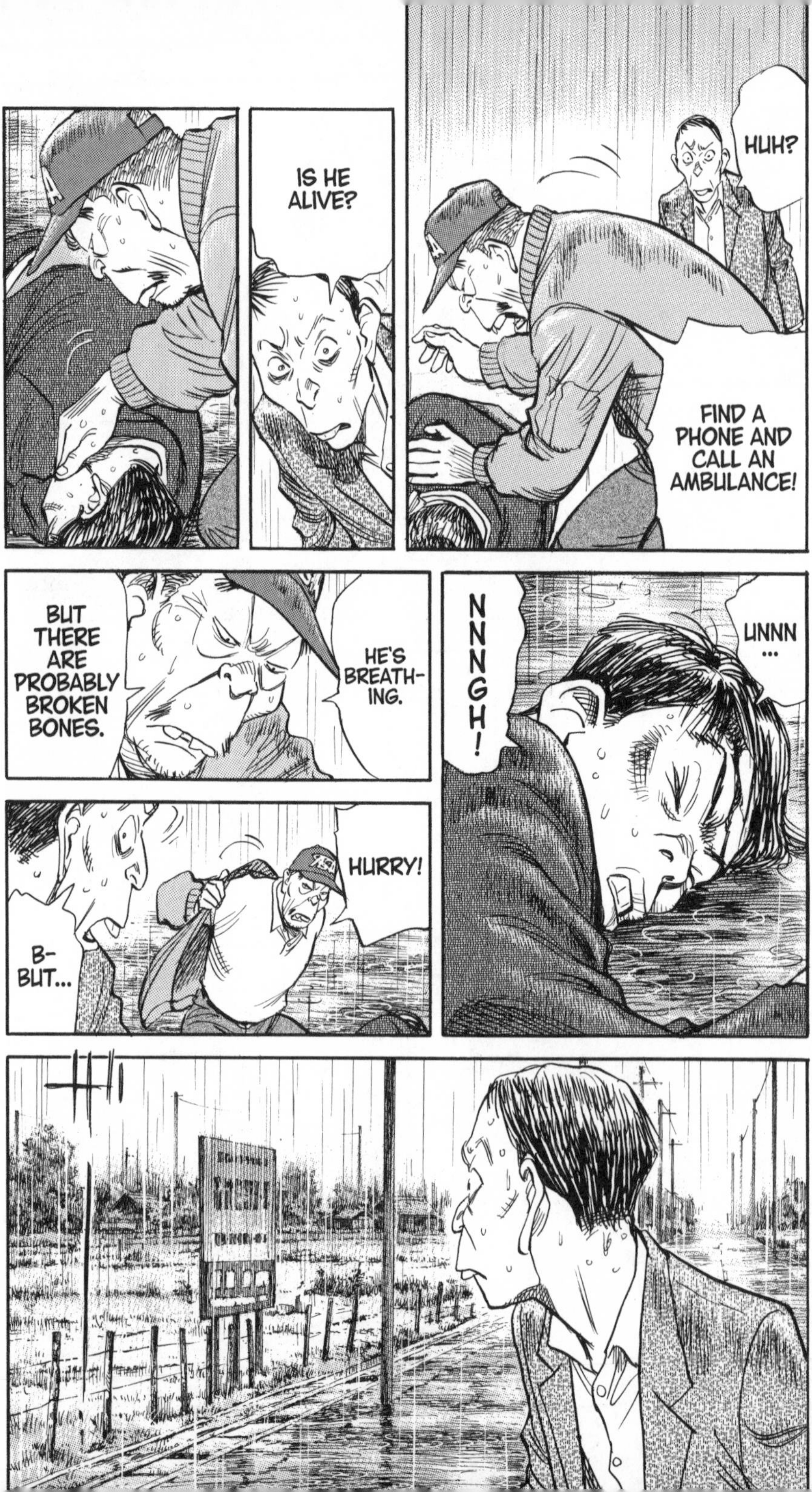
HUH?
FIND A PHONE AND CALL AN AMBULANCE!
IS HE ALIVE?
UNNN...
NNNNGH!
HE'S BREATHING.
BUT THERE ARE PROBABLY BROKEN BONES.
HURRY!
B-BUT...

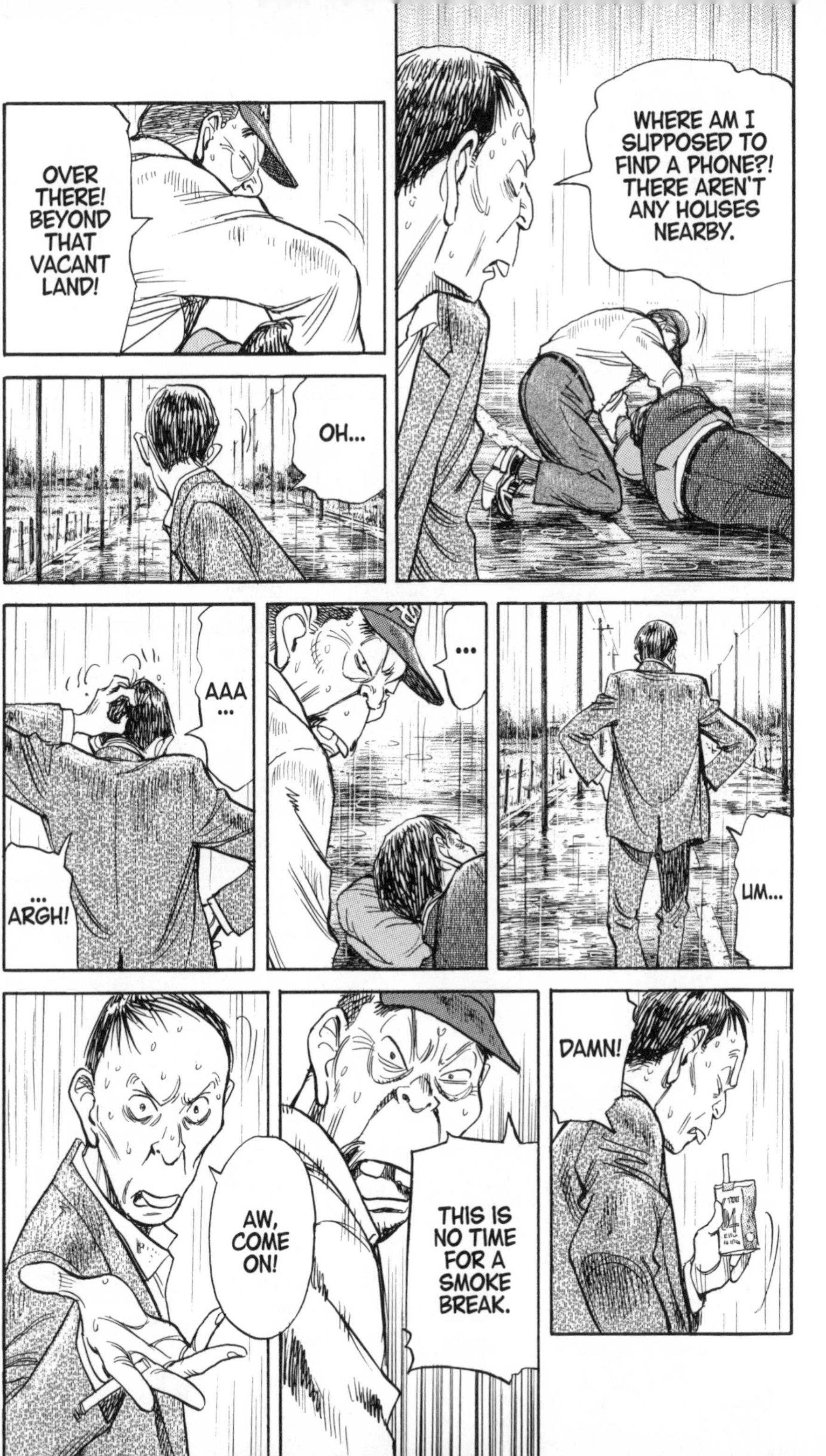
WHERE AM I SUPPOSED TO FIND A PHONE?! THERE AREN'T ANY HOUSES NEARBY.
OVER THERE! BEYOND THAT VACANT LAND!
OH...
UM...
...
AAA ...
... ARGH!
DAMN!
THIS IS NO TIME FOR A SMOKE BREAK.
AW, COME ON!

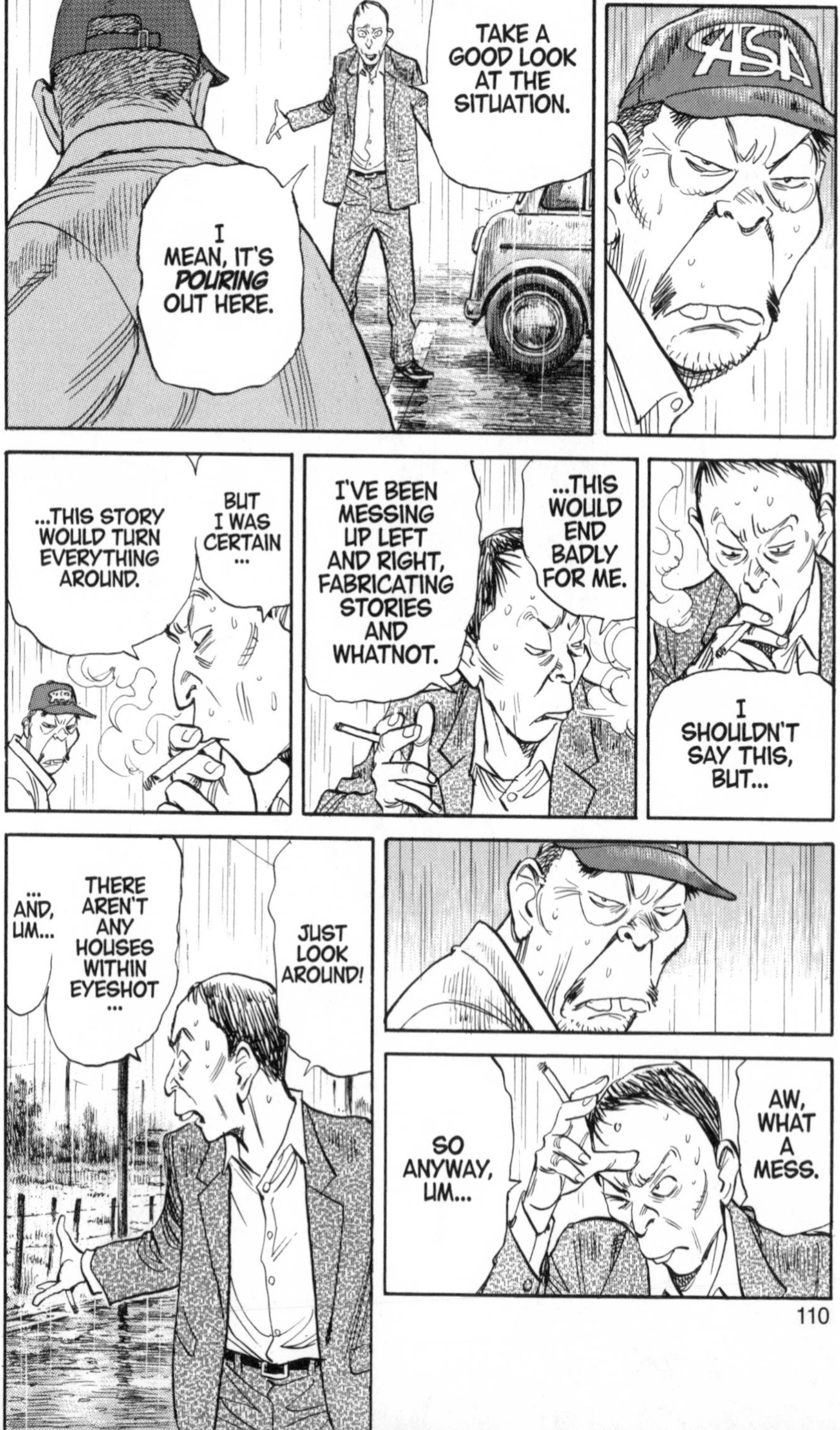
TAKE A GOOD LOOK AT THE SITUATION.
I MEAN, IT'S *POURING* OUT HERE.
I SHOULDN'T SAY THIS, BUT...
...THIS WOULD END BADLY FOR ME.
I'VE BEEN MESSING UP LEFT AND RIGHT, FABRICATING STORIES AND WHATNOT.
BUT I WAS CERTAIN...
...THIS STORY WOULD TURN EVERYTHING AROUND.
AW, WHAT A MESS.
SO ANYWAY, UM...
JUST LOOK AROUND!
THERE AREN'T ANY HOUSES WITHIN EYESHOT...
...AND, UM...

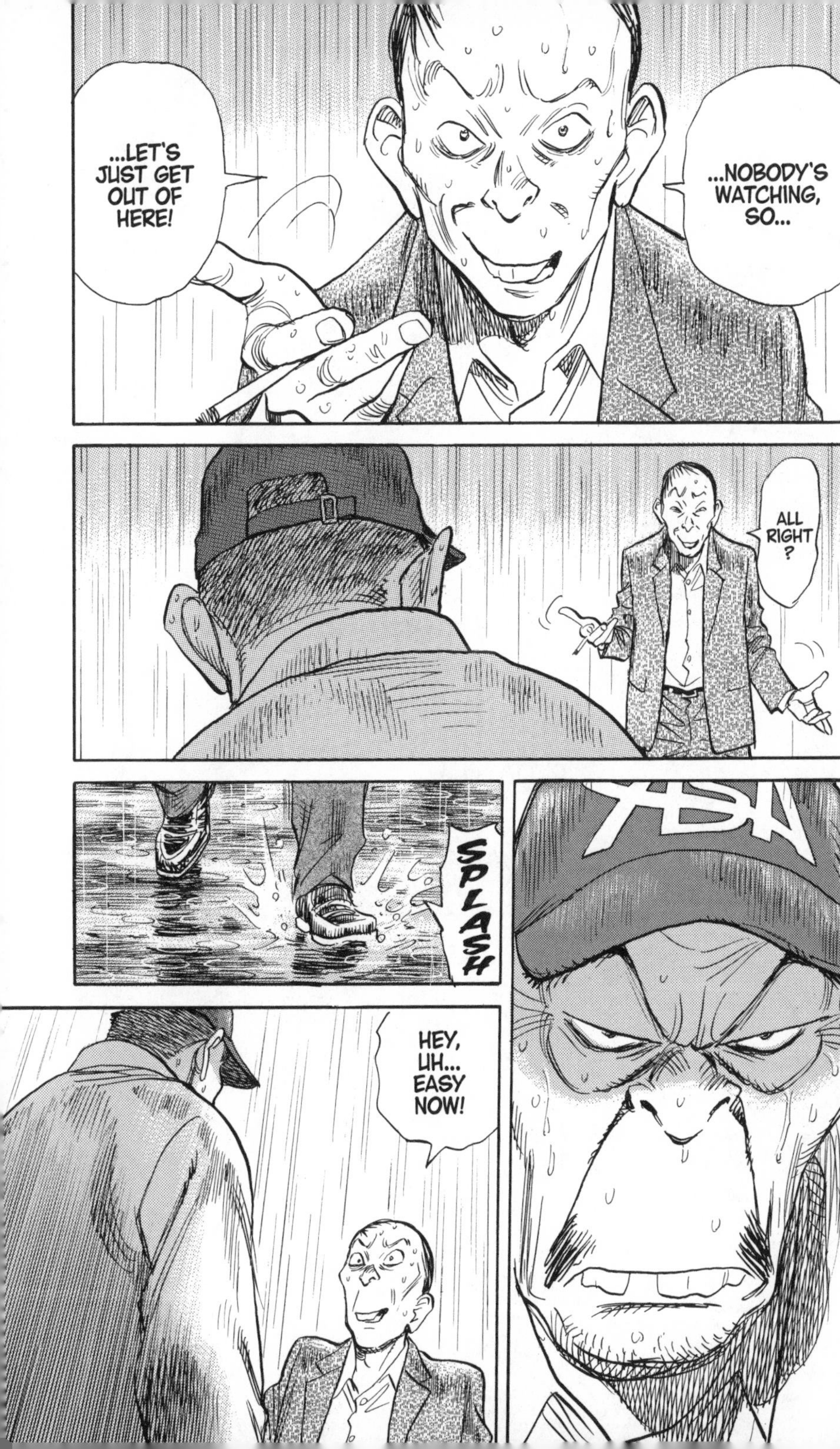
...NOBODY'S WATCHING, SO...
...LET'S JUST GET OUT OF HERE!
ALL RIGHT?
SPLASH
HEY, UH... EASY NOW!

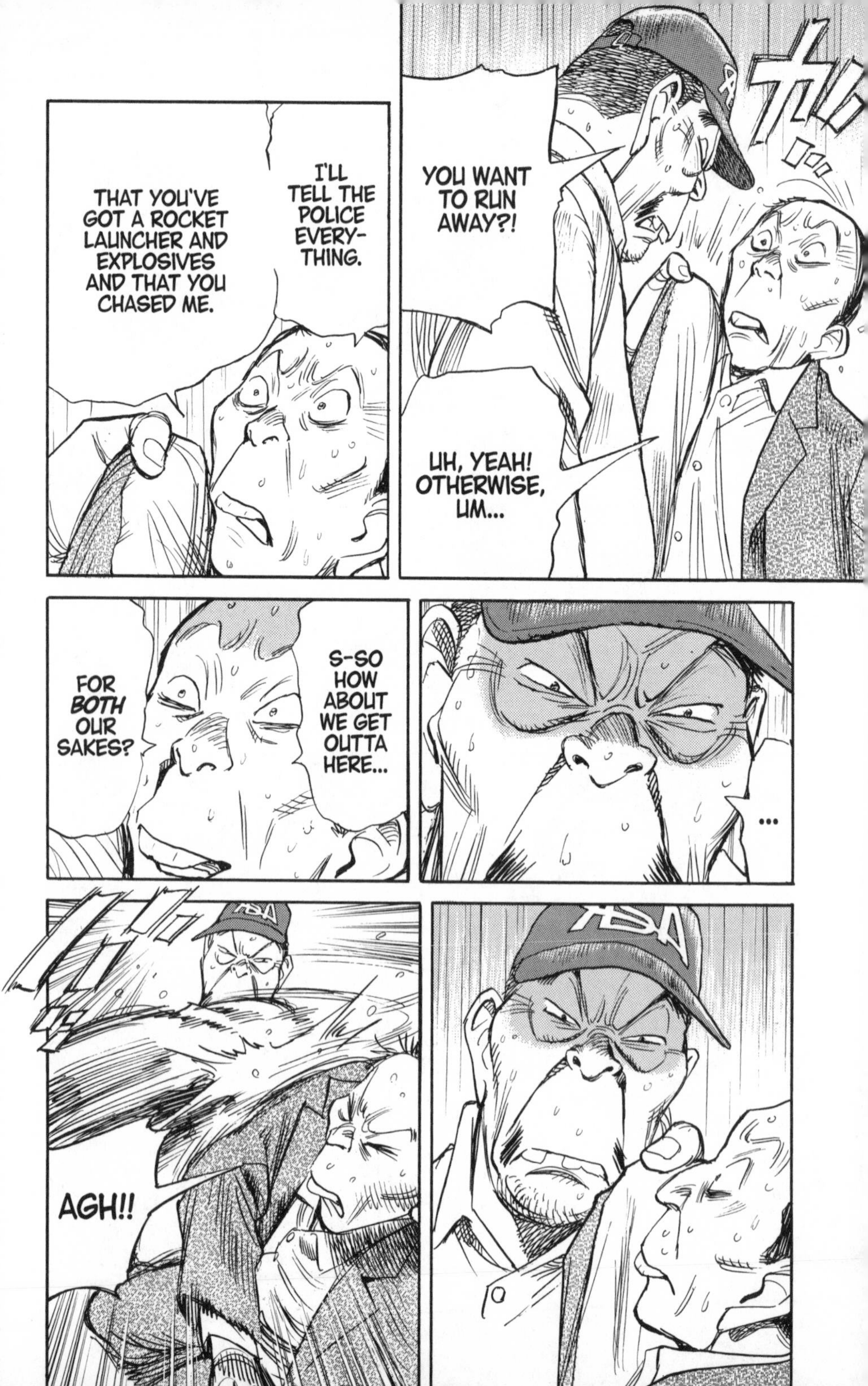
YOU WANT TO RUN AWAY?!
UH, YEAH! OTHERWISE, UM...
I'LL TELL THE POLICE EVERYTHING.
THAT YOU'VE GOT A ROCKET LAUNCHER AND EXPLOSIVES AND THAT YOU CHASED ME.
...
S-SO HOW ABOUT WE GET OUTTA HERE...
FOR *BOTH* OUR SAKES?
AGH!!

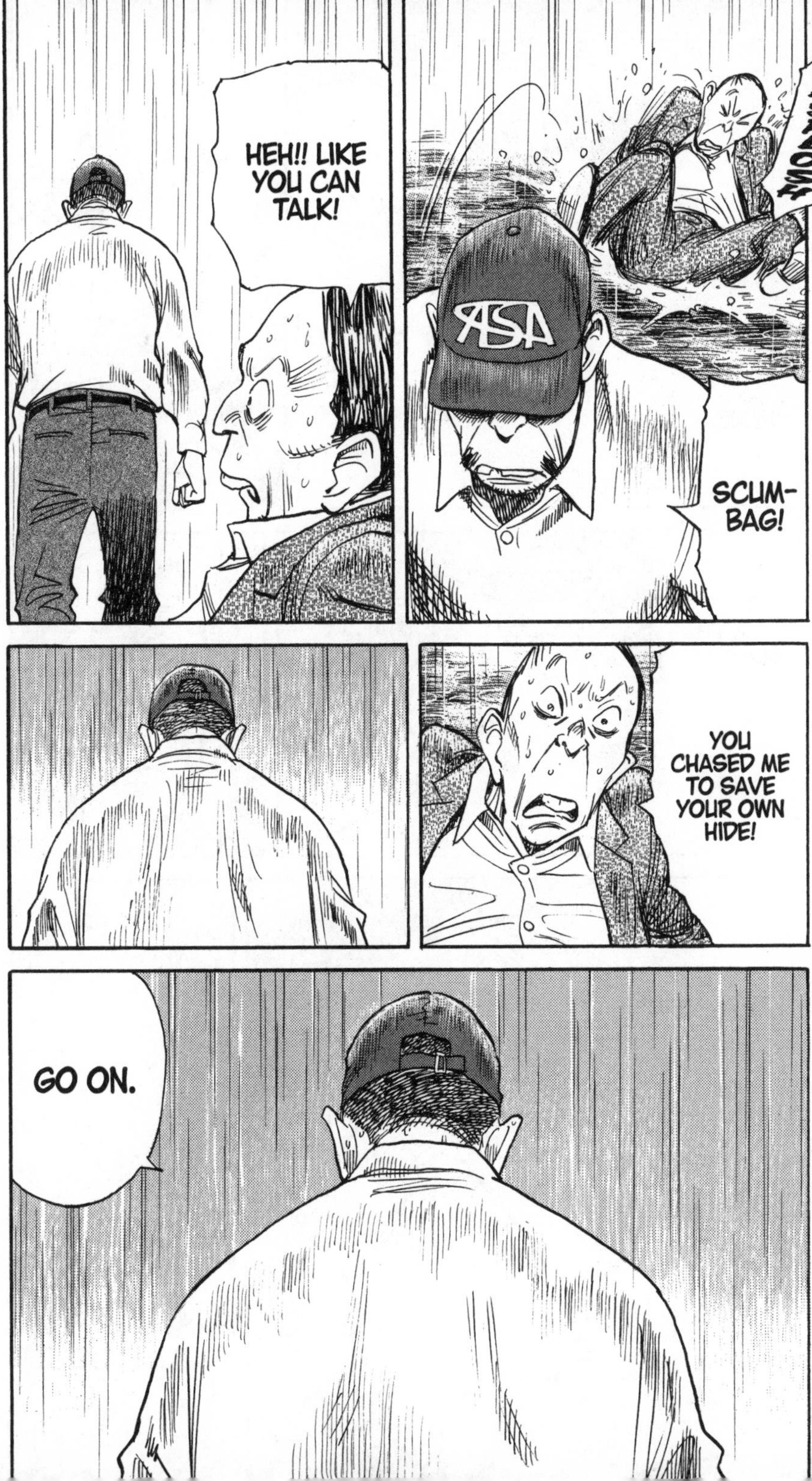
KASPLOSH
SCUM-BAG!
HEH!! LIKE YOU CAN TALK!
YOU CHASED ME TO SAVE YOUR OWN HIDE!
GO ON.

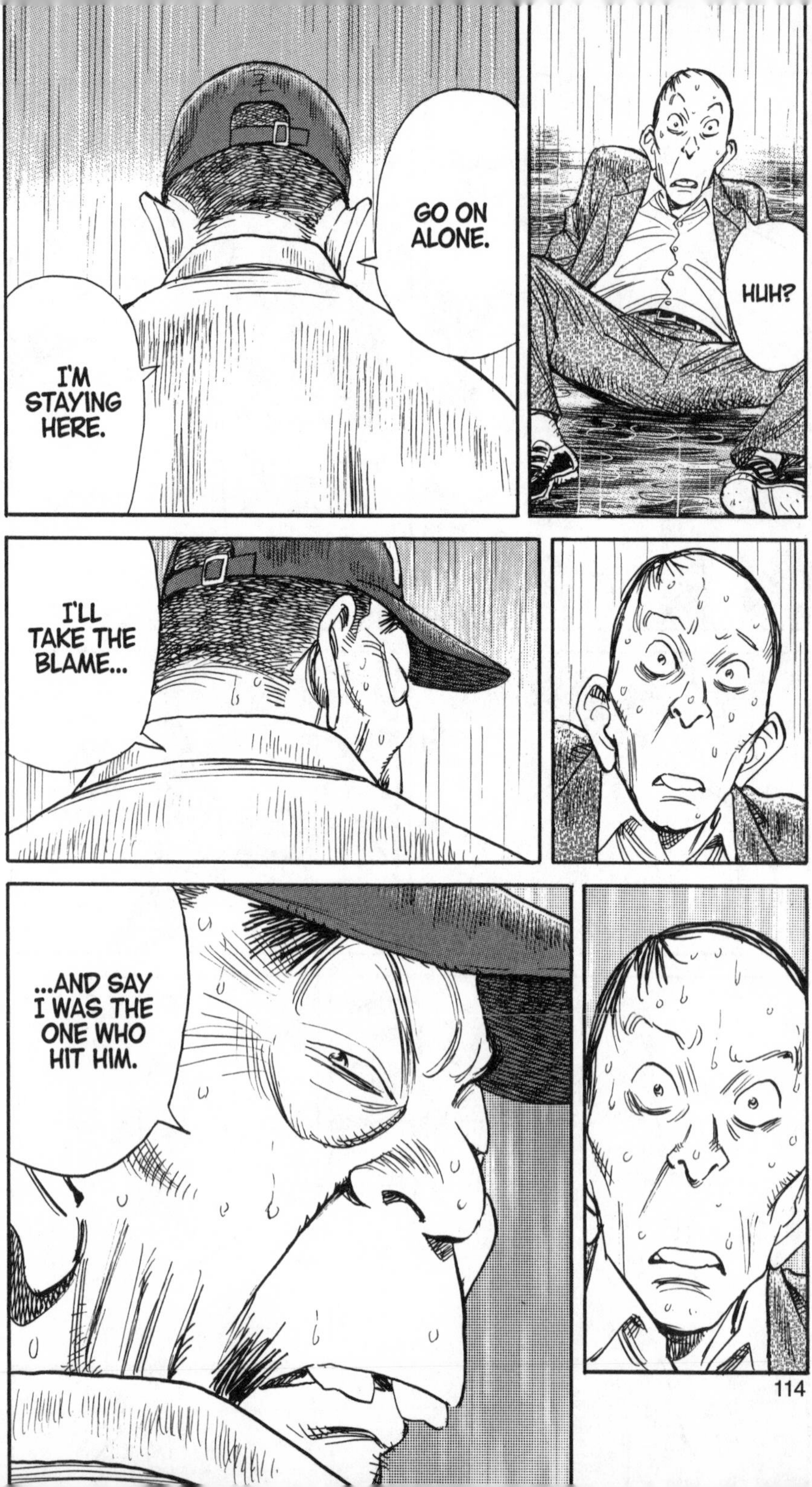
HUH?
GO ON ALONE.
I'M STAYING HERE.
I'LL TAKE THE BLAME...
...AND SAY I WAS THE ONE WHO HIT HIM.

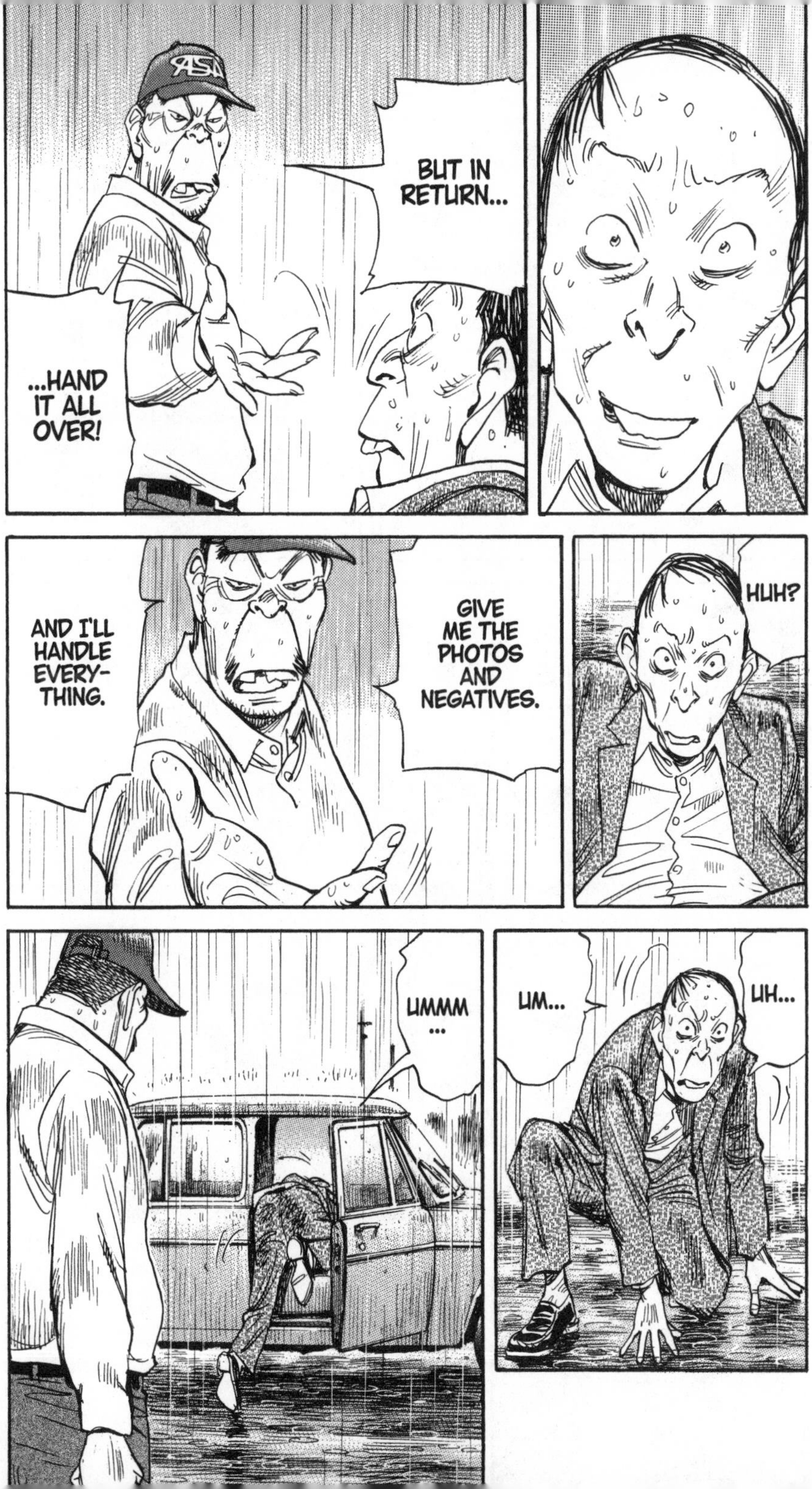
BUT IN RETURN...
...HAND IT ALL OVER!
HUH?
GIVE ME THE PHOTOS AND NEGATIVES.
AND I'LL HANDLE EVERY-THING.
UH...
UM...
UMMM...

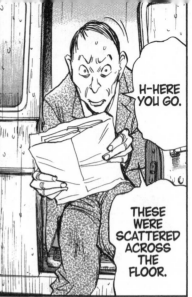

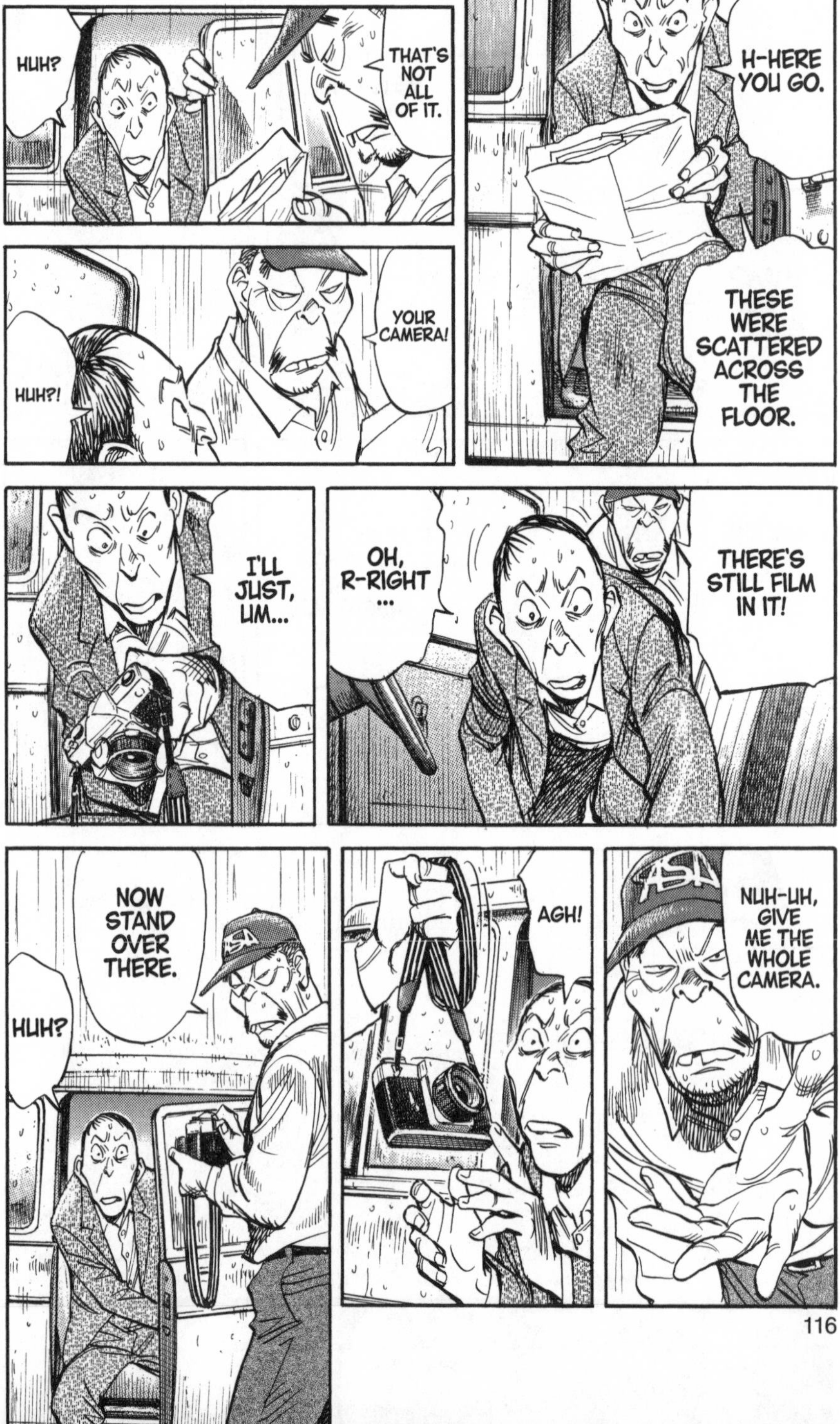
H-HERE YOU GO.
THESE WERE SCATTERED ACROSS THE FLOOR.
THAT'S NOT ALL OF IT.
HUH?
YOUR CAMERA!
HUH?!
THERE'S STILL FILM IN IT!
OH, R-RIGHT ...
I'LL JUST, UM...
NUH-UH, GIVE ME THE WHOLE CAMERA.
AGH!
NOW STAND OVER THERE.
HUH?

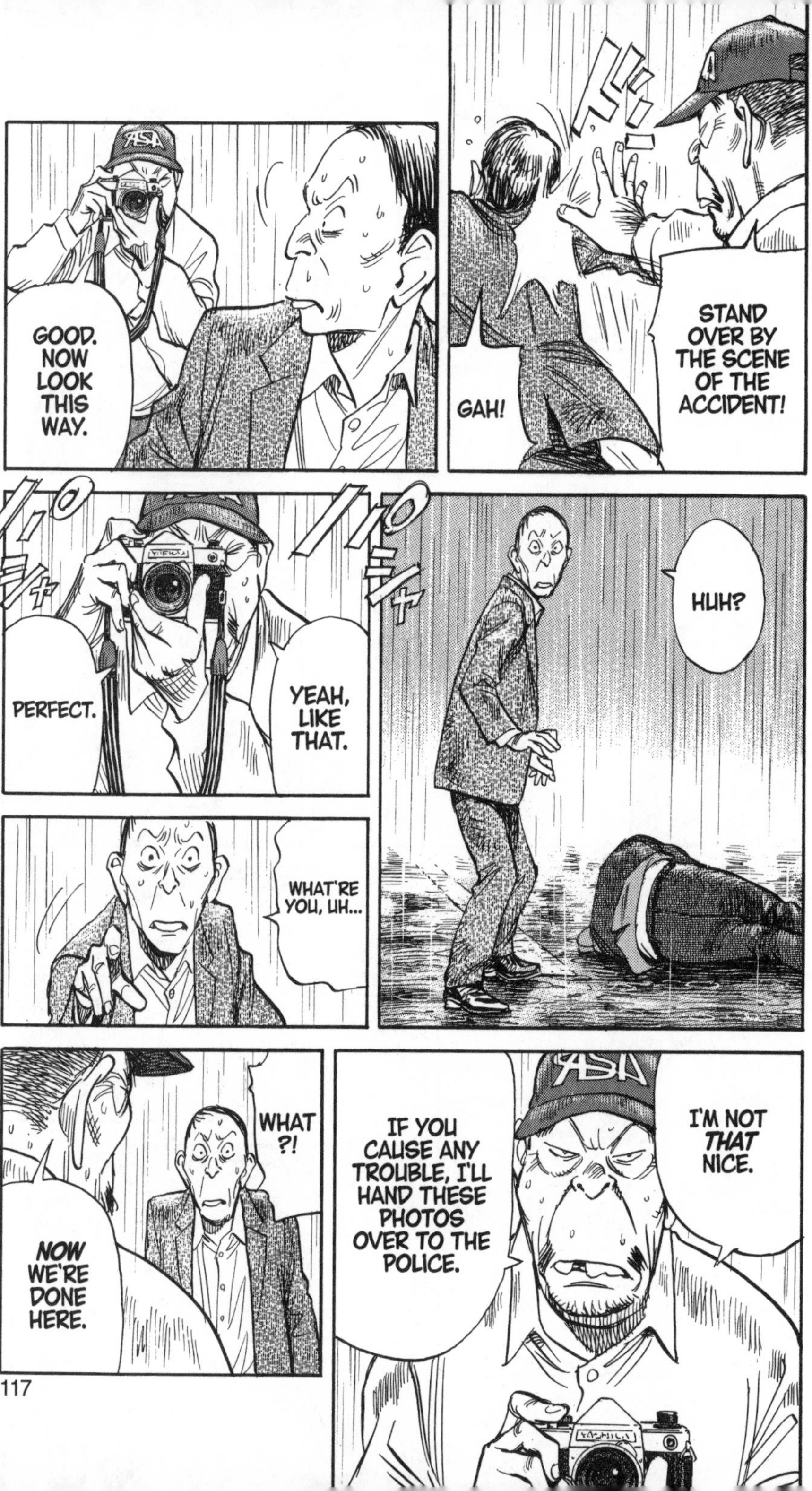
STAND OVER BY THE SCENE OF THE ACCIDENT!
GAH!
GOOD. NOW LOOK THIS WAY.
パシャ
HUH?
パシャ
YEAH, LIKE THAT.
PERFECT.
WHAT'RE YOU, UH...
I'M NOT *THAT* NICE.
IF YOU CAUSE ANY TROUBLE, I'LL HAND THESE PHOTOS OVER TO THE POLICE.
WHAT ?!
NOW WE'RE DONE HERE.

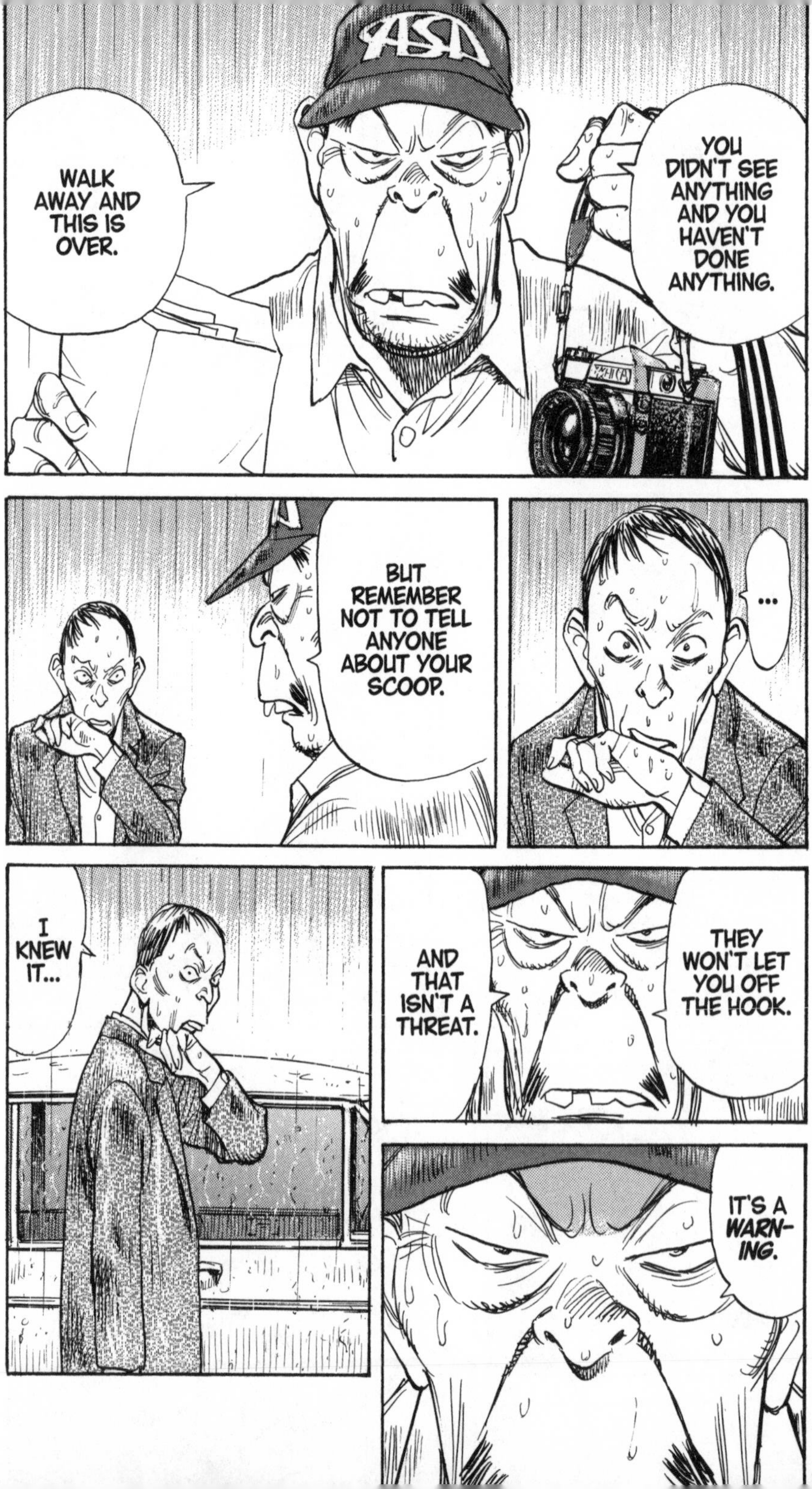
YOU DIDN'T SEE ANYTHING AND YOU HAVEN'T DONE ANYTHING.
WALK AWAY AND THIS IS OVER.
...
BUT REMEMBER NOT TO TELL ANYONE ABOUT YOUR SCOOP.
THEY WON'T LET YOU OFF THE HOOK.
AND THAT ISN'T A THREAT.
IT'S A *WARNING.*
I KNEW IT...

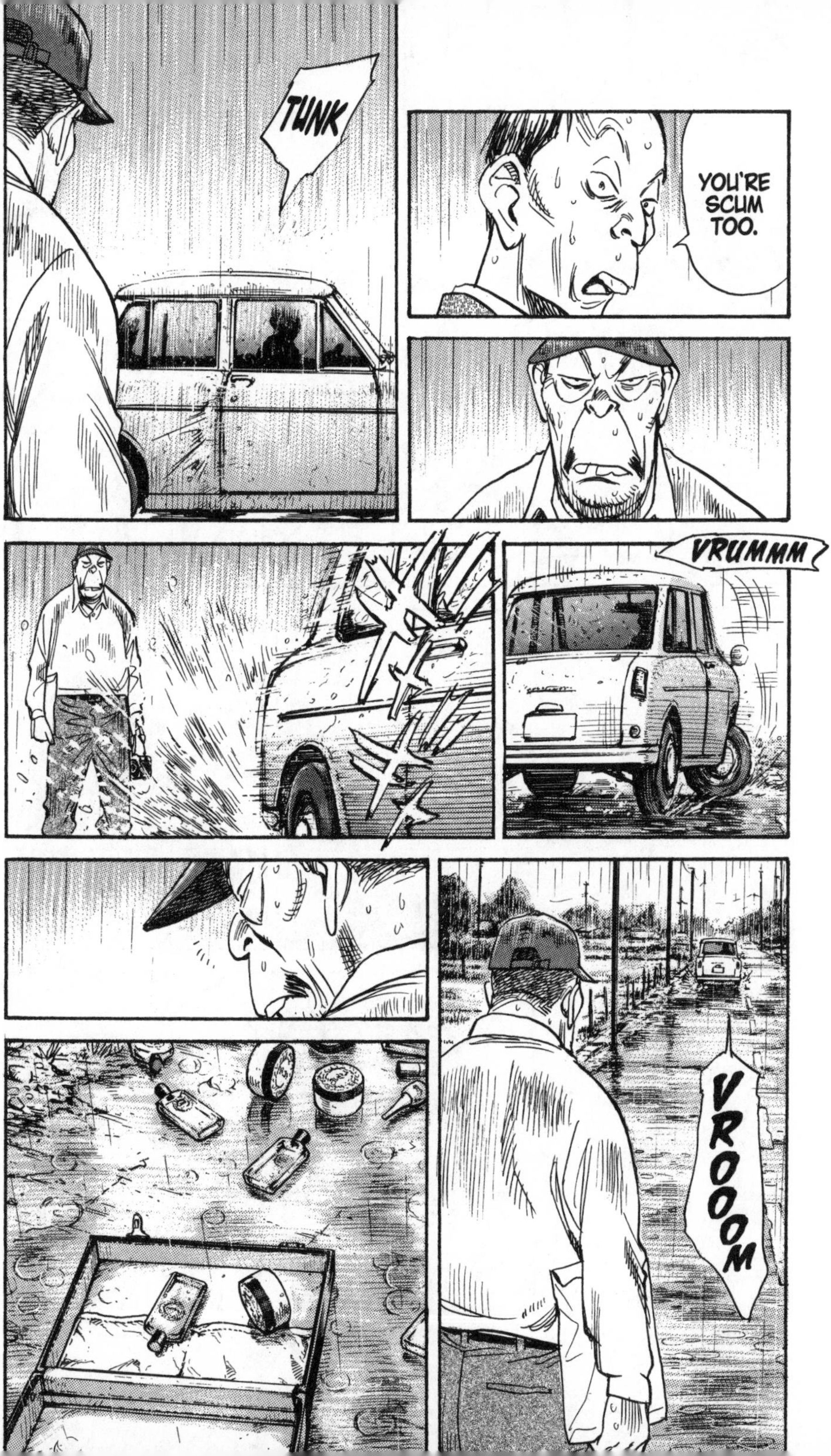
YOU'RE SCUM TOO.
TUNK
VRUMMM
VROOOM

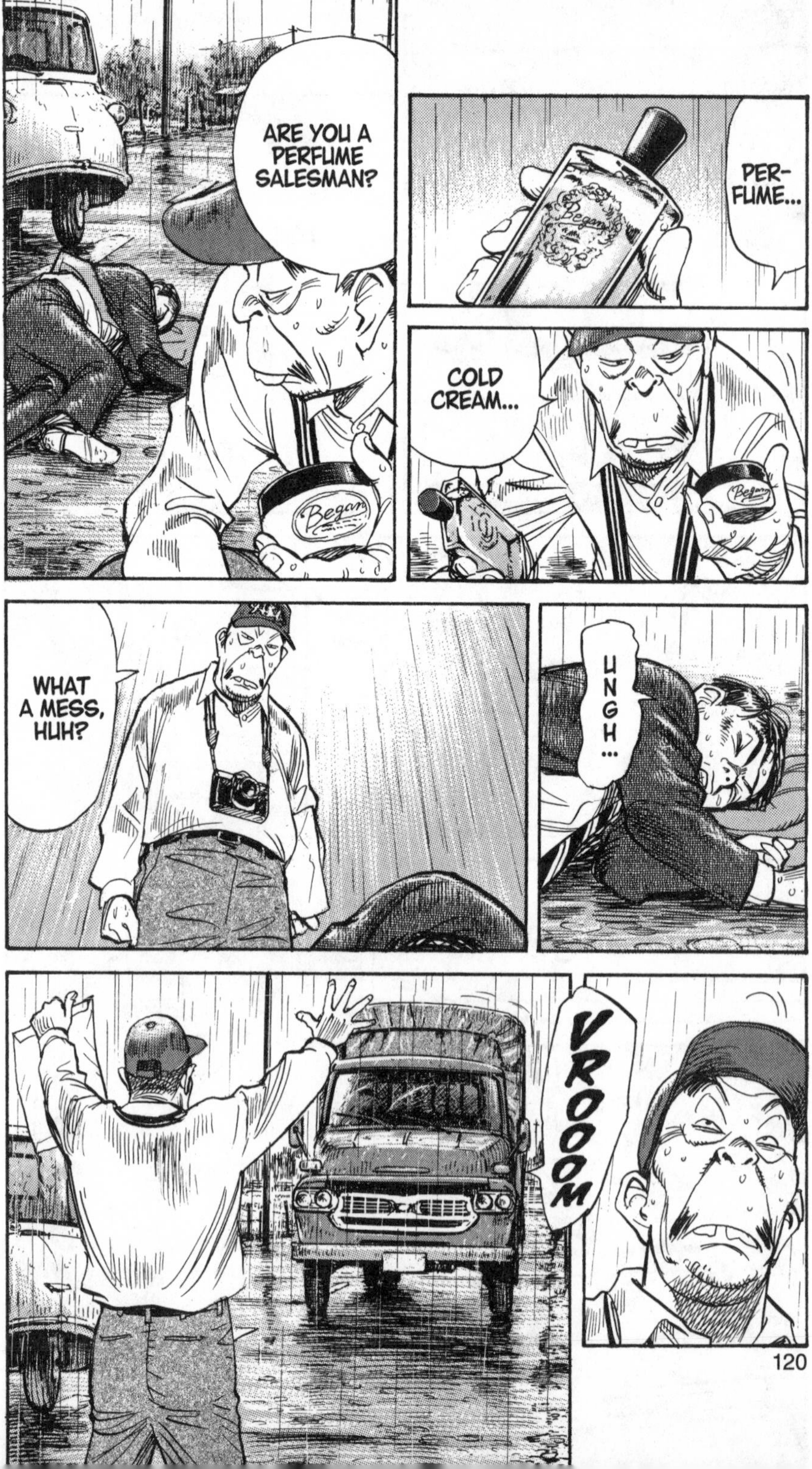
PER-FUME...
COLD CREAM...
ARE YOU A PERFUME SALESMAN?
UNGH...
WHAT A MESS, HUH?
VROOOOM

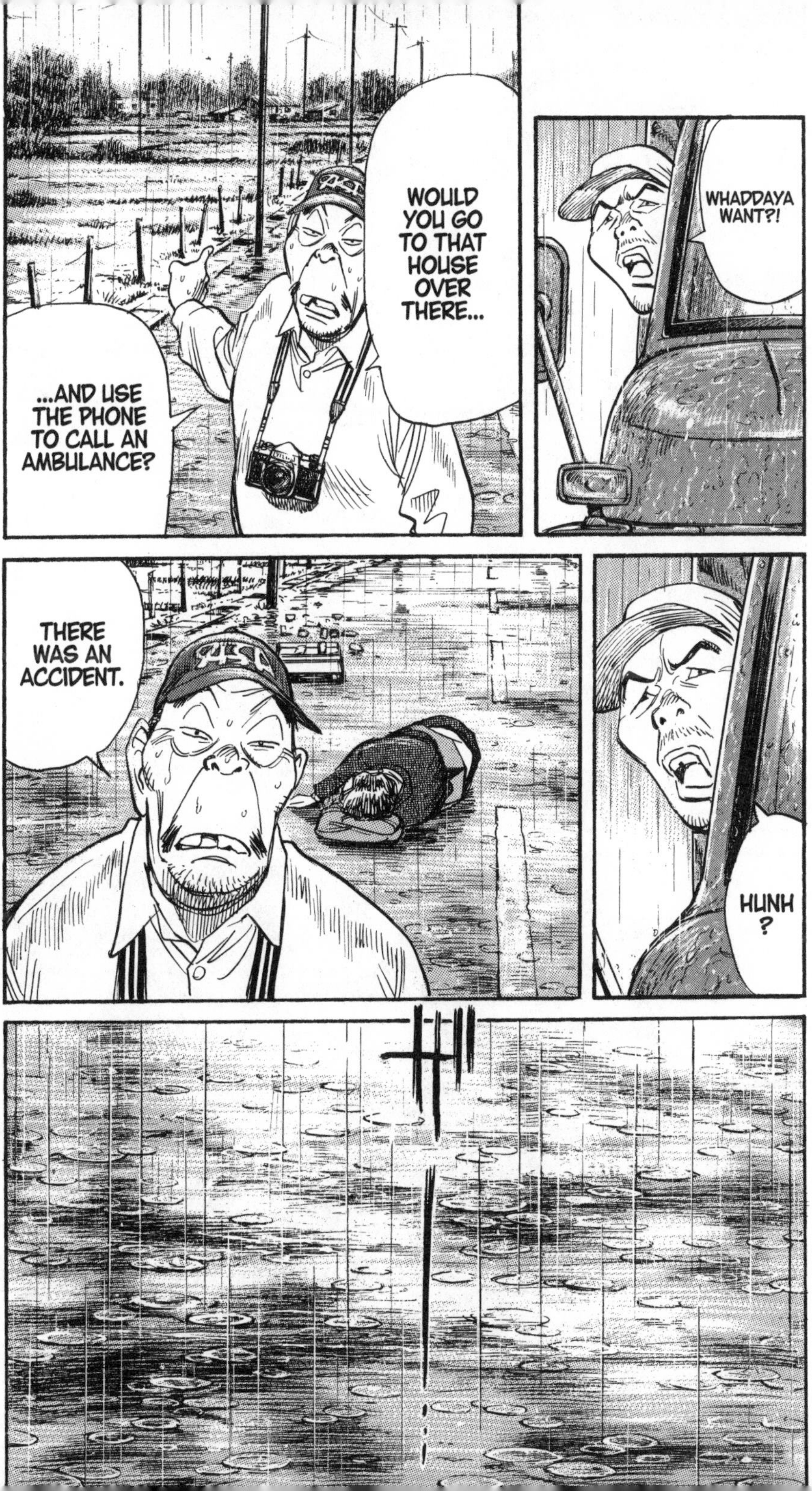
WHADDAYA WANT?!
WOULD YOU GO TO THAT HOUSE OVER THERE...
...AND USE THE PHONE TO CALL AN AMBULANCE?
HUNH?
THERE WAS AN ACCIDENT.

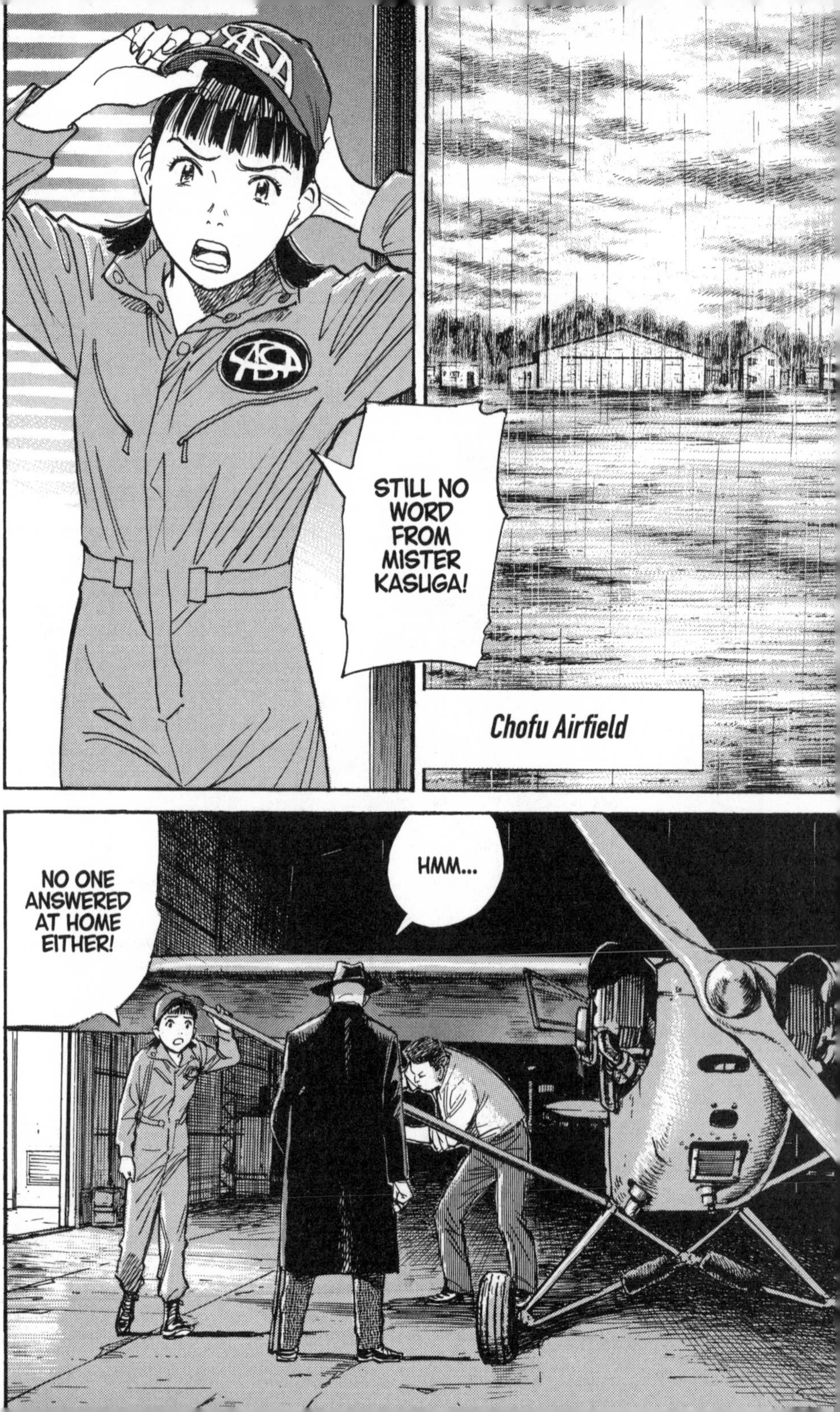
Chofu Airfield
STILL NO WORD FROM MISTER KASUGA!
HMM...
NO ONE ANSWERED AT HOME EITHER!

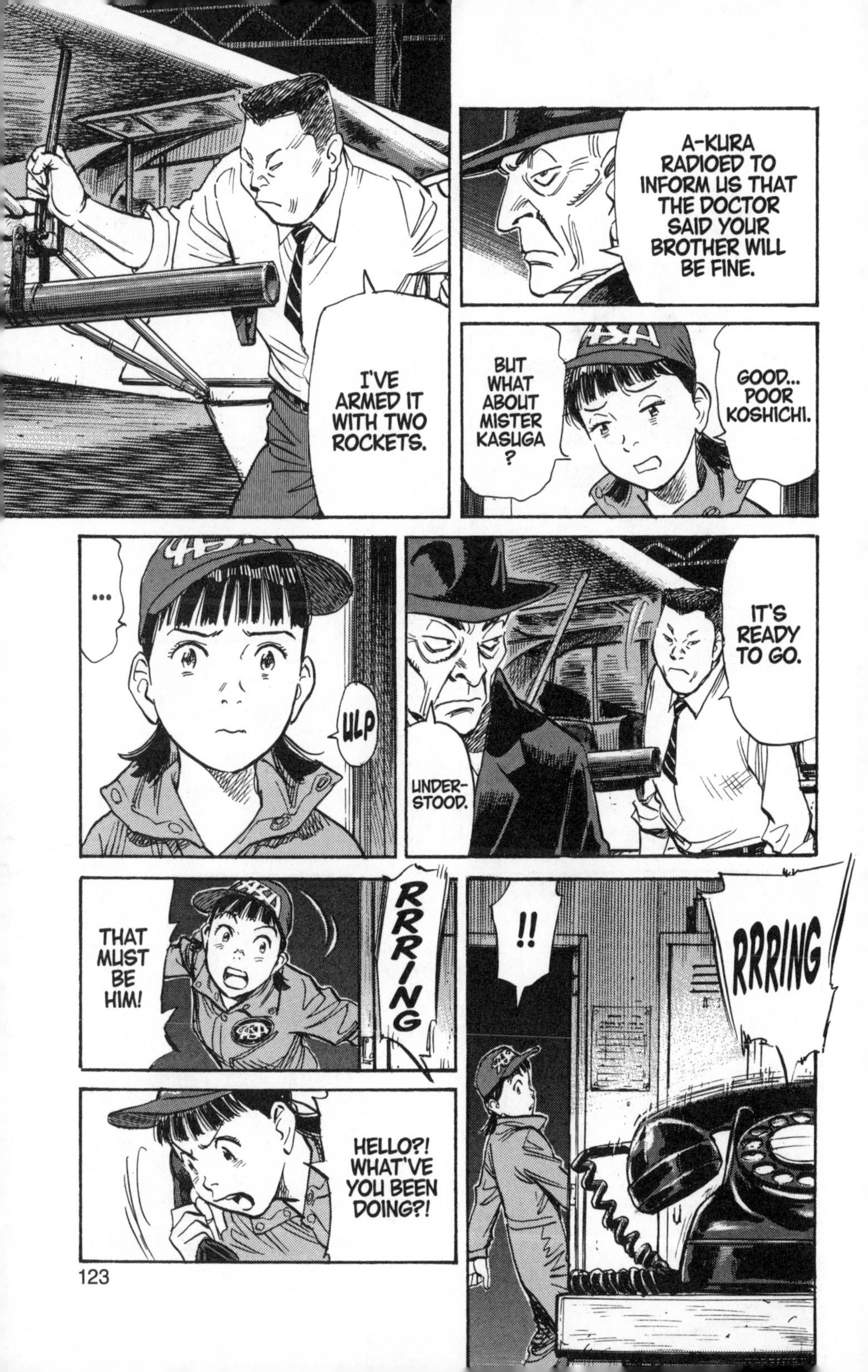
A-KURA RADIOED TO INFORM US THAT THE DOCTOR SAID YOUR BROTHER WILL BE FINE.
GOOD... POOR KOSHICHI.
BUT WHAT ABOUT MISTER KASUGA?
I'VE ARMED IT WITH TWO ROCKETS.
IT'S READY TO GO.
UNDER-STOOD.
...
ULP
RRRING
!!
THAT MUST BE HIM!
RRRING
HELLO?! WHAT'VE YOU BEEN DOING?!

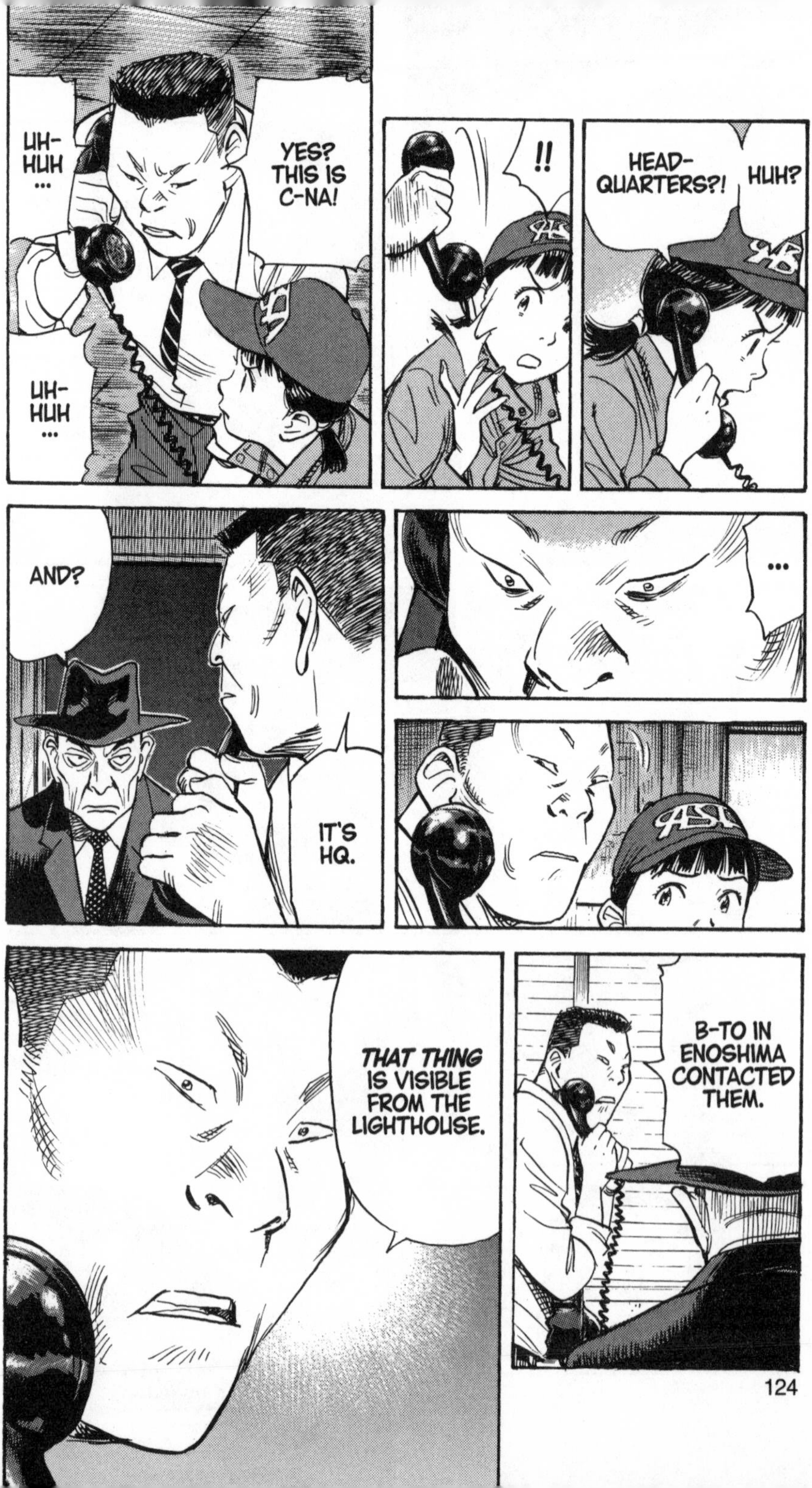
HUH?
HEAD-QUARTERS?!
!!
YES? THIS IS C-NA!
UH-HUH ...
UH-HUH ...
...
IT'S HQ.
AND?
B-TO IN ENOSHIMA CONTACTED THEM.
THAT THING IS VISIBLE FROM THE LIGHTHOUSE.

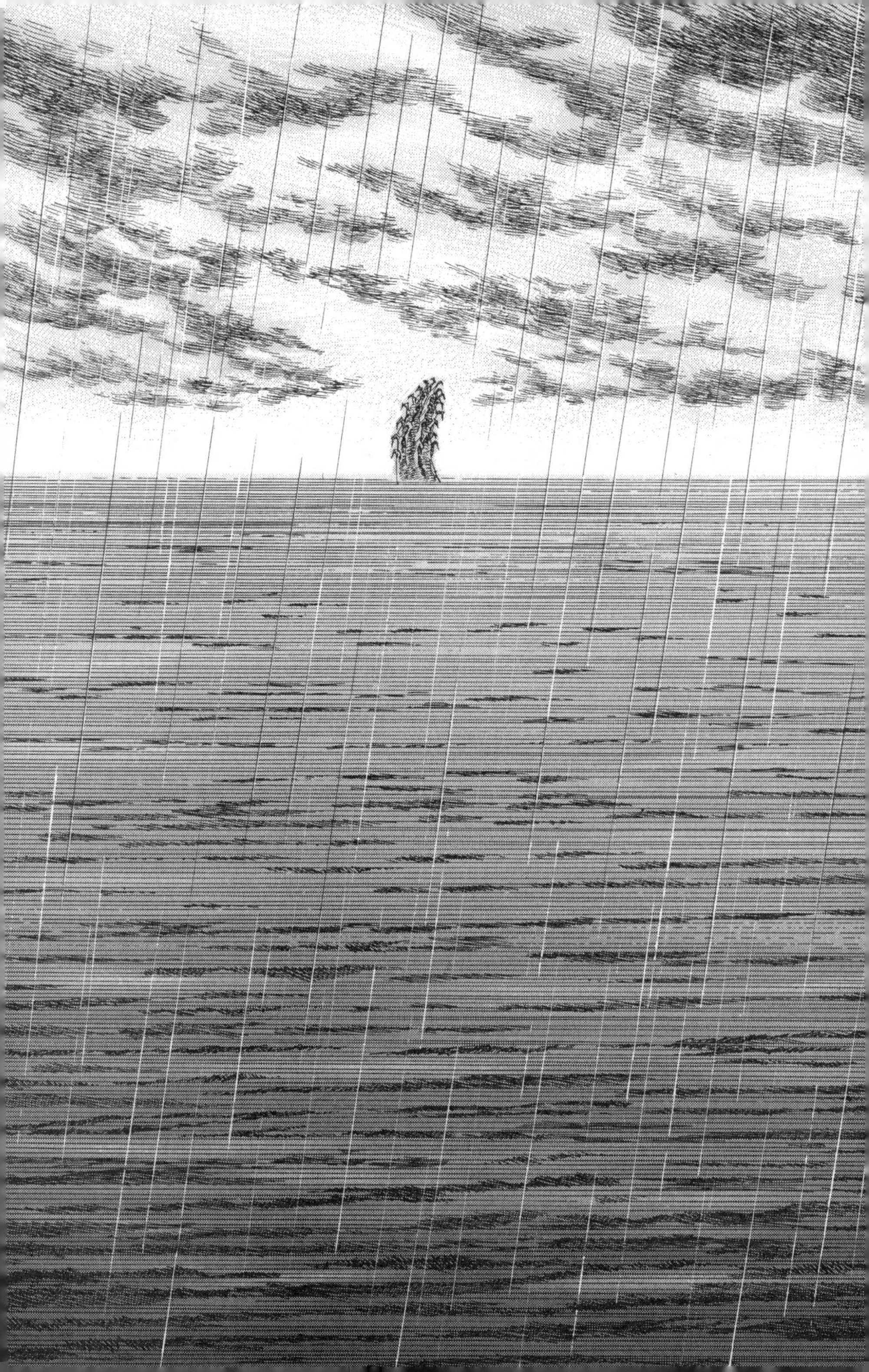

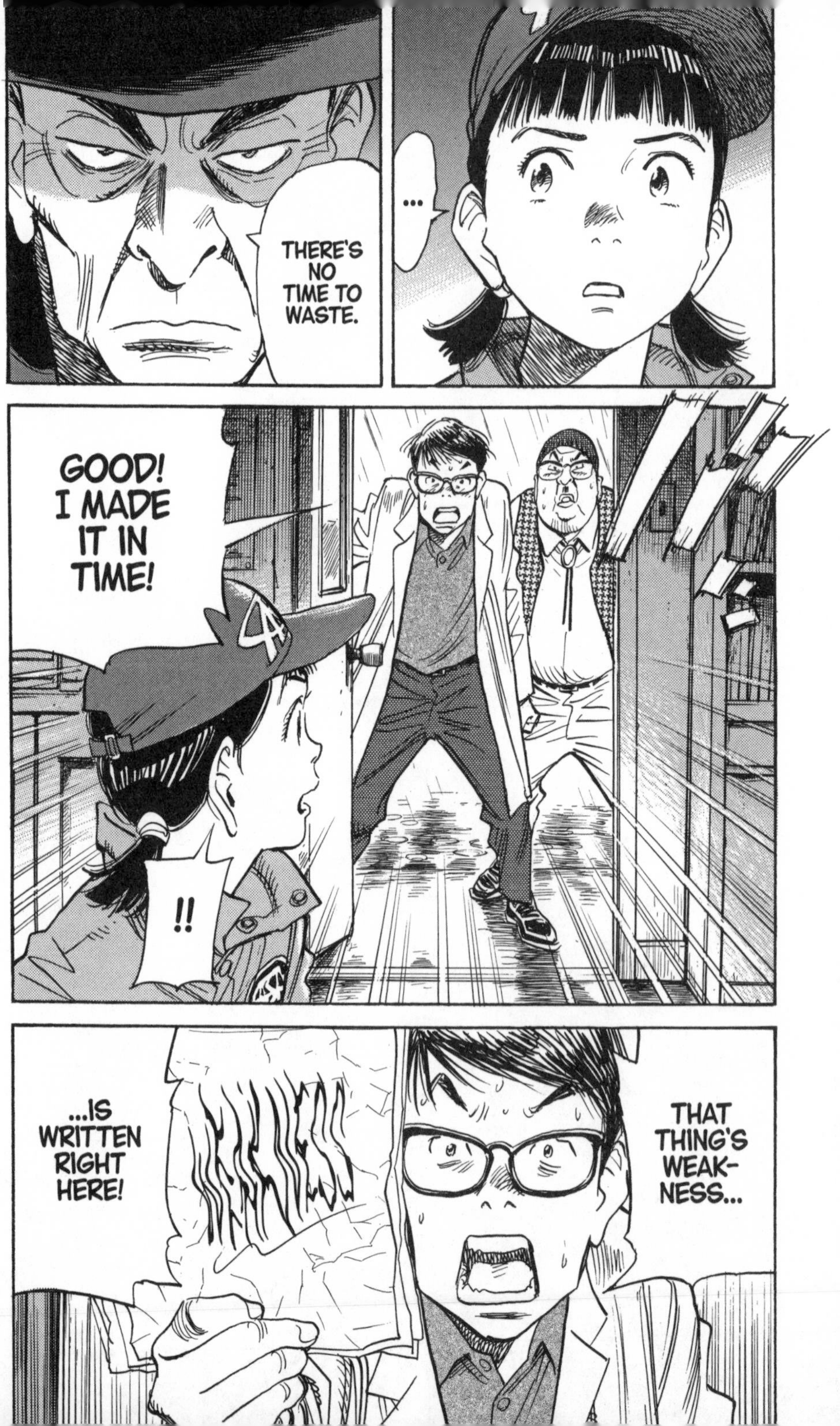
...
THERE'S NO TIME TO WASTE.
GOOD! I MADE IT IN TIME!
!!
THAT THING'S WEAK-NESS...
...IS WRITTEN RIGHT HERE!

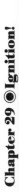

Chapter 29 ● Ignition!

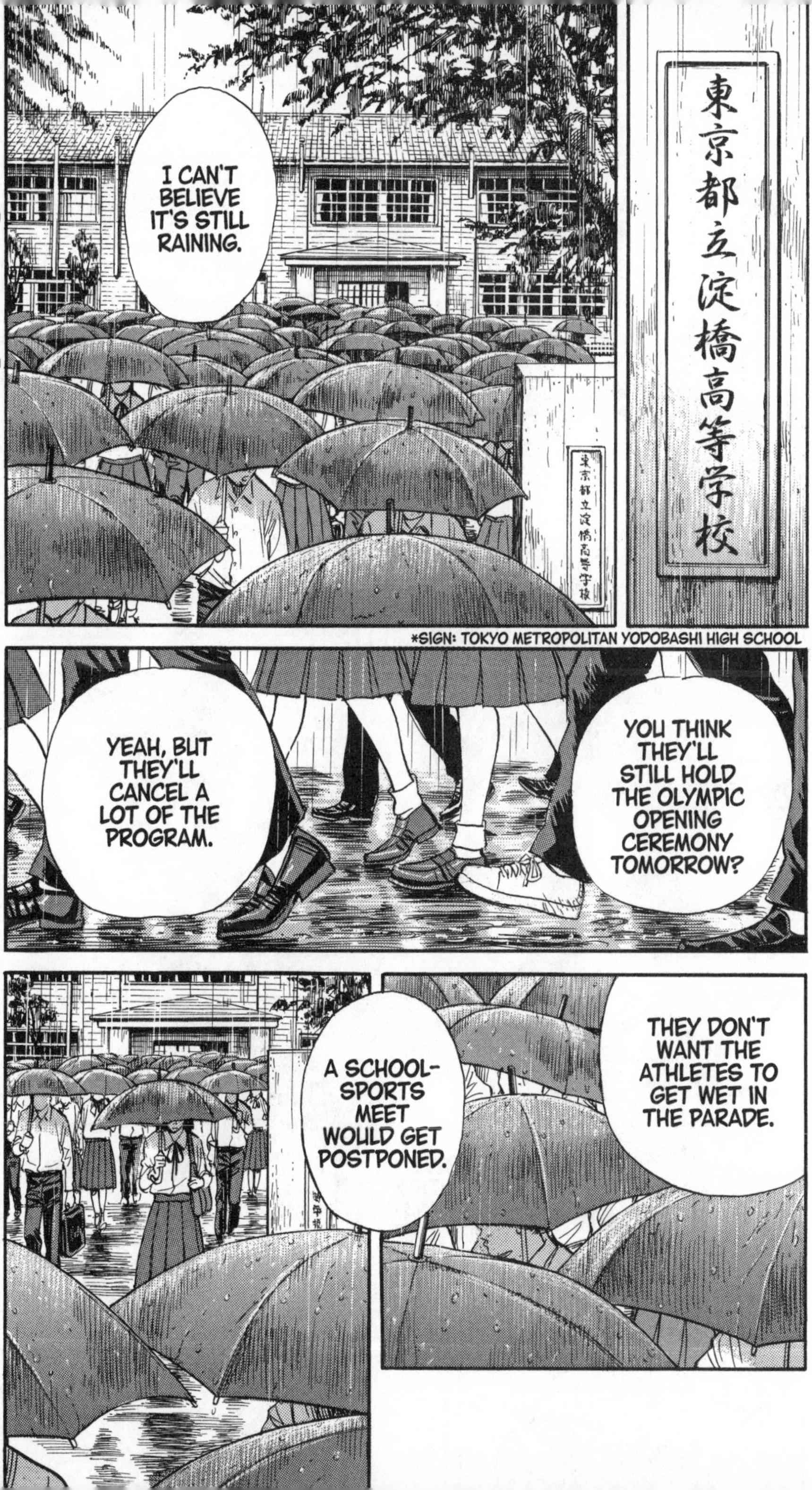
東京都立淀橋高等学校
I CAN'T BELIEVE IT'S STILL RAINING.
*SIGN: TOKYO METROPOLITAN YODOBASHI HIGH SCHOOL
YOU THINK THEY'LL STILL HOLD THE OLYMPIC OPENING CEREMONY TOMORROW?
YEAH, BUT THEY'LL CANCEL A LOT OF THE PROGRAM.
THEY DON'T WANT THE ATHLETES TO GET WET IN THE PARADE.
A SCHOOL-SPORTS MEET WOULD GET POSTPONED.

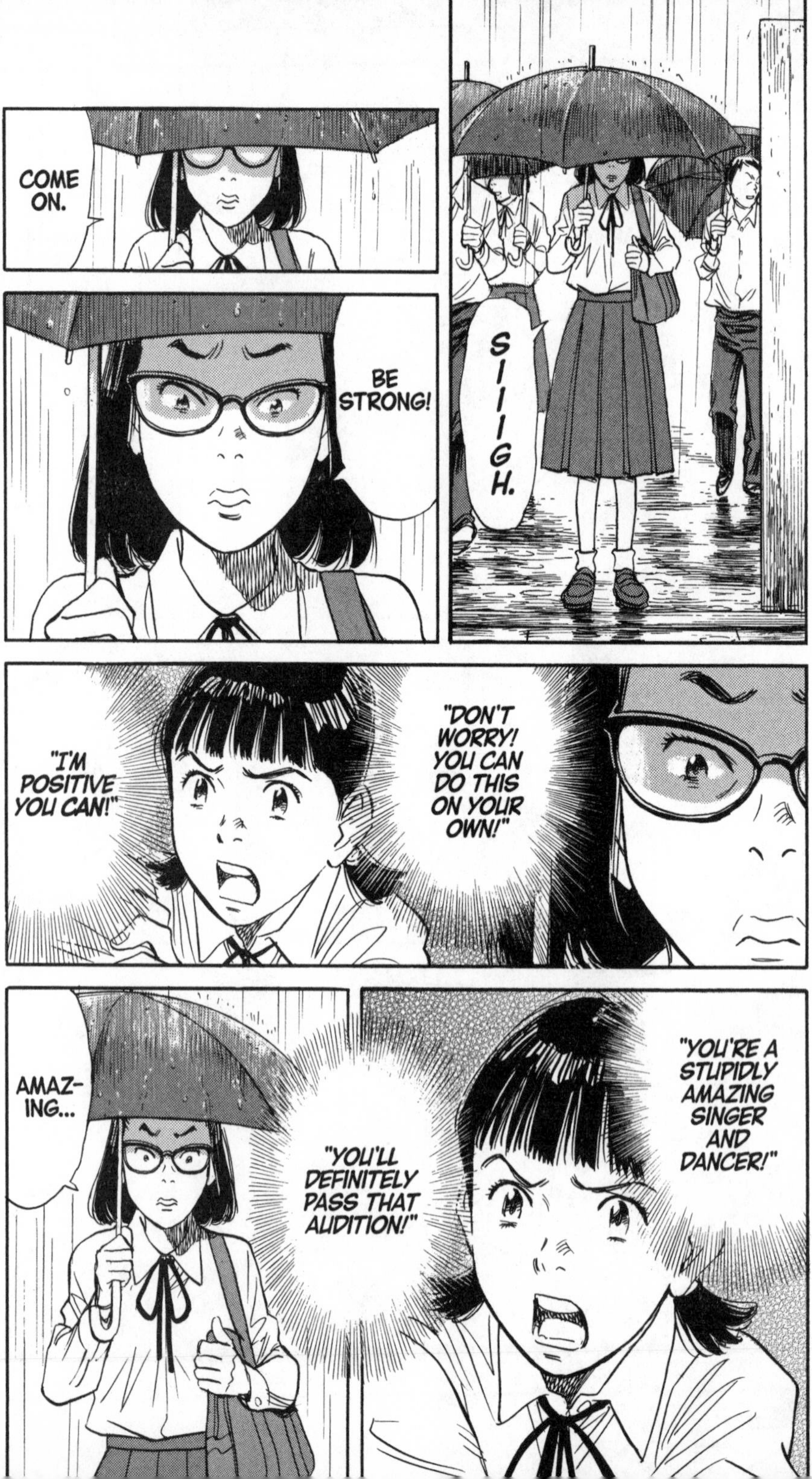
SIIIIGH.
COME ON.
BE STRONG!
"DON'T WORRY! YOU CAN DO THIS ON YOUR OWN!"
"I'M POSITIVE YOU CAN!"
"YOU'RE A STUPIDLY AMAZING SINGER AND DANCER!"
"YOU'LL DEFINITELY PASS THAT AUDITION!"
AMAZ-ING...

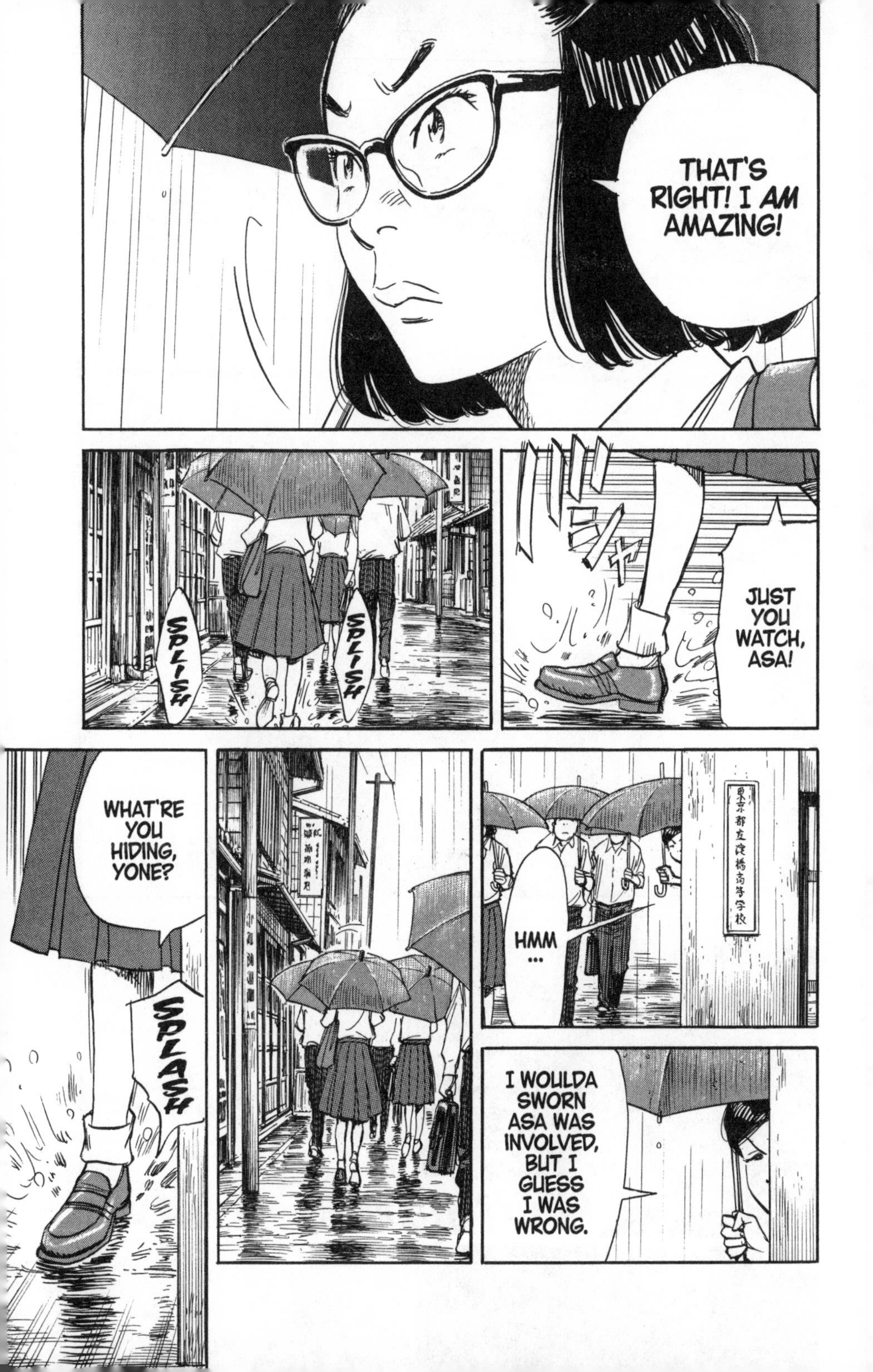
THAT'S RIGHT! I AM AMAZING!
JUST YOU WATCH, ASA!
SPLISH
SPLISH
HMM ...
I WOULDA SWORN ASA WAS INVOLVED, BUT I GUESS I WAS WRONG.
WHAT'RE YOU HIDING, YONE?
SPLASH

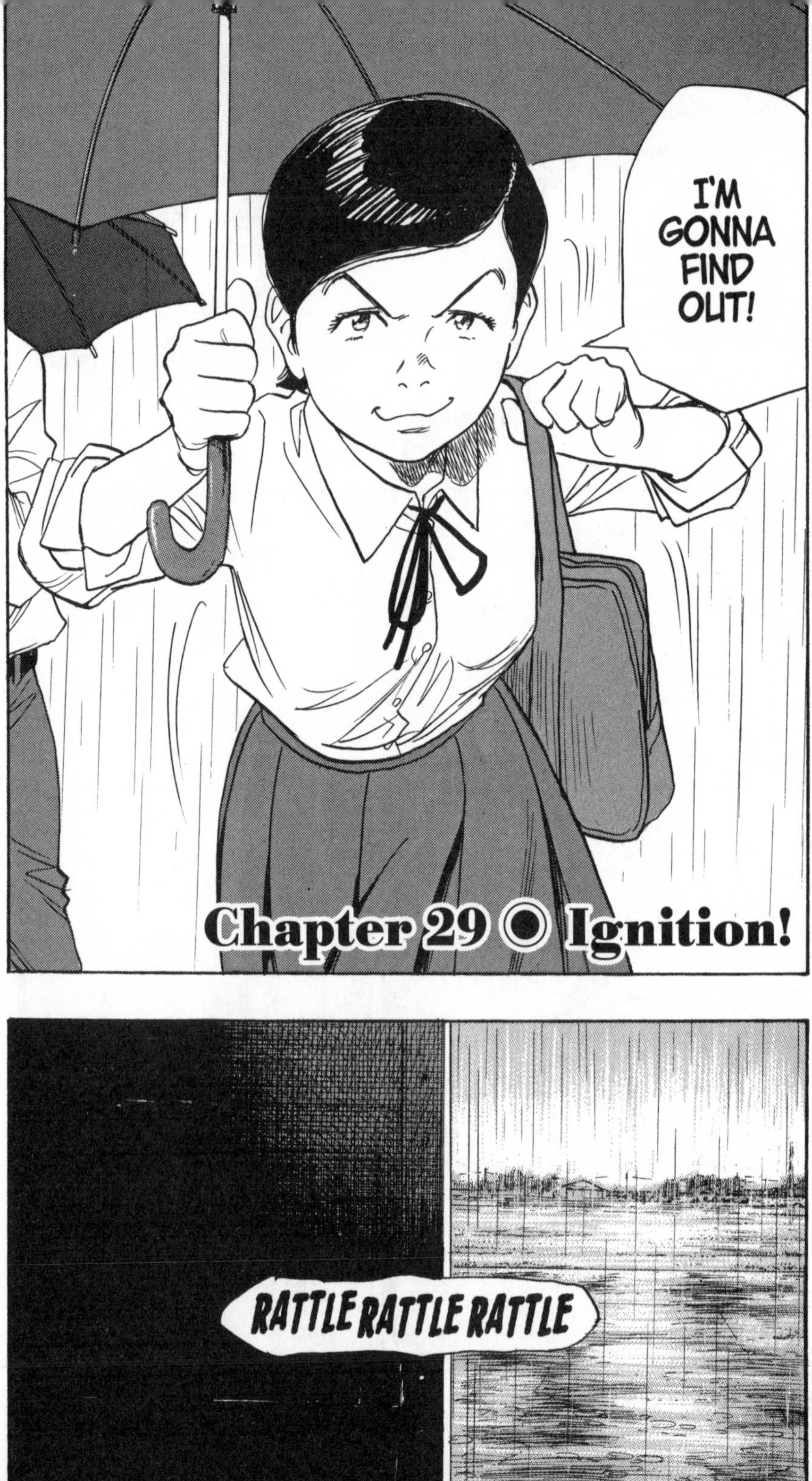
I'M GONNA FIND OUT!
Chapter 29 ◎ Ignition!
RATTLE RATTLE RATTLE

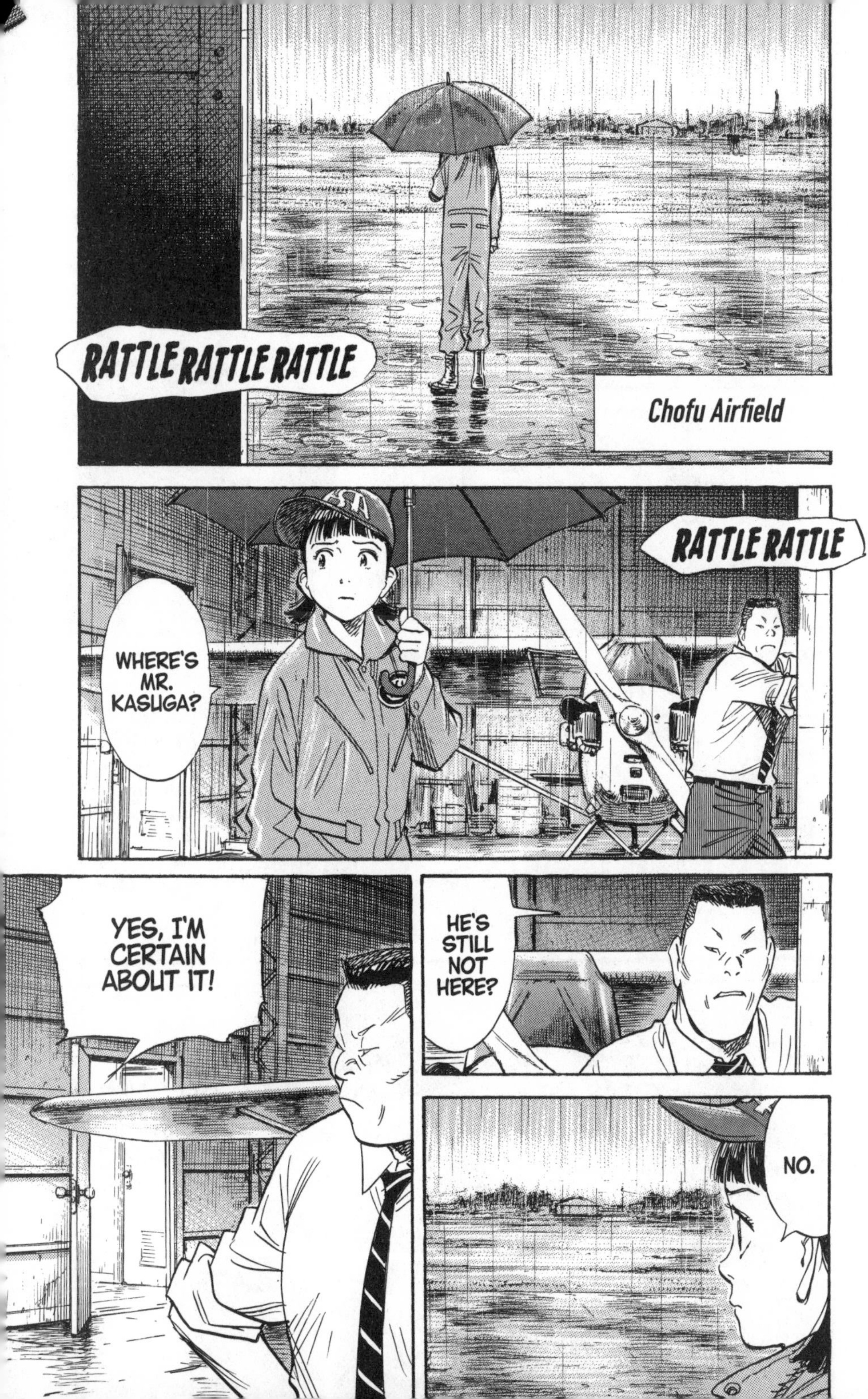
RATTLE RATTLE RATTLE
Chofu Airfield
RATTLE RATTLE
WHERE'S MR. KASUGA?
HE'S STILL NOT HERE?
NO.
YES, I'M CERTAIN ABOUT IT!

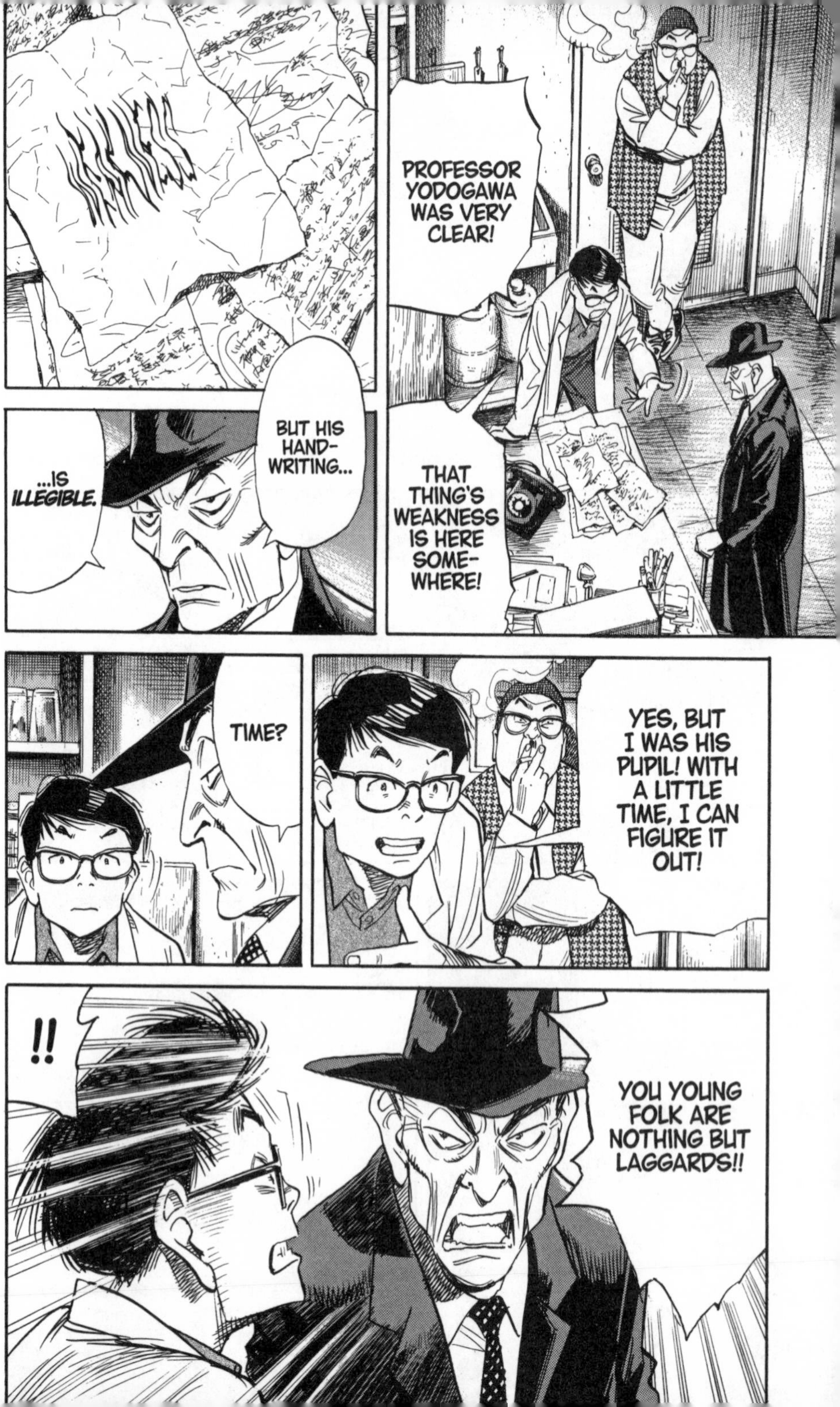
PROFESSOR YODOGAWA WAS VERY CLEAR!
THAT THING'S WEAKNESS IS HERE SOME-WHERE!
BUT HIS HAND-WRITING...
...IS ILLEGIBLE.
YES, BUT I WAS HIS PUPIL! WITH A LITTLE TIME, I CAN FIGURE IT OUT!
TIME?
YOU YOUNG FOLK ARE NOTHING BUT LAGGARDS!!
!!

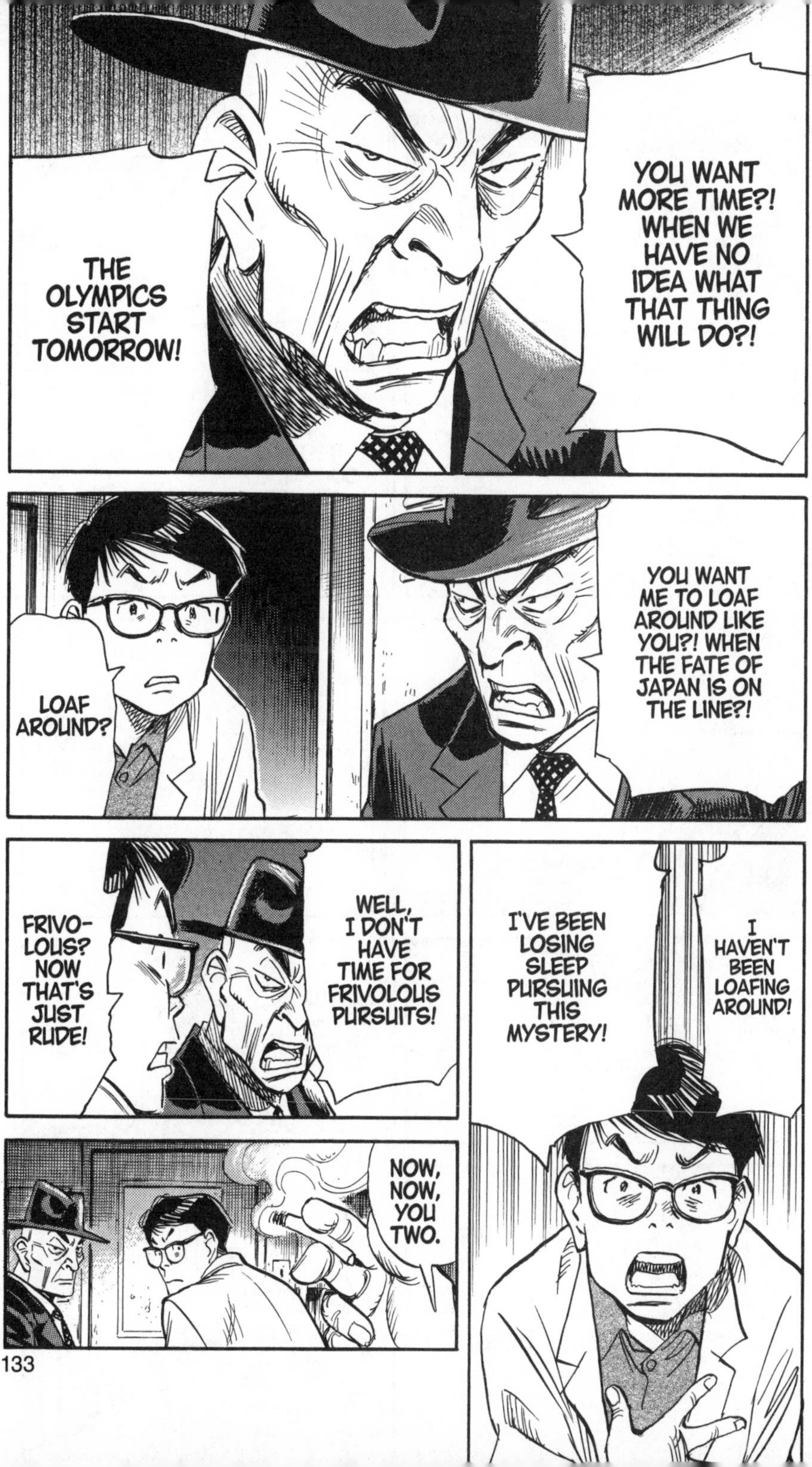
YOU WANT MORE TIME?! WHEN WE HAVE NO IDEA WHAT THAT THING WILL DO?!
THE OLYMPICS START TOMORROW!
YOU WANT ME TO LOAF AROUND LIKE YOU?! WHEN THE FATE OF JAPAN IS ON THE LINE?!
LOAF AROUND?
I HAVEN'T BEEN LOAFING AROUND!
I'VE BEEN LOSING SLEEP PURSUING THIS MYSTERY!
WELL, I DON'T HAVE TIME FOR FRIVOLOUS PURSUITS!
FRIVO-LOUS? NOW THAT'S JUST RUDE!
NOW, NOW, YOU TWO.

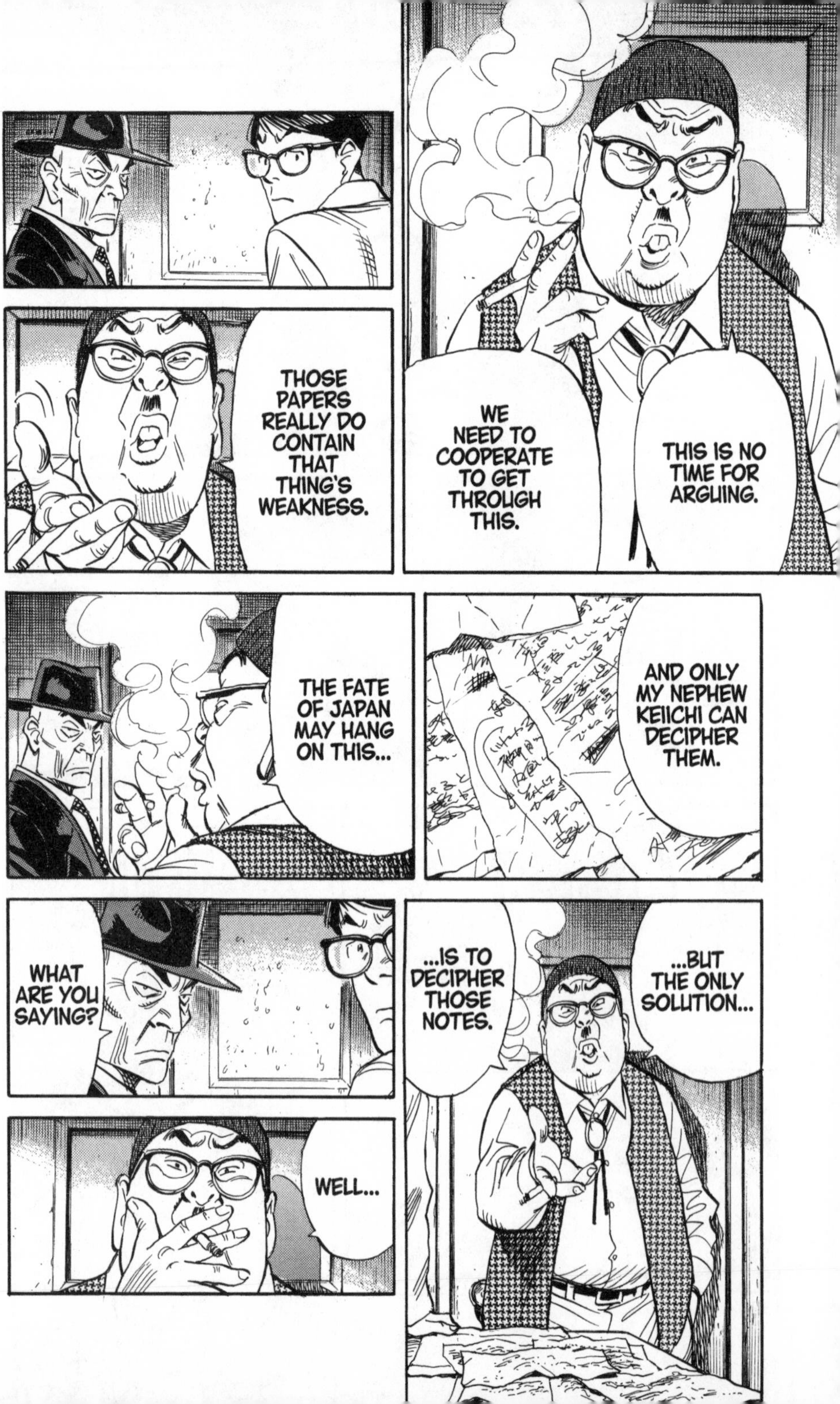
THIS IS NO TIME FOR ARGUING.
WE NEED TO COOPERATE TO GET THROUGH THIS.
THOSE PAPERS REALLY DO CONTAIN THAT THING'S WEAKNESS.
AND ONLY MY NEPHEW KEIICHI CAN DECIPHER THEM.
THE FATE OF JAPAN MAY HANG ON THIS...
...BUT THE ONLY SOLUTION...
...IS TO DECIPHER THOSE NOTES.
WHAT ARE YOU SAYING?
WELL...

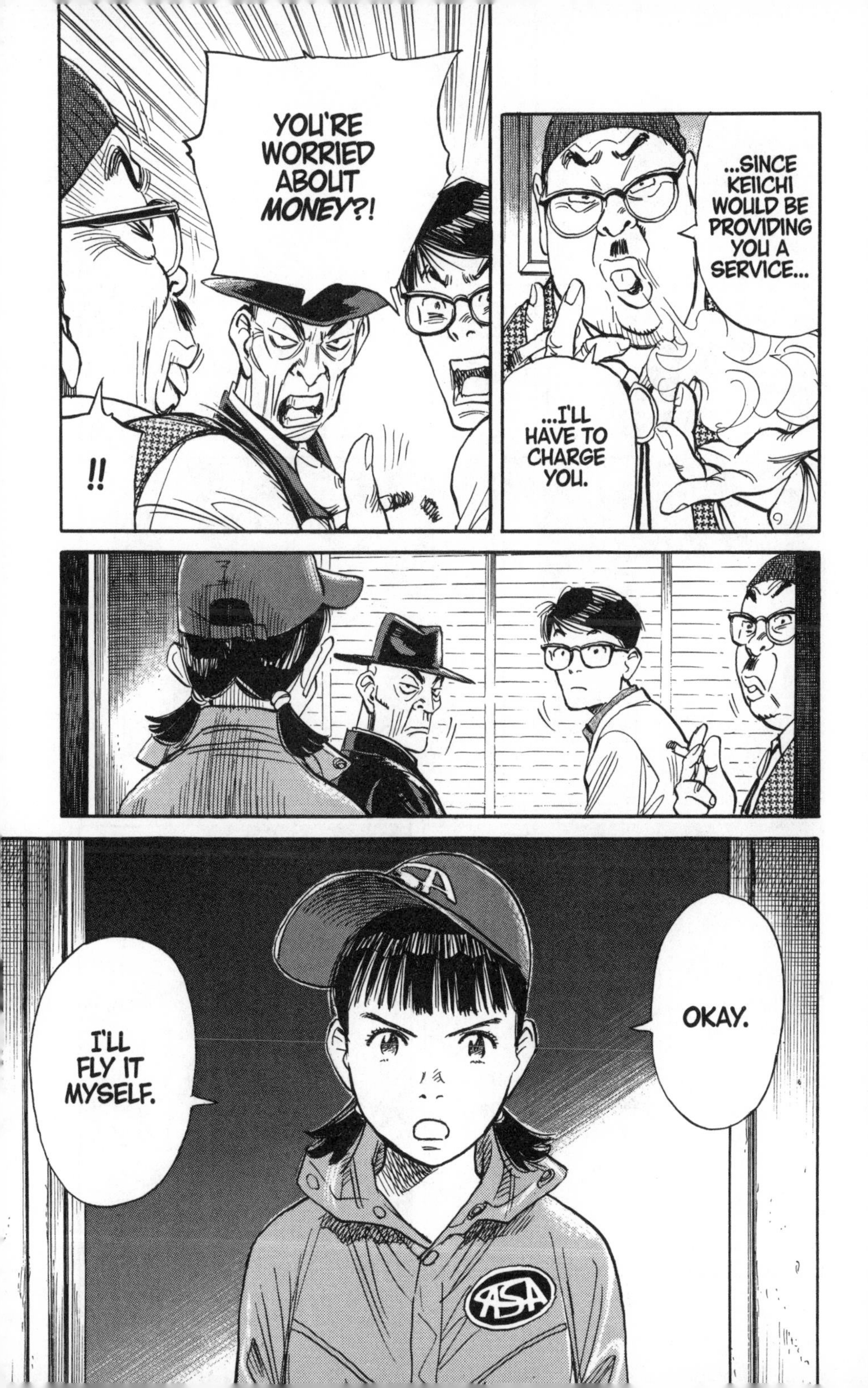
...SINCE KEIICHI WOULD BE PROVIDING YOU A SERVICE...
...I'LL HAVE TO CHARGE YOU.
YOU'RE WORRIED ABOUT *MONEY*?!
!!
OKAY.
I'LL FLY IT MYSELF.

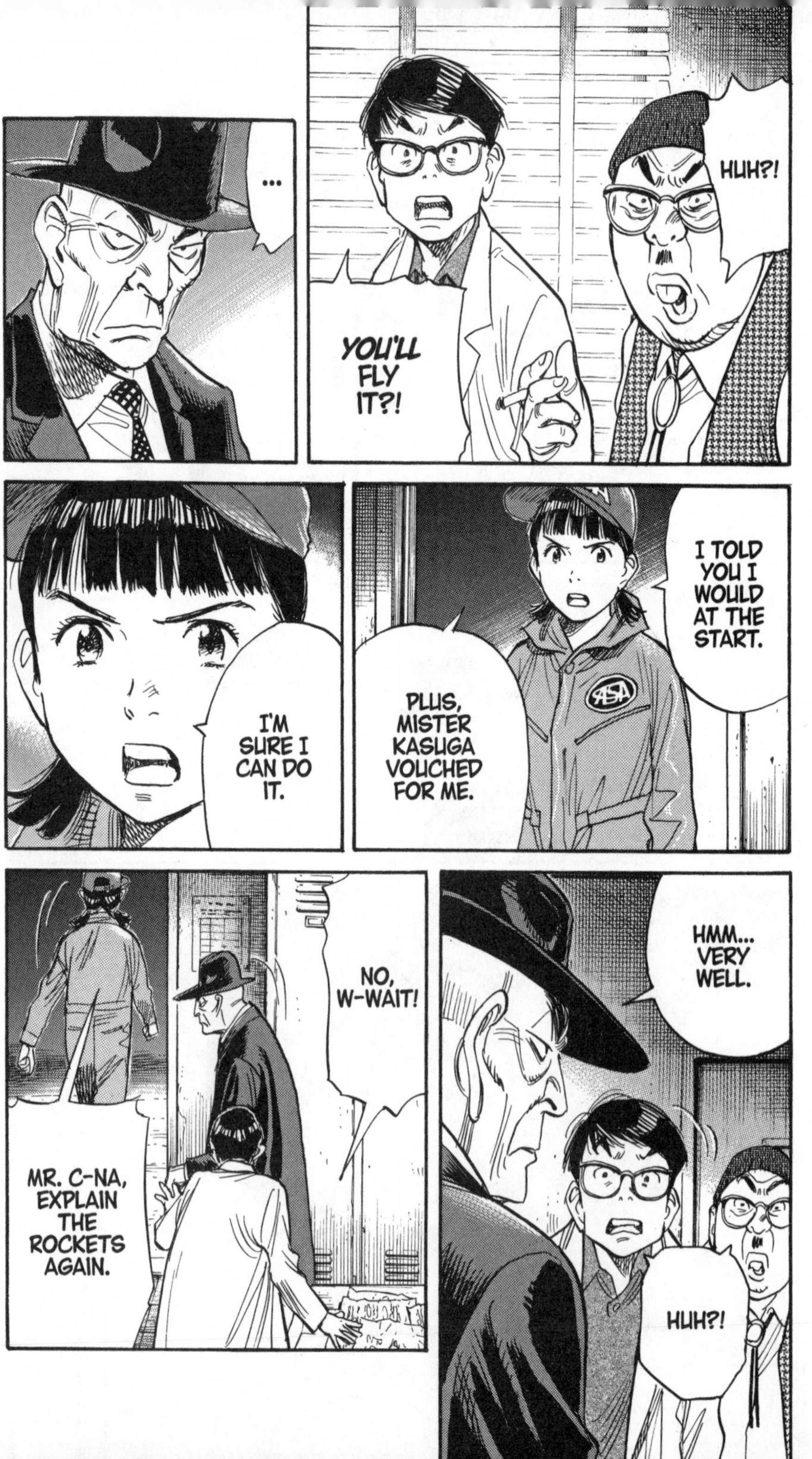
HUH?!
YOU'LL FLY IT?!
...
I TOLD YOU I WOULD AT THE START.
PLUS, MISTER KASUGA VOUCHED FOR ME.
I'M SURE I CAN DO IT.
HMM... VERY WELL.
HUH?!
NO, W-WAIT!
MR. C-NA, EXPLAIN THE ROCKETS AGAIN.

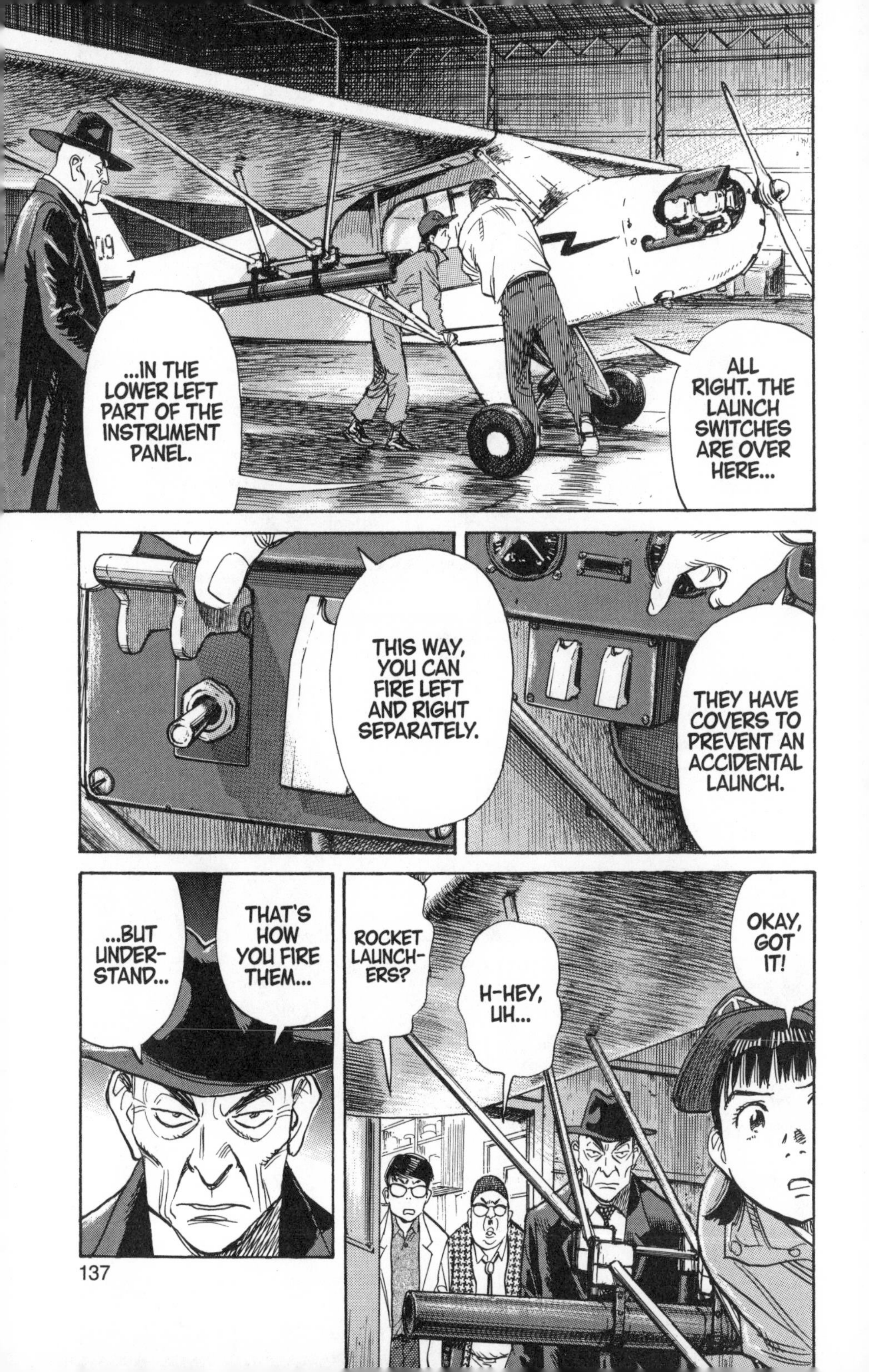
ALL RIGHT. THE LAUNCH SWITCHES ARE OVER HERE...
...IN THE LOWER LEFT PART OF THE INSTRUMENT PANEL.
THEY HAVE COVERS TO PREVENT AN ACCIDENTAL LAUNCH.
THIS WAY, YOU CAN FIRE LEFT AND RIGHT SEPARATELY.
OKAY, GOT IT!
H-HEY, UH...
ROCKET LAUNCH-ERS?
THAT'S HOW YOU FIRE THEM...
...BUT UNDER-STAND...

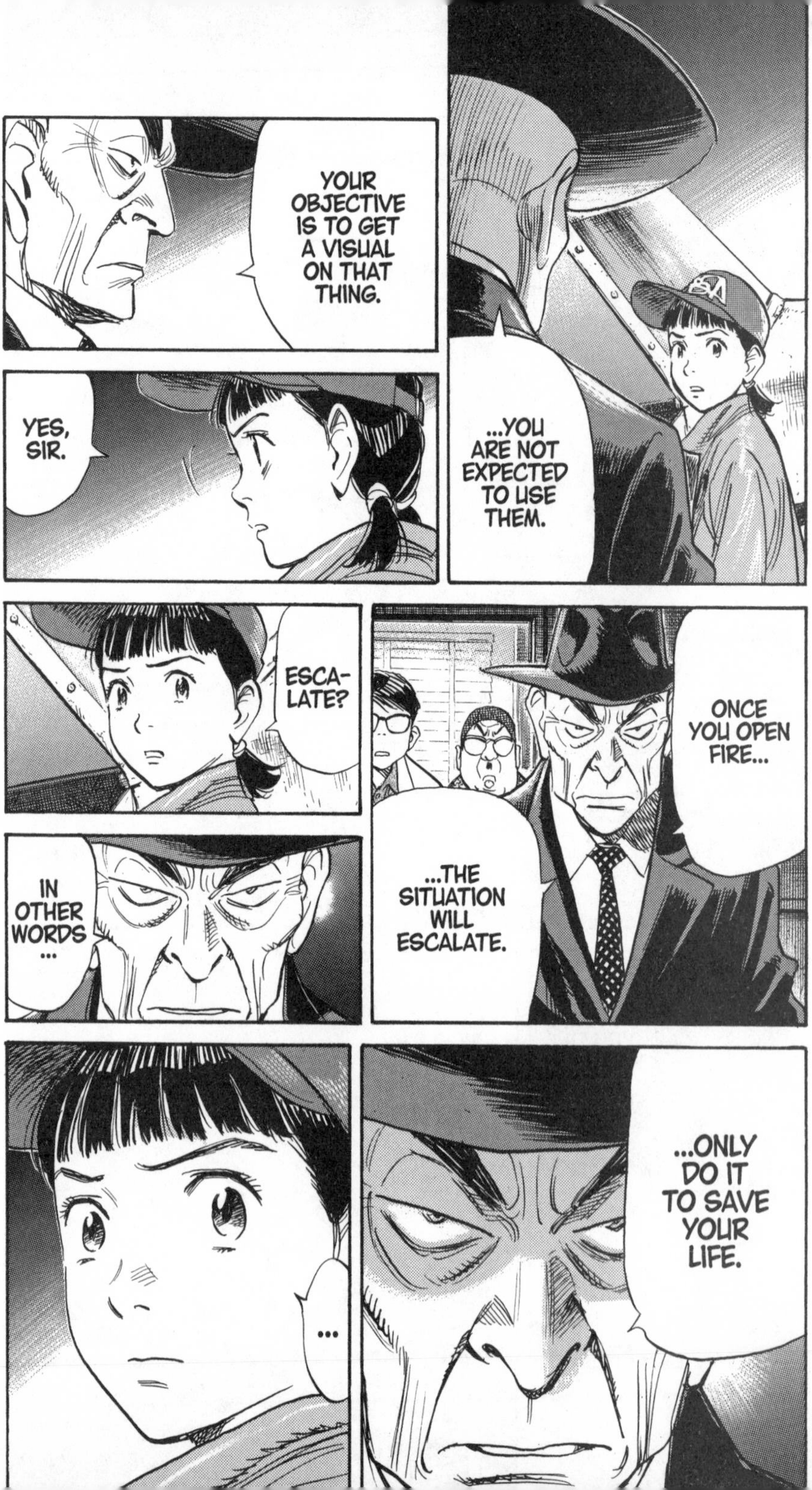
...YOU ARE NOT EXPECTED TO USE THEM.
YOUR OBJECTIVE IS TO GET A VISUAL ON THAT THING.
YES, SIR.
ONCE YOU OPEN FIRE...
...THE SITUATION WILL ESCALATE.
ESCA-LATE?
IN OTHER WORDS...
...ONLY DO IT TO SAVE YOUR LIFE.
...

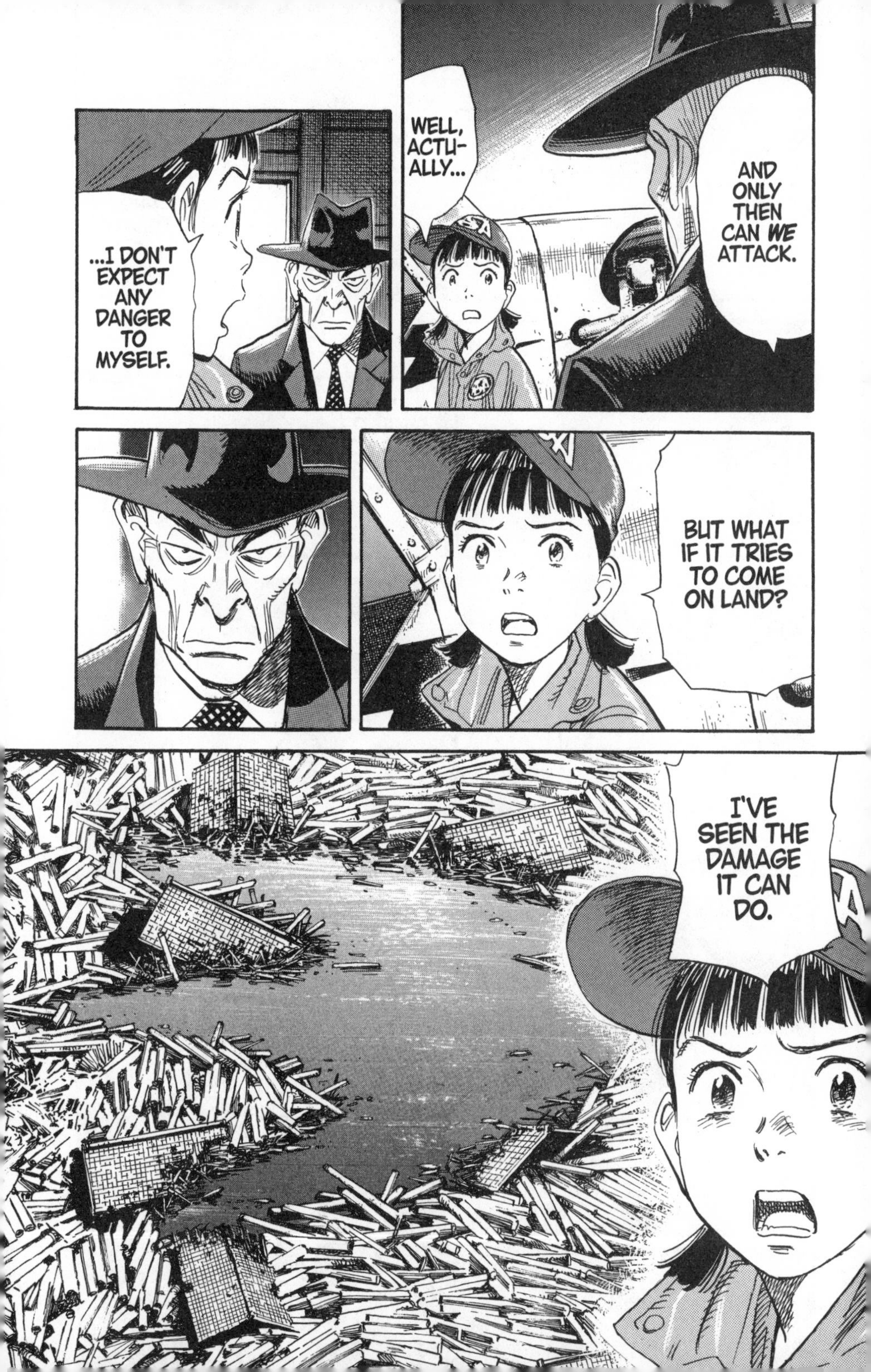
AND ONLY THEN CAN *WE* ATTACK.
WELL, ACTU-ALLY...
...I DON'T EXPECT ANY DANGER TO MYSELF.
BUT WHAT IF IT TRIES TO COME ON LAND?
I'VE SEEN THE DAMAGE IT CAN DO.

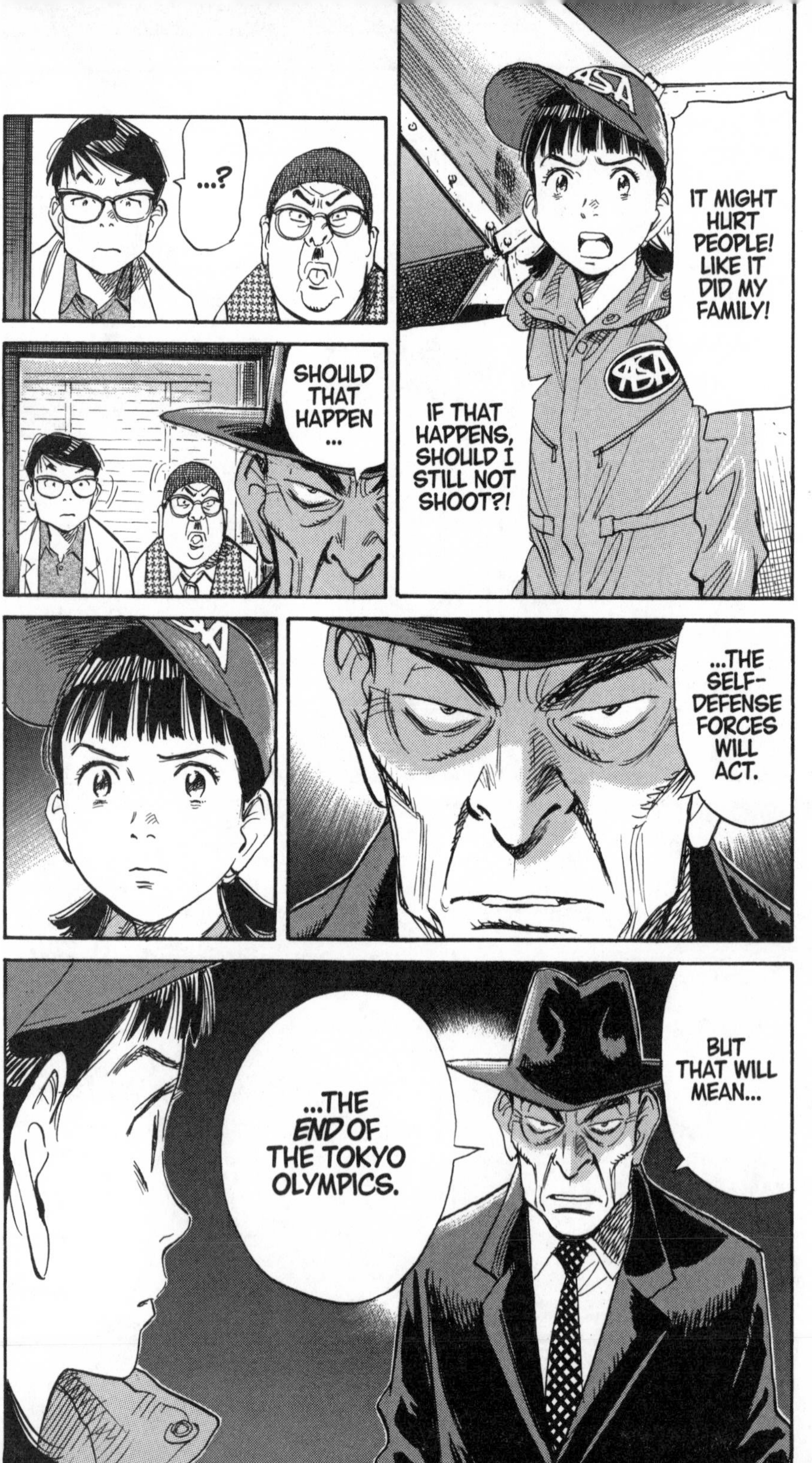
IT MIGHT HURT PEOPLE! LIKE IT DID MY FAMILY!
IF THAT HAPPENS, SHOULD I STILL NOT SHOOT?!
...?
SHOULD THAT HAPPEN ...
...THE SELF-DEFENSE FORCES WILL ACT.
BUT THAT WILL MEAN...
...THE *END* OF THE TOKYO OLYMPICS.

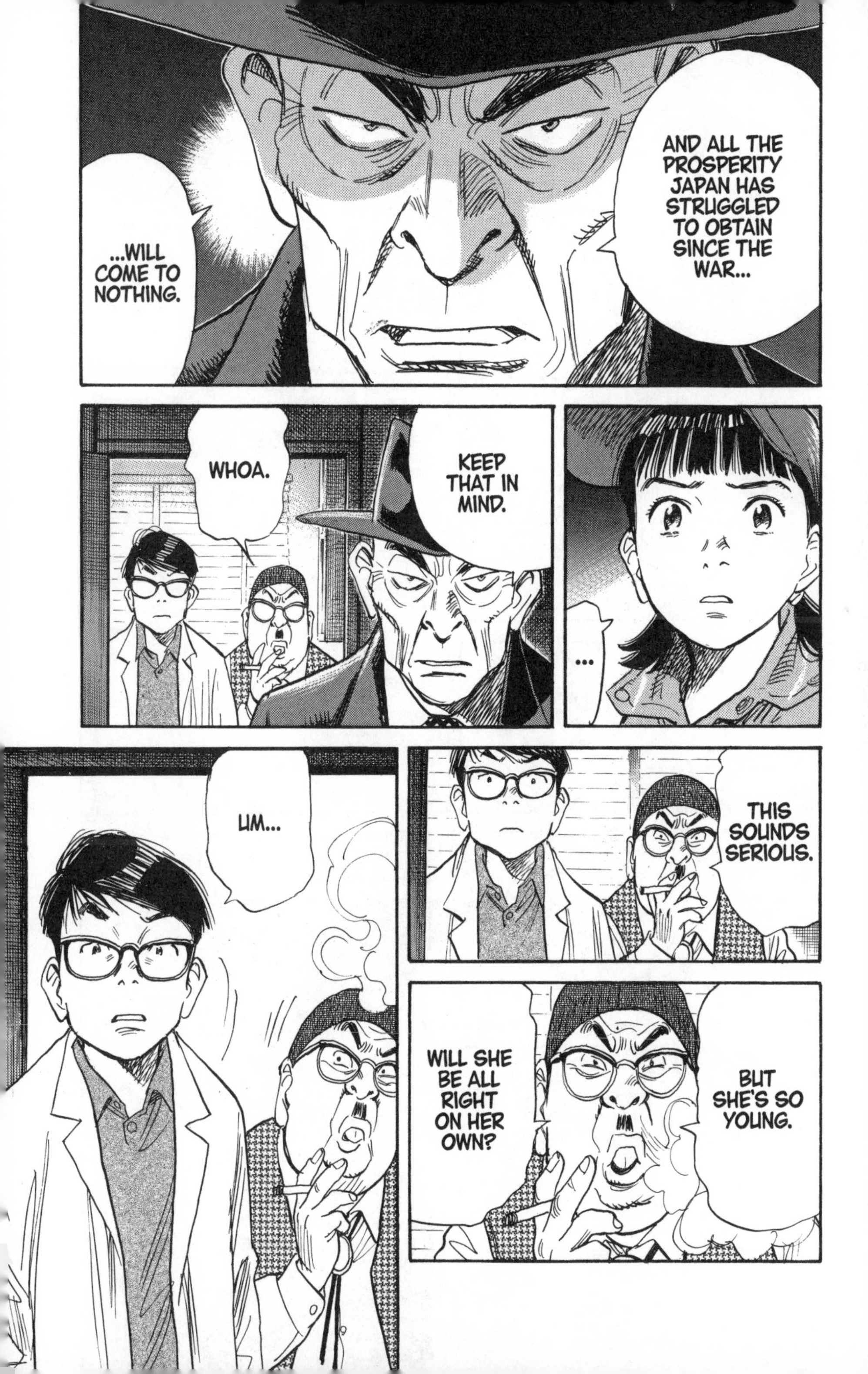
AND ALL THE PROSPERITY JAPAN HAS STRUGGLED TO OBTAIN SINCE THE WAR...
...WILL COME TO NOTHING.
...
KEEP THAT IN MIND.
WHOA.
THIS SOUNDS SERIOUS.
BUT SHE'S SO YOUNG.
WILL SHE BE ALL RIGHT ON HER OWN?
UM...

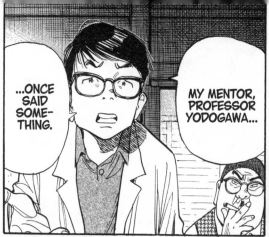

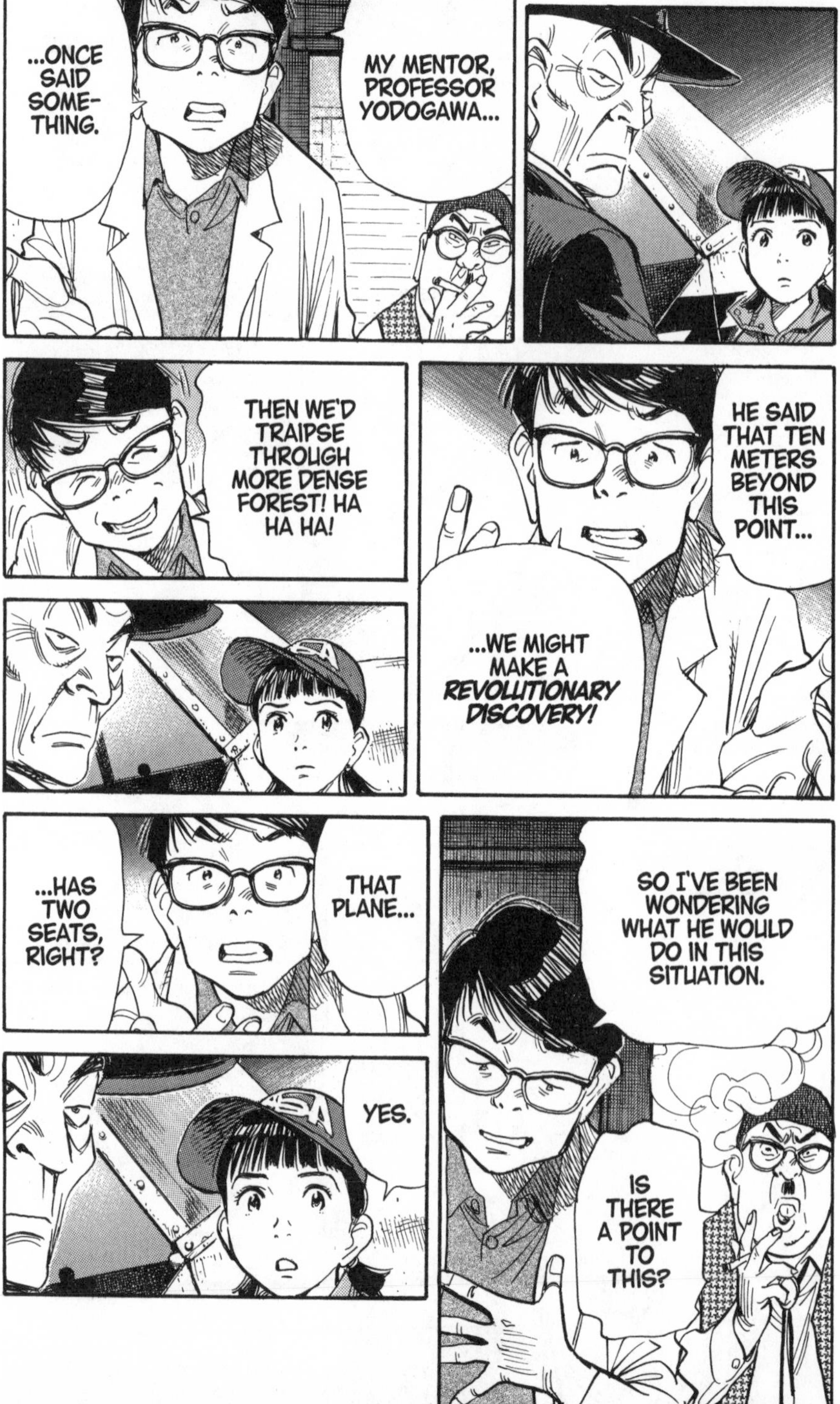
MY MENTOR, PROFESSOR YODOGAWA...
...ONCE SAID SOMETHING.
HE SAID THAT TEN METERS BEYOND THIS POINT...
...WE MIGHT MAKE A *REVOLUTIONARY DISCOVERY!*
THEN WE'D TRAIPSE THROUGH MORE DENSE FOREST! HA HA HA!
SO I'VE BEEN WONDERING WHAT HE WOULD DO IN THIS SITUATION.
IS THERE A POINT TO THIS?
THAT PLANE...
...HAS TWO SEATS, RIGHT?
YES.

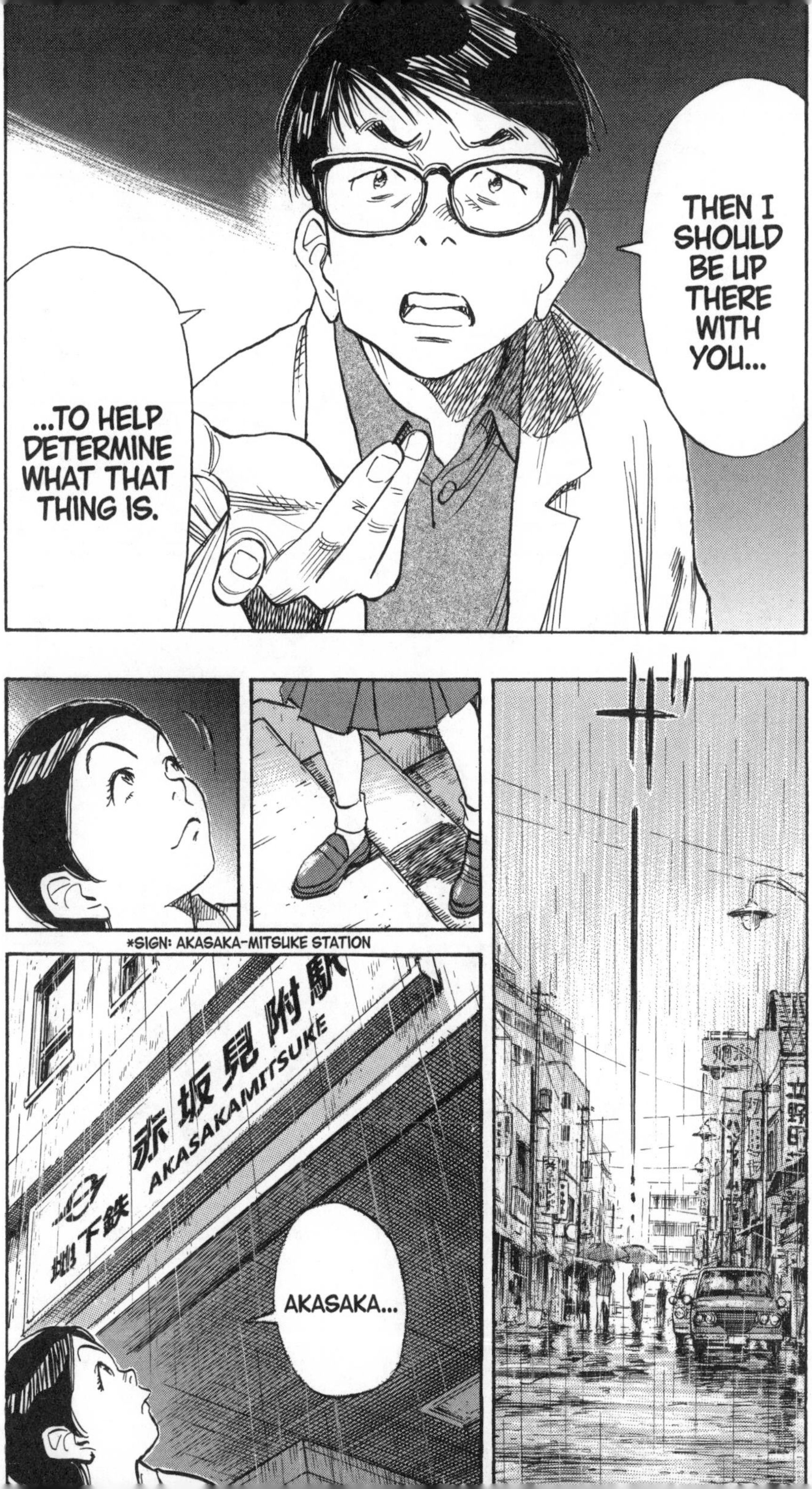
THEN I SHOULD BE UP THERE WITH YOU...
...TO HELP DETERMINE WHAT THAT THING IS.
*SIGN: AKASAKA-MITSUKE STATION
赤坂見附駅
AKASAKAMITSUKE
地下鉄
AKASAKA...

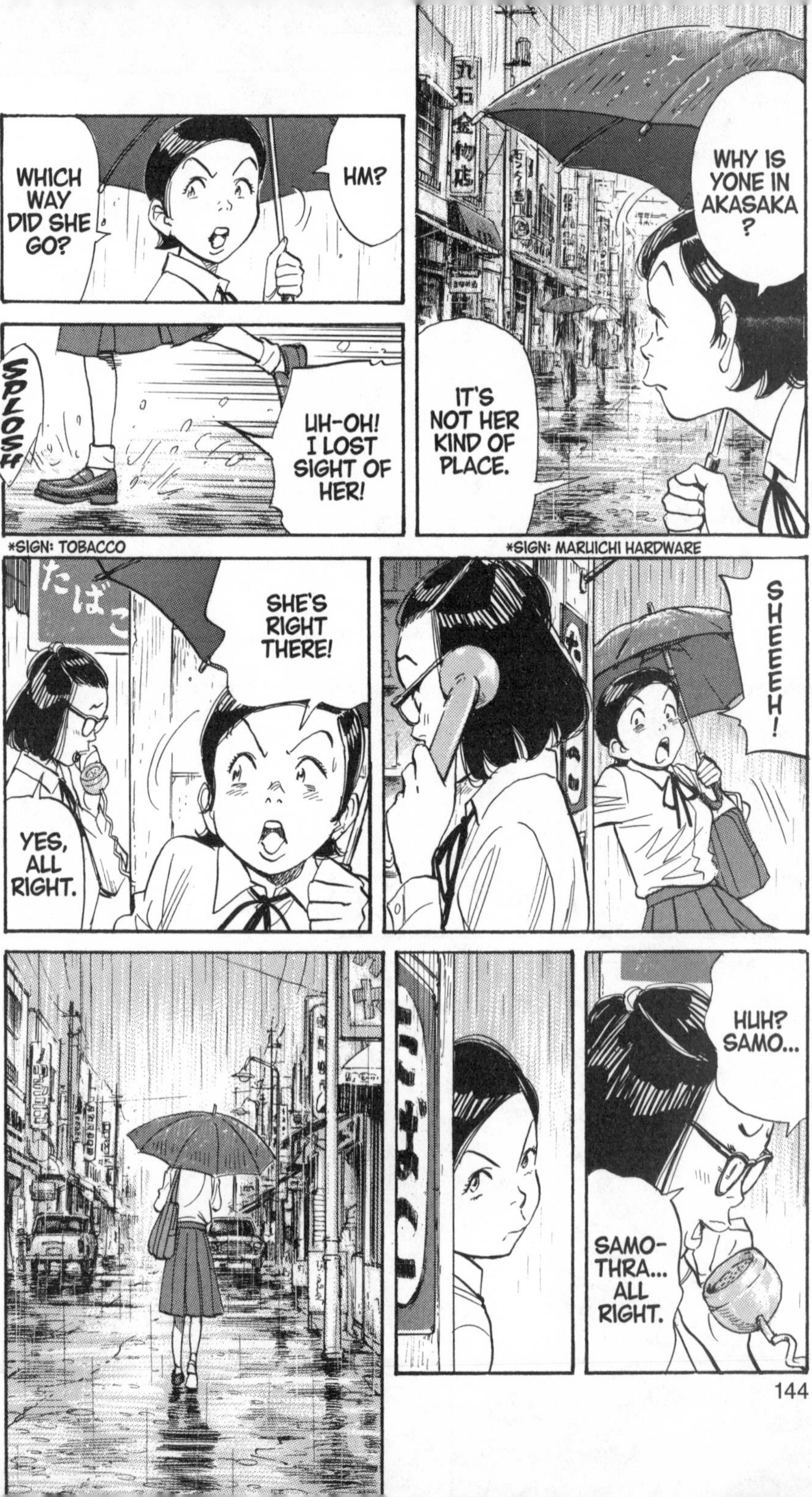
WHY IS YONE IN AKASAKA?
IT'S NOT HER KIND OF PLACE.
*SIGN: MARUICHI HARDWARE
HM?
WHICH WAY DID SHE GO?
SPLOSH
UH-OH! I LOST SIGHT OF HER!
*SIGN: TOBACCO
SHEEEEH!
SHE'S RIGHT THERE!
YES, ALL RIGHT.
HUH? SAMO...
SAMOTHRA... ALL RIGHT.

純喫茶 サモトラケ

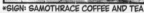

*SIGN: SAMOTHRACE COFFEE AND TEA

TING
TING

!!

THERE SHE IS.

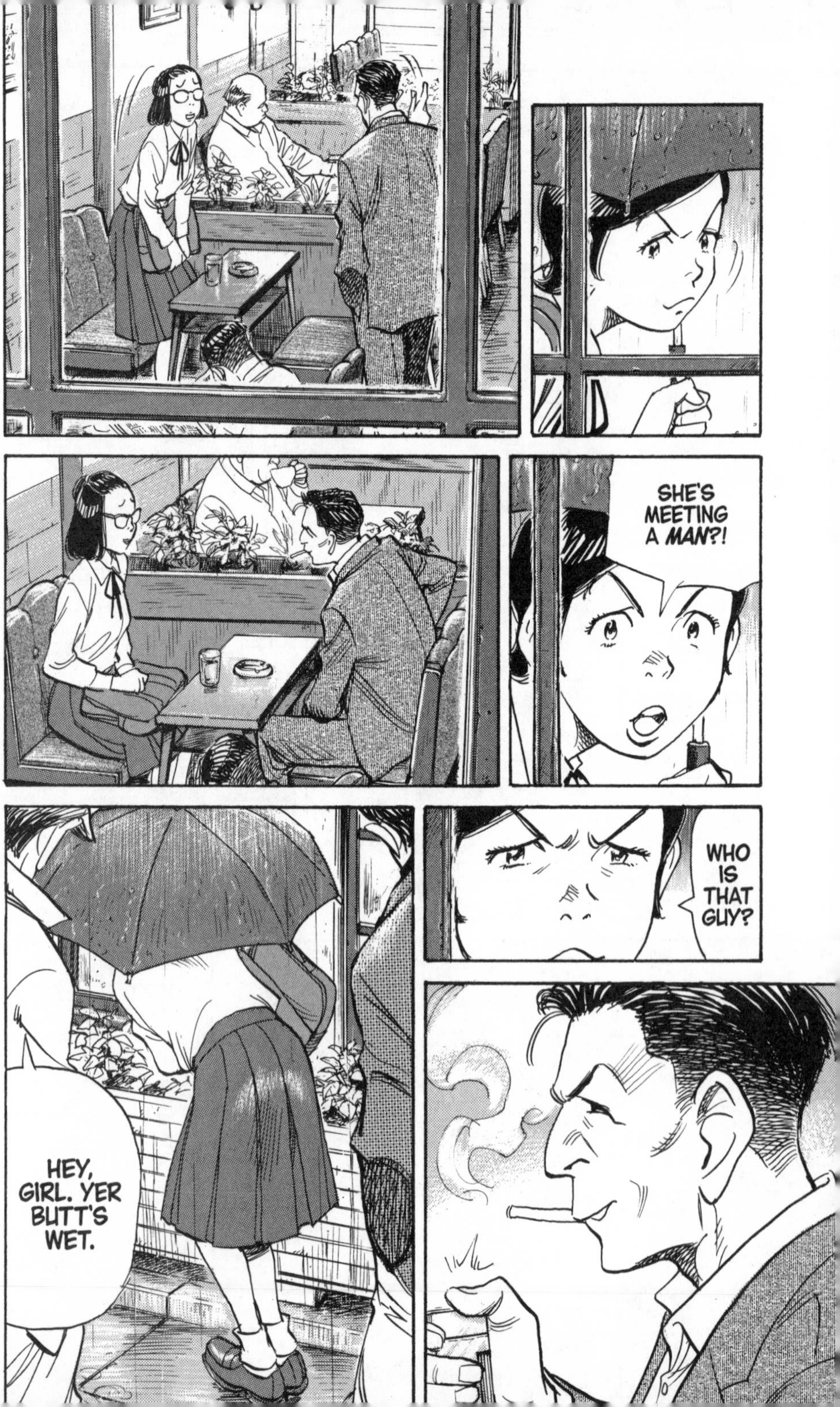
SHE'S MEETING A *MAN*?!
WHO IS THAT GUY?
HEY, GIRL. YER BUTT'S WET.

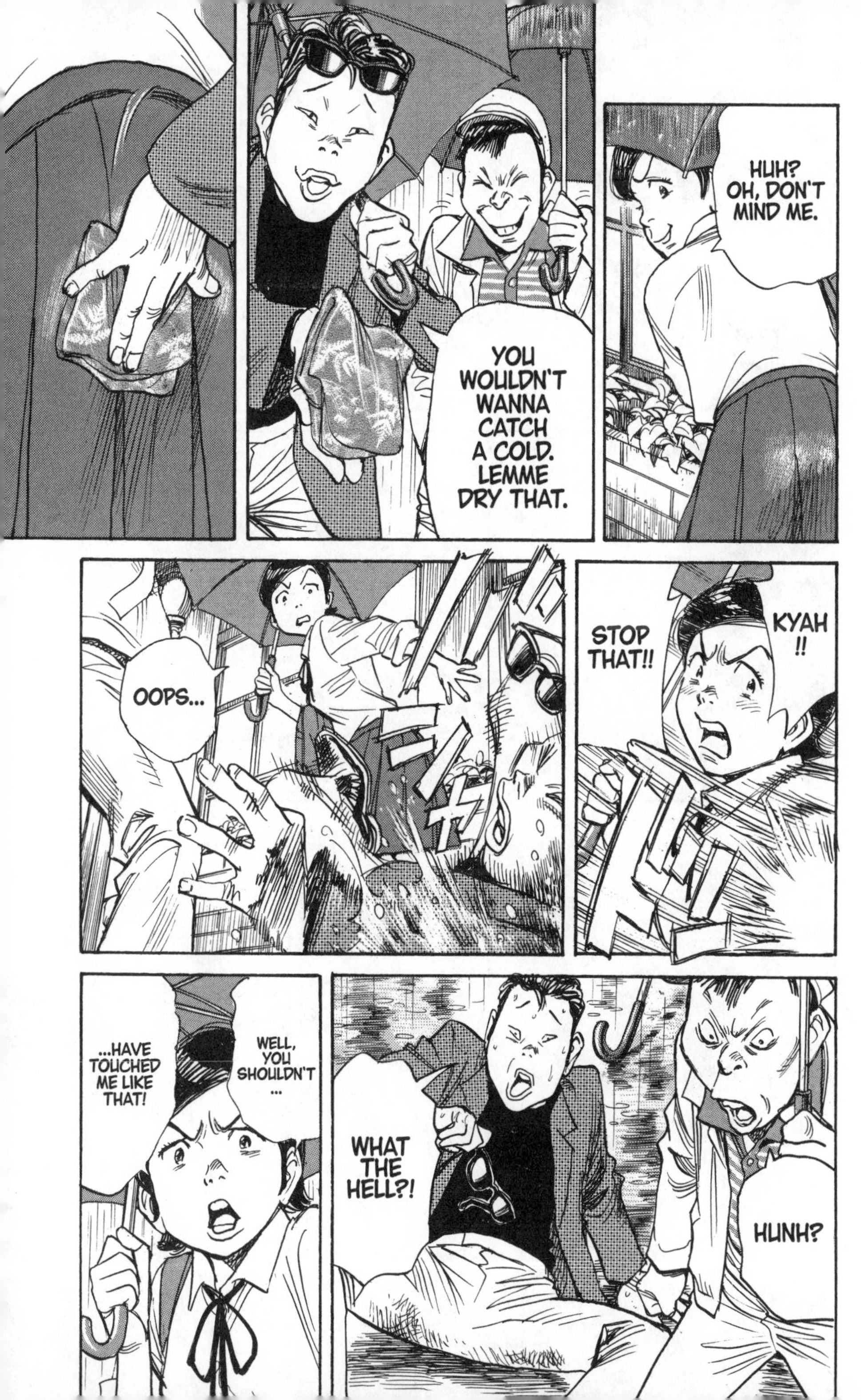
HUH? OH, DON'T MIND ME.
YOU WOULDN'T WANNA CATCH A COLD. LEMME DRY THAT.
KYAH !!
STOP THAT!!
OOPS...
WHAT THE HELL?!
HUNH?
WELL, YOU SHOULDN'T ...
...HAVE TOUCHED ME LIKE THAT!

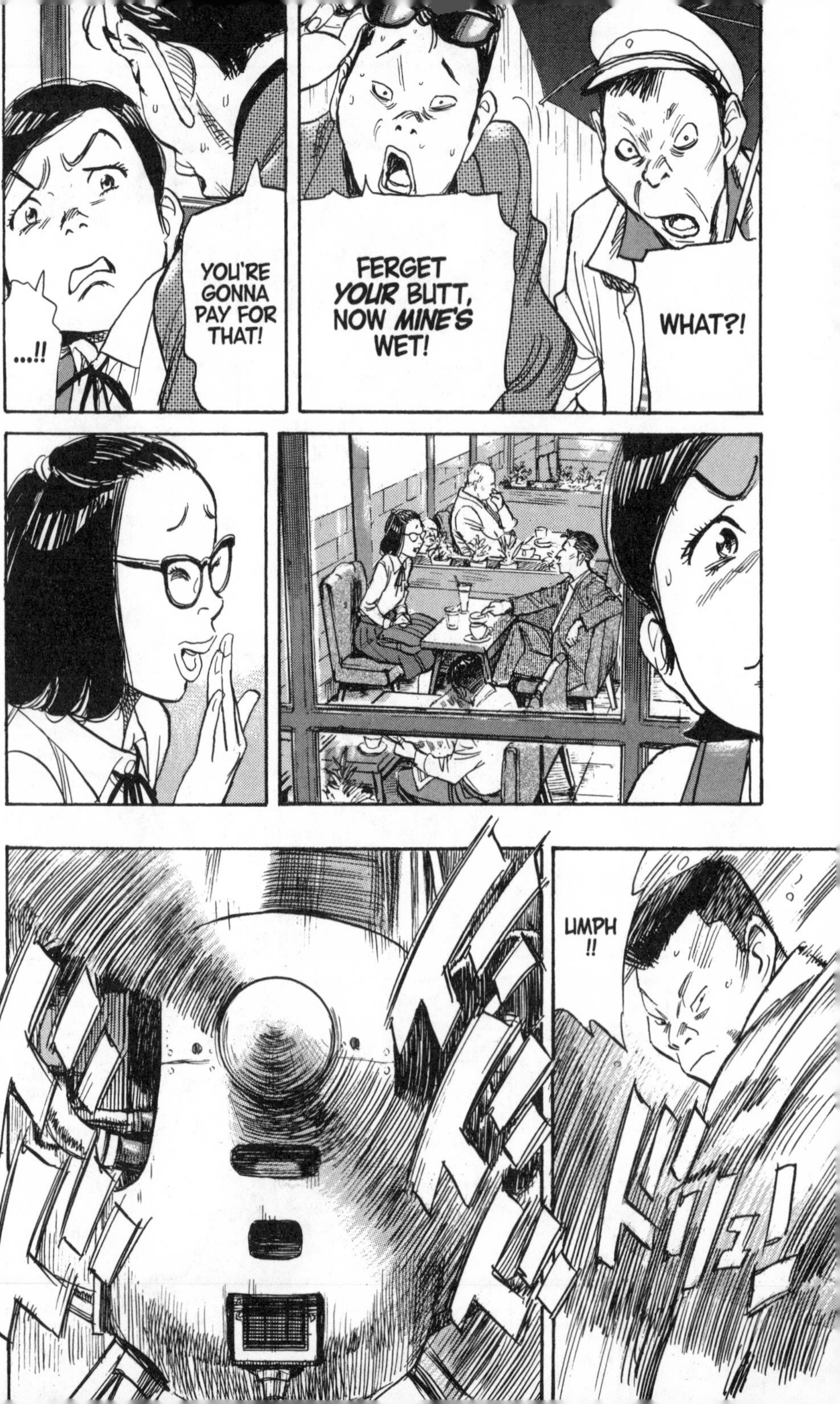
WHAT?!
FERGET *YOUR* BUTT, NOW *MINE'S* WET!
YOU'RE GONNA PAY FOR THAT!
...!!
UMPH !!

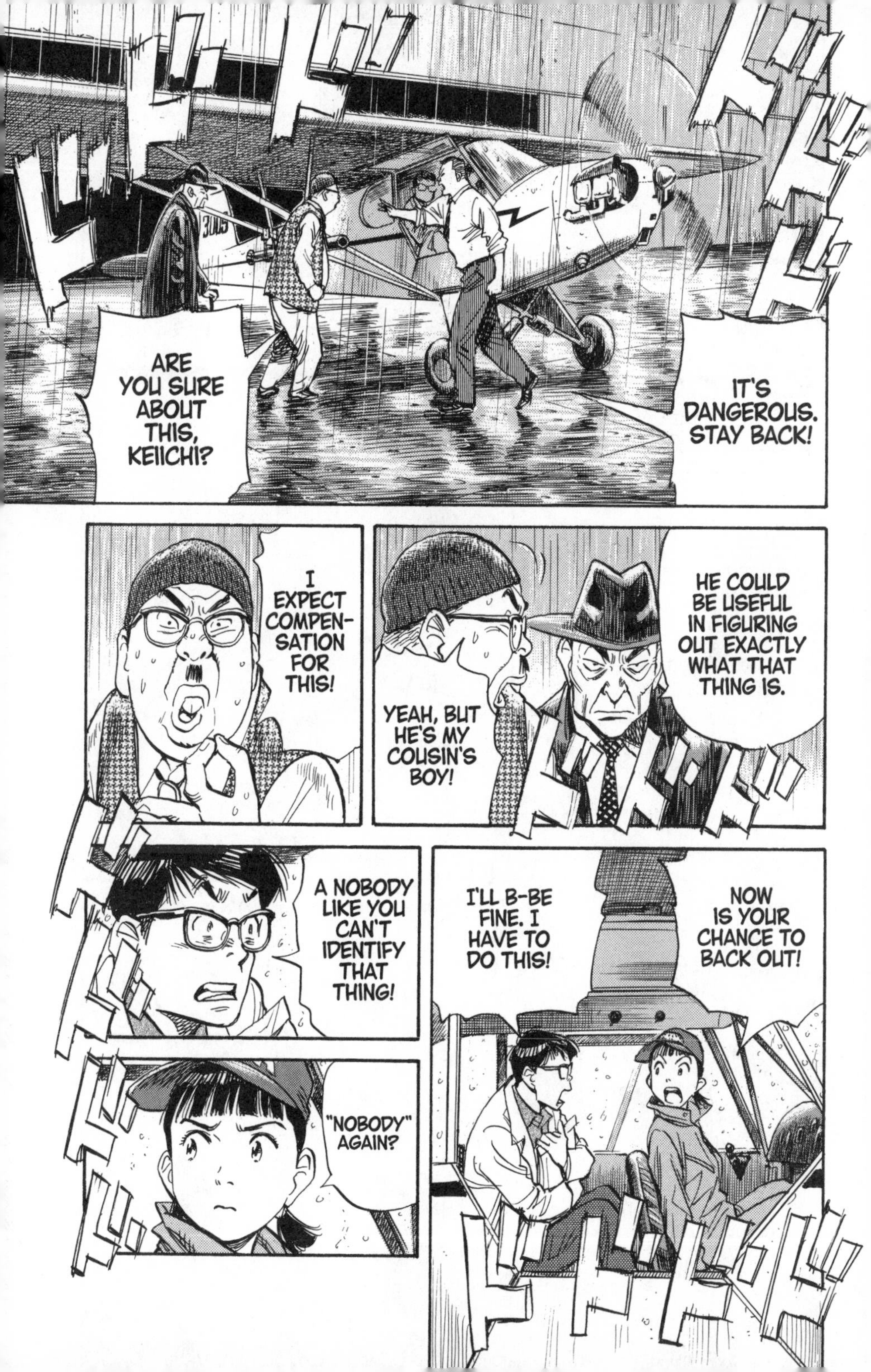
IT'S DANGEROUS. STAY BACK!
ARE YOU SURE ABOUT THIS, KEIICHI?
HE COULD BE USEFUL IN FIGURING OUT EXACTLY WHAT THAT THING IS.
YEAH, BUT HE'S MY COUSIN'S BOY!
I EXPECT COMPENSATION FOR THIS!
NOW IS YOUR CHANCE TO BACK OUT!
I'LL B-BE FINE. I HAVE TO DO THIS!
A NOBODY LIKE YOU CAN'T IDENTIFY THAT THING!
"NOBODY" AGAIN?

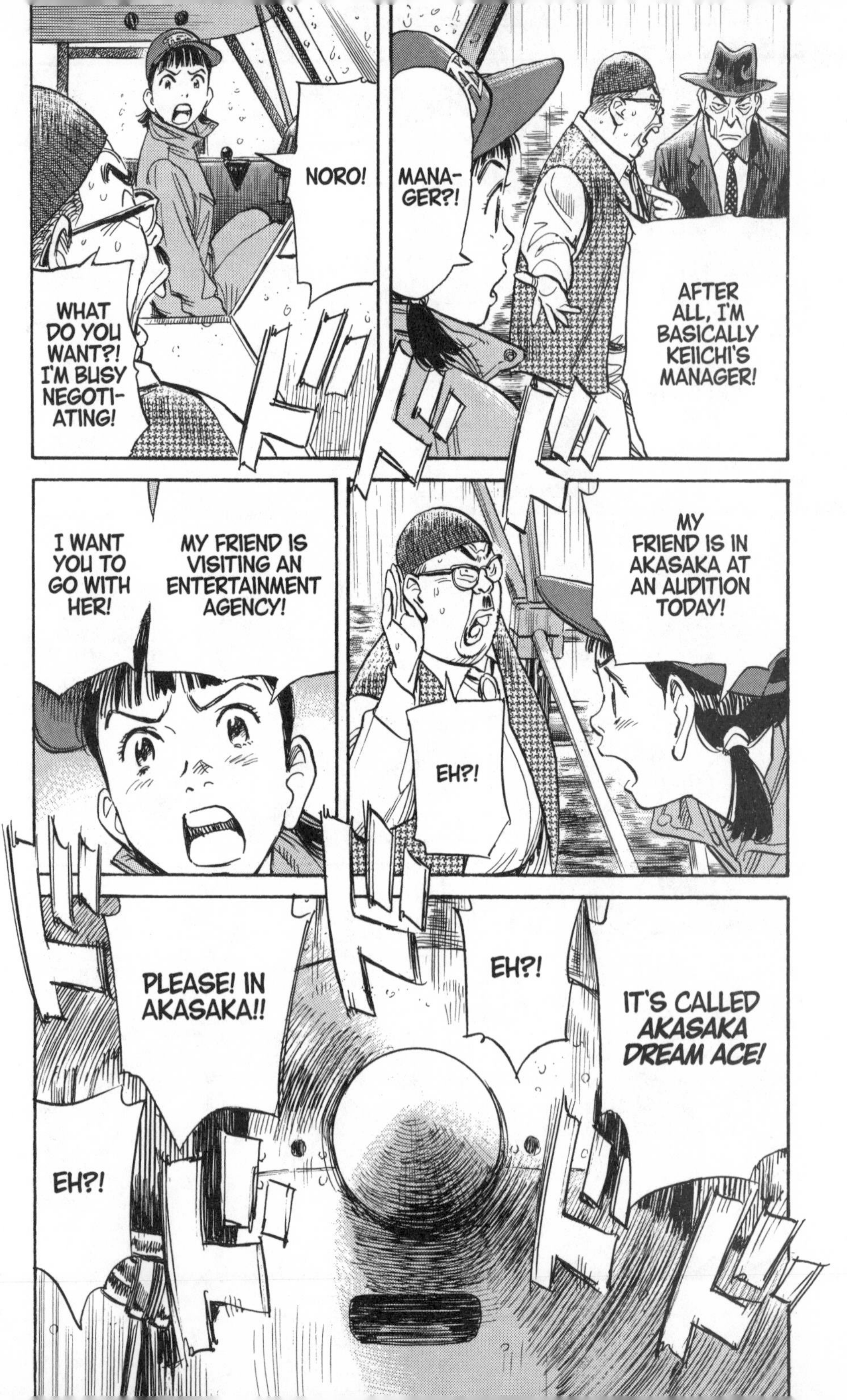
MANA-
GER?!
AFTER ALL, I'M BASICALLY KEIICHI'S MANAGER!
NORO!
WHAT DO YOU WANT?! I'M BUSY NEGOTI-ATING!
MY FRIEND IS IN AKASAKA AT AN AUDITION TODAY!
EH?!
MY FRIEND IS VISITING AN ENTERTAINMENT AGENCY!
I WANT YOU TO GO WITH HER!
IT'S CALLED AKASAKA DREAM ACE!
EH?!
PLEASE! IN AKASAKA!!
EH?!

Chapter 30 ● Close Encounter

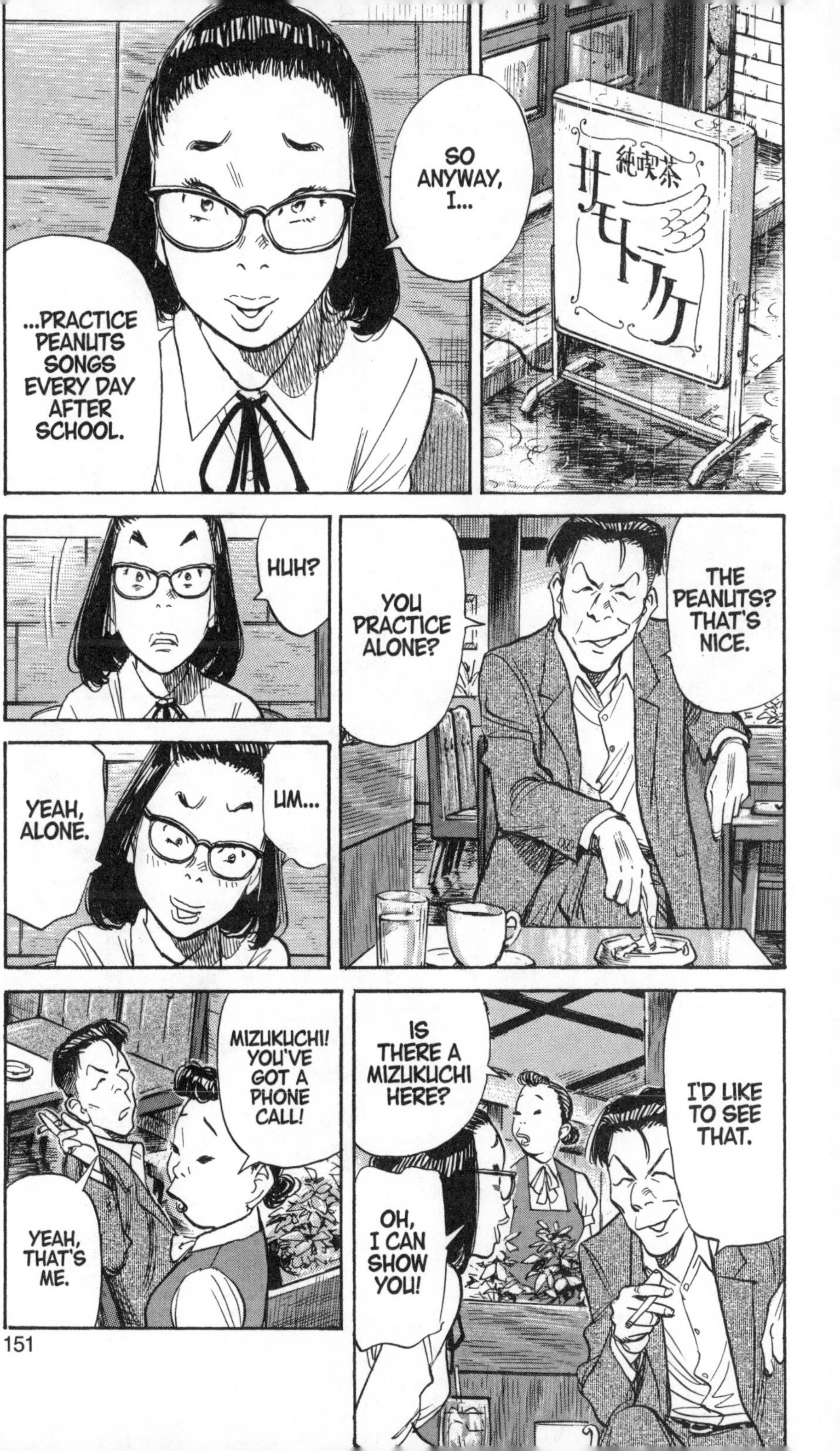

純喫茶
サモトラケ
SO ANYWAY, I...
...PRACTICE PEANUTS SONGS EVERY DAY AFTER SCHOOL.
THE PEANUTS? THAT'S NICE.
YOU PRACTICE ALONE?
HUH?
UM...
YEAH, ALONE.
I'D LIKE TO SEE THAT.
IS THERE A MIZUKUCHI HERE?
OH, I CAN SHOW YOU!
MIZUKUCHI! YOU'VE GOT A PHONE CALL!
YEAH, THAT'S ME.

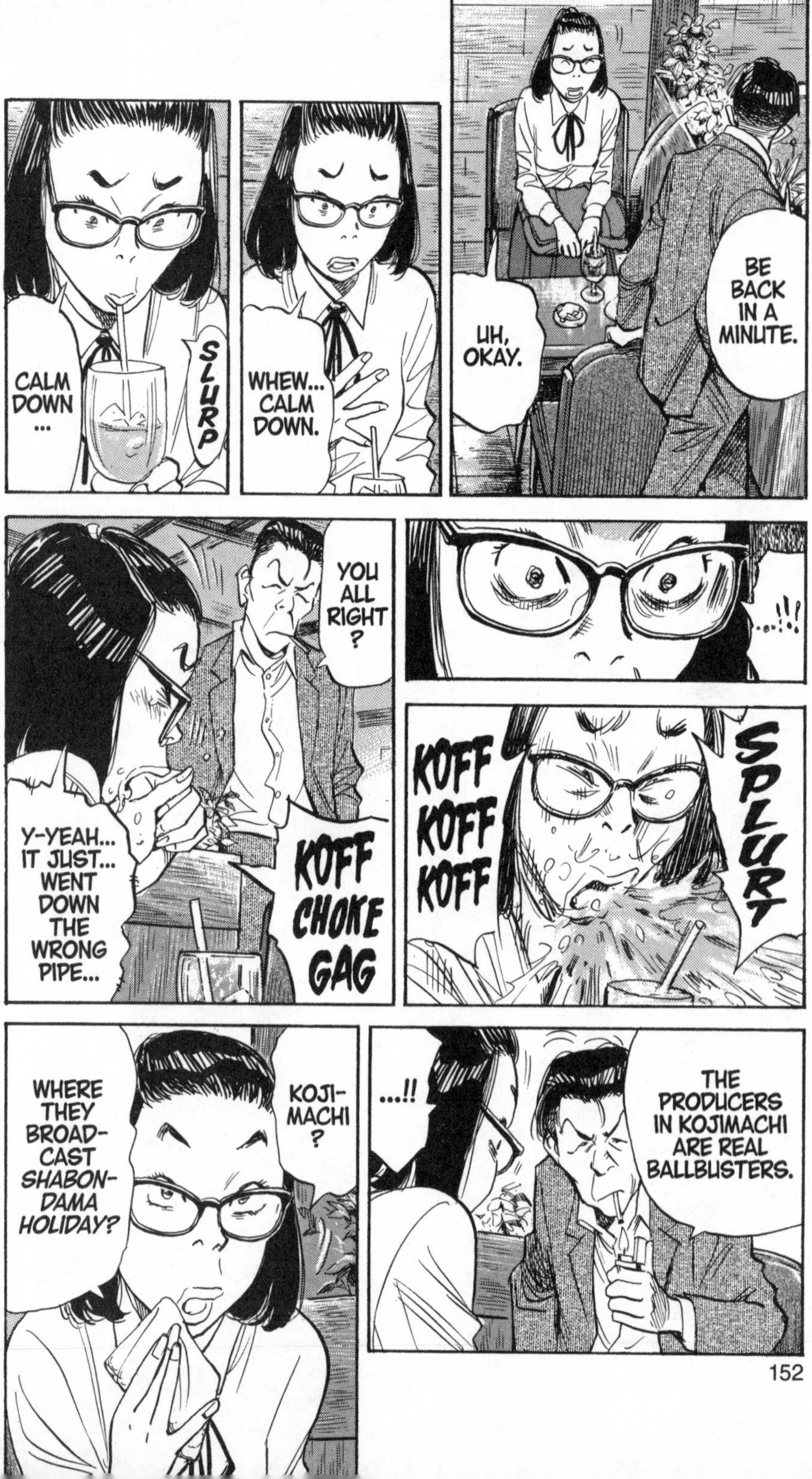
BE BACK IN A MINUTE.
UH, OKAY.
WHEW... CALM DOWN.
SLURP
CALM DOWN ...
...!!?
SPLURT
KOFF KOFF KOFF
YOU ALL RIGHT?
KOFF CHOKE GAG
Y-YEAH... IT JUST... WENT DOWN THE WRONG PIPE...
THE PRODUCERS IN KOJIMACHI ARE REAL BALLBUSTERS.
...!!
KOJIMACHI?
WHERE THEY BROADCAST SHABONDAMA HOLIDAY?

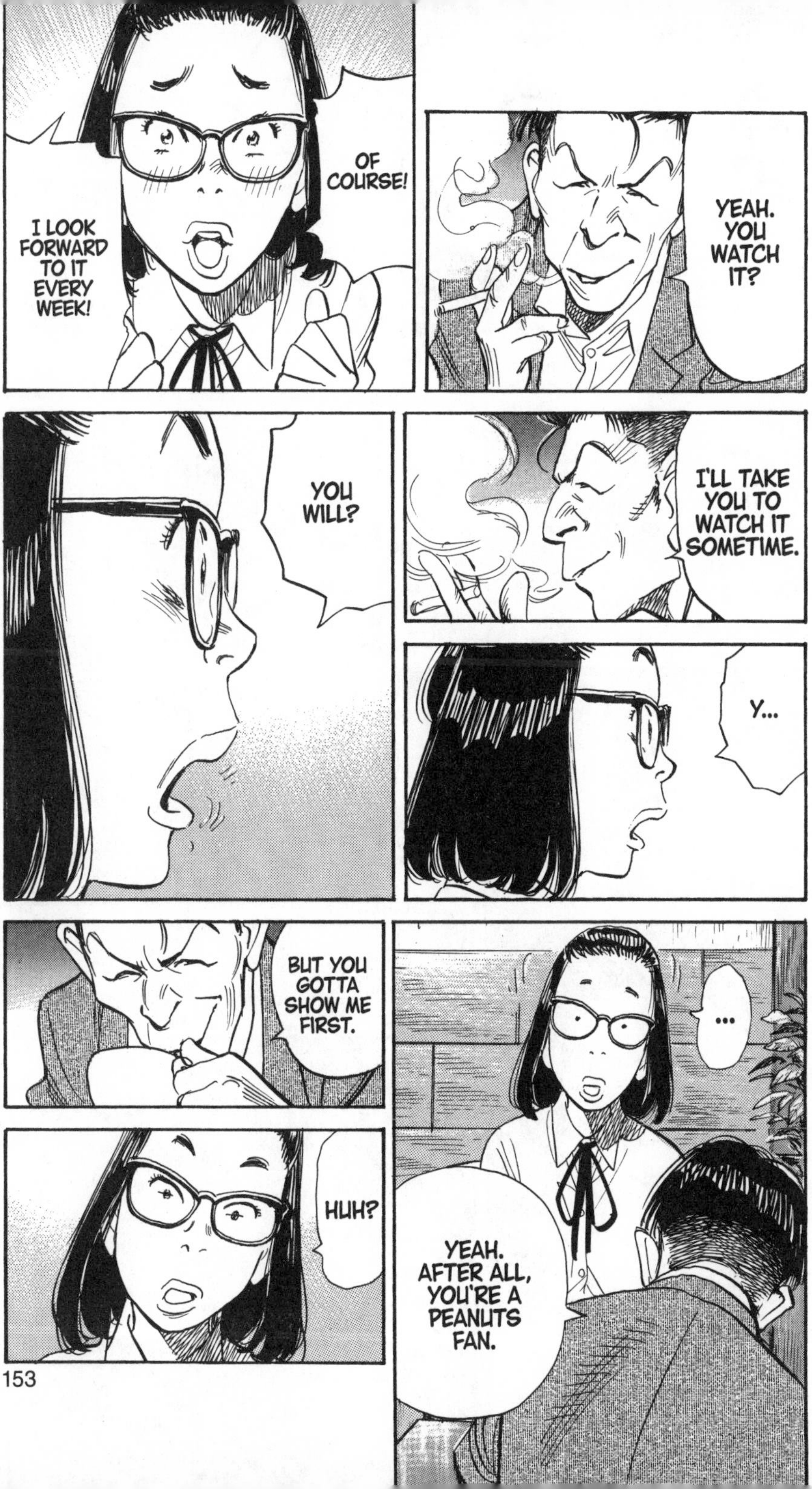
YEAH. YOU WATCH IT?
OF COURSE!
I LOOK FORWARD TO IT EVERY WEEK!
I'LL TAKE YOU TO WATCH IT SOMETIME.
Y...
YOU WILL?
...
YEAH. AFTER ALL, YOU'RE A PEANUTS FAN.
BUT YOU GOTTA SHOW ME FIRST.
HUH?

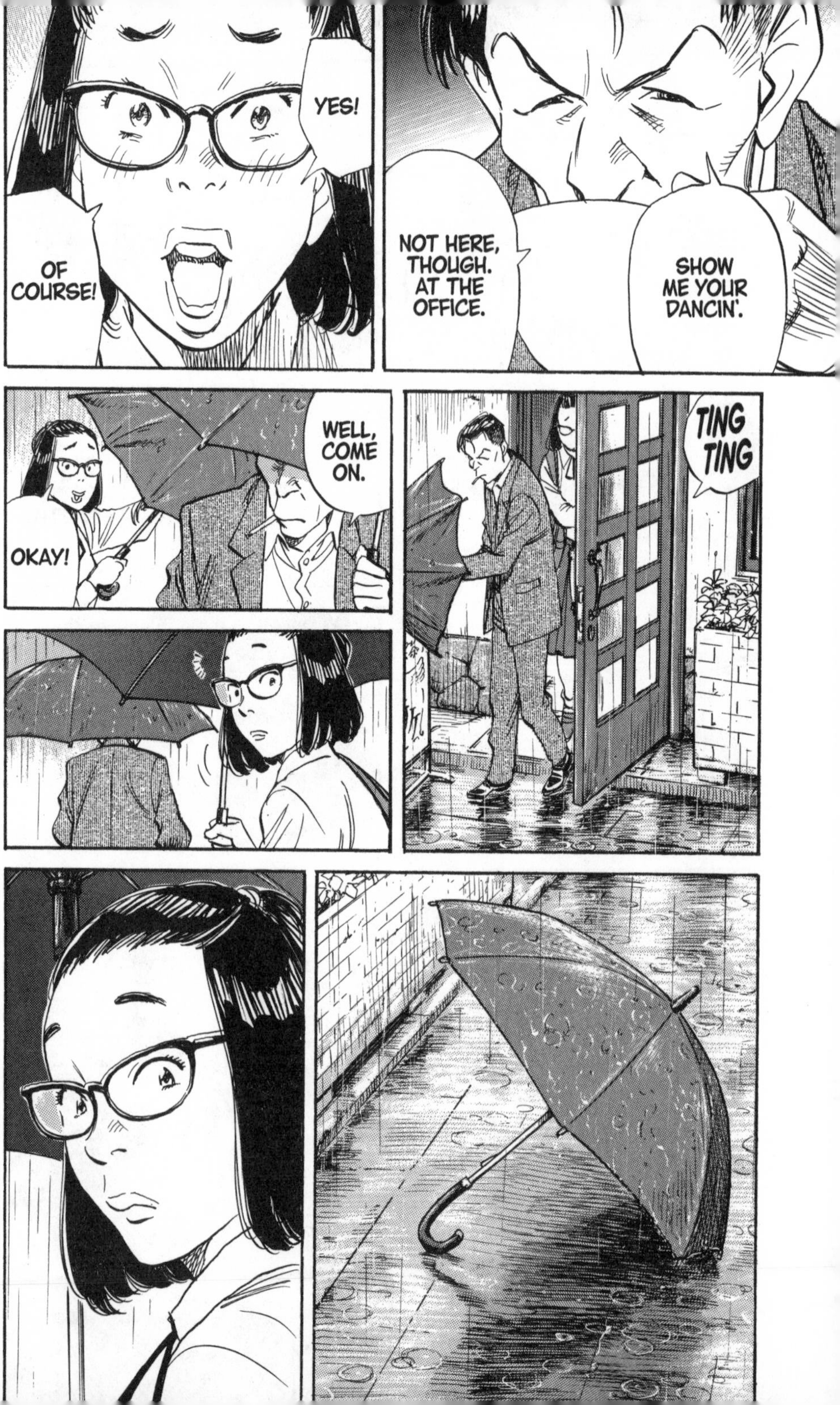
SHOW ME YOUR DANCIN'.
NOT HERE, THOUGH. AT THE OFFICE.
YES!
OF COURSE!
TING TING
WELL, COME ON.
OKAY!

UH, RIGHT!

LET'S GO ALREADY.

*UMBRELLA: MIYAKO

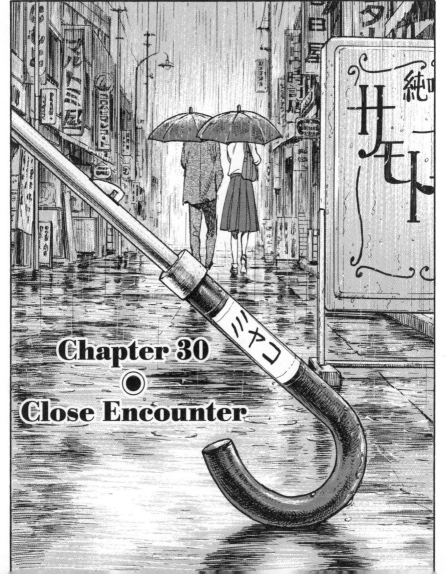

Chapter 30
Close Encounter

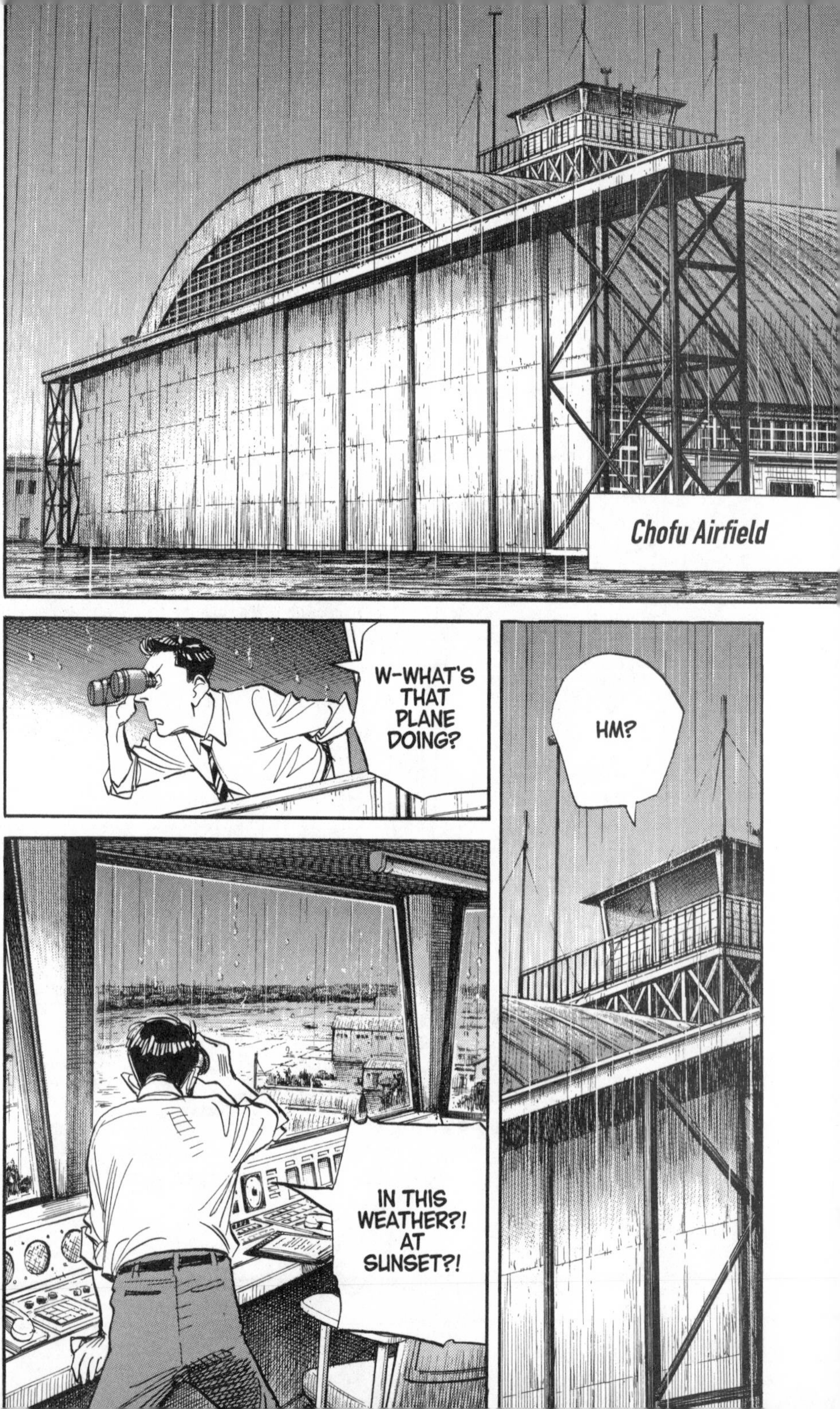
Chofu Airfield
HM?
W-WHAT'S THAT PLANE DOING?
IN THIS WEATHER?! AT SUNSET?!

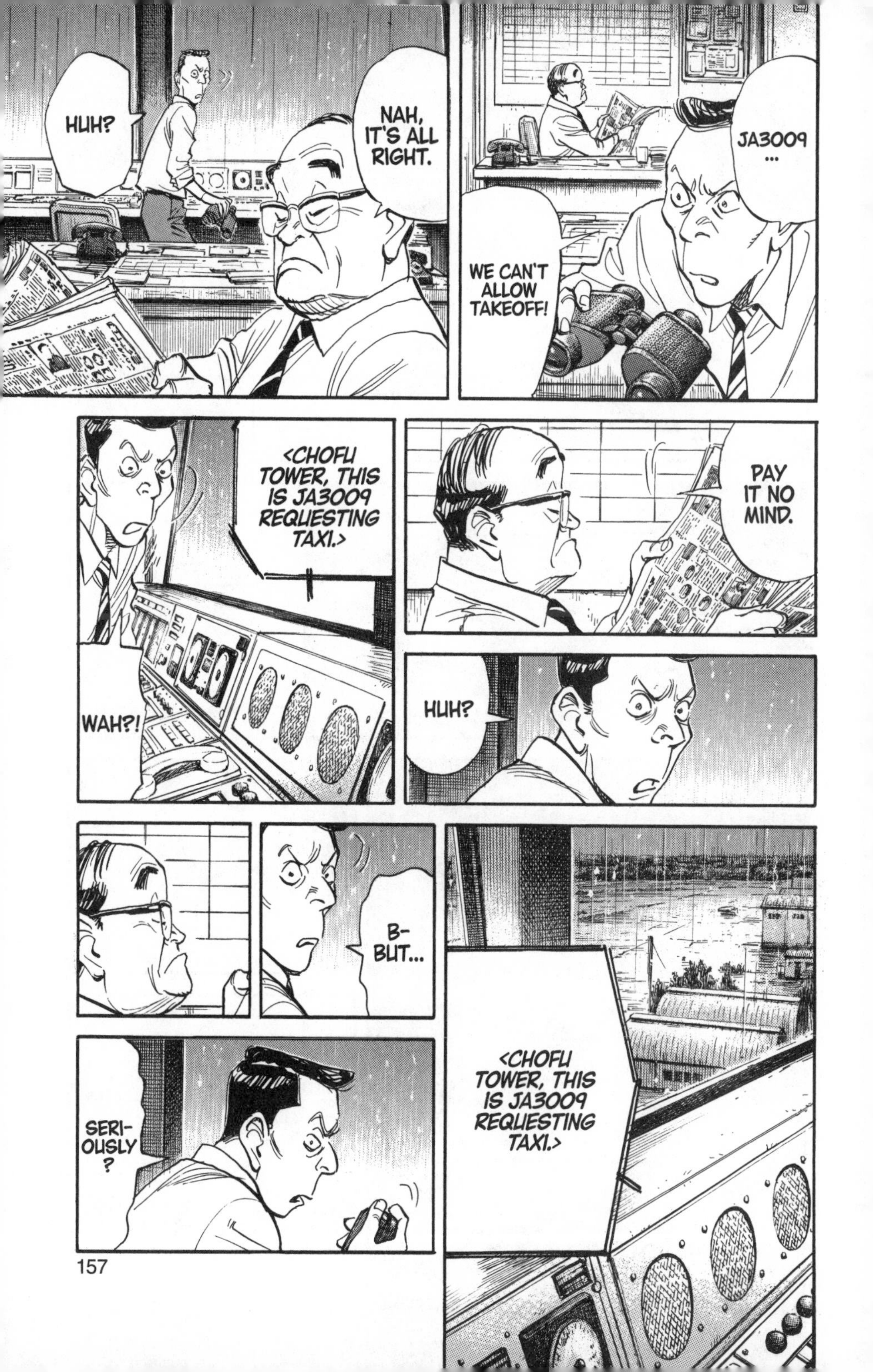
JA3009 ...
WE CAN'T ALLOW TAKEOFF!
NAH, IT'S ALL RIGHT.
HUH?
PAY IT NO MIND.
HUH?
<CHOFU TOWER, THIS IS JA3009 REQUESTING TAXI.>
WAH?!
<CHOFU TOWER, THIS IS JA3009 REQUESTING TAXI.>
B-BUT...
SERIOUSLY?

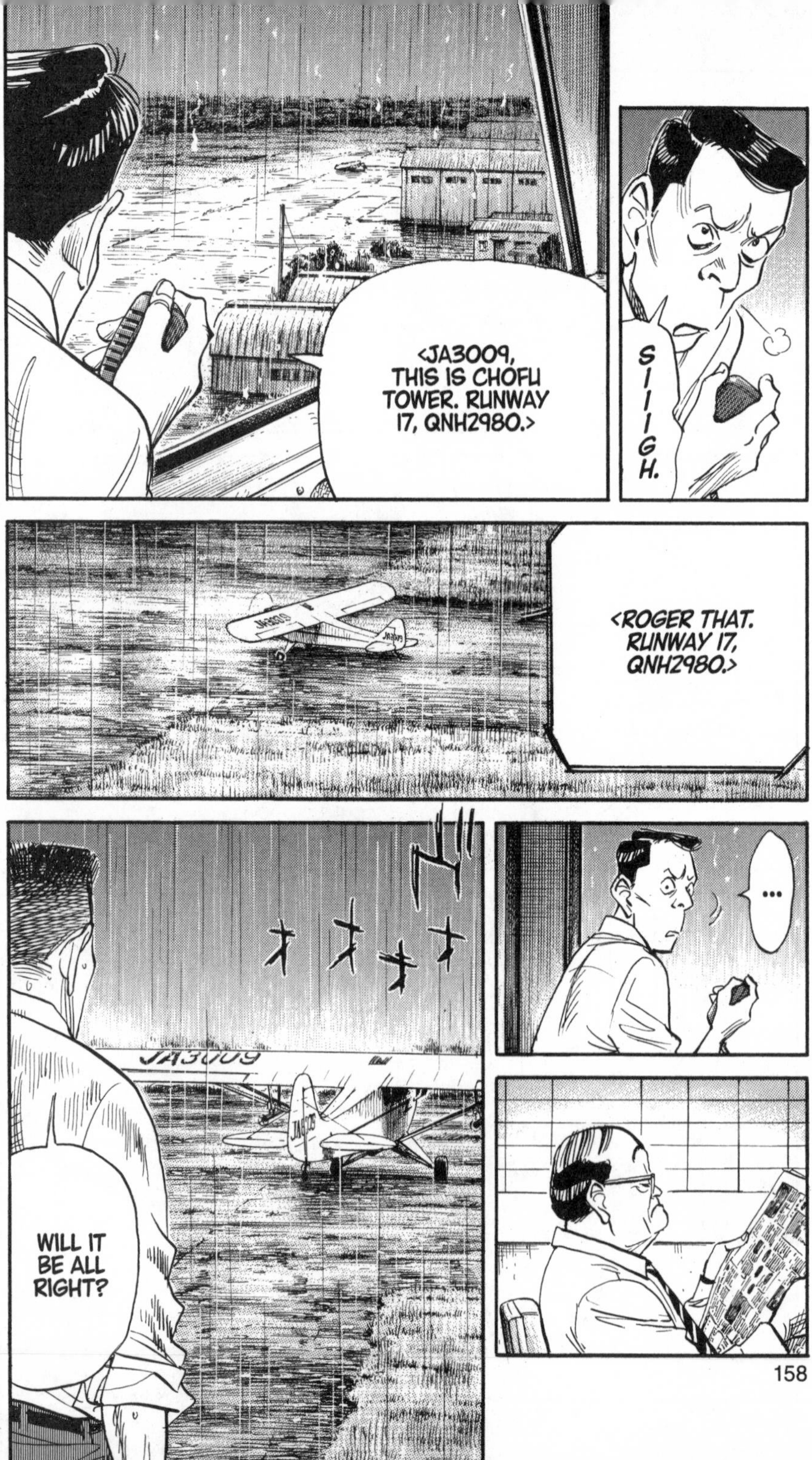
SIIIIGH.
<JA3009, THIS IS CHOFU TOWER. RUNWAY 17, QNH2980.>
<ROGER THAT. RUNWAY 17, QNH2980.>
...
WILL IT BE ALL RIGHT?

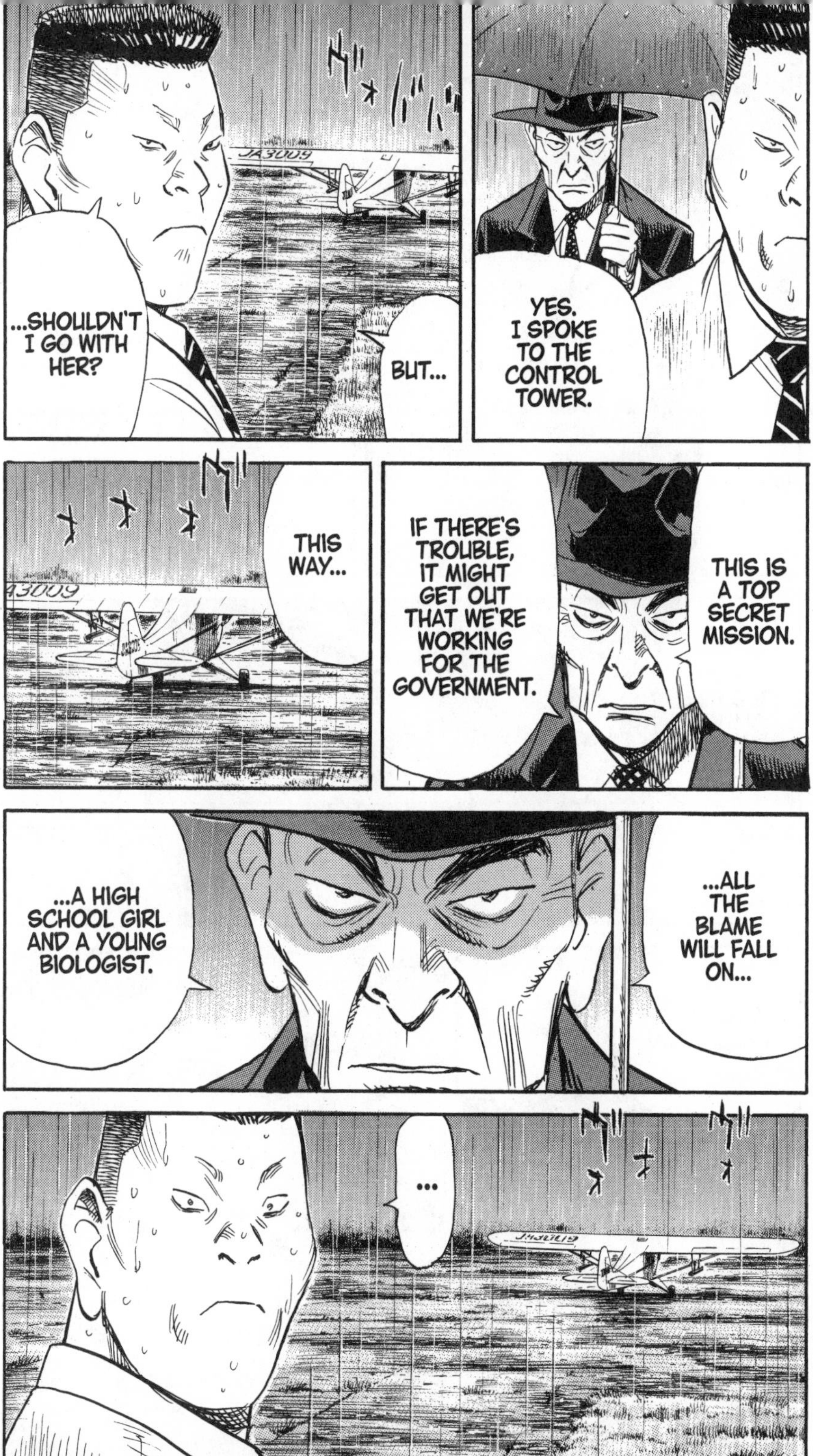
YES. I SPOKE TO THE CONTROL TOWER.
BUT...
...SHOULDN'T I GO WITH HER?
THIS IS A TOP SECRET MISSION.
IF THERE'S TROUBLE, IT MIGHT GET OUT THAT WE'RE WORKING FOR THE GOVERNMENT.
THIS WAY...
...ALL THE BLAME WILL FALL ON...
...A HIGH SCHOOL GIRL AND A YOUNG BIOLOGIST.
...

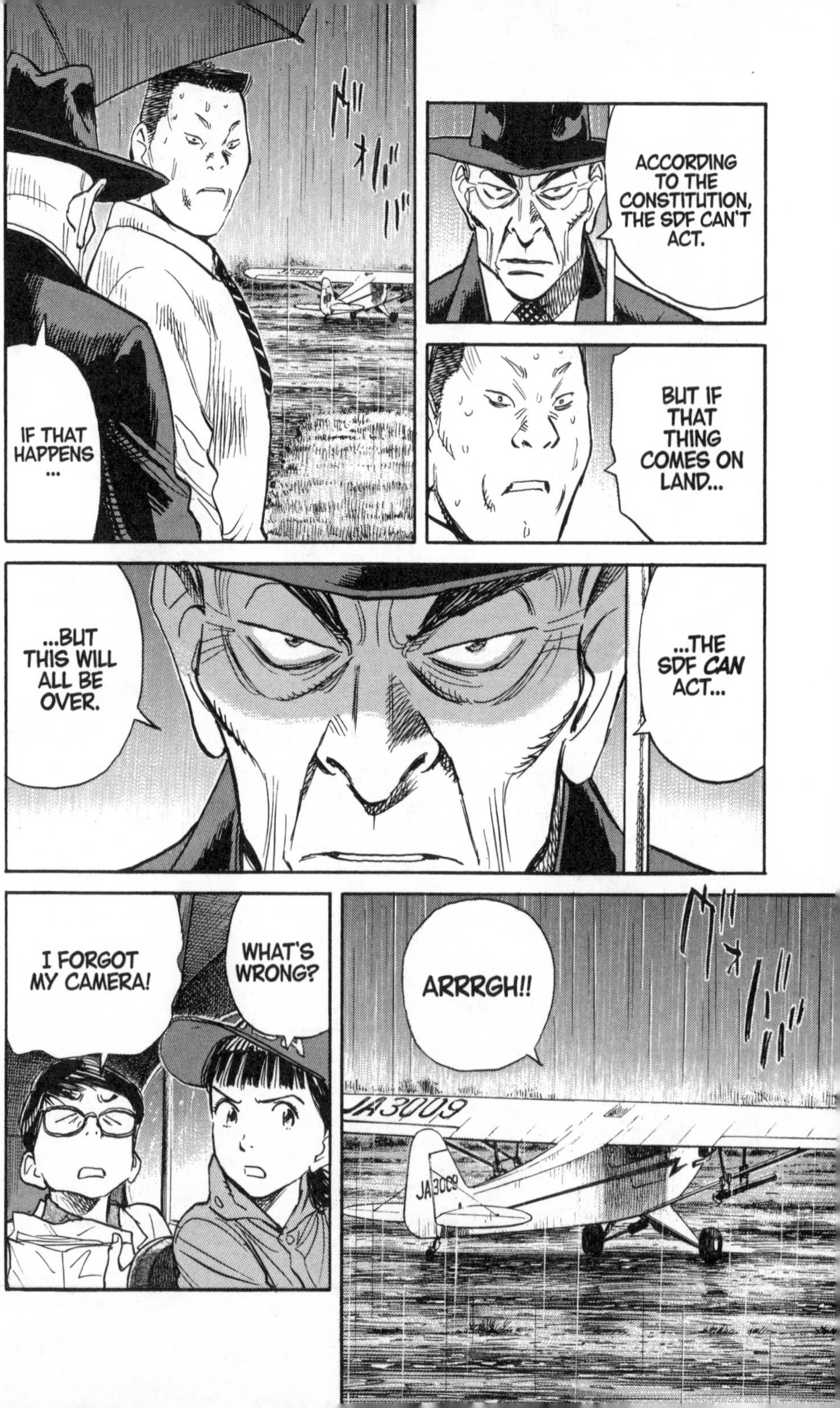
ACCORDING TO THE CONSTITUTION, THE SDF CAN'T ACT.
BUT IF THAT THING COMES ON LAND...
IF THAT HAPPENS ...
...THE SDF *CAN* ACT...
...BUT THIS WILL ALL BE OVER.
ARRRGH!!
JA3009
WHAT'S WRONG?
I FORGOT MY CAMERA!

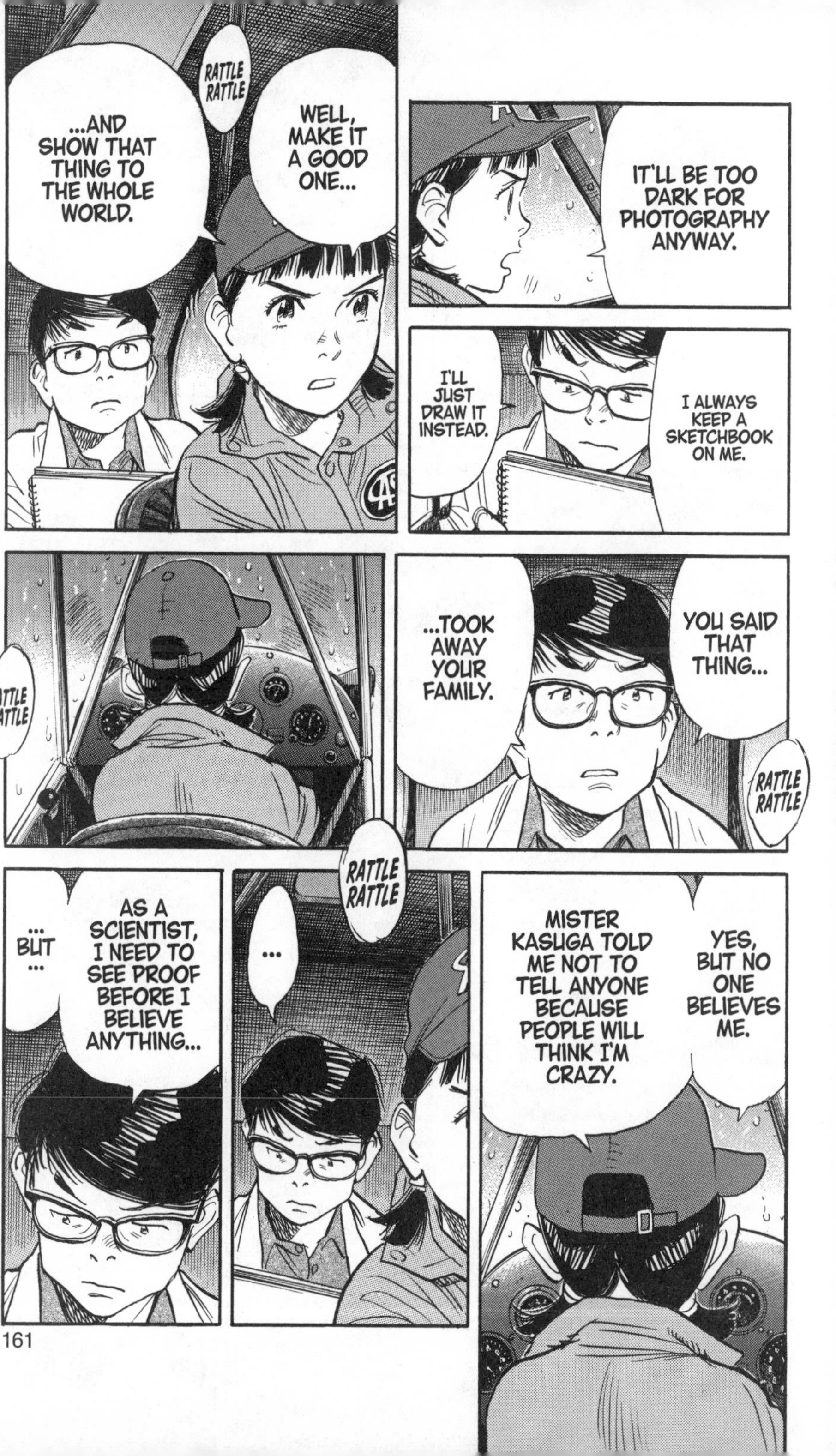
IT'LL BE TOO DARK FOR PHOTOGRAPHY ANYWAY.
I ALWAYS KEEP A SKETCHBOOK ON ME.
I'LL JUST DRAW IT INSTEAD.
WELL, MAKE IT A GOOD ONE...
RATTLE RATTLE
...AND SHOW THAT THING TO THE WHOLE WORLD.
RATTLE RATTLE
YOU SAID THAT THING...
...TOOK AWAY YOUR FAMILY.
RATTLE RATTLE
YES, BUT NO ONE BELIEVES ME.
MISTER KASUGA TOLD ME NOT TO TELL ANYONE BECAUSE PEOPLE WILL THINK I'M CRAZY.
RATTLE RATTLE
...
AS A SCIENTIST, I NEED TO SEE PROOF BEFORE I BELIEVE ANYTHING...
... BUT ...

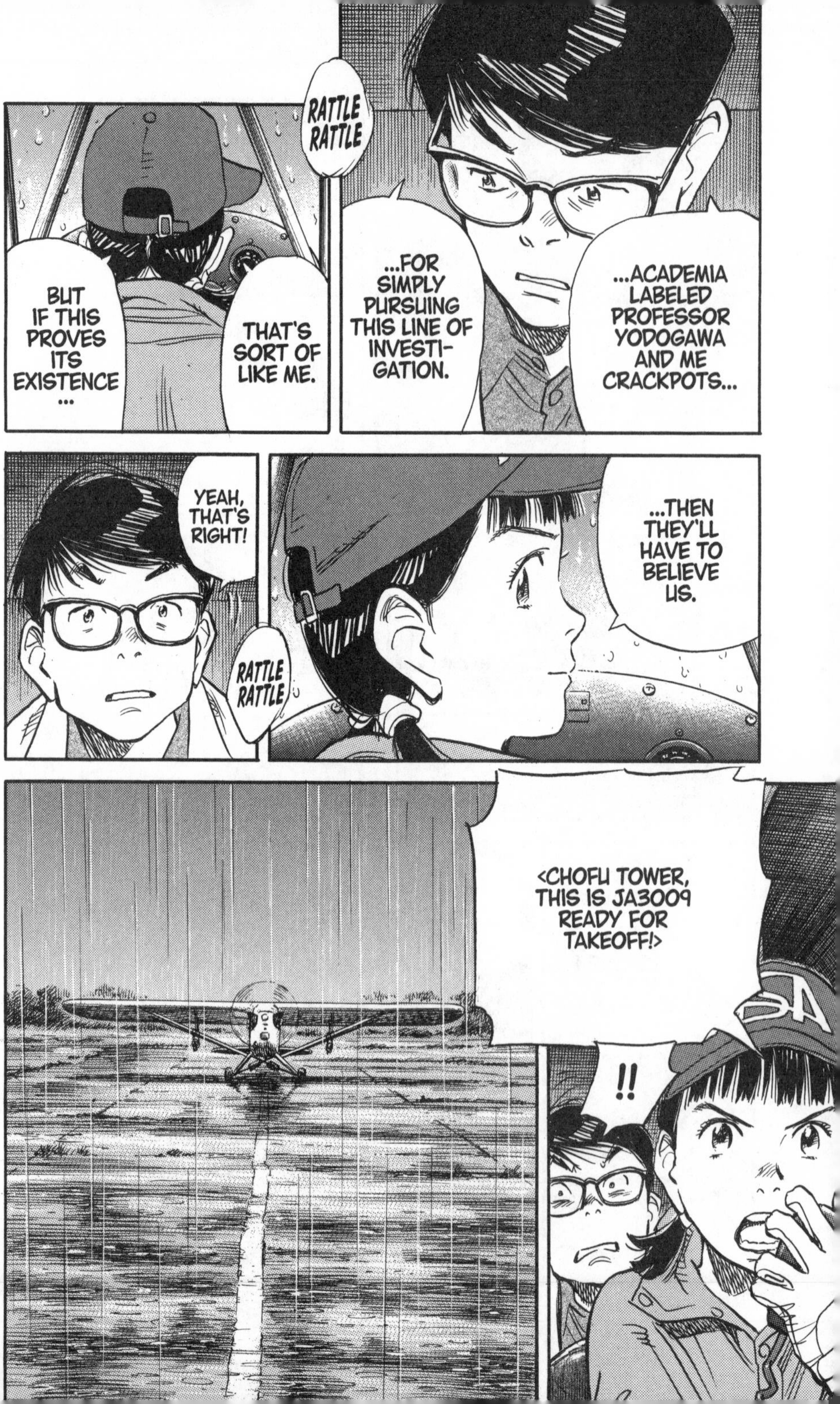
RATTLE RATTLE
...ACADEMIA LABELED PROFESSOR YODOGAWA AND ME CRACKPOTS...
...FOR SIMPLY PURSUING THIS LINE OF INVESTIGATION.
THAT'S SORT OF LIKE ME.
BUT IF THIS PROVES ITS EXISTENCE ...
...THEN THEY'LL HAVE TO BELIEVE US.
YEAH, THAT'S RIGHT!
RATTLE RATTLE
<CHOFU TOWER, THIS IS JA3009 READY FOR TAKEOFF!>
!!

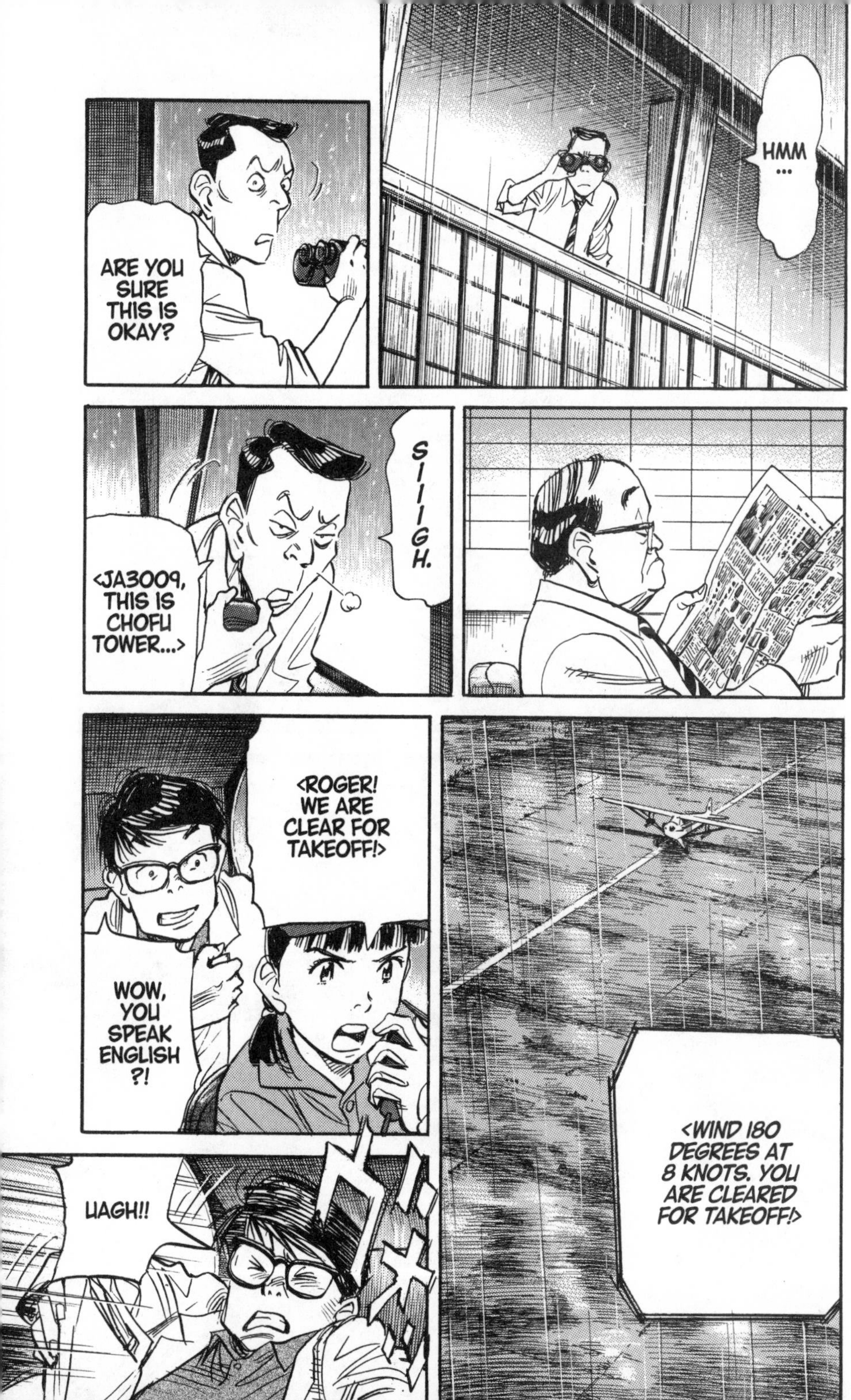
HMM...
ARE YOU SURE THIS IS OKAY?
SIIIGH.
<JA3009, THIS IS CHOFU TOWER...>
<WIND 180 DEGREES AT 8 KNOTS. YOU ARE CLEARED FOR TAKEOFF!>
<ROGER! WE ARE CLEAR FOR TAKEOFF!>
WOW, YOU SPEAK ENGLISH?!
UAGH!!

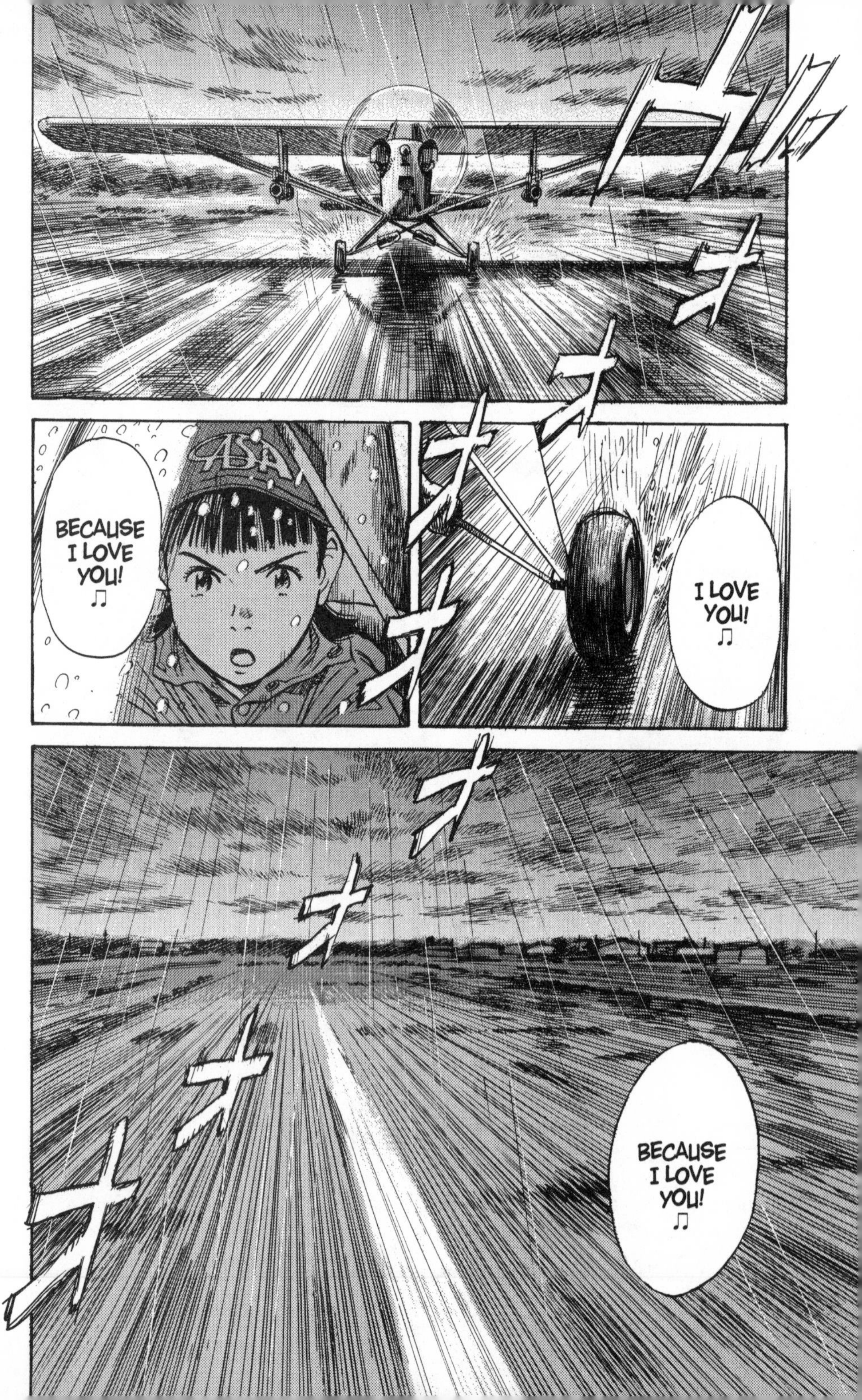
I LOVE YOU! ♫
BECAUSE I LOVE YOU! ♫
BECAUSE I LOVE YOU! ♫

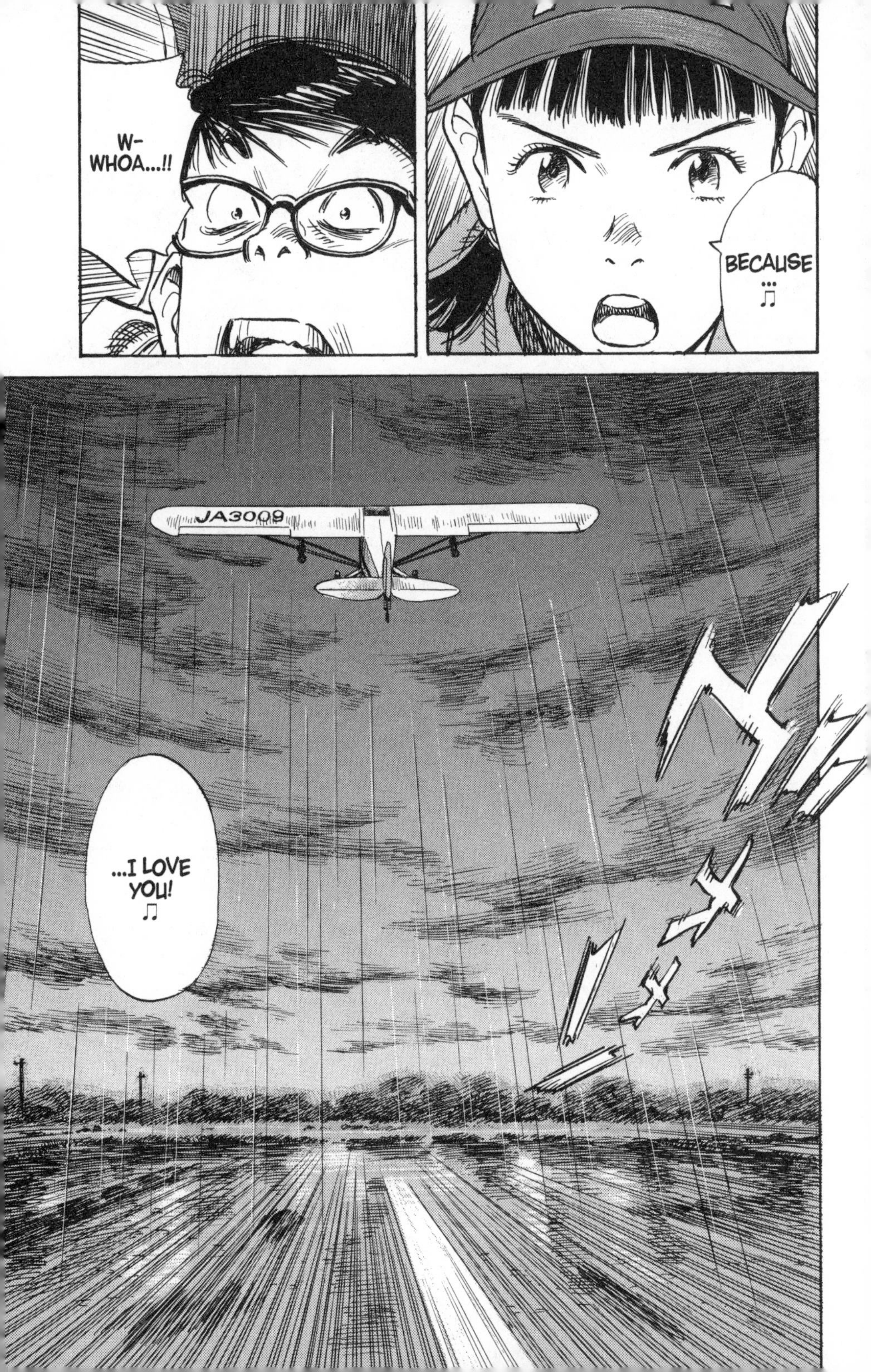
BECAUSE ... ♫
W-WHOA...!!
JA3009
...I LOVE YOU! ♫

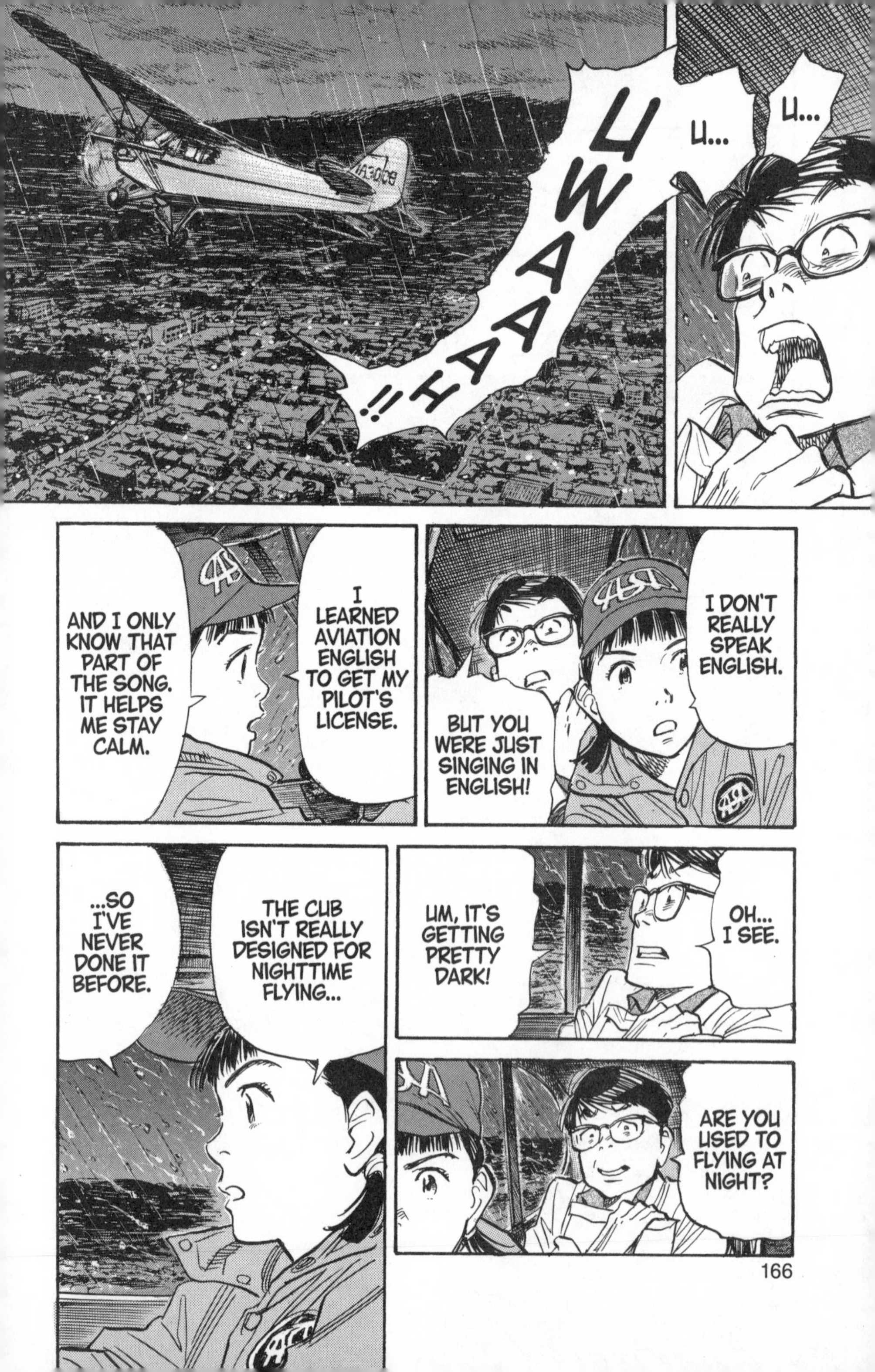
U...
U...
UWAAAH!!
I DON'T REALLY SPEAK ENGLISH.
BUT YOU WERE JUST SINGING IN ENGLISH!
I LEARNED AVIATION ENGLISH TO GET MY PILOT'S LICENSE.
AND I ONLY KNOW THAT PART OF THE SONG. IT HELPS ME STAY CALM.
OH... I SEE.
UM, IT'S GETTING PRETTY DARK!
ARE YOU USED TO FLYING AT NIGHT?
THE CUB ISN'T REALLY DESIGNED FOR NIGHTTIME FLYING...
...SO I'VE NEVER DONE IT BEFORE.

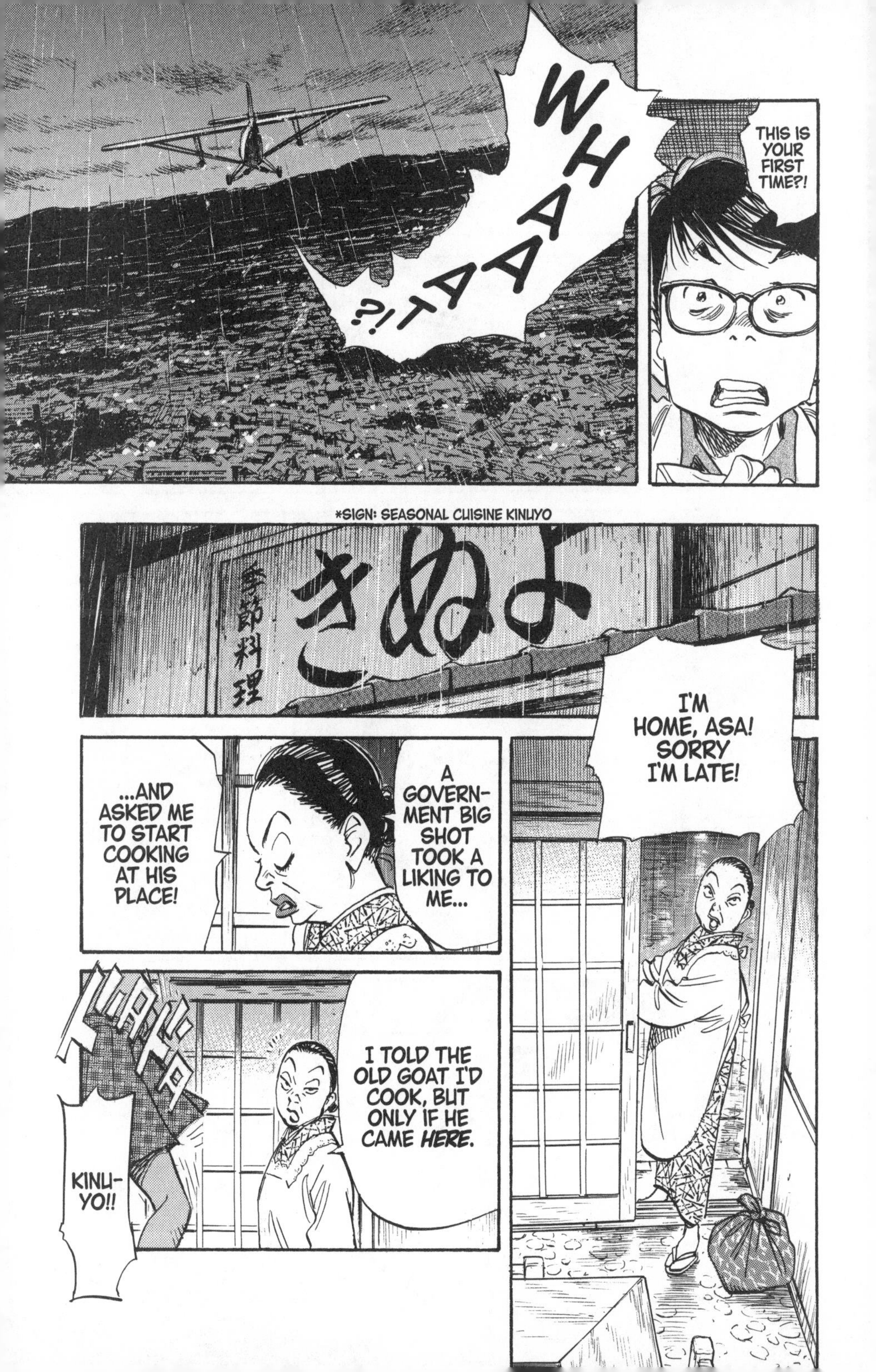
THIS IS YOUR FIRST TIME?!
WHAAAAT?!
*SIGN: SEASONAL CUISINE KINUYO
季節料理
きぬよ
I'M HOME, ASA! SORRY I'M LATE!
A GOVERNMENT BIG SHOT TOOK A LIKING TO ME...
...AND ASKED ME TO START COOKING AT HIS PLACE!
I TOLD THE OLD GOAT I'D COOK, BUT ONLY IF HE CAME *HERE*.
KINU-YO!!

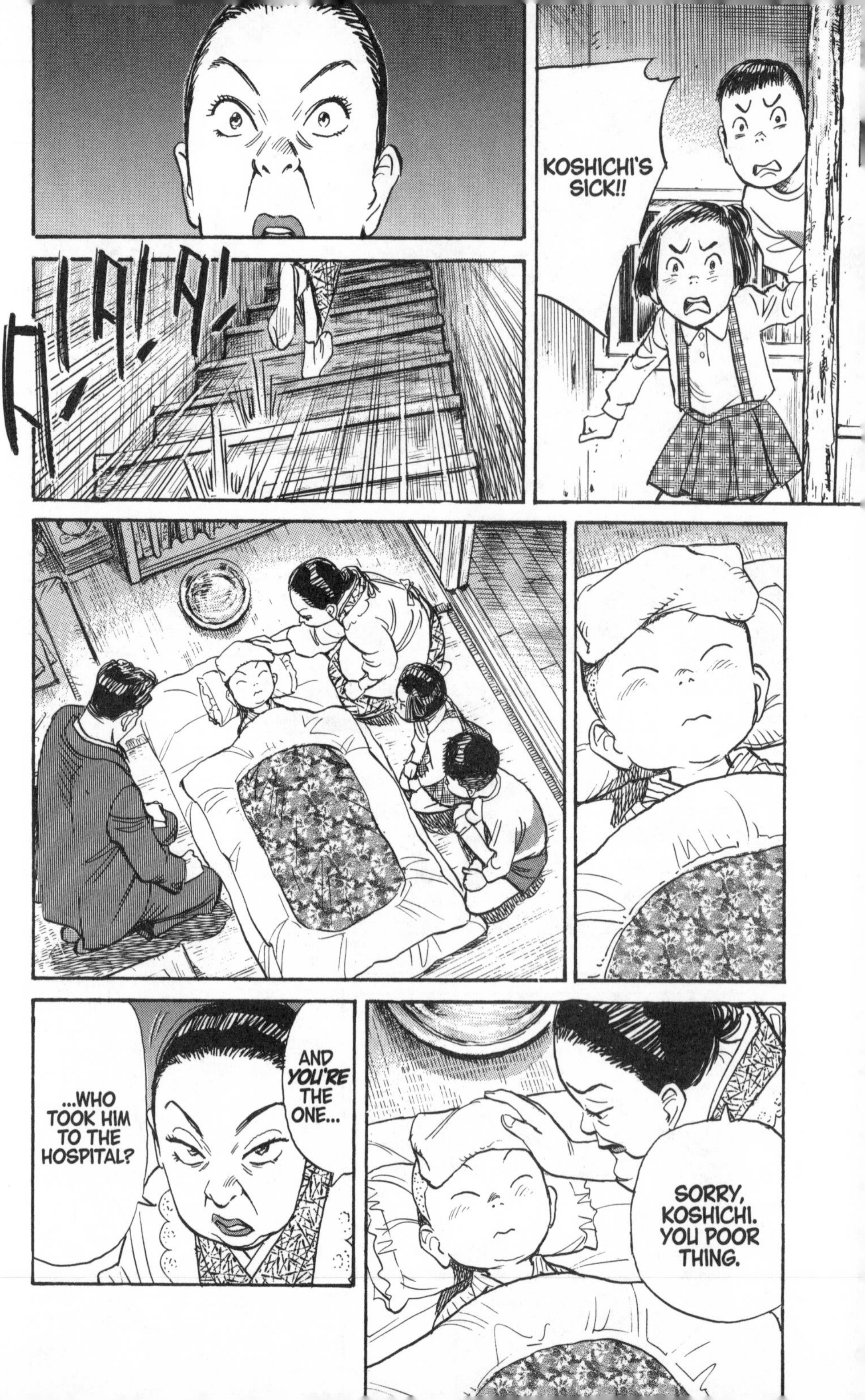
KOSHICHI'S SICK!!
SORRY, KOSHICHI. YOU POOR THING.
AND *YOU'RE* THE ONE...
...WHO TOOK HIM TO THE HOSPITAL?

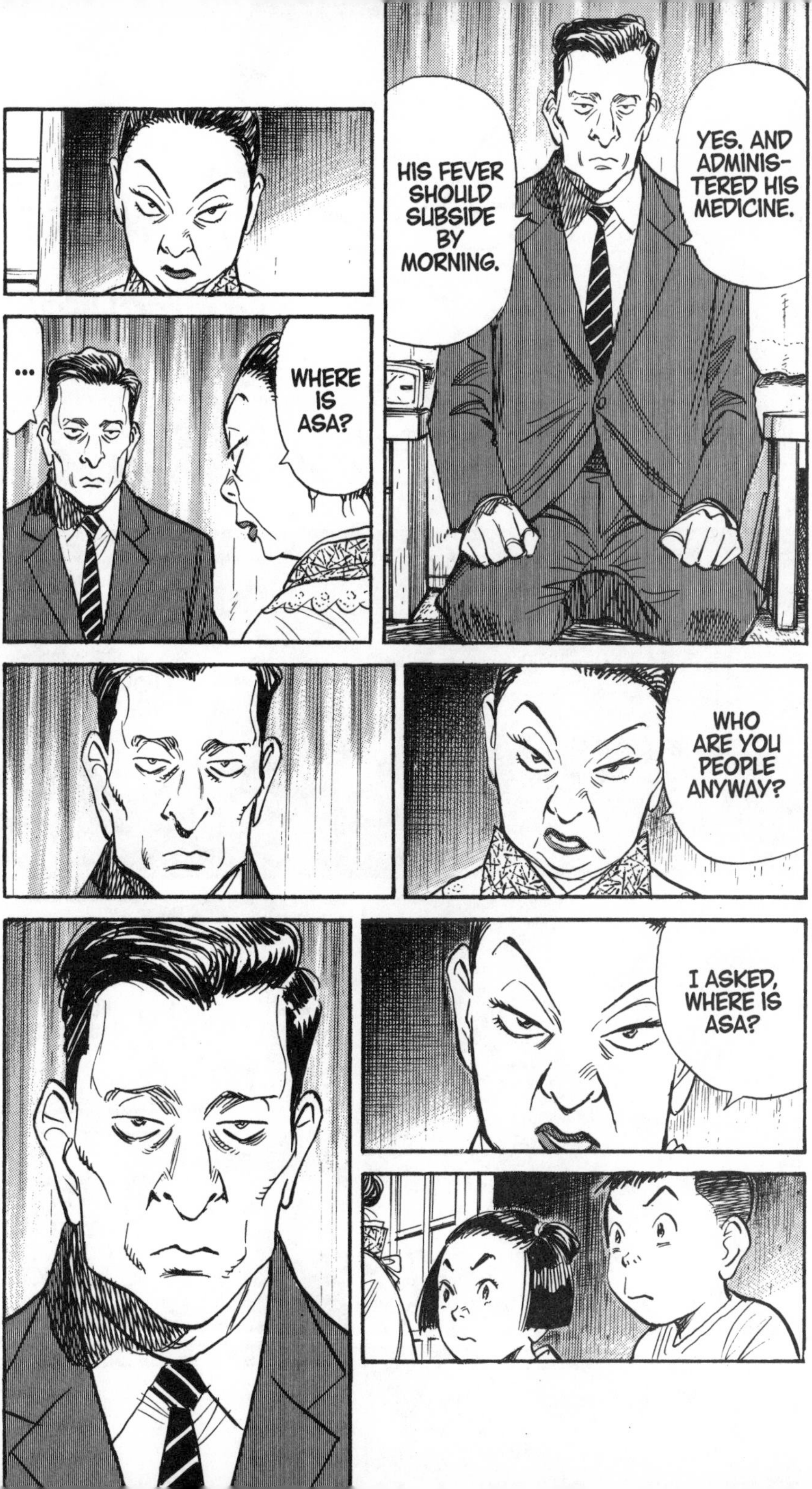
YES. AND ADMINIS-TERED HIS MEDICINE.
HIS FEVER SHOULD SUBSIDE BY MORNING.
WHERE IS ASA?
...
WHO ARE YOU PEOPLE ANYWAY?
I ASKED, WHERE IS ASA?

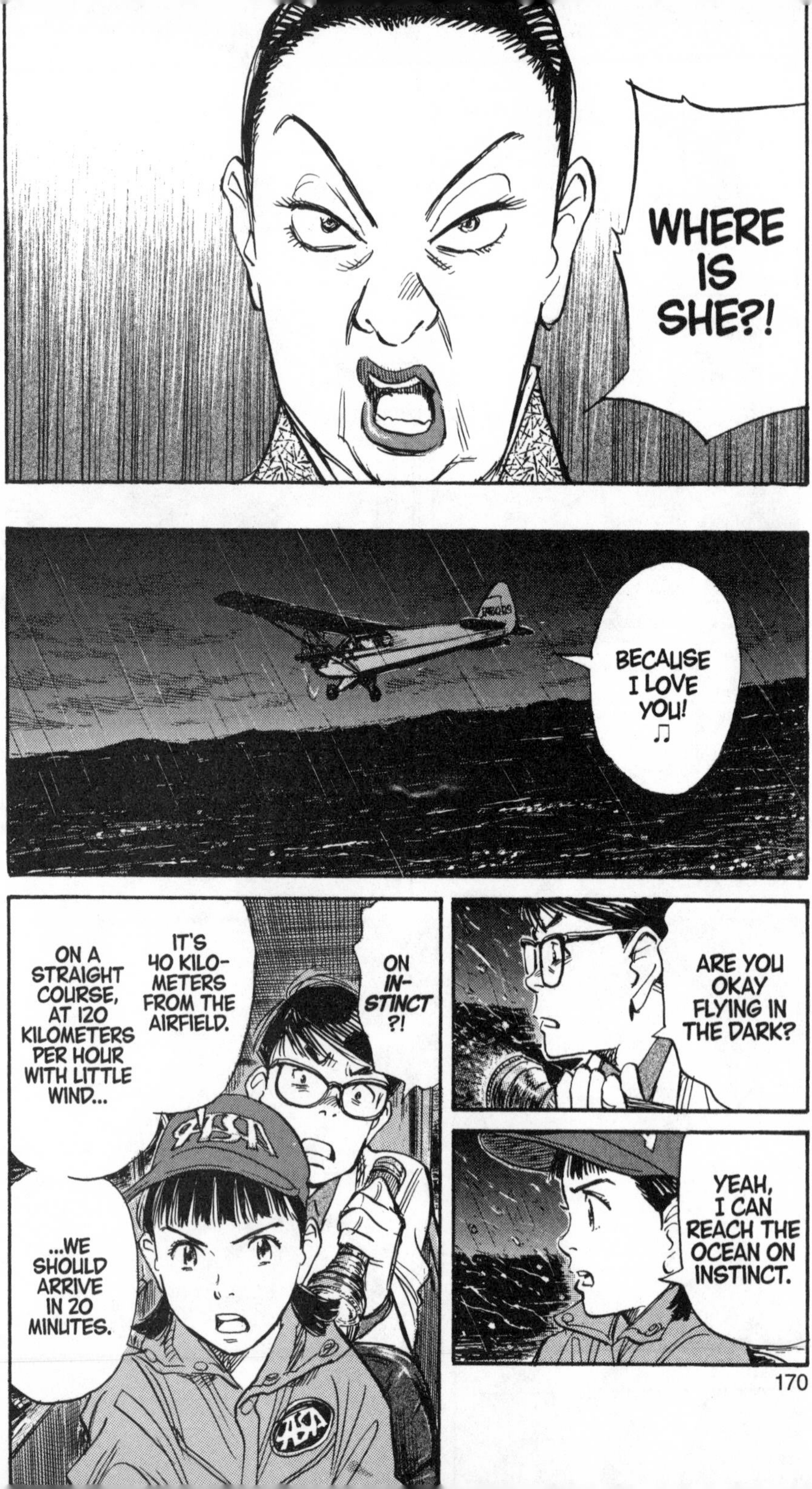
WHERE IS SHE?!
BECAUSE I LOVE YOU! ♫
ARE YOU OKAY FLYING IN THE DARK?
YEAH, I CAN REACH THE OCEAN ON INSTINCT.
ON IN-STINCT?!
IT'S 40 KILO-METERS FROM THE AIRFIELD.
ON A STRAIGHT COURSE, AT 120 KILOMETERS PER HOUR WITH LITTLE WIND...
...WE SHOULD ARRIVE IN 20 MINUTES.

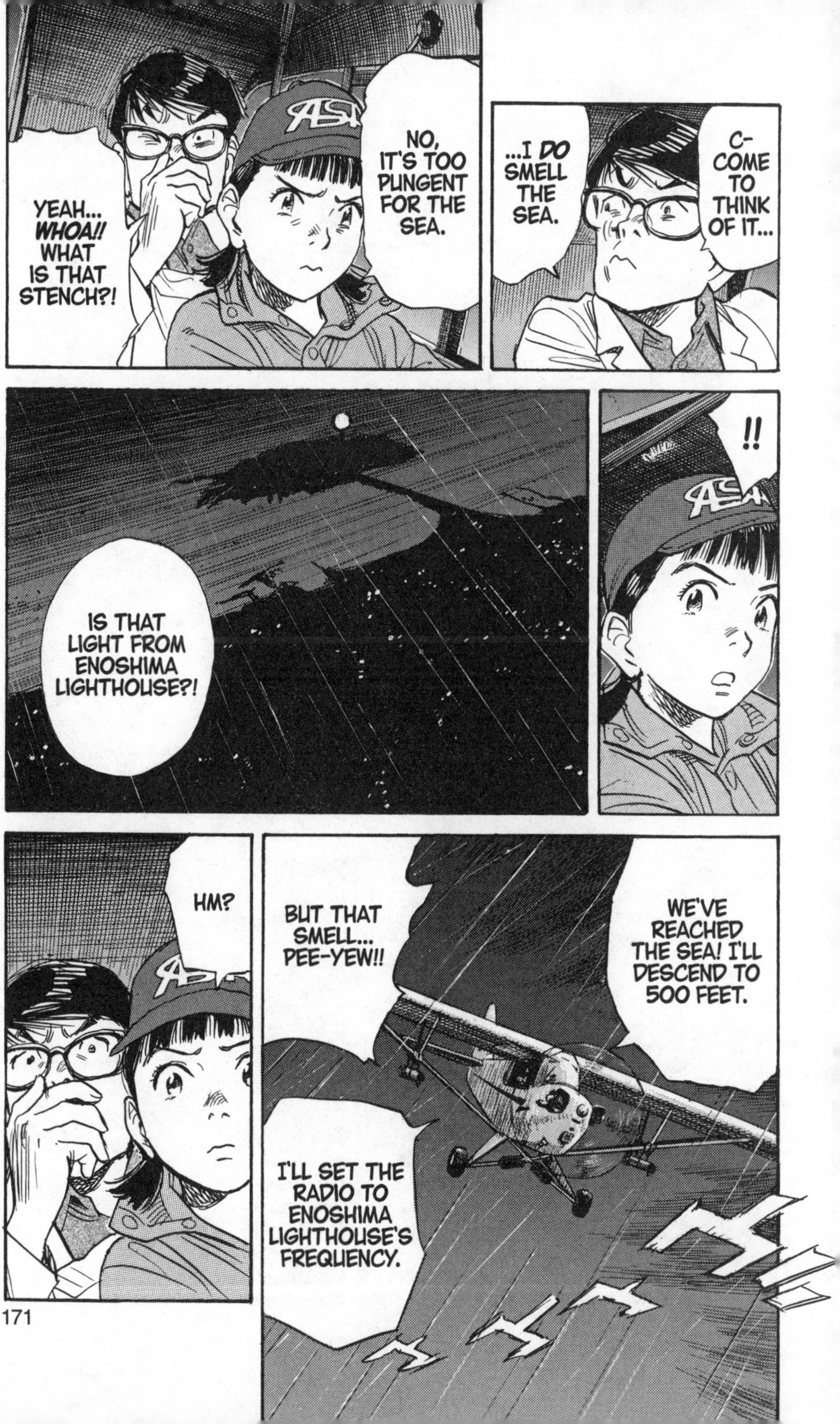
C-COME TO THINK OF IT...
...I DO SMELL THE SEA.
NO, IT'S TOO PUNGENT FOR THE SEA.
YEAH... WHOA!! WHAT IS THAT STENCH?!
!!
IS THAT LIGHT FROM ENOSHIMA LIGHTHOUSE?!
WE'VE REACHED THE SEA! I'LL DESCEND TO 500 FEET.
BUT THAT SMELL... PEE-YEW!!
I'LL SET THE RADIO TO ENOSHIMA LIGHTHOUSE'S FREQUENCY.
HM?

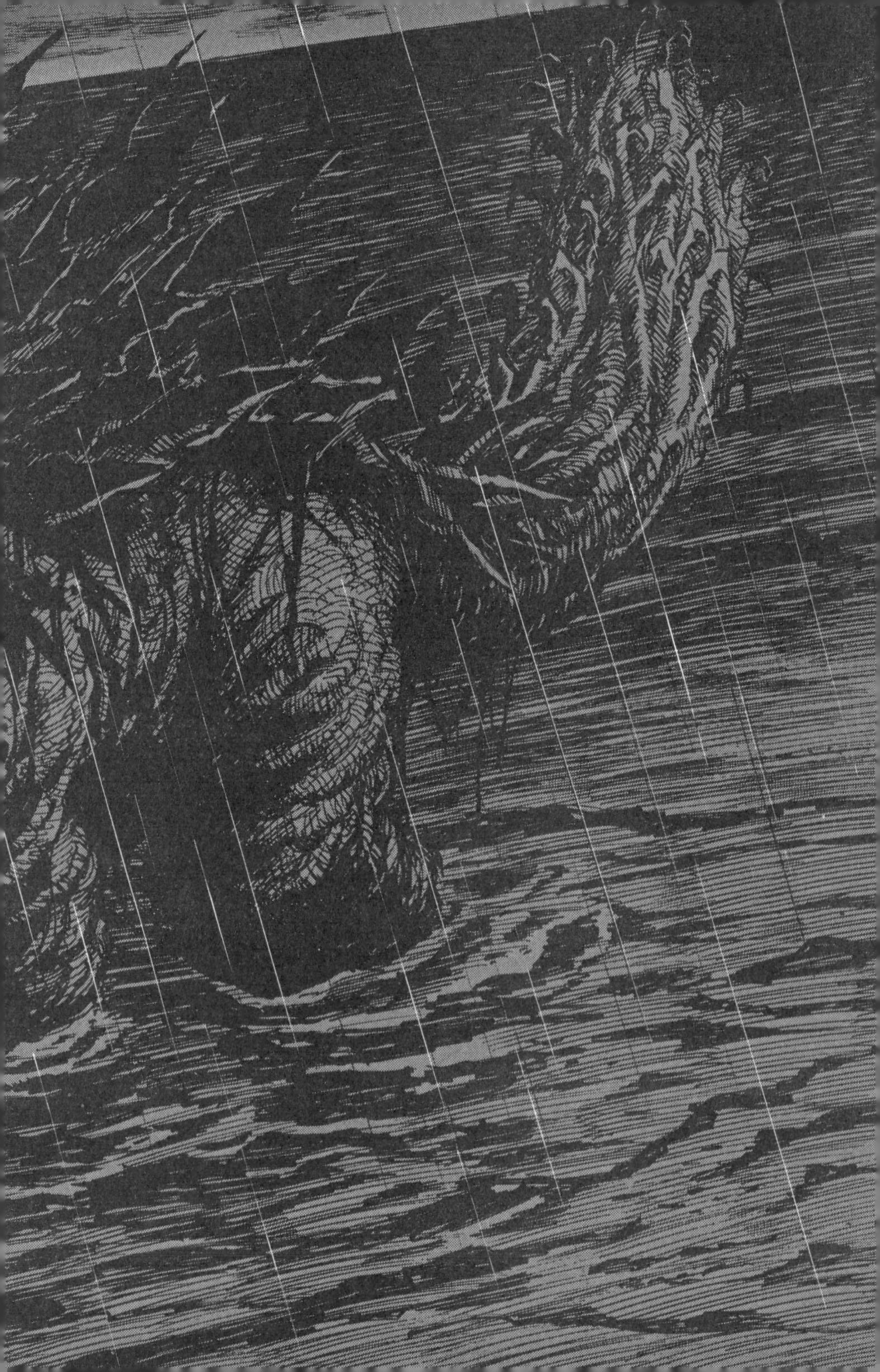

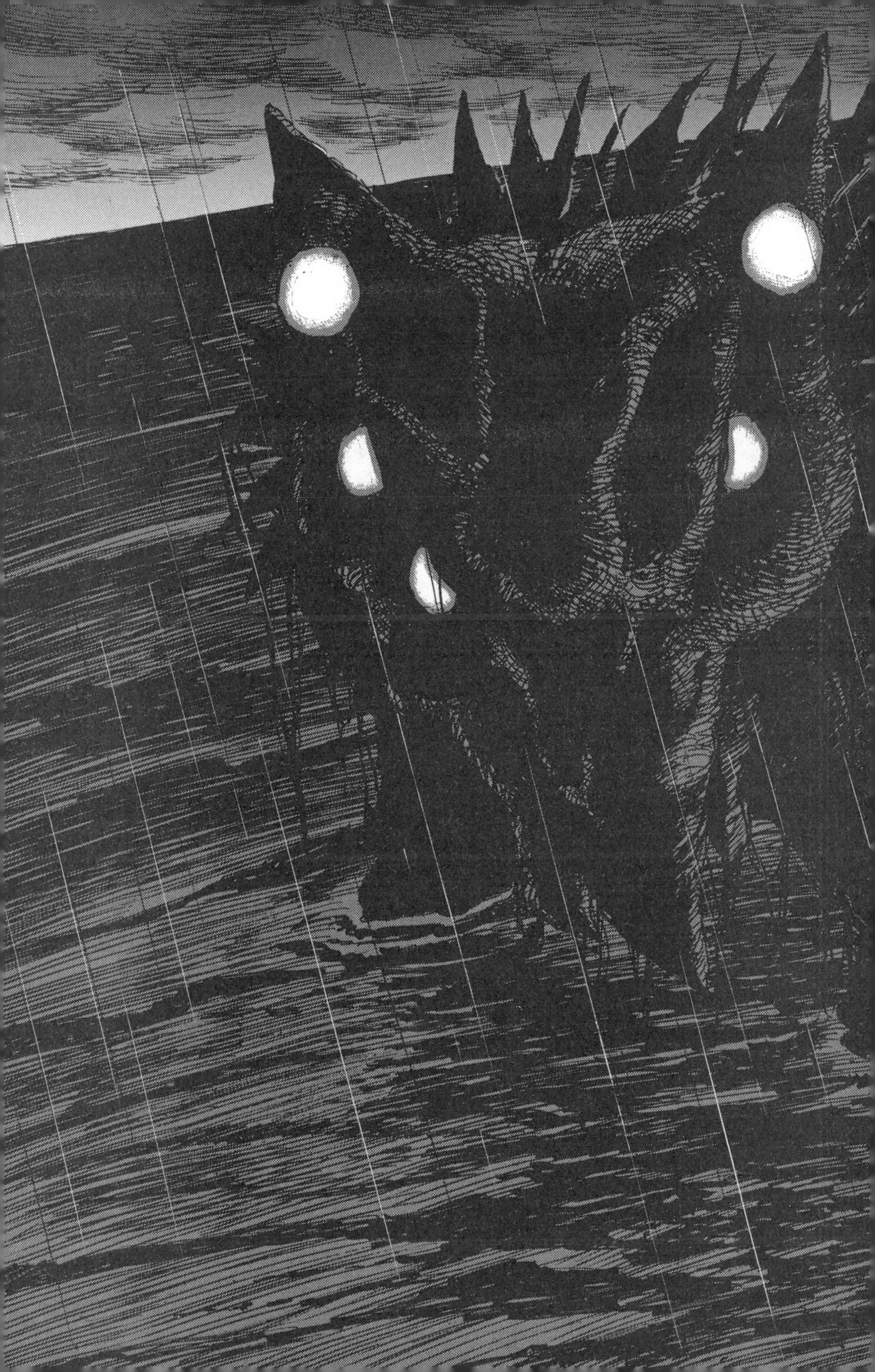

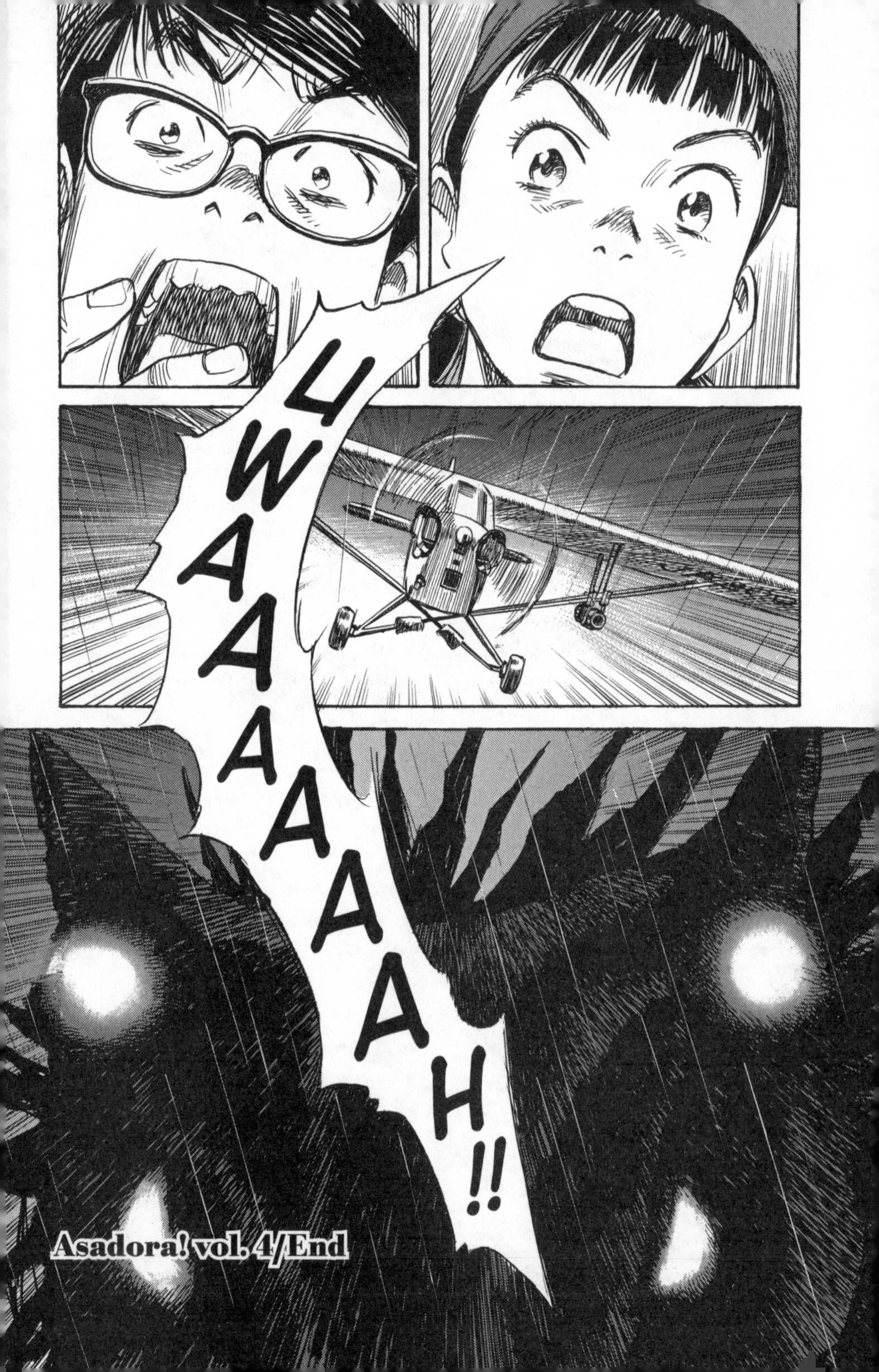
UWAAAAAAAH!!
Asadora! vol. 4/End

To be continued...

Production Staff:
Hideaki Urano
Tohru Sakata

Cooperation:
Satoshi Akatsuka (TAC Photography)
Jun Takahashi
Yorimasa Takeda
Hidetaka Shiba
Nagoya Times, Archives Committee
Japan Aeronautic Association, Aviation Library
Hajime Matsubara (The University Museum, The University of Tokyo)
National Museum of Nature and Science
Takeshi Ijichi (Ikaros Publications, Ltd.)
Akatsuka
Satomi Danno

Editor:
Haruka Ikegawa, Noboru Masaoka

References:
Takahashi, Jun. *Jun-san no Ozora Jinsei, Oreryu* (Jun's Life in the Skies, My Way).
Assisted by Masahiro Kaneda. Ikaros Publications, Ltd.

Takeda, Yorimasa. *Blue Impulse: Ozora o Kakeru Samurai-tachi*
(Blue Impulse: Samurai Who Fly Across the Sky). (Bungeishunju Ltd.)

Thank you to everyone else who offered help.

PAGE 86: *Tamagoyaki* is a Japanese omelette made by rolling several layers of fried egg together. In Japan, it is commonly served as a breakfast dish, but it also appears in many types of sushi rolls.

PAGE 90: The Yoshinobu kidnapping was a famous kidnapping that occurred in 1963 in Tokyo's Taito Ward. It marked the first time that the media in Japan agreed not to cover an incident out of fear for the victim's safety. However, extensive television and radio coverage began during the criminal investigation. Unfortunately, the four-year-old kidnap victim was murdered before the police could find the suspect. The story moved the nation's people, and it became the most notorious kidnapping in postwar Japan.

PAGE 144: "Sheeeh!" is the cry of the gag character Iyami from Fujio Akatsuka's manga *Osamatsu-kun*. An Iyami lookalike constantly belts out this iconic cry in Naoki Urasawa's previous work, *Mujirushi: The Sign of Dreams*. In Japanese, this sound is one of surprise or frustration, similar to words like "argh" and "gyah."

Translation Notes

PAGE 32: Enoshima Lighthouse was originally built in 1951. However, on New Year's Eve 2002 it was replaced by the Enoshima Sea Candle after a ceremony to transfer lighthouse duties was held. The original lighthouse has since been dismantled.

PAGE 38: *Koko San Nensei* (High School Third-Years) is a 1963 Japanese film about the ups and downs of high school life. The movie is based on the debut song of the same name by Enka singer Kazuo Funaki, who also appears in the film. "Classmates are forever" is a line from the song.

PAGE 64: Marilyn Monroe (1926–1962), born Norma Jeane Mortenson, was an American actress, model, and singer famous for the comedic blonde bombshell characters she portrayed on the big screen. She is still considered a pop culture icon to this day. The first part of her stage name, "Marilyn," came from 20th Century Fox executive Ben Lyon, who said Norma Jeane reminded him of Broadway star Marilyn Miller. The last name, "Monroe," was the maiden name of Norma Jeane's mother.

Sound Effects Glossary

The sound effects in this edition of *Asadora!* have been preserved in their original Japanese format. To avoid additional lettering cluttering up the panels, a list of the sound effects is provided here. Each sound effect is listed by page and panel number; for example, "6.3" would mean the effect appears in panel 3 of page 6.

7.5 - whsh (ba: rushing out)

7.6 - thump (da: running)

25.4 - wham (doga: shouldering open door)

36.4 - tump tomp tomp (suta suta suta: walking)

39.3 - slam (batan: closing door)

51.3 - whoosh (da: running)

51.7 - tshhhhh (zaa: running)

55.4 - bam (gon: colliding)

60.2 - fwush (ba: scattering papers)

60.5 - gwup (ga: grabbing arm)

73.2 - splosh (basha: stepping in puddle)

73.6 - slam (bamu: closing car door)

74.2 - bam bam (ban ban: hitting window)

74.3 - bam bam (ban ban: hitting window)

74.6 - skrrrid (gyagya: wheels spinning)

75.1 - vroosh (baa: car)

75.4 - slam (ban: closing car door)

75.6 - skroosh (gyagya: skidding)

76.3 - vwoosh (baa: driving fast)

88.2 - sloosh (zaa: driving on wet road)

91.2 - vwoosh (zaa: car)

91.3 - tshhhhh (zaa: rain)

91.4 - screech (gyagya: sliding)

91.5 - vroom (vuoo: driving fast)

91.6 - screech (gyagya: sliding)

91.6 - vroosh (ooo: driving fast)

92.5 - skroosh (gyagya: rounding corner)

93.4 - skiddd (gyagyagya: sliding)

93.6 - hroosh (ooo: driving fast)

94.3 - splosh splosh
(basha basha: running through puddles)

101.2 - whoosh (baa: driving fast)

102.1 - wham (gon: collision)

102.2-3 - screech (gyagyaa: sliding)

102.4 - tshhhhh (zaa: rain)

108.7 - tshhhhh (zaa: rain)

112.1 - gwup (ga: grabbing)

112.6 - hwap (ba: pushing away)

117.1 - shuv (don: pushing)

117.4 - click click (pasha pasha: taking photos)

119.5 - screech (gyagya: tires spinning)

121.5 - tshhhhh (zaa: rain)

126.3 - bam (ba: throwing open door)

129.2 - splosh (basha: stepping in puddle)

143.2 - tshhhhh (zaa: rain)

147.4 - wham (don: colliding)

147.5 - kasplosh (basha: falling into puddle)

148.5 - vwush (doryun: spinning propeller))

148.6 - thrummm (dodododo: plane engine)

149.1 - vmmmmm (dododododo: plane engine)

149.2 - vmm (dodo: plane engine)

149.4 - vmmm (dodododo: plane engine))

149.5-6 - vmmm (dodododo: plane engine)

150.1-2 - vmm (dodododo: plane engine)

150.5 - vrumm (dododododo: plane engine)

158.6 - vrrrr (vuoooo: airplane)

159.2 - vrr (vobaba: airplane)

159.4 - vrrr (vuooo: airplane)

159.6 - vrrrr (vovuoo: airplane)

160.3 - vrrr (vobaba: airplane)

160.5 - vrr (vobaba: airplane)

163.7 - whump (vuo: falling back)

164.1-4 - vrrrrrrrr (vuoooooooo: increasing speed)

165.3 - vwoosh (vuoon: lifting off)

167.6 - fump bump (dota dota: commotion)

168.3 - tump tump tump (tan tan tan: footsteps)

171.5 - vrrr (vuuuu: flying)

ASADORA!

Volume 4
VIZ Signature Edition

By Naoki URASAWA/N WOOD STUDIO

Translation & Adaptation John Werry
Touch-up Art & Lettering Steve Dutro
Design Jimmy Presler
Editor Karla Clark

ASADORA! Vol. 4
by Naoki URASAWA/N WOOD STUDIO
© 2019 Naoki URASAWA/N WOOD STUDIO
All rights reserved.
Original Japanese edition published by SHOGAKUKAN.
English translation rights in the United States of America, Canada,
the United Kingdom, Ireland, Australia and New Zealand arranged with SHOGAKUKAN.

Original Cover Design: Isao YOSHIMURA + Bay Bridge Studio

The stories, characters and incidents mentioned in this publication are entirely fictional.

Printed in Canada.

Published by VIZ Media, LLC
P.O. Box 77010
San Francisco, CA 94107

10 9 8 7 6 5 4 3 2 1
First printing, October 2021

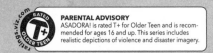

PARENTAL ADVISORY
ASADORA! is rated T+ for Older Teen and is recom-
mended for ages 16 and up. This series includes
realistic depictions of violence and disaster imagery.

 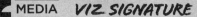

viz.com   vizsignature.com

This is the last page.

Asadora! **has been printed in the original Japanese format to preserve the orientation of the artwork.**

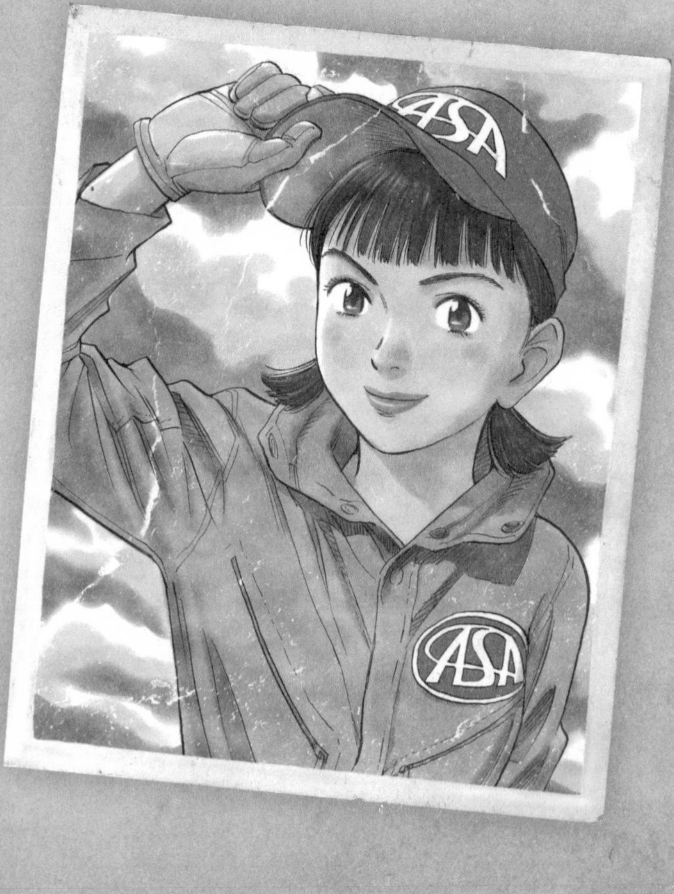
ASA
ASA